# LESBIAN PSYCHOLOGIES

# LESBIAN PSYCHOLOGIES

*Explorations and Challenges*

*Edited by the*
Boston Lesbian Psychologies Collective

University of Illinois Press
*Urbana and Chicago*

Illini Books edition, 1987

© 1987 by the Board of Trustees of the University of Illinois
Manufactured in the United States of America
1  2  3  4  5  C  P  5

*This book is printed on acid-free paper.*

Library of Congress Cataloging-in-Publication Data

Lesbian psychologies.

Includes bibliographies and index.
1. Lesbians—Psychologies.   2. Lesbians—United States—
Psychology.   3. Interpersonal relations. I. Boston
Lesbian Psychologies Collective. [DNLM: 1. Homosexuality.
WM 615 L6236]
HQ75.5.L445 1987      306.7′663      86-30736
ISBN 0-252-01403-0 (cloth : alk. paper)
ISBN 0-252-01404-9 (paper : alk. paper)

*Members of the Boston Lesbian
Psychologies Collective*

Mary Bragg
Rosemary Dunn Dalton
Buffy Dunker
Phyllis Fisher
Norma Garcia
Loraine K. Obler
Lucinda Orwoll
Pat Paiser
Sarah F. Pearlman

# Contents

# Introduction

THE BOSTON LESBIAN PSYCHOLOGIES COLLECTIVE

This book is a feminist re-vision of the lesbian experience. It grew out of a number of concerns and frustrations: the paucity of written material on clinical work with lesbians; the limited opportunities for lesbians in psychology to discuss their work and their concerns; and the growing awareness of certain themes and patterns in lesbian relationships that were difficult to compare and confirm when working in isolation.

A group of us began to discuss the possibility of working toward a feminist understanding of lesbians — as individuals, in relationships, and as community members. Work by researchers and theorists in the psychology of women — particularly Nancy Chodorow, Carol Gilligan, and Jane Flax — offered insights into female development and relationship styles that we thought could be applied explicitly to the lesbian experience.[1] We hoped that a volume such as this would add to the understanding of our multiple identities, challenge our thinking, and inspire further theorizing and research, and we organized a conference to bring together theorists and practitioners who had worked in this area. We believed that in coming together the participants would have an opportunity to recognize the bravery of lesbian authenticity and to celebrate the richness, joy, and vitality of lesbian lives. Our hopes were realized first in the conference and then with the essays we present in this book.

We have worked on our collective editing in a challenging historical context. We faced a problem lesbians often face: whatever we do must necessarily be new. Past psychological literature on lesbians, particularly psychoanalytic theory, with Freud as an example, has been nonfeminist at best, and usually makes us look pathological.[2] Feminist work on the psychology of women ignores lesbian issues; it focuses on concerns of

1

women with regard to men and the patriarchy: sex roles, achievement, careers, dual role families, gender differences in abilities, and nonsexist therapy practices. Virtually all of these issues affect lesbians too, but they are experienced in a different context because lesbians use women, not men, as a reference point. There are additional and sometimes more pressing issues as well. The lesbian is often invisible in the psychology of women, or even in feminist psychology papers and courses. Her particular perspective on these women's issues has been ignored.

Apart from some articles in family therapy journals, discussion about lesbian psychological issues has primarily taken place outside of the field of psychology in journals such as *Conditions* and *Heresies* and in fiction and coming-out stories. To speak and write about the feelings and experiences of lesbians in the language of psychology, we have had to consider our words carefully. The language we inherit from our professional journals is oppressive, while the language of feminist analysis must be developed to express those psychological concepts that we choose to explore. In addition, we wanted to choose our words and essays to avoid the possibility of exploitation of this book for titillating purposes, as we feel has happened with *Lesbian Nuns*.[3]

We have put this book together in a climate of homophobic fear and anger that has been exaggerated by the AIDS epidemic. In Massachusetts, for example, two foster children were removed from the home of a well-respected gay male couple. The Massachusetts Department of Social Services had known that the couple was active in the gay community when it made the placement, but it then responded to a public outcry by transferring the children to a "traditional" home. In the wake of this incident, Massachusetts has moved to limit foster parenting to traditional families with mother at home and father at work—a policy that cuts out a very large percentage of those previously employed as foster parents: not only gay individuals and couples, but also heterosexual working mothers. These events have weighed heavily on us as we made decisions about essays submitted to us.

As a result, we have been particularly concerned in this volume about the focus on lesbians' "problems." Most chapters were written by clinicians who see lesbians in times of distress, and who, as clinicians, have chosen to try to understand the nature of that distress. None of our authors considers the choice to be a lesbian in any way pathological. They recognize that most lesbian problems arise from societal hatred and oppression. However, as editors, we were aware of the possible negative effect that a book dealing with these problems may have in a time of increased anti-gay hysteria. Despite the possibility that our book could be misrepresented by the media and the courts, we decided that it offered substantial benefits to lesbians and to clinicians working with them, and that it was worth publishing.

We have chosen to structure this book into sections that focus primarily on issues of identity, relationships, community, and struggle. We considered dividing the book into theoretical and clinical sections, but realized that most of the chapters include both perspectives. As the index makes clear, many topics, such as responses to homophobia, coming out, intimacy, and sexuality, cut across all sections of the book.

The book addresses the following questions: Who is the healthy lesbian? What do we know about her identity, her couple relationships, her relationships with family and community, and her psychological strengths and struggles? What does the lesbian who chooses to work with a psychotherapist or counselor bring to discussion? What do mental health workers need to know about lesbians? And what stereotypes about lesbians must be discarded as mental health workers and others consider the diversities of the lesbian experience?

*Lesbian Identity*

Of all the topics covered in this book, the issue of lesbian identity has been most written about by scholars of the patriarchy, and thus has been the most misrepresented. Toward the end of the last century, medical and psychological theorists characterized lesbian development as related to biological abnormalities, either genetic or hormonal, or to psychological "deficits" such as arrested psychosexual development or constitutional inferiority. Sadly, lesbian authors such as Radclyffe Hall, in *The Well of Loneliness*, espoused such notions and used them as a plea for tolerance.[4]

Today, following the well-developed arguments of lesbian and gay professionals, more enlightened members of the psychological and psychiatric professions have redefined homosexuality so that it is no longer regarded per se as an indicator of mental illness. This viewpoint, which is embodied in the *Diagnostic and Statistical Manual of Mental Disorders* (DSM-III), contradicted the entire previous education of psychiatrists—both formal and societal—and no doubt had little effect on practices. Even the more enlightened psychological professionals have not moved in a positive direction. Their discussions about the individual lesbian ask whether she is "ego-syntonic" or "ego-dystonic"—that is, does she "accept" her lesbianism or not.[5] Discussion is scant, however, of the complexity of her acceptance or not as it relates to systematic homophobia and her actual life situation. Moreen if the diagnostic categories have changed, theorizing about development is still solidly in the realm of looking for "causes" of this 'psychopathology.'' It does not look for the causal events that permit or encourage or constrain a woman to live a lesbian or heterosexual life in adulthood. These theorists look for early "trauma" or developmental difficulties for their explanations, and these explanations focus only on the lesbian choice.

The recent literature that demonstrates that lesbians are less pathological than nonlesbian women receives scant attention. Mark Freeman in *Homosexuality and Psychological Functioning* and Andrea V. Oberstone and Harriet Sukoneck in their 1976 article demonstrate convincingly that lesbians are healthier than heterosexual women on a variety of standard psychological variables such as self-esteem, and not significantly different on all other important ones.[6] But these voices are still the minority in standard psychology literature.

In contrast to the bulk of traditional homophobic literature, the voices of lesbians speaking in the 1970s and 1980s express the multiplicity of ways in which the choice of lesbian identity leads to a happy and healthy life. The work toward authenticity by the lesbian can result in a thoughtful, well-examined life. In fact, she is virtually obliged to engage in this process because the patriarchy has carefully rendered invisible role models for being in the world as a lesbian. We hardly see such models in literature or films, or during our childhood.

There is no single lesbian identity, nor is there a single lesbian identity development. Indeed we have chosen to use the plural form, *Lesbian Psychologies*, in the title of this book to emphasize the diversity of the ways of being a healthy lesbian. Some of us choose to be lesbians because we found that in our relationships with women the spiritual qualities and psychological or emotional connections give us great satisfaction and empower us in our own potentials. Some of us choose to be lesbians for more strictly political reasons, in order to counter heterosexual privilege and to develop nonaggressive and nonhierarchical structures for interpersonal relationships—that is, to live in egalitarian relationships with our lovers, friends, and community. Others of us feel that our connections and attractions have always been exclusively to women and that a lesbian identity has led us to discover who we are despite the lack of models available to us. Others feel we were born lesbians. Some of us recognize our ability to relate intimately, sexually, and emotionally to both men and women.

Two chapters in this book specifically address the diversity of our sexual identities: Rebecca Shuster considers bisexuality within the lesbianism matrix, and Carla Golden discusses the variety of ways in which middle-class college students identify their sexuality, which may or may not line up with their overt sexual behavior. Buffy Dunker reminds us of other diversities, of the different ages at which we come out and of different ways of being a lesbian at different ages. The chapter by Norma Garcia, Cheryl Kennedy, Sarah Pearlman, and Julia Perez articulates the tensions that may result from differences in our racial and ethnic identities.

Being *out* in the face of the severe homophobia in our society is difficult. Our invisibility and our minimal pool of positive role models means that we must find our way to positive self-image often alone and against a negative stereotype. Unlike many minority people who have no choice in whether they will be identified as belonging to their minority, many of us have the choice whether to pass or to identify ourselves, subtly or more overtly, as lesbians.[7] Lee Zevy and Sahli Cavallero in their contribution to this book make vivid the various pulls shaping our developing sense of lesbian identity. Different attitudes toward the healthiness or "goodness" of being out of the closet are also reflected in the book. Sherry Zitter's chapter on coming out to one's mother assumes that this is something we will all want to do. Yet Dunker maintains that it is not necessarily healthy for every lesbian to be out in every situation.

As a consequence to these many stresses involved in choosing the way she presents herself and experiences her authenticity, the healthy lesbian may often decide to enter counseling or therapy to focus on the specific issues that arise for her. Before we consider those concerns, however, we need to discuss how a lesbian enters into relationships with a partner, her family, and her community.

## Couple Relationships

For many lesbians, entering a relationship is the event that signals the choice of a lesbian life. The lesbian couple relationship is probably the most intense of all romantic relationships and the most egalitarian.[8] Conflict within the relationship is a concern of our contributors. The lovers' vitality and electricity is described in a number of chapters in this volume—especially those by Margaret Nichols and Beverly Burch, who suggest that the joy and happiness in bodily contact with another woman springs from a buried primal experience. Burch expands our theories in explaining the positive aspects of lesbian relationships. To date, most of those trying to understand the lesbian couple have considered only problems such as dependency, power imbalance, and sexual incompatibility.

One expression of conflict in the couple relationship is problems of sexual compatibility. Experiencing differing desires for sexual activity brings many couples to therapy. For example, Pepper Schwartz and Philip Blumstein report in *American Couples* that lesbian couples tend to show diminishing sexual activity and interest after the second year.[9] Nichols and others in this volume offer a number of answers to the question of why this happens, as well as suggestions that can facilitate the continuation of a rewarding sexual relationship. Deeper issues that trigger surface arguments or their equivalent include the pulls both toward and against dependency, discussed (by Sue Vargo and Beverly Burch) in terms of "fusion" or "enmeshment" and consequent distancing within the couple.

Conflicts in a couple's relationship may be resolved both inside and outside of traditional counseling or therapy. Vargo discusses conflict resolution in terms of enhanced communication and a clarified sense of self as distinct from "us" in a relationship. For couples terminating relationships, Bonnie Engelhardt and Katherine Triantafillou discuss ways in which negotiation allows the partners to understand personal and psychological dimensions of the conflict and attain a sense of closure.

It is, we discover, impossible to consider lesbian couple relationships apart from the question of identity, and ways of relating to community, family, and society. Because outside groups rarely offer recognition and respect for a lesbian couple, couple boundaries are often indistinct, and as Sally Crawford points out, individual lesbians in couples must spend time deciding how to establish themselves as a family. Working on these issues as a couple can serve to bind the couple. No one, to our knowledge, has determined the extent to which response to these pressures serves as an emotional glue to hold a couple together, and the extent to which such stresses can push the couple to terminate their relationship.

## Relationship of the Lesbian to Her Family

Lesbians often choose friendship groups that function in many of the same ways as families do for heterosexuals. However, many of us continue to relate, for better and for worse, to families of origin, and a number of us have children from prior heterosexual relationships. Many of us have children by choice as declared lesbians. Alongside our lovers and friends, we consider all of these people our extended family.

Most older lesbians grew up in heterosexual families, yet discussion of the experience of the lesbian child in the nuclear family has been silenced. If the lesbian chooses to be out, her family's initial reaction may be to ignore her statement, or to banish her from the family. Lesbians who choose *not* to be out, or not to act on a lesbian life choice, have long served family roles as "spinsters" providing support for the rest of the family, as reflected somewhat pathetically in Radclyffe Hall's *The Unlit Lamp*.[10] Few families know how to be truly supportive. However, there are some who try, and who join organizations of parents or families and friends of gays and work together on our behalf. For some of us, the choice to live a lesbian life-style is an explicit choice not to live the lives of our parents, and more particularly the lives of our mothers.

Coming out within the family, as Zitter points out in her chapter, raises issues for ourselves and for our parents and has an impact on family dynamics. Families that pride themselves on openness must deal with this previously unmentionable topic. Will the parents appreciate that the daughter will have a greater potential for having her needs met, as Zitter phrases it, or will they assume that the daughter can never be happy unless she leads a life just like theirs?

Our relationships with our siblings are also virtually unexplored, although it is our sense that lesbians will often first come out to their siblings, whether or not they have siblings who are themselves gay, and may actually have closer relationships over time with siblings than heterosexual children do.

If our first role to negotiate within a family is as a child and sibling, our adult role in our society is assumed to involve parenting children. However, many people assume that lesbians do not have children. Lesbians often have children and make extraordinary efforts to keep custody of their children from previous marriages, for example, facing unpleasant court cases or deciding not to be out until the children are out of the home. A number of young lesbians today are choosing to have children on their own or with partners.

Even if they know that some lesbians do have children, the homophobic element in our society often asserts that lesbians should not have them, or be allowed near them. Part of this prejudice derives from the belief that children are not (or at least should not be) tainted by sex, combined with the false assumption that sex is what lesbians are all about. A significant aspect of the prejudice has to do with the fear that the child of the lesbian will not grow up to play the appropriate heterosexual sex role. This would threaten the patriarchal roots of our society that vest power in men and establish women and children as their property.

Another component of the prejudice assumes that the child of the lesbian will suffer a social stigma, as any child must who is different in our conformity-demanding culture. Marjorie Hill points out that it is not necessarily a disadvantage to grow up "different" in our society, however. Lesbian mothers, for example, provide many positive qualities for their children, such as a lowering of sex role expectations and valuing independence and self-sufficiency. Hill's study demonstrates that if we do our research ourselves instead of having it done *to* us, we can frame the questions and appreciate and interpret the answers in ways that counter homophobia and document our special qualities.

Because lesbian parenting has remained so invisible, the lesbian parent has the challenge of creating new family structures and family processes from scratch, as Sally Crawford points out. The lesbian family must counter the fact that it is at best invisible, is often assumed to be impossible, and at worst meets true hostility. We are in the process of creating ways for lovers to relate to each other as parents and to relate to each other's children. We are starting to create rituals to celebrate our coming together and our decisions to add new family members. We are working to balance carefully our roles regarding our children, and their roles and ours regarding a society that has a hard time seeing our choices as healthy. Much thought therefore goes into the development of lesbian families with children, leading to the iden-tification and resolution of questions taken for granted by many het-erosexuals.

Families, then, may hold a greater diversity of strong meanings for lesbians than they do for others. Our struggles to create alternative ways of interacting with our various family members may be painful and stressful at times, as any therapist will recognize. But there are many joys in making conscious decisions about our lives and in creating new kinds of relationships with others outside the limited roles of the "traditional" nuclear family. Through these struggles we make new structures and models familiar for ourselves, for our community, and in the long run for the society in which we find ourselves.

*Struggles/Clinical Issues*

In the course of realizing her identity, engaging in relationships, and participating in community, the healthy lesbian will encounter many psychological struggles. A few essays in this volume look at specific concerns that confront women in special ways, and lesbians in additional ways. Lee Nicoloff and Eloise Stiglitz suggest that alcoholism has been a greater problem in the lesbian community than for the heterosexual woman because for so long lesbian bars served as the major place to meet other lesbians in Western culture. Moreover, alcohol and drugs may be used as a reaction to external and internal homophobia. Issues of sexuality for lesbians and heterosexually active women would appear to be different on the basis of the Blumstein and Schwartz data.[11] Two chapters in this volume point out that it is not age per se that diminishes sexual desire in lesbian couples (Dunker), but rather relationship dynamics and female socialization (Nichols).

Laura Brown discusses the eating issues that arise for some lesbians. Perhaps more than many heterosexual women, lesbians are prepared to confront society's prescriptions for the way a woman's body is supposed to look; as feminists and lovers of women's bodies, lesbians come to recognize that we are responsible for feeding ourselves appropriately. Thus if alcoholism, sexual difficulties, and eating problems may exacerbate the stresses of being a lesbian, at the same time being a lesbian may also provide a woman with special strengths for dealing with these issues.

Intricacies of women's relations with family members take on a special light for the lesbian. What we learned from our parents about misogyny—either subtly through our parents' heterosexual relationships, or more vividly through incest as Eileen Starzecypyzel details, often remains to be sorted out in therapy.

Although differentiation may be a problem for many women in relationships and perhaps for some men, we suspect it is a particular concern for many lesbians, because it turns up so often in lesbian counseling and therapy, as Burch and Vargo point out. Merging, or permeating ego boundaries, is an exciting and powerful experience. It is an experience of closeness and being together, and demands new levels of understanding the phenomena of relationships. But merging also has costs as one's separate sense of self is upset. While independence and autonomy may represent male bias in psychological concepts, the subjective experiencing of an upset sense of separate self is distressing in a culture that prizes independence.

The struggle with homophobia has been mentioned at numerous points in this introduction, as it is in numerous points in the book. The overt and covert fear of lesbians in our society is conveyed to all of us at an early age in many ways. Moreover, many of us are rewarded for staying in the closet. As a result, a lesbian must struggle with her desire to be authentic not only to herself, but also publicly and with her too-often contradictory desire to get along comfortably in the world.

The lesbian must deal by herself, in couples, and in community with the homophobia we have all internalized, as the chapter by Liz Margolies, Martha Becker, and Karla Jackson-Brewer makes clear.

For the mental health worker dealing with lesbian clients, it is important to recognize and understand the many issues of lesbian identity, relationships, and struggles we discuss in this book. In addition, the clinician, counselor, or therapist must at a minimum appreciate the ideology from which the lesbian is operating, and respect and espouse it. Factors such as race, class, and culture that cut across strictly "lesbian" and "women's" issues must be recognized for their place in the psychological being of the lesbian. Struggles of the individual lesbian or the lesbian couple and the economic consequences of homophobia must be considered as well in therapy.

## Lesbian Community

For the lesbian, *community* has a variety of meanings. *Lesbian community* in the 1950s meant everybody you ran into at your local lesbian bars; more recently it includes the spectrum of people you see at lesbian and women's concerts, the theater, conferences, and at parties. It also means friendship groups and support groups. Communal groups develop to deal with life's circumstances, from organizations such as the Daughters of Bilitis to lesbian mothers' groups. In one major U.S. city, the Lesbians Considering Motherhood group got so large, with a mailing list of five hundred, that it divided into six support groups: one for lesbians considering adoption, one for lesbians currently being inseminated, and so forth. Community is also being expressed in terms of neighborhood lesbian groups in many cities. These meet both for social purposes and to take on political issues that express our power to the larger society.

This lesbian community has all the advantages and potential problems of a small town, as Susan Krieger records in her book, *The Mirror Dance*.[12] It offers social support for both the individual lesbian and for the couple. In the community we can share such common experiences as coming out, and we can gain an understanding of the stages through which family members and co-workers will go in response to our coming out.[13] In addition, individuals within the community can be counted on to provide many services in a nonhostile way, from counseling and legal assistance to crafts, child care, bookstores, restaurants, bars, and printing presses.

Because community provides us with support, assistance, and affirmation, we often have idealistic expectations of what it can offer, as

Sarah Pearlman and Francine Rainone point out in their chapters. The community in turn has expectations of its members. Rules on "political correctness" result in conflict and decreasing loyalty to community. Pearlman offers some theoretical explanations for this lack of respect for diversity; Rainone proposes that lesbian community develop at a spiritual level.

Identification as a lesbian poses special problems for lesbians who also identify with other communities. Moreover, certain single lesbians have complained of a couple imperative within the community, which means that couples will choose to associate with other couples, and not to associate with single individuals.

As Oliva Espín points out in her chapter, the choice to identify as a lesbian primarily or as a Latina primarily is a problematic one. Both communities pull the individual to behave in ways that are often contradictory. For different pairings of communities, moreover, and in different historical times, the conflicting weights we give to our several communities-of-reference may be different.

*Lesbian Psychology*

We have debated among ourselves as to how the study of lesbian psychology relates to the field of psychology generally, and to the field of psychology of women more particularly.

If lesbian psychology were a discipline it would, like all disciplines, include cognitive dimensions, normative dimensions, and an evaluative dimension.[14] The cognitive dimensions would include a body of knowledge about the psychology of lesbians, as well as a body of knowledge about the techniques applied in research and in clinical work on the psychology of lesbians. It would also include an articulated sense of the necessary training for the individual lesbian psychologist. The normative dimensions would elaborate a description of the range of psychological function of lesbians. They would also include a sense of the functions of lesbian psychologists and a discussion of the ethics of the field. The evaluative dimension would include a professional association, a structure and system for publications, and a recognized, unique identity with regard to related fields such as psychology generally and psychology of women.

Lesbian psychology may eventually develop into such a field. There are indications that it already meets certain requirements for it. For example, there is a new professional organization within the American Psychological Association, Division 44, the Society for the Psychological Study of Lesbian and Gay Issues; a new journal, *Lesbian Ethics*, that goes beyond but includes psychological issues; and a relatively recent literature on feminist clinical psychology that sometimes deals with lesbian concerns, including special issues of journals.[15] But many of the other aspects which would define lesbian psychology as a full-fledged discipline or profession do not exist, and may never come to exist. Indeed, we are not sure that they are desirable; perhaps ours should remain an interdisciplinary field in order to take advantage of all that has developed of value in the feminist study of the psychology of women.[16] The psychology of women has articulated the many ways in which models and assumptions within psychology generally are inadequate for accurate understanding of women. We maintain that this is all the more true for the lesbian, and we touch on this in the final section of this introduction.

The psychology of women offers us many aspects of a discipline and a profession: research methods, modes of scholarship, ethics, training, techniques and skills, professional associations, journals, and a recognized unique identity. It also offers us a corpus of knowledge about women's experience pertinent to most women and thus to many lesbians, but the special issues of lesbians have been slighted.

Historically, feminist psychologists and political organizations have not and could not focus on lesbian issues if they were to be taken seriously by the larger, not yet feminist society. If we examine causes, however, we realize that it is because the mere existence of lesbians — women who succeed in living relatively apart from men — is too threatening to the patriarchy and to heterosexual women. For precisely this reason, we would propose that lesbian psychology be seen as the core of psychology of women, toward which this discipline has been moving. The study of lesbian psychology, we are convinced, poses a fundamental challenge to psychology. It permits us to view woman in her "purest" form, that is, as untainted by the patriarchy as possible. It permits us to view her not only in her various personal aspects, but also in relation to other women and communities of women, and to build entirely new models of how women relate in the world.

Many of the issues discussed in the chapters of this book are issues on which solid work has been done in feminist psychology: issues of relationships, sexuality, identity, conflict resolution, women's relations to parents and children. For each of these issues, contributions to our book discuss the particular implications for lesbians: Vargo, for example, discusses how the principles of feminist counseling may be extended for use with the lesbian individual and the lesbian couple. Other issues would seem unique to lesbians. One theme that is a key issue throughout the book is the response to homophobia in our society. Studies remain to be done of the ways in which response to homophobia may be similar to, and different from, the other prejudices in our society based on race, color, ethnicity, religion, and class. Evaluation of how much we can learn about homophobia from societal misogyny and its repercussions for women generally needs study.

Within the field of psychology of women there is, if not a debate, a divergence of opinions; for example, Are Freud's psychodynamic theories and the object relations theories useful ways to think about the psychology of women, or dangerous ones?[17] Rather than attempt to come to a collective decision on the relative merits and difficulties with these theories, we have chosen to incorporate the several essays on these issues as an example of diversity: the diversity of approach even within the feminist psychology community as it considers lesbians.

In principle we do not resolve the somewhat different explanations for the decrease in sexuality in lesbian relationships offered by the chapters by Vargo and Nichols. Of course, a part of each of us would like to know what the "right answer" is. If we had it, we could get to work on it, correcting any problems, assuming we agree that decreased sex in a relationship *is* a problem. But in this spirit of opening up discussion, and with the feminist sense that there will always be a certain context-dependency making inappropriate our expectations that there will be a single, true answer, we have chosen to include chapters representing somewhat different views. Readers will no doubt find numerous other such examples in the course of the chapters that follow, and perhaps they will discover entire topics that should be included in the matrix for studying lesbian psychology that are not represented here. In any event, we are sure that the topics we have included are necessary for a study of lesbian psychology. Discussion of the individual lesbian as she relates to herself, to other lesbians in couple relationships, to her family of origin and her family of choice, to various communities and society and to her therapist or clients, must surely form core points for studies in the psychology of lesbians, whether the enterprise is regarded as a separate discipline, or as the touchstone for the psychology of women.

## New Directions

This work represents a beginning effort to capture the experience of contemporary American lesbians. The chapters in this volume draw on a limited body of existing research, theory, and clinical data from the psychology of women and traditional psychology. In presenting these essays that articulate and share experiences, raise questions, challenge traditional assumptions, and offer new perspectives, our goal has been to start a continuing discussion out of which will develop a dynamic, growing lesbian psychology.

In this book, lesbians come out to psychology. And just as an individual's coming out is a process in which there is commitment and clarity and the need for maturation, so in the coming out of a group there is the need for growth. In this final section of our Introduction, we want to suggest some directions for development.

Feminism has an important lesson for lesbians: the necessity of questioning traditional assumptions. Cultural models of male-female differences are deeply embedded in clinical thought and clinical processes. Awareness of those assumptions will lead to a valuing and prizing of the diversities of women's experience. For example, feminist enlightenment might lead to a relaxation of the nonpluralistic assumptions that there are standards for frequency and amount of sex in successful, long-term lesbian relationships, and there are appropriate and inappropriate amounts of food that women should feed themselves (see Brown's discussion of eating problems in this volume). Similarly, awareness of male power, motives, and social manipulations can serve as a liberating agent, enabling lesbians to see how we and our mothers have been victimized and led to devalue ourselves and each other.

Gender biases in psychological models have started to be explored by feminists. What had previously been seen as truth has been shown to derive from models contaminated by masculine ideas of objectivity and control. Awareness of this gender bias will lead us to ask further how our views of our own experience and how lesbian research and theory are colored by traditional views and assumptions. It will make it possible for us to expand our inquiry into the ways that external forces have shaped our internal psychologies—how patriarchy, homophobia, heterosexism, and social manipulations in policy, function, and belief have influenced lesbian experience.

Detailed analyses of external forces have not been a major concern in this book. The focus has been primarily on intrapsychic processes and interpersonal dynamics. Such analyses are important. As we have said, it does not make sense to ignore the importance of the mother and father in understanding individual development. Revisions of object relations theory, as it may apply to the lesbian experience, offer therapists a useful orientation and are in keeping with clinical traditions in psychology. However, the impact of the external world is equally important; it shapes and influences us and becomes internal. Within lesbian psychology, therefore, and in psychology in general, the impact of the external requires substantial further analysis of how the political becomes personal.

As the impact of social and political forces such as homophobia and patriarchy become central to our understandings, we can begin to introduce and revise other nonpsychodynamic theories, and we can invent new models. Drawing on social learning theory and developing pluralistic, women-valuing psychological models, for example, would add not only a fresh perspective, but also one that does not lead to labeling behavior as pathological. Variations in the coming-out process and in the ways we form couples might then be interpreted as creative, women-centered modes of living and not as "problems" to be dealt with in psychotherapy. For example, fusion might not be seen as pathological, but rather as a healthy development of boundaries that serve to protect the couple from a homophobic culture.

The social and political forces that make it necessary for a couple to fuse in order to protect themselves from a homophobic culture may also limit our vision so that the creative potential of fusion is not seen. The merged state in which fusion occurs may in fact be an example of an optimum state of human interaction—one that transcends isolating ego boundaries. Such a viewpoint is a long way from our standard psychodynamic conceptualization.

Implicit in the psychodynamic models that underlie much current thinking is the notion that discomfort means something is amiss—something that must be overcome by the lesbian individual, couple, or community. In contrast, views that take account of both the external forces impinging on lesbians and the impact of those forces on internal responses might interpret discomfort as a critical indication of awareness and coping. Thus, discomfort would become an indicator of creative adjustment rather than pathology.

As lesbian psychology matures, it will integrate the political analysis and theoretical challenge of feminism, producing lesbian-affirming clinical orientations. The merging of feminist perspectives, politics, and values with clinical thinking is perhaps the greatest need in carrying forward the discussion that is opened and invited by this book.

## NOTES

1. Nancy Chodorow, *The Reproduction of Mothering: Psychoanalysis and the Sociology of Gender* (Berkeley: University of California Press, 1978); Carol Gilligan, *In a Different Voice: Psychological Theory and Women's Development* (Cambridge: Harvard University Press, 1982); and Jane Flax, "The Conflict between Nurturance and Autonomy in Mother/Daughter Relationships and within Feminism," *Feminist Studies* 4 (Spring 1978): 171–89.

2. Sigmund Freud, *Three Essays on Sexuality*, Standard Edition, vol. 18, 1955; *Fragments of an Analysis of a Case of Hysteria*, Standard Edition, 1953; *The Psychogenesis of a Case of Homosexuality*, Standard Edition, vol. 18, 1955; *Leonardo da Vinci: A Study in Psychosexuality*, Standard Edition, 1959 (all published in London by Hogarth Press).

3. Rosemary Curb and Nancy Monahan, *Lesbian Nuns: Breaking Silence* (Tallahassee: Naiad Press, 1985).

4. Radclyffe Hall, *The Well of Loneliness* (London: Jonathan Cape, 1928).

5. *Diagnostic and Statistical Manual of Mental Disorders*, 3d ed. (Washington, D.C.: American Psychiatric Association, 1980).

6. Mark Freeman, *Homosexual and Psychological Functioning* (Belmont, Calif.: Brooks/Cole, 1971); Andrea V. Oberstone and Harriet Sukoneck, "Psychological Adjustment and Lifestyle of Single Lesbians and Single Heterosexual Women," in *Psychology of Women Quarterly* 1 (Winter 1976): 172–88.

7. Julia Penelope, "The Mystery of Lesbians," in *Lesbian Ethics*, vol. 1, no. 3 (Venice, Calif.: LE Publications, 1985).

8. Philip Blumstein and Pepper Schwartz, *American Couples* (New York: William Morrow, 1983).

9. Blumstein and Schwartz, *American Couples*.

10. Radclyffe Hall, *The Unlit Lamp* (New York: Deal Press, 1981).

11. Blumstein and Schwartz, *American Couples*.

12. Susan Krieger, *The Mirror Dance* (Philadelphia: Temple University Press, 1983).

13. Penelope, "The Mystery of Lesbians"; Casey Adair and Nancy Adair, *Word Is Out* (San Francisco: New Glide Publications, 1978).

14. Magali S. Larson, *The Rise of Professionalism: A Sociological Analysis* (Berkeley: University of California Press, 1977).

15. Sara Sharratt and Lilian Bern, "Lesbian Couples and Families: A Co-Therapeutic Approach to Counseling," in *Handbook of Feminist Therapy: Women's Issues in Psychotherapy*, ed. Lynne B. Rosewater and Lenore Walker (New York: Springer, 1985); Jean Israel, "A Feminist Works with the Nontraditional Client," in *Women and Mental Health*, ed. Elizabeth Howell and Marjorie Bayes (New York: Basic Books, 1981); and Del Martin and Phyllis Lyon, "Lesbian Women and Mental Health Policy," in *Women and Mental Health Policy*, ed. Lenore Walker (Beverly Hills, Calif.: Sage Publishing, 1984).

16. Susan Sturdivant, *Therapy with Women* (New York: Springer, 1980); Mary Ballou and Nancy Gabalac, *A Feminist Position on Mental Health* (Springfield, Ill.: Charles C. Thomas, 1985); Rosewater and Walker, eds., *Handbook of Feminist Therapy*; Muriel Greenspan, *A New Approach to Women and Therapy* (New York: McGraw Hill, 1981); and Walker, ed., *Women and Mental Health Policy*.

17. Sigmund Freud, *Three Essays on Sexuality*; Donald W. Winnicott, *The Maturational Processes and Facilitating Environments* (New York: International University Press, 1965); Heinz Kohut, *The Restoration of the Self* (New York: International University Press, 1977); and Margaret Mahler, *The Psychological Birth of the Human Infant* (New York: Basic Books, 1975).

# I

# IDENTITY

# 1

## *Diversity and Variability in Women's Sexual Identities*

CARLA GOLDEN

Psychologists and feminists alike tend to assume that most persons can be neatly categorized according to membership in one of four groups: heterosexual, homosexual, bisexual, or asexual (celibate). Furthermore, they tend to accept uncritically the notion that when a person's behavior fits into one of those four sexual preference categories, that person adopts a corresponding sexual identity to match the behavior. If such beliefs are not questioned, it seems logical to assume that a person whose sexual behavior is exclusively heterosexual would also assume a heterosexual identity, and conversely, that a person with a heterosexual identity would only engage in heterosexual behavior. The same connection between sexual behavior and sexual identity would be assumed of homosexuality as well.

The relation between sexual behavior and sexual identity may not be so clear-cut, however. For women, sexuality may be an aspect of identity that is fluid and dynamic as opposed to fixed and invariant. I came to think of women's sexuality in this way as a function of interviews and more general discussions with young college women who were exploring their sexuality. Many of these women were defining themselves as lesbians despite the fact that their current or previous sexual experience was heterosexual. I was confused by this, because I had tended to think of sex between women as rather central to the definition of lesbianism. However, as I read more feminist literature on sexuality and spoke with women who were feminists and/or lesbians, I came to see that the definition of a lesbian is both problematic and far from unambiguous. As a psychologist, I am primarily interested in how women subjectively experience their identities, and how they react when their personally constructed identities are not concordant with social definitions. Exploring these issues led me to a new view of women's sexuality.

I will review here some of the controversial definitional issues that have been identified in the feminist sexuality literature, and then will present the findings from interviews with college women. These interviews suggest that there is enormous diversity and variability in women's self-defined sexual identities, and that these identities are often at odds with social definitions. Finally, I will discuss how the exploration of sexuality from the perspective of a "deviant" group (i.e., lesbians) sheds some important light on the nature of women's sexuality in general.

How do feminist theorists interested in women's sexuality define lesbianism? Adrienne Rich's conception of the lesbian continuum provides an interesting introduction to the problematic nature of the term.[1] Instead of using the word *lesbianism*, which for her has connotations both clinical and pejorative, Rich suggests thinking in terms of a lesbian continuum. She notes that across history and cultures, women have in a variety of ways been primarily committed to other women, and she uses the term *lesbian continuum* to refer to the range of such women-identified experiences. That a woman has actually had, or has consciously desired, genital sexual experience with another woman is but one point on the lesbian continuum. By conceiving of lesbianism in these terms, Rich suggests that many more forms of primary intensity between and among women (including emotional bonding) can be included than would be possible with a narrower definition based solely on sexual behavior. Furthermore, according to Rich's definition, a woman need not identify herself as a lesbian in order to be considered one. By defining lesbianism in terms of primary intensity between women, she allows for women from previous historical periods to be considered as lesbians, even though at the time when they lived there may have been no cultural conception of lesbianism.

Rich's formulation holds that neither sexual relations nor sexual attraction between women is necessary for inclusion in the category *lesbian*. It should be noted that such a contention is not new. In 1973, the Radicalesbians, in their "Woman-Identified Women" article, focused on the political, as opposed to specifically sexual, nature of lesbianism when they defined it as "the rage of all women condensed to the point of explosion."[2] Blanche Wiesen Cook, in her *Chrysalis* article on "Female Support Networks and Political Activism," defined a lesbian as "a woman who loves women, who chooses women to nurture and support and to create a living environment in which to work creatively and independently, whether or not her relations with these women are sexual."[3] Such definitions, which have de-emphasized sexual feelings and behavior, have not been uncontroversial. Not only do they suggest that with whom one has sexual relations is not critical, but they also imply that a woman who never consciously considers herself to be a lesbian may in fact be thought of as one.

Ann Ferguson has argued that defining lesbianism in such a manner incorrectly downplays the importance of sexual feelings and behavior.[4] Such a definition in effect unsexes lesbianism and makes it more agreeable to some people by diminishing what is undeniably a significant difference. Furthermore, Ferguson argues that it isn't meaningful to talk about a woman as a lesbian if she doesn't acknowledge herself to be one. She suggests that, because before the twentieth century there was no cultural conception of lesbianism, one cannot and should not attempt to consider women lesbians who did not consider themselves to be such. As an alternative, Ferguson offers the following definition: "A lesbian is a woman who has sexual and erotic-emotional ties primarily with women or who sees herself as centrally involved with a community of self-identified lesbians whose sexual and erotic-emotional ties are primarily with women *and* who is herself a self-identified lesbian."[5] Without de-emphasizing the role of sexual behavior, this definition includes both celibate and bisexual women as lesbians, as long as they identify themselves as such.

The issue of self-conscious acknowledgment of lesbian identity is important, especially if we are talking about contemporary women for whom a definite cultural category of lesbian exists. The issue of sexual behavior is a bit more complicated, and Ferguson's definition reflects this in her use of the word "primarily," which allows for inclusion in the category *lesbian* women whose sexual relations are not exclusively with women. It is my observation that within certain lesbian communities there has tended to be more ready acceptance of celibate and of sexually inexperienced women who choose to call themselves lesbians than there has been of bisexual women who choose to identify themselves as lesbians. Thus, it seems that for some members of the lesbian community the critical issue in determining the "legitimacy" of a woman's claim to a lesbian identity is not whether or not she is sleeping with women, but whether she is sleeping with men. This kind of thinking is problematic because women's relations to men are given greater weight than are women's own self-conscious voices.

Some have argued that attempts to define who is and who is not a lesbian will only be divisive, and it seems undeniable that to a certain extent it has been. Jacquelyn Zita has aptly referred to this judging and weighing of who does and does not qualify for membership as the "Lesbian Olympics."[6] However, it does seem both intellectually important and socially useful for groups to define themselves. It is critical for any minority or oppressed group to break free from the confining definitions of the dominant culture and to create their own. In collectively resisting oppression, minority groups need to foster not only a positive group identity, but also a sense of the cohesiveness of the group based at least partially on shared characteristics and self-definitions.

While acknowledging that it is important for minority groups to define themselves (as opposed to being defined by the dominant group), it must be recognized that it is a sociopolitical task to do so, and that there are certain limitations inherent in such an enterprise. That is, to construct a definition is to identify a set of criteria according to which individual women can be considered to fit or not. Describing a social group is quite different from the psychological task of understanding what it means to any particular woman to identify as a member of that group. In fact, the construction of a categorical definition of lesbian is bound to obscure the personal and variable meanings of lesbian identity as it is experienced by real women. I say this because sexual feelings, attractions, and behavior are not necessarily fixed and invariant with regard to the sex of the person toward whom they are directed. When definitions of lesbian are conceptualized with primary reference to sexual feelings and activities, it may be difficult (if one wishes to allow for the complexity of lived experience) to construct unambiguous criteria that would specify who does and does not belong in the category *lesbian.*

A precise definition of lesbian that establishes unchanging sexual criteria according to which individual women can be judged as legitimate members of the category may not have the flexibility to account for the diversity and variability in subjectively experienced lesbian identities. One serious problem that results is that individual women may find their experience of themselves at odds with the socially constructed category, even when it emanates from the lesbian community. At this point in history when so many women are self-consciously asking who they are and how they can understand their place in society, it is possible to explore these issues with them directly.

Between 1977 and 1983, I taught at a northeastern women's college, where I served, albeit unofficially, as a counsellor to young women exploring their sexual and personal identities. For many of the women I spoke with over the years, these were times of change and transition, and among the most prominent changes were those in their sexual feelings, activities, and identities, and in their sense of possibilities for the future. Although many of these young women had been sexual (in varying degrees and with different sexual object choices) before coming to college, several features of their new environment converged to make the issue of sexuality in general, and their own sexuality in particular, more salient than it had been in their high school years.

One important aspect of their new environment was that they were away from their parents and had the option of engaging in sexual relations without having to be overly concerned about their parents' discovery of their behavior. Second, they were in an all-women's environment where close connections between women were valued, and where they were free to develop in ways not often matched in co-educational environments. In women's colleges, relationships between women can and do flourish; women have the opportunity to live, love, learn, work, and grow together. Although such environments are special in any historic time period, there was something unique about their atmosphere in the last ten years. As a result of the women's movement, the visibility of a small but dedicated number of feminist faculty, and the presence in the curriculum of women's studies courses, a certain self-consciousness about being women existed among a majority of the students. This consciousness gave rise to both self-exploration and a broader consideration of women's lives and possibilities, including the variety of vocational choices and sexual life-styles available to women. Added to this was a highly visible and active Lesbian Alliance on campus. At a time when many students were having to deal with themselves as sexual beings, they were also being exposed to "out" lesbians, many of whom were in more than a few respects indistinguishable from themselves. Workshops conducted by the Lesbian Alliance did a tremendous job in raising consciousness, and they also served, for some students, to heighten questions and thinking about their own sexuality.

Let me digress to address the issue of lesbianism at women's colleges, specifically whether it is more prevalent at such institutions than at coeducational colleges. Although the president and public relations officials at the college where I taught have steadfastly maintained that the proportion of lesbians at the college is not higher than in the population at large, it is still the case that alumnae, parents of prospective students, and some of the prospective students themselves, express strong concern about both the prevalence and the visibility of lesbianism on campus. Although I did not make a systematic survey, it is my impression that the incidence of lesbianism at this women's college was higher than in the population at large, even significantly so. Young women who had previously thought of themselves as heterosexual, as well as those who had suspected that they were lesbians but had tried to deny it, found in their four years at this college that there was something positive and good in lesbian relationships, and some of them began to identify proudly as lesbians. I believe that the environment at a women's college is both structurally and psychologically conducive to lesbianism. But I do not think that the concern expressed by alumnae, parents, and students is entirely attributable to the existence and visibility of lesbianism on campus. At least some of their concern is actually unrelated to the level of lesbianism on campus. For one thing, it is still considered unusual for a woman to choose to spend four years in an all-women environment, especially now that there are equivalently excellent coeducational liberal arts colleges. As is typically the case with women who make different choices, who choose to take themselves and other women so seriously that they decide not to organize four years or more of their lives around men, they get labeled deviant. And we all know what that means. Expressed concern about lesbianism at women's colleges is at least partially based on a failure to understand why women would choose to be together and on a fear of what that kind of choice suggests.

Second, I think fear or concern about lesbianism is at least partially a displaced fear among parents about their daughters' sexuality. Parents know that their daughters are going to engage in sexual explorations while away at college, and for a great many of those daughters, the explorations will involve heterosexual sex. I think it may be difficult for both mothers and fathers to conceive of this consciously; even if they do, it may be difficult to express to themselves, each other, and their daughters, some of their real concerns (e.g., that their daughters may be coerced or taken advantage of). Psychologically, parental concerns about their daughter's sexuality (in the broadest sense) may get displaced and expressed in relation to something about which, in a homophobic culture, concern can more readily be articulated and discussed, that is, lesbianism. I have often had the sense that parental preoccupation with lesbianism serves to assuage more deeply hidden or more difficult to acknowlege fears about the (hetero)sexual behavior of daughters.

Whether or not lesbianism is more prevalent at women's colleges is difficult to establish, and the expressed concern about it may in fact mask other issues and fears concerning women's choices. What is abundantly clear, however, is that at the women's college where I taught, there was a significant minority of young women who were actively engaged in the process of sexual self-definition. Let me return to some of the definitional concerns that emerged as particularly salient in my discussions with these women. I had extensive contact with students who were active members of the Lesbian Alliance (and who were thus viewed as "the lesbian community" on campus), as well as with students who were not publicly affiliated with the Alliance. I will articulate as well as I can from their perspective some of the ways in which these young women were defining themselves, and how they made sense of their pasts, their present, and their futures.

One major distinction that emerged from interviews with women who defined themselves as lesbian was between those who felt their lesbianism was essentially beyond their control and those who felt it was self-consciously chosen. Some of these women had from an earlier age (usually between six and twelve) considered themselves to be different from other girls. Whether or not they had a label for it, they experienced themselves as different in that they felt sexually attracted to and oriented toward other girls or women. Their feelings could be independent of actual sexual experiences. In other words, they may or may not have had lesbian relationships, and they may even have had heterosexual ones, but regardless, they felt themselves to be different in that they were attracted to females. Furthermore, this was experienced either at the time, or in retrospect, as something beyond their control; these women had not chosen to be attracted to women, they just were. Some of these women offered comments to the effect that they were "born" lesbians and would spontaneously contrast themselves with women who described their lesbianism as resulting from a conscious decision. Following a distinction made by Barbara Ponse in her study of a southern lesbian community, I have characterized these women as primary lesbians; that is, women who from an early age have a conscious sense of difference based on sexual attraction toward members of the same sex, and who do not perceive this difference to be based on any kind of conscious choice.[7]

In contrast to primary lesbians were women who could be characterized, again following the distinction made by Ponse, as elective lesbians. For these women, their lesbian identity is perceived as consciously chosen. This is not to imply that it is strictly a political choice; for the majority it is experienced as an erotic choice as well. Unlike primary lesbians, these women did not have a conscious sense of being different from other girls at a younger age. But in similarity with primary lesbians, their sense of identity was independent of their actual sexual history. As girls, some of these elective lesbians had crushes on other girls; they may even have engaged in sexual play and exchanges with other girls. Despite such lesbian-like experiences, they did not think of themselves as different. No one had ever labeled their behavior as deviant, and it had not occurred to them that others might consider it to be.

These women usually had some heterosexual experience as they got older, and even when they had not, they had heterosexual identities. However, regardless of their actual sexual experience, they never thought of themselves as different from the "average" female in terms of their sexual orientation. Although they may never have explicitly called themselves heterosexuals, neither did they consider the possibility that they were anything else (much in the manner of white people who never give much explicit thought to their race). I have characterized as elective lesbians women who perceive of their lesbianism as a conscious choice, and who do not have a history of thinking of themselves as different from other females in the realm of sexual inclinations.

Among elective lesbians, I found two distinctive sub-patterns that suggested another salient dimension of lesbian identity. Some of these women viewed their sexual attraction to women as a central, basic, and unchanging aspect of who they were, and it seemed to me that this was not merely a political stance but a strongly experienced subjective feeling about their essential natures. In light of this sense of themselves, their past heterosexual behavior and identity presented an inconsistency. Unwilling to accept this apparent discontinuity and given their belief in the stability and enduring quality of their sexual orientation, they repeatedly expressed the view that there was something "unreal" about their previous heterosexuality. This was reflected in their tendency to reinterpret their past history to suggest a continuity between past and present senses of self. As one woman put it, "In high school when I had a steady boyfriend, the real me, the lesbian, was suppressed. I just wasn't my real self back then." For other women, their less-than-satisfactory heterosexual experiences confirmed that they had really been lesbians all along. Still others pointed to their intense friendships with girlfriends as suggestive of their true lesbian identities. Sexual feelings and behaviors were central to the lesbian identities of these women, and they believed in the essentiality of their lesbianism.

Other elective lesbians did not view their lesbianism as an essential and enduring aspect of who they were. They did not show any tendency to reinterpret their past history, and did not experience dissonance or contradiction in describing themselves as lesbians with heterosexual pasts. As one woman put it quite simply, "Then I was heterosexual, and now I'm a lesbian." These women expressed the view that there was nothing inconsistent or in need of explanation about their present identity and the one they had assumed in the past. Some of these women revealed, upon questioning, that they had engaged in childhood sexual play with other girls or had had strong attachments to camp counsellors and teachers, but had never thought of these as lesbian feelings. Although they currently identified themselves as lesbians, they saw no reason to reconstruct their pasts as implicitly lesbian. Unlike the elective lesbians previously described, they did not view sexual attraction to women as an essential and unchanging aspect of who they were, although they strongly believed they would continue to have their primary (if not all) relationships with women. Some women said they considered themselves to be lesbians whose sexual feelings could be most accurately characterized as bisexual, or just sexual; however, these comments tended to be private as opposed to publicly stated. Other lesbians in this subgroup defined themselves as lesbian and let its essentiality be assumed, while privately they experienced their sexuality as fluid, or potentially so.

To summarize, in the sample of college women with whom I worked, one major difference that emerged was in whether their lesbianism was experienced as determined (i.e., primary) or self-consciously chosen (i.e., elective). Another major difference had to do with whether their lesbianism was experienced as a central and enduring aspect of who they were, or whether it was experienced as more fluid and dynamic in nature. These two dimensions of difference were not entirely independent of one another. Among those lesbians whose identity was a chosen one, some experienced their sexuality as essential, others as fluid; among those lesbians whose identity felt determined, sexuality was experienced as essential by definition.

With respect to these dimensions of sexuality, there appear to be some interesting age differences. I have spoken with elective lesbians in their late twenties, thirties, and forties who described shifts in their thinking about the nature of their lesbianism. Some had at an earlier age experienced their sexuality as essential and fixed, that is, invariantly focused on women, but later in the development of their lesbian identity had come to feel that their sexuality was in fact more fluid. For a few, this shift resulted from bisexual experiences later in life. Others who felt this way had continued to have relationships only with women. They attributed their earlier position to their more adamant lesbian feminist politics or to what they thought was a developmental phase many lesbians go through.

Alternatively, some elective lesbians felt that in their younger years, when they were engaged in sexual exploration and discovery, their sexuality was more fluid, but that in the context of lesbian culture and relationships they had developed a very explicit preference for women. These women thought of their sexuality as having become more fixed as they got older. Whereas the college women with whom I worked characterized their sexuality as either fixed or fluid, some older women had experienced shifts over the life-cycle in this aspect of their sexuality.

It seems that as lesbians engage in the continuing process of self-definition, their sense of the essentiality or fluidity of their sexuality may change. In contrast, the distinction between primary and elective lesbianism seems to remain more dichotomous over the course of development. Women of all ages with whom I have spoken made reference to such a distinction; they tended to identify as one or the other, and experienced this identification as one that was stable.

Let me return to my discussion of these differing dimensions of lesbian identity as they were experienced by the students with whom I spoke. Because among themselves some of these students discussed lesbianism and their differing experiences of it, they were often aware that not all lesbians described themselves similarly. Sometimes they had distinct opinions about themselves in relation to other lesbians who described themselves differently. For example, some women whom I have characterized as primary lesbians referred to themselves as "born" or "real" lesbians with the implicit designation of elective lesbians as "fake."

It was not uncommon for an elective lesbian to express to me privately her speculations about whether she was "really" a lesbian. At times she wondered whether she wasn't "really" bisexual, or even heterosexual. While some primary lesbians interpret such uncertainty as difficulty in coming out, unwillingness to give up heterosexual privilege, or internalized homophobia, it seems to me that at least some of the elective lesbian's uncertainty can be traced back to the belief within the campus lesbian community that women who choose to be lesbians are somehow less real, or legitimate, than those who felt they had no choice about it.

Despite this belief, there did seem to me to be a tolerance within the community for differences based on primary, compared with elective, lesbianism. In contrast, the issue of whether sexuality was thought of as essential or fluid was a much more sensitive one. For example, there was a noteworthy asymmetry in the application of the concept of the fluidity of sexual attractions when discussed in relation to lesbian and heterosexual women. I spoke with more than a few lesbians who were quite intolerant of (some) heterosexual women's insistence that they simply were not sexually attracted to women and that they couldn't imagine ever feeling differently. Implied in their intolerance was the belief that, despite heavy socialization pressures, sexual attraction is never so fixed and unmalleable as to be irrevocably focused just on persons of one sex. Yet some of these same women were equally intolerant of the opposite stance, that sexual feelings could exist toward persons of either sex, when expressed by a lesbian.

The assumption was often made about lesbians who were unwilling to state that they were (forever) uninterested sexually in men, that they must be having difficulty coming out, or were unwilling to accept a stigmatized identity. Sometimes they were assumed to be going through a bisexual phase, or worse yet, to be male-identified and operating under a false consciousness. The assumption that bisexuality is simply a phase in the coming-out process of lesbians, and that those who call themselves bisexuals are really lesbians unwilling to call themselves that, has been countered by the contention from self-proclaimed bisexuals that their lesbianism was a phase in their coming out as bisexuals.[8]

The problem with all of these assumptions is that one person or set of persons presumes an attitude of knowing and understanding the meaning of another person's experience better than the person who is herself experiencing it. In this climate, individual women may have a difficult time finding their own voices and defining their own experiences. To the extent that lesbianism is very narrowly defined, the categories will restrict, rather than give full expression to, the diversity among women who subjectively define themselves as lesbian.

The question of sexual identity and how it is formed is not well understood, but some of our psychological conceptions do not do justice to the complexity of the process. We have often simplistically assumed that people have sexual attractions to persons of one or the other sex (but not both), that they act on those exclusive attractions, and that they eventually come to adopt the identity appropriate to their sexual activities, although there may be resistance when that identity is a stigmatized one. It appears to be the case, however, that sexual feelings and activities change; they can be fluid and dynamic. And furthermore, the reality is that feelings, activities, and self-conscious identities may not at all times be congruent. It has been suggested by social psychologists that people strive for congruence between their thoughts and feelings,[9] and that with respect to sexual identity in particular, we are motivated to achieve congruence between our feelings, activities, and self-proclaimed identities.[10] This suggestion, however, does not accord with what I observed during my six-and-a-half years at a women's college in the late seventies and early eighties.

What particularly struck me, among this select sample of college women, was the diversity in self-definitions and the degree of incongruence between their sexual activities and their sexual identities (as expressed both publicly and privately). Every possible permutation of feelings and activities existed within each sexual identification category. Further, I was impressed by the way in which these young women were able to tolerate the ambiguity without significant internal distress.

Let me elaborate on the observation that every possible permutation existed. Among women who identified themselves to me as lesbians, there were some whose sexual behavior was explicitly and exclusively lesbian, and some whose behavior was exclusively heterosexual or bisexual (these latter also described themselves as "political lesbians"). In addition, I spoke with sexually inexperienced women who considered themselves to be lesbians. Although no student ever self-consciously identified herself as a celibate lesbian, this is a distinct possibility and has been described by Susan Yarborough.[11] Thus, among women who call themselves lesbians, a wide range of sexual behavior is evident.

Far fewer women described themselves to me as having a bisexual identity, and those who did made it quite clear that this was a confidential disclosure. The small number of self-identified bisexuals was particularly interesting in light of the findings from a survey of sexual behavior and attitudes taken in a psychology of women class I taught. The survey was constructed by students in the class and administered in such a way as to insure complete anonymity. In response to the question of how they would label their sexuality to themselves, regardless of their actual sexual experiences, 65 percent (of 95 students) identified as heterosexual, 26 percent identified as bisexual, and 9 percent identified as lesbian. When asked what their actual sexual experiences were, the responses were as follows: 72 percent heterosexual, 20 percent bisexual, 4 percent lesbian, and 4 percent lacking sexual experience. Two things are interesting about these figures. First, they reveal that the way in which women sexually identify themselves does not always coincide with their actual sexual experience. Second, although three times as many women privately considered themselves to be bisexual as contrasted with lesbian, their concerns were never publicly raised, nor were their bisexual identities ever acknowledged in class. In comparison, lesbian concerns and identities were much more visible in the classroom. It began to occur to me that acknowledging one's bisexuality, or raising such issues publicly, was as stigmatized as discussing lesbianism, if not more so.

To return to the question of the various permutations of sexual activity and identity: Among those interviewed women who identified themselves to me as bisexual, some were engaged in exclusively lesbian activity, some were engaged in exclusively heterosexual activity, while others actually had bisexual experience. Some women who were sexually inexperienced considered themselves on the basis of their potential sexual behavior to be bisexual.

Finally, to complete consideration of the various permutations, consider women who identified themselves to me as heterosexual. Here too, I found women whose current sexual behavior was exclusively lesbian (of the "I just love Mindy; I'm not a lesbian" variety) as well as those whose sexual behavior was exclusively heterosexual. A few women considered themselves to be basically heterosexual even though they had had bisexual experience. And again, some women who were sexually inexperienced nevertheless asserted that they knew they were heterosexual.

The point I wish to make by describing these combinations is not simply that one's sexual identity is not always predictable on the basis of one's sexual behavior, but rather that the assumption that we inherently strive for congruence between our sexual feelings, activities, and identities may not be warranted, and that given the fluidity of sexual feelings, permanent congruence may not be an achievable state. The women with whom I spoke were not personally distressed by the fact of discrepancies between sexual behavior and sexual identity. For example, women who identified as lesbians but found themselves to be occasionally sexually attracted to men were made more uncomfortable by the thought of what other lesbians might think than by their own fluid and changing attractions. These were women who wanted to be considered legitimate members of the lesbian community, but who often felt that they were not welcome, or that if they were, they were not trusted. Although very often they felt compelled to identify themselves publicly and unequivically as lesbians whose sexuality was stable and enduring and exclusively focused on women, they privately experienced their sexuality in a more fluid and dynamic manner. The pressure to be congruent and to proclaim an identity that was in line with their sexual activities was often more externally than internally motivated.

These women are real, not hypothetical. Although the kind of lesbian they represent did not constitute a majority of the self-defined lesbians with whom I spoke, I think that the way they experienced their identities and their relation to the community has implications for how psychologists talk about sexuality and sexual identity.

Identity is constructed both societally and psychologically; it is both a social and a personal process. The process of psychological self-definition takes place within the context of existing dominant culture definitions as well as those that emanate from within the minority community itself. Not only are lesbians a stigmatized and oppressed group, with the result that many have internalized negative images of self, but they are also a group whose central characteristic is debatable and not altogether invariant. Hence its boundaries are more permeable than those of other minority groups. Unlike one's sex or race, which is typically both highly visible and unchanging, one's sexuality (like one's class) is less visible and not so static over the course of a lifetime. Thus, the process of lesbian identity formation is complicated not only because of homophobia, but also because of the nature of sexuality itself.

When counselling women who are engaged in the act of sexual self-definition, therapists need to be aware of the variations in the process of identity formation. On the basis of the findings presented here, it is suggested that psychologists need to take a more serious look at the assumptions inherent in the phrase "coming out." It is not uncommon to hear clinicians talk about women who are in the process of coming out, or who have difficulty with coming out, as if they know what the "right" result looks like. We should begin to question not only whether there is a "right" way to come out, but also whether there is some static end point at all. Liberal teachers and clinicians often think their appropriate role with lesbians is to help them deal with coming out, but I would urge us to think seriously about the relationship between coming out and self-definition. It seems to me that the aim ought to be to encourage each woman as she struggles to define herself. This may mean facilitating her search for authenticity rather than assuming a fixed sexuality that the therapist will help her discover. If being authentic entails accepting the fluidity of one's sexual feelings and activities and identifying as a lesbian, therapists should support this rather than convey the impression that the woman is confused or unwilling to accept a stigmatized identity.

These interviews suggest that sexuality is experienced by some women (both heterosexual and lesbian) as an aspect of identity that may change over the course of their lives. Although there has not been research on this issue with male homosexuals, from reading gay male literature, speaking with a small sample of gay men, and exchanging views with therapists who work with them, my sense is that gay men do not experience their sexuality in the fluid manner that some lesbian and heterosexual women do. I have no strong data on this, but I suspect that very few gay men could be characterized as elective homosexuals. Although this observation might at first seem puzzling and lead one to wonder why the nature of sexuality would be different for women and for men, I think it becomes more understandable with reference to psychoanalytic theories of mothering that place emphasis on the primary human need for social relationship and then examine the expression of that need in terms of the infant's first love object: its mother. Specifically, object relations theory can provide the framework for understanding how the conditions of early infancy might lead women to have greater bisexual potential than men. Dorothy Dinnerstein has discussed how the first relationship with a woman establishes a homoerotic potential in women,[12] and Nancy Chodorow has elaborated on the early psychic foundations of women's homoemotional needs and capacities.[13] The writings of both of these authors can provide the basis for formulation of a new question: Why do so many women become exclusively heterosexual as opposed to bisexual or lesbian?

One of the most important insights of both feminist psychology and the women's movement is that our being born female does not mean that we automatically and naturally prefer certain roles and activities. We have recognized that the category *woman* has been socially constructed, and that societal definitions notwithstanding, women are a diverse group with interests, attitudes, and identities that do not always conform to what is traditionally considered feminine. We have long been told that we are not "real" women unless we are wives and mothers, and to counter this, feminists have been forceful and articulate in asserting that one's sex is not related in any inevitable or natural way to one's sexual preference or societal role. In a similar vein I suggest, on the basis of my discussions with a select sample of college women, that sexual feelings and activities are not always accurately described in either/or terms, nor do they exist in a simple one-to-one relation to our sexual identities. Just as we have protested the constricting social definition of what a real woman is, precisely because it has served to oppress women and to limit the expression of our diverse potentials, so too must we be careful in our social construction of sexuality not to construct categories that are so rigid and inflexible that women's self-definitions put them at odds with the social definitions. To do so only limits the expression of the diversities and variabilities in women's sexual identities.

### NOTES

1. Adrienne Rich, "Compulsory Heterosexuality and Lesbian Existence," *Signs* 5 (Summer 1980): 631–60.
2. "Radicalesbians, Woman-Identified Women," in *Radical Feminism,*

ed.  Ann Koedt, Ellen Levine, and Anita Rapone (New York: Quadrangle Books, 1973).

3. Blanche Wiesen Cook, "Female Support Networks and Political Activism," *Chrysalis* 3 (1977): 43–61.

4. Ann Ferguson, "Compulsory Heterosexuality and Lesbian Existence: Defining the Issues," *Signs* 7 (Autumn 1981): 158–72.

5. Ferguson, "Compulsory Heterosexuality," 166.

6. Jacquelyn Zita, "Compulsory Heterosexuality and Lesbian Existence: Defining the Issues," *Signs* 7 (Autumn 1981): 172–87.

7. Barbara Ponse, *Identities in the Lesbian World* (Westport, Conn.: Greenwood Press, 1978).

8. Lisa Orlando, "Loving Whom We Choose: Bisexuality and the Lesbian/ Gay Community," *Gay Community News*, Feb. 25, 1984.

9. Leon Festinger, *A Theory of Cognitive Dissonance* (Evanston, Ill.: Row, Peterson, 1957).

10. Vivienne Cass, "Homosexual Identity Formation: A Theoretical Model," *Journal of Homosexuality* 4 (Fall 1979): 219–35.

11. Susan Yarborough, "Lesbian Celibacy," *Sinister Wisdom* 11 (Fall 1979): 24–29.

12. Dorothy Dinnerstein, *The Mermaid and the Minotaur: Sexual Arrangements and Human Malaise* (New York: Harper & Row, 1976).

13. Nancy Chodorow, *The Reproduction of Mothering: Psychoanalysis and the Sociology of Gender* (Berkeley: University of California Press, 1978).

# 2

## Issues of Identity in the Psychology of Latina Lesbians

OLIVA M. ESPÍN

Identity development for persons of ethnic or racial minority groups involves not only the acceptance of an external reality that can rarely be changed (e.g., being black, Puerto Rican, Jewish, or Vietnamese), but also an intrapsychic "embracing" of that reality as a positive component of one's self. By definition in the context of a heterosexist, racist, and sexist society, the process of identity development for Latina lesbian women entails the embracing of "stigmatized" or "negative" identities. Coming out to self and others in the context of a sexist and heterosexist American society is compounded by coming out in the context of a heterosexist and sexist Latin culture immersed in racist society. Because as a Latina she is an ethnic minority person, she must be bicultural in American society. Because she is a lesbian, she has to be polycultural among her own people.

The dilemma for Latina lesbians is how to integrate who they are culturally, racially, and religiously with their identity as lesbians and women. The identity of each Latina lesbian develops through conscious and unconscious choices that allot relative importance to the different components of the self, and thus of her identity as woman, as lesbian, as Latina.

### Identity Development

The term *identity* is understood here as that which each woman tells herself about who she is when she is alone with herself. The term is also understood as that which each context to which she is field sensitive

calls forth in a given moment. In other words, identity is also associated
with social image.

According to Erik Erikson, the crises conducive to the development
of an integrated identity consist of "a state of being and becoming that
can have a highly conscious (and, indeed, self-conscious) quality and
yet remain, in its motivational aspects, quite conscious and beset with
the dynamics of conflict." Because a "part of identity must be accounted
for in that communality within which an individual finds himself"
there might be "fragments that the individual had to submerge in
himself as undesirable or irreconcilable or which his group has taught
him to perceive as the mark of fatal 'difference' in sex role or race in
class or religion."[1] For both lesbians and ethnic minority persons of
both sexes and, indeed, for ethnic minority lesbians, the process of
identity development is full of vicissitudes, and it frequently demands
the submerging of different fragments of the self.

However, as Erikson has written, "certain historical periods present
a singular chance for a collective renewal which opens up unlimited
identities for those who, by a combination of unruliness, giftedness,
and competence, represent a new leadership, a new elite, and new
types . . . in a new people."[2] We seem to be living in such a period,
and ethnic minority lesbians seem to be at a crucial point of this
psychohistorical process.

Obviously, different individuals are at different stages of identity
development: that is to say, different stages of clarity about who they
are, or are finding different ways of embracing the labels—imposed
or chosen—by which people classify each other and themselves, including embracing those aspects of identity considered to be negative
by the group or groups to which the individual belongs. The process
is not necessarily linear for any given individual. In fact, identities are
fluid as is the process of developing them. Donald Atkinson, George
Morten, and Derald Wing Sue have evolved a model of identity development for ethnic minorities that captures the fluidity of the process
and describes its phases in a clear and concise way (Table 1).[3] Vivienne
Cass has developed a similar theoretical model in reference to homosexual identity formation.[4] Both models incorporate the different possible reactions to a negative identity that ethnic minority persons and
homosexuals can have at different points in life.

In the Atkinson, Morten, and Sue model, stage one, Conformity,
is characterized by a preference for dominant cultural values over one's
own culture. The reference group is likely to be the dominant cultural
group, and feelings of self-hatred, negative beliefs of one's own culture,
and positive feelings toward the dominant culture are likely to be strong.

TABLE 1. Minority Identity Development Model

| Stages of minority development model | Attitude toward self | Attitude toward others of the same minority | Attitude toward others of different minority | Attitude toward dominant group |
|---|---|---|---|---|
| State 1: conformity | Self-depreciating | Group depreciating | Discriminatory | Group appreciating |
| State 2: dissonance | Conflict between self-depreciating and appreciating | Conflict between group depreciating and group appreciating | Conflict between dominant-held views of minority hierarchy and feelings of shared experience | Conflict between group appreciating and group depreciating |
| Stage 3: resistance and immersion | Self-appreciating | Group appreciating | Conflict between feelings of empathy for other minority experiences and feelings of culturocentrism | Group depreciating |
| Stage 4: introspection | Concern with basis of self-appreciation | Concern with nature of unequivocal appreciation | Concern with ethnocentric basis for judging others | Concern with the basis of group depreciation |
| Stage 5: synergetic articulation and awareness | Self-appreciating | Group appreciating | Group appreciating | Selective appreciating |

From D. R. Atkinson, G. Morten, and D. W. Sue, *Counseling American Minorities: A Cross-Cultural Perspective*, Dubuque, Iowa: William C. Brown, 1979, 198.

The second stage, or Dissonance, is characterized by cultural confusion and conflict. Information and experiences begin to challenge accepted values and beliefs. Active questioning of the dominant-held values operates strongly. In stage three, Resistance and Immersion, an active rejection of the dominant society and culture and a complete endorsement of minority-held views become evident. Desires to combat oppression become the primary motivation of the person. There is an attempt to get in touch with one's history, culture, and traditions. Distrust and hatred of dominant society is strong. The reference group is one's own culture. Stage four, Introspection, is characterized by conflict at the too-narrow and rigid constraints of the previous stage. Notions of loyalty and responsibility to one's own group and notions of personal autonomy come in conflict. In stage five, Synergetic Articulation and Awareness, individuals experience a sense of self-fulfillment with regard to cultural identity. Conflicts and discomfort experienced in the Introspective stage have been resolved, allowing greater individual control and flexibility. Cultural values are examined and accepted or rejected on the basis of prior experience gained in earlier stages of identity development. Desire to eliminate all forms of oppression becomes an important motivation of the individual's behavior.[5]

Vivienne Cass's model proposes six stages of development that individuals move through in order to acquire a fully integrated identity as a homosexual person. In stage one, Identity Confusion, the individual realizes that feelings, thoughts, or behavior can be defined as homosexual, and this realization presents an incongruent element into a previously stable situation in which both the individual and the environment assumed the person to be heterosexual. As a result of this incongruency the individual arrives at a self-identity potentially that of a homosexual.[6] "Where the task of stage one was to resolve the immediate personal identity crisis of Who am I?' the task of stage two, Identity Comparison, is to handle the social alienation that now arises." In stage three, Identity Tolerance, there is an increased level of commitment to the homosexual self-image. "At this stage, contacting homosexuals is viewed as something that has to be done in order to counter the felt isolation and alienation from others. The individual tolerates rather than accepts a homosexual identity." Stage four, Identity Acceptance, is "characterized by continued and increasing contacts with other homosexuals. These allow [the person] to feel the impact of those features of the subculture that validate and 'normalize' homosexuality as an identity and a way of life. [The individual] now accepts rather than tolerates a homosexual self-image." Entrance into stage five, Identity Pride, is characterized by the incongruencies that exist between a concept of self as totally acceptable as a homosexual and society's rejection of this concept. In order to manage this incongruency, heterosexuals and heterosexuality are devalued. A combination of anger and pride is developed, and confrontation with the environment may occur. More and more strategies previously used to conceal a homosexual identity are deliberately abandoned. Disclosure becomes a strategy for coping. Stage six, Identity Synthesis, starts "with an awareness that the 'them and us' philosophy espoused previously, in which all heterosexuals were viewed negatively and all homosexuals positively, no longer holds true. . . . Personal and public sexual identities become synthesized into one image of self receiving considerable support from [the] environment. . . . Homosexual identity. . . instead of being seen as the identity, is now given the status of being merely one aspect of the self. This awareness completes the homosexual identity formation process."[7]

Although these two models are not identical, they describe a similar process that must be undertaken by people who must embrace negative or stigmatized identities. This process moves gradually from a rejected and denied self-image to the embracing of an identity that is finally accepted as positive. Both models describe one or several stages of intense confusion and at least one stage of complete separatism from and rejection of all representatives of the dominant society. The final stage for both models implies the acceptance of one's own identity, a committed attitude against oppression, and an ability to synthesize the best values of both perspectives and to communicate with members of the dominant group.

## Latina Lesbians

It can be reasonably asserted that the development of identity in Latina lesbians must follow patterns similar to those described by these two models. However, I do not know of any studies on this topic. Indeed, the literature on Latina lesbians is scarce.

A professional presentation by Hortensia Amaro discussed the issue of coming out for Hispanic lesbians,[8] and some literary discussions that address the experiences of Latina lesbians have been published by Cherríe Moraga.[9] Although there might be studies in progress on this population, very few have been published. Hilda Hidalgo and Elia Hidalgo-Christensen have published two versions of a study of Puerto Rican attitudes toward lesbianism.[10] Yvonne Escaserga and her collaborators studied the attitudes of Chicana lesbians toward psychotherapy.[11] To my knowledge, no other research studies focus particularly

on Latina lesbians or on the specific aspect of their identity development.

Although emotional and physical closeness among women is encouraged by Latin culture, overt acknowledgment of lesbianism is even
more restricted than in mainstream American society. Hidalgo and
Hidalgo-Christensen, for example, discuss the importance of *amigas
íntimas* (intimate female friends) for Puerto Rican women, and contrast
it with the results of their research that show that most members of
the Puerto Rican community strongly reject lesbianism. They found
that "rejection of homosexuals appears to be the dominant attitude in
the Puerto Rican community."[12] At a meeting of Hispanic women in a
major U.S. city in the early 1980s, one participant expressed the opinion
that "lesbianism is a sickness we get from American women and American culture." This is, obviously, an expression of the common belief
that homosexuality is chosen behavior acquired through the bad influence of others. Socialist attitudes with respect to homosexuality are
extremely traditional, as the attitudes of the Cuban and other revo-
lutions clearly manifest. Thus, Latinos who consider themselves radical
and committed to civil rights may remain extremely traditional when
it comes to gay rights. In a book entitled *Pleasure and Danger: Exploring
Female Sexuality*, I have discussed the impact of the prevalent Latin
attitudes on Hispanic women who have a lesbian orientation.[13] These
attitudes clearly add further stress to the lives of Latina lesbians who
are invested in participating in the life of their communities. Although
these attitudes may not seem different from those of the dominant
culture, some important differences experienced by Latina lesbians are
directly related to Hispanic cultural patterns. Latin families tend to treat
their lesbian daughters or sisters with silent tolerance: Their lesbianism
will not be openly acknowledged and accepted, but they are not denied
a place in the family, either. Very seldom is there overt rejection of
their lesbian members on the part of Hispanic families. The family may
explain away the daughter's lesbianism by saying that "she is too
intelligent to marry any man" or "too dedicated to her work to bother
with dating, marriage or motherhood." Nevertheless, because frequent
contact and a strong interdependence among family members, even in
adult life, are essential features of Hispanic family life, leading a double
life may become more of a strain. Because of the importance placed
on family and community by most Hispanics, the threat of possible
rejection and stigmatization by the Latin community becomes more of
a psychological burden for the Hispanic lesbian. Rejection from mainstream society does not carry the same weight. As Cherríe Moraga puts

it, "that is not to say that Anglo culture does not stigmatize its women for 'gender transgression'—only that its stigmatization did not hold the personal power over me which Chicano culture did."[14]

To avoid stigmatization by the Latin community, Hispanic lesbians frequently seek other groups or networks in which their lesbian orientation will be more accepted than it is in their family and its community. However, as Hortensia Amaro states, "reliance on alternative support groups outside the Hispanic community would not occur without a cost. Loss of contact with the ethnic community and culture will mean lack of support for their identity as a Hispanic. On the other hand, staying within the Hispanic community and not 'coming out' will represent a denial of the identity associated with sexuality and intimate love relationships."[15] To be out of the closet only in an Anglo context deprives them of essential supports from their communities and families, and, in turn, increases their invisibility in the Hispanic culture, where only the openly "butch" types are recognized as lesbian. To complicate matters even further, Latina lesbians sometimes experience discrimination or more subtle forms of racism, not only from the mainstream of American society, but also within the context of the Anglo lesbian communities in which they continue to be in numerical minority.

Many Latina women who are lesbians choose to remain closeted among their families, their colleagues, and society at large. Coming out may jeopardize not only the strong family ties, but also the possibility of serving the Hispanic community. This is particularly difficult because the talents of all members are such an important asset for any minority community. Because most lesbian women are single and self-supporting and not encumbered by the demands of husbands and children, it can be assumed that the professional experience and educational level of Hispanic lesbians will tend to be relatively higher than that of other Hispanic women. Because there are no statistics on Hispanic lesbians, this assertion cannot be easily proved. But if it is true, professional experience and education will frequently place Latina lesbians in positions of leadership or advocacy in their community. Their status and prestige, and thus the ability to serve their community, will be easily threatened by the possibility of being found out by the same people they are trying to serve.

## Cuban Lesbians

Having provided some background on the development of identity in minority persons and on the experience of Latina lesbians, I will present what a group of Cuban lesbians have to say about the different components of their identity. I was prompted by a recognition of the problems encountered by Latina lesbians to study the relative importance of these identity components in a group of such women. I wanted to assess the relative degree of cultural and lesbian identity for this group. How did these women integrate the different components of the self in the process of identity formation? I decided to limit my study to Cuban women in order to reduce the number of intervening factors that may differentiate among Hispanic subgroups. Although the study focuses on Cuban women, the results serve to illustrate general principles relevant to the identity development of other Latinas and minority lesbians.

## THE STUDY

I distributed a questionnaire (Appendix) through friendship pyramiding among Cuban lesbians in several cities in the United States and analyzed the responses primarily through the use of qualitative methods. Qualitative methodology provides a legitimate and flexible format for an exploratory study, based on a sample of convenience obtained through friendship pyramiding such as this one.[16]

I kept both the Atkinson, Morten, and Sue model of ethnic minority identity development and the Cass model of homosexual identity development as background for understanding the process of identity formation of the respondents. However, I made no effort at coding questions on the basis of the stages described in these two models. Because there is no other study published on this specific population of lesbians, I saw value in examining how they themselves described their experience without superimposing any previously determined model of analysis.

I mailed thirty-five questionnaires: fifteen to specific individuals and twenty in small packets of five to people who had offered to contact others. Sixteen completed questionnaires were returned.[17] The respondents expressed great enthusiasm for the study, and almost all of them asked to be sent results and to be kept informed about any future studies on this matter.

It is important to acknowledge the possibility that respondents are only among those women who have embraced the multiple components of their identity enough to be willing to answer and return the questionnaire. In fact, I heard through the grapevine that some of the prospective respondents felt that their lesbianism was a "trial" sent by God, which they had to suffer and endure and thus found the questionnaire too difficult and decided not to answer it. In addition, because the questionnaire was written in English, it presupposes literacy in English on the part of prospective respondents, at least to be able to read it. (Respondents were encouraged to answer in Spanish if they preferred. However, although some Spanish was used, questionnaires were primarily answered in English.) A further consideration is that respondents were highly educated and perhaps not representative of the population of Cuban lesbians in the United States.

The questionnaire was brief. It consisted of three pages preceded by a demographic fact sheet in which questions such as occupation, place of residence, and age were asked. Because I wanted to make the questionnaire easy and to the point, some richness of data may have been lost. If the study is to be expanded in the future, in-depth interviewing should be used to follow up. The questionnaire was completely anonymous. Respondents who were interested in the results of the study were asked to submit a request under separate letter or postcard.

Before presenting the data I must reiterate that both sexuality and ethnicity, regardless of how "in-born," "born into," or "given at birth," are, in fact, fluid, life-long processes. What I think of myself today in terms of either ethnicity or sexuality may not be what I thought yesterday or what I will think tomorrow. Because "what each woman thinks of herself" is what I define as identity for my purposes here, I have included those women who consider themselves appropriate participants of this study by responding to the questionnaire. That is why one of the respondents, a twenty-three-year-old woman born in Hialeah, Florida, a short while after her family immigrated into the United States, is included in the study. She defines herself as Cuban, so she can be considered as such for the purposes of this study.

## Characteristics of the Group

The ages of the sixteen respondents range from twenty-three to forty-five with a mean of thirty-two years. Fifteen of the respondents were born in Cuba, and one was born in Florida. Eleven of the sixteen are either the oldest child or the oldest daughter in the family. Their places of residence are fairly evenly distributed across the United States. Responses came from Florida, California, the Midwest, and the Northeast.

On the basis of their parents' occupation and education in Cuba and in the United States, it can be estimated that three come from an upper-middle-class socioeconomic background, seven from a middle-class background, and six from a low-middle or working-class background. The occupations of the respondents varied, but they were all highly educated. Three of the respondents held doctorates, one was a physician, one was a lawyer, and two were law students. Five had master's degrees and five bachelor's degrees, and one was a professional writer. This high level of education may be an effect of the friendship pyramiding process of recruiting participants for the study. On the other hand, it may be that the high level of education found in this group is a confirmation of what was hypothesized earlier in this chapter concerning the level of education of Latina lesbians compared to a general population of Latinas in the United States. Fourteen of the sixteen women were raised Catholic, one was Methodist, and one Episcopalian. Only three of them practiced their religion at the time of the study. These three women were members of Dignity, a national organization of gay and lesbian Catholics.

Of the sixteen women, fifteen were involved in a committed relationship. Nine of them were in relationships with Cuban or other Hispanic women, five in relationships with Jewish women, one with an Afro-American woman, and one with a white Anglo woman.

The fifteen women who were born in Cuba had arrived in the United States between 1956 and 1972. Thus their length of residence in this country ranged from seven to twenty-eight years, with a mean of eighteen years. Their age at leaving Cuba ranged from three to twenty-two. Twelve participants left Cuba between three and thirteen years of age, one left at seventeen, two at twenty, and one at twenty-two. Most of them left Cuba during their childhood years, and only three left in early adulthood.

Coming out as a lesbian occurred from twenty-one years earlier (1962) to as recently as a few months before the questionnaire was filled out. The ages of coming out ranged from sixteen to thirty-three years old. As is usual with a lesbian population, chronological age does not correlate with the number of years of being out, except for those who had been out twenty-one or eighteen years, who, obviously, were among the oldest respondents. Five of the women were out to all members of their family, including parents. Six were out to siblings or other relatives, and five were not out to anyone in their families. Most of them were out to friends, and most of them preferred to socialize with people who know they are lesbians.

## Responses to the "Core" Questions

Several questions were considered to be the core questions of the study. Questions 5 and 6 asked the participants if they identified as Cuban and as lesbian, respectively. Questions 7 and 8 asked for a brief description of their process of identifying as Cuban and as lesbian. Questions 9 and 10 asked about the influence that living in the United States may have had on them as lesbians and as Cubans. Question 11 asked for the relative importance that being Cuban or being lesbian had in their lives. Question 12 asked about their decision making in choosing friends among Latin people who are not gay or among Anglo lesbians. This last question was intended to elicit reflections on the process of emotional costs involved in this decision.

Fourteen of the women, including the young woman born in Florida, identify as Cuban. The two respondents who do not identify as Cuban live in Florida. One of them is thirty-one years old. She came to this country in 1956, before the larger waves of Cuban migration, and was raised, in her own words, "as an Anglo among Anglos." The other woman who does not identify as Cuban is forty-two years old and came to Miami from Cuba in 1962, when she was twenty. She was the only woman in the group who was in a relationship with a white Anglo woman. Although she came to the United States as an adult and lives in the geographical area where the largest concentration of Cubans in the country is, she strongly rejects Cuban ways. In her words,

> It is great to be able to know and share black beans and rice and talk Spanish, but if we cannot be ourselves, we cannot share with one another if our waves do not click—to what good is Spanish if we cannot communicate? I am afraid black beans and rice are not enough. Latins are provincial, nonworldly, ignorant, superstitious, with no room for individuality, self-expression, nonprogressive, politically oppressive, bound by archaic traditions that enslave people. Come to Miami, see butch/femme still alive and well. Very disturbing. These are 17 to 25 year olds.

Among the descriptions of their process of self-definition as Cuban, two responses seem to express the general sentiment more precisely. A thirty-three-year-old woman who had lived in the United States for twenty-three years describes her process in the following way:

> As a child this self-definition was not conscious, since there was no need for awareness of ethnic identity while I lived in Cuba. Coming to the United States instantly brought to my awareness at the age of 10 what being Cuban meant in this country. I would say that the need to assert that identity was strengthened by the racism of the United States. In my teens, I passed through a period of acculturation in which to some

extent I internalized society's view of ethnic groups in a very subtle way. During college, I became active in political and community activities and went through a "militant" phase in which I came to understand the nature of racism and oppression more deeply. Presently, I consider myself to have a more universal or humanistic perspective and I am able to appreciate as well as critically analyze aspects of my cultural heritage.

This woman's description of her process as an ethnic minority person clearly fits Atkinson, Morten, and Sue's model of ethnic minority identity development described earlier. When confronted with a culture different from her own, she evolved from a conformity stage as an adolescent to a more synergetic stage at this point in her life.

Another respondent, a forty-five-year-old woman, who had lived in the United States for twelve years, said the following about being Cuban in this country: "It is difficult to be cut off from the Cuban community while not feeling fully understood by Americans and sometimes even by other Latins. Being Cuban at this point in history is not easy!"

The vicissitudes of the process of self-identification as a lesbian woman are described best by the following two responses:

First, total unawareness. Then, after sleeping with a woman, total rejection of her; as if she was an addiction. I knew this was "sick." I never went to bed with so many men in my life as I did during that period. Then, I started realizing that I was denying my own happiness. Now I am almost totally out. I feel whole.

Although I had been intensely involved with another woman, we both denied it. When I became involved with a woman who defined herself as lesbian, I thought I was not lesbian, only "in love with her." Then, I started feeling attracted to other women, became involved in gay groups. I'm now out at work and to friends. Family is impossible, though.

The internal journeys described by these two women, as well by other respondents, fit the processes involved in developing a homosexual identity as described in Vivienne Cass's model.

Interestingly, one of the respondents does not identify as a lesbian. According to her, "No, my sexual preference does not rule my life. I like women, I love women, that is called being a lesbian, but I don't define myself as one." In spite of these words, this woman, who at forty years old had been out for eighteen years, chose to answer the questionnaire knowing that it was about lesbians.

When asked what was more important for them, being Cuban or being lesbian, twelve women responded that both were equally important. Three women responded that being lesbian was more important and one responded that "being a Latin woman" was most important, because "being a Latin woman gives me a broader perspective—culturally and politically." This person is the same one who said she did not define herself as lesbian.

When confronted with the choice of being among Latins without coming out, or living among lesbians who are not Latin or who are unfamiliar with Latin culture, eleven of the women said they had chosen or would choose the second alternative. However, this choice is not made without ambivalence. A twenty-nine-year-old woman from San Francisco explained her choice in this way: "*¡Una pregunta muy difícil!* (A very difficult question!) I have done both. I think being able to be a lesbian is too much a part of me for me to repress. I can still be Cuban if I'm around Americans."

A twenty-seven-year-old woman from Miami expressed not only the ambivalence, but also the pain and anger associated with choosing between different parts of herself:

> I guess that if the choice were absolute, I would choose living among lesbians. This answer may invalidate my answer to question 11 in which I said that being Cuban and being lesbian were both equally important for me. But I want to point out that I would be extremely unhappy if all my Latin culture were taken out of my lesbian life. I had a hard time with all the questions that made me choose between Cuban and lesbian, or at least, made me feel as if I had to choose. It made it real clear to me that I identify myself as a lesbian more intensely than as Cuban/Latin. But it is a very painful question because I feel that I am both, and I don't want to have to choose. Clearly, straight people don't even get asked this question and it is unfair that we have to discuss it, even if it is just a questionnaire.

Two of the respondents said that when confronted with the choice, they prefer to be among Latinos. The reason given by one of them for her choice was, "I feel comfortable with my people—gay or not."

Three women said that they would not choose, without explaining how they have integrated both alternatives in their lives. One woman expressed a strong rejection against the possibility of such a choice: "I would refute that choice and insist on the third alternative of not denying either aspect of myself. This is a false dichotomy as we all know, sort of like saying are you a woman or an ethnic person, such choices arise out of racism and homophobia and I refuse to even postulate such possibility for myself."

It is not clear if this woman has in fact answered the question in terms of her own personal choices, or if she is primarily making a statement about what she considers to be correct, or taking a political position. On the other hand, this woman was the most out person in the group. Perhaps because she was out to parents and family as well as to all the important people in her life, she could actively act out her refusal to choose in a better way than others.

From the responses of this small group, we can conclude that it is impossible to determine that one aspect of the identity of these Cuban lesbians is more important for them than the other. The relative importance given to the different components of their identity does not appear to be related, at least in this group, to factors such as age, years of residence in the United States, place of residence, or any other factors. In fact, the two most extreme and definite positions, that of not wanting to identify as Cuban or as lesbian, are espoused by two women who are more than forty (forty-two and forty, respectively), who have been living in the United States for more than twenty years and out as lesbians for twenty or eighteen years, respectively. The woman who rejects her Cuban identity lives in Miami. The woman who rejects her lesbian identity lives in New York.

Most of the respondents, although regretting their decision, choose behaviorally to be among Anglo lesbians rather than among straight Latinos. The possibility of "passing" or not must be a factor in this decision. Obviously, they cannot hide their Hispanic identity among Anglos as they can hide their lesbian identity among Hispanics. But even when they believe that it is easier to be Cuban among lesbians than it is to be lesbian among Cubans, they do not feel fully comfortable not being both. In fact, what most of them say is that they feel more whole when they can be out both as Cubans and as lesbians. However, because of the realities of racism and heterosexism that they have to confront, they are forced to choose for their lives those alternatives that are more tolerable or less costly to them. Some may choose to live in Miami among Cubans, even if that implies "staying in the closet." Others may choose to live in other areas of the country among Anglo lesbians, without feeling fully supported in terms of their Cuban identity.

However, as expressed by one of the women, "eating black beans and rice while speaking in Spanish with other Latina lesbians makes those beans taste like heaven!"

## Implications for Psychotherapy

Some implications for the practice of psychotherapy with Latina lesbians can be derived from the discussion of the specific factors influencing the identity development of Latina lesbians and from the results of this brief study. Like all other individuals who seek psychotherapy, Latina lesbians who come to therapy do so for a variety of reasons. As with all other individuals, the formation of their identity occurs in a specific cultural, class, and historical context. For the therapist working with Latina lesbians, it is essential to understand the impact of these specific contextual variables on the individual client. But the understanding of the unique vicissitudes of identity development for Latina lesbians should be tempered by the understanding that certain processes are similar to those encountered by any lesbian woman from any cultural background who is in the process of coming out.

It is essential that the therapist understands the anger, frustration, and pain that the Latina lesbian experiences both as a lesbian and as an ethnic minority member. If the therapist is a white Anglo, it is essential that she develop awareness and understanding of how her own cultural background influences her responses to her Latina lesbian client. If the therapist has a heterosexual orientation, particularly if the therapist is also Hispanic, freedom from heterosexist biases and male-centered cultural values and from Latin stereotypes of homosexuals is essential for effective therapy. Of particular importance is the use of language in therapy when the client's associations to Spanish words that refer to her lesbian identity may all be negative.

As with all clients, it must be remembered that each woman's choices express something about who she is as an individual as well as what her cultural values are. Lesbian choices, as any behavior that violates strict cultural norms, can present a high personal cost to any woman. In the case of Latinas, this high personal cost may additionally involve a loss of support from their ethnic group. Any encouragement of their coming out as lesbians should be done with sensitivity to the other components of their identity.

The therapist should keep in mind that there is as much danger in explaining individual differences away as culturally determined as there is in ignoring or rejecting the impact of cultural influences on each woman's choices. As always in therapy, validation of each woman's identity and of all the components of her total self is provided through the expansion of feeling states and encouragement to understand their meaning. To understand the multiplicity of tasks involved

in identity development for Latina lesbians and to provide the opportunity for the accomplishment of those tasks is the first step in therapy
with Latina lesbians.

## NOTES

I wish to thank Lourdes Rodriguez-Nogues for her help with the development
of the questionnaire and study and the members of my Feminist Research
Methodology Group for their useful comments.

1. Erik H. Erikson, *Life History and the Historical Moment* (New York: W.
W. Norton, 1975), 19–20.

2. Erikson, *Life History,* 21.

3. Donald R. Atkinson, George Morten, and Derald W. Sue, *Counseling
American Minorities* (Dubuque, Ia.: William C. Brown, 1979).

4. Vivienne C. Cass, "Homosexual Identity Formation: A Theoretical
Model," *Journal of Homosexuality* 4 (Spring 1979): 219–35.

5. Derald Wing Sue, *Counseling the Culturally Different* (New York: Wiley,
1981), 66–68.

6. Cass, "Homosexual Identity Formation," 222–23.

7. Ibid., 225, 229, 231, 233, 234–35.

8. Hortensia Amaro, "Coming Out: Hispanic Lesbians, Their Families
and Communities," paper presented at the National Coalition of Hispanic
Mental Health and Human Services Organizations (COSSMHO), Austin, Texas,
1978.

9. Cherrie Moraga, *Loving in the War Years: Lo que Nunca Pasó por sus
Labios* (Boston: South End Press, 1983).

10. Hilda Hidalgo and Elia Hidalgo-Christensen, "The Puerto Rican Lesbian and the Puerto Rican Community," *Journal of Homosexuality* 2 (Winter
1976–77), 109–21; Ibid., "The Puerto Rican Cultural Response to Female
Homosexuality," in *The Puerto Rican Woman,* ed. Edna Acosta-Belén (New
York: Praeger Publishers, 1979), 110–23.

11. Yvonne D. Escaserga, E. C. Mondaca, and V. G. Torres, "Attitudes
of Chicana Lesbians towards Therapy." Master's thesis, Department of Social
Work, University of Southern California, Los Angeles, 1975.

12. Hidalgo and Hidalgo-Christensen, "The Puerto Rican Lesbian and
the Puerto Rican Community," 120.

13. Oliva M. Espín, "Cultural and Historical Infleunces on Sexuality in
Hispanic/Latin Women: Implications for Psychotherapy" in *Pleasure and Dan-
ger: Exploring Female Sexuality,* ed. Carole Vance (London: Routledge and Kegan
Paul, 1984), 149–63.

14. Moraga, *Loving in the War Years,* 99.

15. Amaro, "Coming Out: Hispanic Lesbians," 7.

16. See, for example, Robert Bogdan and Steven J. Taylor, *Introduction
to Qualitative Research Methods* (New York: Wiley, 1975); W. J. Filstead, *Qualitative Methodology: First Hand Involvement with the Social World* (Chicago:
Markham, 1970); and Barney G. Glaser and Anselm Strauss, *The Discovery of
Grounded Theory: Strategies for Qualitative Research* (Chicago: Aldine, 1967).

17. Although the sample is obviously small, it is important to remember that obtaining respondents in a population surrounded by secrecy while searching for a specific ethnicity, as in this case, is not a minor task. A response rate of almost half of questionnaires sent is not considered a low response rate in itself. In addition, ten subjects or even smaller numbers are considered to be sufficient in qualitative studies when the sample is saturated (see Glaser and Strauss, *The Discovery of Grounded Theory*).

# Appendix: Questionnaire Distributed to Latina Lesbian Respondents

## Part 1. FACT SHEET

1. Age_____

2. Place of birth_____

3. Birth order (e.g. oldest daughter of three brothers)_____
_____

4. Present place of residence_____

5. Father's education_____

   Father's occupation_____

   Mother's education_____

   Mother's occupation_____

6. How long have you lived in the United States?_____

7. When did you leave Cuba?_____

   How old were you when you left Cuba?_____

8. Your present education_____

   Your present occupation_____

9. Religion of your parents_____

   Your present religion_____

   Do you practice it?_____

10. Are you presently in a relationship?  Yes_____   No_____

    Is your partner   Cuban_____  Latin_____  North American_____

                      Other_____ (specify)_____

11. Do you date mostly   Cuban women_____ Latin women_____

                         North American women_____  Other_____

                         (specify)_____

## Part 2. QUESTIONNAIRE

### (Answer in English or Spanish)

1. When did you first came out?_____

   How old were you when you came out?_____

Where were you living at the time?   Cuba_____

United States_____

other Latin American country_____

other (specify)_____

2. Are you out to your immediate family?   Yes_____ No_____

2a. If your answer is yes,

Who in your family are you out to?_____

_____

Why did you decide to come out to them?_____

_____

_____

2b. If you are not out to your family, can you explain briefly why you have chosen not to come out to them?_____

_____

_____

_____

3. Are you out to: most of your Latin friends_____

some of your Latin friends_____

none of your Latin friends_____

most of your Anglo-American friends_____

some of your Anglo-American friends_____

none of your Anglo-American friends_____

other_____ (specify)_____

4. Who do you socialize with?

mostly women_____      mostly men_____

mostly Cuban_____      mostly Latin_____

mostly Anglo-American_____

mostly gays/lesbians_____

mostly heterosexuals_____

other (please specify)_____

5. Do you identify as Cuban?

    Yes_____ because_____

    _____

    No_____ because_____

    _____

6. Do you identify as a lesbian?

    Yes_____ because_____

    _____

    No_____because_____

7. Can you describe your process of self-definition as a Cuban?_____

    _____

    _____

    _____

8. Can you describe your process of self-definition as a lesbian?_____

    _____

    _____

    _____

9. Does living in the U.S.A. have any effect on you as a lesbian?

    Yes_____ Explain briefly_____

    _____

    No_____ Explain briefly_____

    _____

10. Does living in the U.S.A. have any effect on you as a Cuban?

    Yes_____ Explain briefly_____

    _____

    No._____ Explain briefly_____

    _____

11. Which is more important to your self-definition?

    being Cuban_____ because_____

    _____

    being lesbian_____ because_____

    _____

both_____      because_____

_____

other (specify)_____

because_____

_____

12. If presented with the choice of being among Latins without coming out as a lesbian, or living among lesbians who are not Latins or who are unfamiliar with Latin culture, what would you choose and why?

_____

_____

_____

_____

_____

13. Have you ever been involved in political, cultural, gay rights or other type of organizations?

No_____ Yes_____

political_____ which?_____

cultural_____ which?_____ gay rights_____ which?_____

women rights_____ which?_____ other_____

14. Do you have any additional comments?

# 3

## *Sexuality as a Continuum: The Bisexual Identity*

REBECCA SHUSTER

Understanding bisexuality is essential to lesbian psychology. Descriptions and theoretical frameworks of bisexuals' lives provide vital information toward a comprehensive understanding of the origins and lifelong evolution of sexual choice, the parameters and potentials of relationships, and the mechanics of heterosexist oppression and effective methods of eliminating it. In addition, many bisexual-identified women[1] define themselves and visibly function as members of the lesbian community.[2] A complete picture of lesbian psychology—examining personal identity, interpersonal relationships, and the social institutionalization of and political resistance to oppression—must include these women.

I have used interviews, survey results, observation, and a review of what psychological research exists to consider the nature and implications of bisexual-identified women's experience. I will focus here on women who, at least privately, call themselves bisexual. I will not address the experience of those who are actively bisexual without consciously adopting that identity. I will use the term *bisexual women* hereafter to refer to women who identify as bisexual. To generalize from bisexual-identified to all bisexual women, however, risks creating a distorted image of bisexuals as self-defined feminists and deliberate activists. Many bisexually and homosexually active women do not consider their lives in terms of conscious identities, deliberate political decisions, or intentional affectional communities, and feminist literature frequently excludes their experience.

56

## Defining Bisexuality

Bisexual women make individual, contextual decisions to love and make love with women and men in their lives. They make complex choices within and across different periods of their lives. By definition, bisexuals defy categorization. Some of them, sometimes, are contemporaneous bisexuals in intimate relationships with both a woman and a man. Some of them, sometimes, are sequential bisexuals in a series of relationships with people of both genders. Others are indefinitely monogamous or sexually involved with a series of people of one gender; they define themselves as bisexuals on a theoretical basis. There is no bisexual prototype: that is the center of both their significance and their challenges.

I am going to present as particular examples the case histories of two bisexual women, Allison and Barbara.[3] Both Allison and Barbara use an open-ended definition of bisexuality. Barbara, a thirty-year-old health care worker, defines bisexuality this way: "For me bisexuality is having partners of different genders. . . . It doesn't mean having multiple partners at the same time, but it means being open and having the possibility of men and women in intimate relationships."

Allison, a thirty-six-year-old child care worker and parent, similarly states: "[Bisexuality means] being open to having a relationship with either a female or male person. . . . And that covers all facets of a relationship." So the term *bisexual* is used colloquially among bisexual women to refer to both activity and potential activity, both sexual and platonic relationships.

## Bisexuality and Lesbian Oppression

With few exceptions, twentieth-century American girls have been raised within the constraints and expectations of social, political, and economic heterosexual culture. Therefore, to choose a bisexual identity (or any identity other than heterosexual) is subversive, and each stepwise thought or action toward a bisexual identity is an act of subversion. Although most people have at least occasional desires (fantasies, dreams) for sexual partners of both genders,[4] perhaps a third have sexual contact with partners of both genders at some time in their lives,[5] and few openly identify as bisexual. An infinite array of internal and external circumstances influence tentative or consistent bisexual experience and identity. Margaret Mead points to lesbian activity at one-sex institutions as evidence of cultural limitations on bisexuality.[6] For example, female prison inmates whose behavior has been exclusively heterosexual develop lesbian relationships during detention and then return to heterosexual relationships upon release. Other women who consider themselves heterosexual or lesbian may participate in repeated or long-term relationships contrary to their usual gender choice.

Allison explains her transition from a heterosexual to a bisexual identity in terms of simply becoming aware of that possibility.

> We're taught that we're heterosexual. . . . The movies you see, the books you read: all are about how this "girl" falls in love with this "young man." That's the whole direction you're pushed in. I would say, definitely in my case, that if someone had said both [genders] are possibilities [as sexual partners] a long time ago, I probably would have said, "Oh, both are possibilities." And it really would have been "You're a person and therefore I can be with you." . . . If . . . somewhere I had read one book that said this is a possibility, it would have been a possibility.

Women who identify as bisexual see themselves as sexual dissidents allied with lesbians, refusing to conform to heterosexual culture. Barbara expresses it this way:

> I think it feels just as alientating to me [as it does to lesbians]. . . . It doesn't make me feel any more a part of the heterosexual group to consider myself a bisexual. I still feel like I'm out on the fringe. That my lifestyle is very different. . . . If I was mated to a man I don't know if I would go the white veil route with a diamond ring. I probably would have felt alienated in an average group of heterosexuals even with a male partner. That's who I am in terms of my lifestyle as opposed to my sexuality per se. . . . I feel more like the token dyke even if I do consider myself bisexual. I don't think that gives me any more comfort.

So a bisexual's experience is one of nonconformity, a personal choice to act against heterosexist cultural constraints.

Mass culture, psychology, and history invariably leave bisexuals hidden among heterosexuals and lesbians. Research on the lesbian community has been confounded by substantial numbers of bisexually active individuals characterized as lesbian based on even just one lesbian relationship.[7] In addition, many women reclaimed as lesbians by feminist historians actually led bisexual lives. Bisexuals will gain public and theoretical visibility as the lesbian and gay liberation movement successfully legitimizes all that is not heterosexual.

Thus, bisexual women owe their growing visibility and freedom to act on their lesbian desires to lesbian and gay activists and feminists who have demanded sexual rights. A 1984 poll of Boston Bisexual Women's Network (BBWN) members revealed that bisexual-identified women are predominantly young (nearly half under thirty, 99 percent under forty).[8] These women reached adulthood in a period of lesbian rights activism, necessarily recognizing lesbianism—and thus bisexuality—as an option in their lives.

Public bisexuals endure much of the same oppression as their lesbian friends and lovers, often losing jobs, family, friends, and emotional security. Their experiences echo lesbian experiences of coming out: They are misunderstood and mistreated because they break cultural rules about intimacy, sex, and gender. The core of bisexual women's oppression *is* lesbian oppression. Heterosexist society defines bisexuals based on their lesbianism. They are not 50 percent oppressed.[9] Coming out publicly is a risk Allison is just beginning to take: "First I talked to a couple of women friends who I knew were sympathetic to gay people. . . . With my mother I've talked about my cousins who are gay and how I really want Carla [her daughter] to be whoever she wants to be. . . . At work right now it would be absolutely crazy for me to talk about it [but] at some point in my life . . . I don't want it to be a dishonesty." Allison's comments are barely distinguishable from those of a lesbian in the common context of heterosexist culture.

### Coming Out as Bisexual

Bisexuals undergo an internal as well as external coming-out process, gradually arriving at their personal identity and gradually sharing it with others. The diversity of bisexuals' individual histories makes it difficult to generalize about those processes. Informal discussion with bisexual women discloses a wide variation in early, adolescent, and adult sexual development; events leading to identification as bisexual; patterns of monogamy or nonmonogamy; structure of primary and additional relationships; and current visibility as bisexual. Allison and Barbara's stories, although by no means representing the range of bisexual experience, provide two examples.

Allison's first memory of sex play was an attempt to act out the content of sexual jokes she learned at Girl Scout camp as an eleven year old: "I remember a [female] friend of mine came over and we wanted to take pictures of each other with no clothes on, and I remember we tried doing whatever it was those jokes were about. I'm not even sure whether we were clothed or not, and we didn't touch each other's genitals. We were just sort of moving together, and we decided the whole thing was out of our realm. Somehow we were going to get in trouble for that. It didn't have a label of lesbianism or anything." Although Allison believes she has a "tendency to want to . . . bias [her sexual history] toward homosexuality," she describes a series of adolescent crushes on women. "Teacher after teacher," she says, "and some mothers of friends . . . though not in sexual terms at all." At fifteen Allison had her first boyfriend: "I remember not being the least bit impressed [with a heterosexual relationship]. The idea was that I had a boyfriend, and that was something important to tell a friend of mine."

When Allison was seventeen she met Dave, her first male lover, and, she relates, "It became very important to me that Dave and I were together." Two years later, after a period of nonmonogamy (which Dave initiated), they were married. Later, while Dave wanted a monogamous marriage, Allison "wanted independence [and] was involved with some other men." After a crisis in 1974, Allison and Dave "made a decision that we were going to survive as a couple [and] became monogamous." Their daughter, Carla, was born in 1976.

Eight years later, Allison became interested in sexual relationships with women:

> It started in my sociology class where a woman came in and talked to us about her childhood [as] an abused child—it had nothing to do with sexuality—but I was fascinated by her as a person. Later we had a class about lesbianism, and she came [again]. It was the first time in my adult years that I had thought about the whole subject or issue [of lesbianism]. . . . And then I read *Coming Out Stories* and everything I could get my hands on for about a year and [began] feeling more and more as though that was who I was. Only that didn't fit with the fact that I was married.

In 1984, Allison saw an ad for a meeting of a local bisexual women's organization and attended it: "It was such a relief to find a group of people who said you don't have to choose one way or the other. You can love all people. Gender doesn't have to be the basis on which you decide."

Within a year, Allison developed a sexual relationship with another bisexual woman, Elaine. Dave supported the relationship, and Allison was happy to continue her marriage while spending up to three nights a week with Elaine. "I had in my own [mind hoped] I would be involved with both of them for a long time. I felt as though I had the energy to cope with it." Elaine, however, decided after several months that she wanted to return to being friends with Allison. Allison describes that change as a painful one, and remains in a period of healing and uncertain introspection about her future relationships.

Barbara tells her story beginning in high school, when she thought of herself as heterosexual: "I never did have a lot of relationships. In high school I pretty much kept to myself, did a lot of babysitting. I had one involvement with a man who was very sensitive, fit the gentle man kind of role. In my first couple of years of college I was embarrassed that I had gotten to college and was still a virgin, and therefore kept myself isolated. Because of that fear of having to admit that I still had a lack of experience. And finally [I] had my first sexual relationship [with a man] when I was twenty or twenty-one." After college Barbara continued a series of sexual relationships with men. Meanwhile, she was exposed to feminist and leftist political thinking. She began working in a feminist health center in 1979 among both heterosexual and lesbian feminists, and by 1981 sought "a feminist household where there was a lot of flexibility and openness" to various sexual preferences.

Barbara fell in love with one member of her new household: "I began to feel that I wanted to share more [than a friendship] because we shared such a common life and dreams about living . . . I didn't feel like I was that definite about women, but that this one woman was a woman I wanted to pursue relating to [sexually]. So it was a real individual choice, and then I've slowly become more woman-identified and more interested in women." In the course of that relationship, which lasted a few months, Barbara began calling herself bisexual. During the same time period, she built a circle of friends who actively supported her in that relationship and a subsequent series of sexual relationships with women. Barbara now hopes to find one woman who will become her lifelong "partner." She calls herself a "bisexual lesbian," presently interested in women, but acknowledging an attraction to men she may someday choose to act upon.

Little research has investigated the route bisexuals take to this identity, or any common qualities of those who identify themselves as bisexual.[10] Often women fall in love with someone of an unexpected gender, and the power of that relationship pulls them to re-evaluate their identity. For both Allison and Barbara, that "aha!" occurred within the context of a developing consciousness of lesbian and women's rights. In order to arrive at a bisexual identity, a woman must confront her images of dichotomous sexual options, societal lesbian oppression, her own internalized homophobia, and particular myths about (and resulting mistreatment of) bisexuals.

Allison exemplifies bisexual women who retrace their histories for early precedents of attraction and love for women and men, and relate stories of temporary struggle to conform to a heterosexual or lesbian identity. Some, like Barbara, settle (or hope to settle) into a long-term monogamous relationship with a woman or a man. Meanwhile, such women maintain a bisexual identity in order to remain personally honest about their bisexual desires or to present a political vision of utopian relationships. Bisexuals define their identity in terms of their particular personal relationships rather than as an abstract gender preference. Their common thread is their willingness to incorporate flexibility into their identity.

## Sexuality as Choice

At this moment in human sexual history, the presence of bisexuals conspicuously reopens the issue of sexual choice.[11] Bisexuality undoes the rigid lesbian/heterosexual dichotomy. What emerges is a continuum of sexual choices, a continuum that is threatening to those who have imposed a categorical definition on their sexuality (versus those — probably those few — who are in reality completely lesbian or completely heterosexual). Bisexuals do more than reveal a third sexual category. They uncover a range of sexual and emotional attraction and closeness of infinite variety. To place all human beings into one of two — or three — sexual boxes is then absurd, denying the breadth and individuality of human sexuality. Such categorization, whether as a theoretical standpoint or a political stance, reinforces societal divisions that form the mainspring of lesbian and gay oppression.

Furthermore, bisexuality unravels traditional notions of the immutability of sexual identity. Bisexuals contemporaneously or sequentially select sexual partners of the same or different genders, demonstrating that these choices can vary over time and opportunity. Sexuality, then, differs from race, ethnicity, or class background. Underlying any bisexual identity is an assumption that all sexuality can be chosen apart from cultural — or countercultural — expectations. The more spontaneous and contextual a woman's choices are, the more free she is from societally imposed and internalized limitations. Her self-determination is her full intelligence, transcending reactive responses to social constructs of sexuality.

Many bisexuals believe that, given the flexibility of sexual choices, even the vision of a continuum falls short of the possible. Sexual identities can become an acknowledgment of one's lifetime's loves, rather than an inflexible dictation to select some particular proportion of relationships with women or men. As gender roles dissolve, individuals can begin to love and make love with particular human beings rather than with "a woman" or "a man." As heterosexism and sexism dissipate (the assumption here is that both will), sexual preference will become unimportant.

Bisexual women are often aware of the implications of choosing their identity. Barbara: "I've always been one to hate labels. . . . Even though bisexuality is a label . . . it's a label which allows me to be flexible. That's . . . the way I've lived my life. [People get threatened] because someone that says they're bisexual allows that openness and fluidness of identity. That can be threatening because it means that you can relate to anybody, that you have a connection to anybody that's willing to relate on an intimate level."

Until sexual relationships are selected in an atmosphere of total freedom, using the labels *lesbian, bisexual,* or *heterosexual* makes sense as personal, psychological, and political tools. Such labels are useful to organize information about sexual experience, to establish cohesive communities, and to mobilize activists on behalf of sexual freedom.

## A New Vision for Closeness

Because bisexuals consider all people potential friends and lovers, they break down cultural rigidities about sexual and emotional closeness. Bisexuals seek closeness without concession to the constructed obstacles of socialization. They can become close to any person along a fluid line from acquaintance to intimacy, deciding whether sex will be part of a relationship or not. A bisexual's relationships can spontaneously shift along the line of affection, having distinctions between closeness and sex and unintentionally or intentionally creating new forms of relationships. Often, bisexuals define themselves as much by their constellation of committed friendships as by their sexual relationships. Many choose to ask themselves more complex questions about short- and long-term relationships and monogamy and nonmonogamy than their lesbian and heterosexual peers. Thus, they call into question society's values, as well as rules, of relationship.

Bisexuals relate stories of relationships that transcend traditional boundaries between romance and friendship. Allison: "Right now [I'm close to] a woman . . . with whom I've agreed not to have a sexual relationship. We've agreed to sort of surrogate mother each other. . . . There's an intimacy line, and on one end there's sexuality. . . . What's going on is that there are *people* in my life, and sexuality isn't the highest thing in my world."

Bisexuals describe complex networks of friends: One might spend one night a week sleeping with someone she has no sexual relationship with, one might maintain several friendships she considers lifelong, one might live and co-parent with a committed friend. Bisexuals reinterpret social constructions of friendships, romances, and families.

### Bisexuality and Women's Liberation

A substantial majority of bisexual-identified women consider themselves feminists (90 percent in the BBWN poll)[12] and see their sexual and emotional self-determination within the context of the empowerment of women. Bisexuals' spontaneous selection of relationships with both women and men relies on an assumption that although sexism remains ubiquitous, men are not the enemy. Within the identity of a bisexual feminist there is an awareness and firm stance against sexism, as well as an acceptance of heterosexual relationships as a viable option. Allison says: "People are people. That's probably my highest reality in terms of my politics. . . . No matter what color you are you're people, and no matter what gender you are you're people."

Bisexuals perceive distinct challenges in relationships with men versus relationships with women and assume both experiences are valuable. In relationships with women they grapple with homophobia, lesbian oppression, and internalized sexism among women such as competition and insecurity. In relationships with men they grapple with heterosexism, their anti-male feelings, and sexism, both external and internalized.

The particular obstacles in relationships with either gender are significantly different in a sexist society, and bisexuals' choices to love and make love with women or men have real effects on their lives. Relationship choices influence their daily sexuality, their livelihoods, their political work, and their sense of self. Many bisexual women think out the ramifications of these decisions carefully. They select relationships with particular people, conscious of but often not deferring to the resulting societal costs and benefits; envisioning that as sexism and heterosexism fade, such choices will become personal preferences without political underpinnings. Thus, bisexuals aim to stretch past "man-identified," past "woman-identified," to a new capacity to self-identify: to define themselves by their selves.

Many bisexuals respect those women throughout history who have chosen separatist life-styles, making sensible choices given vicious sexism and few options for escaping the severe limitations imposed on them by society. Bisexual women, however, choose relationships with men who act out relatively little sexism and are willing to unlearn the sexist conditioning that was passed down to them. Barbara describes her former male lovers this way: "I always tended to relate to men that were more womanly in a lot of ways, who had more characteristics that were feminine. More sensitive, more gentle." Allison and Dave have deliberately structured their relationship outside of sex role constraints: "I'm the one who's bringing home the money. He has dinner cooked, and he listens to me and cares what happens to me. [Sexually] he waits for me to make the move. Which is a pretty phenomenal thing, I think, in a man." In loving both women and men, bisexuals violate social rules about womanhood and manhood.

## Between Both Worlds

Bisexual women are mavericks within both the heterosexual and lesbian communities. Bisexuals struggle to defy myths of their self-delusion ("you're really a heterosexual" or "you're really a lesbian"), promiscuity, and indecisiveness, myths that arise amid widespread confusion about sexuality and closeness. Allison and Barbara both come up against such myths. Allison: "[One myth] is the question of loyalty or monogamy. Even though plenty of bisexuals are monogamous, just the word itself puts that into question. There's always a question no matter what you're doing. The word somehow implies that there's a conflict."

Barbara: "There's another myth that bisexuality is just a transition time. . . . when you're really gay but you're afraid to admit it. You're on the fence and when you eventually decide what you really want to do you'll realize that you want to be a lesbian. Which doesn't give us a whole lot of validation for who we are . . . I feel like if I come out to my family as bisexual they'll hold on to the bisexual [versus lesbian] end of it and still be thinking that I'm going to get married. See it as a phase, or that it's not valid as much."

Bisexuality can in fact be a transitory stopping point for some, just as heterosexuality and lesbianism can be for others. Bisexual-identified women may avoid a frightening lesbian identity just as lesbian-identified women may avoid a frightening bisexual identity. Like others, bisexuals choose to act on *some* of their sexual attractions. No evidence exists that bisexuals have any more or less sex than anyone else, nor that they require simultaneous female and male lovers for sexual satisfaction. While Allison exemplifies a nonmonogamous bisexual at points in her sexual history, Barbara explicitly seeks a monogamous relationship: "To me [nonmonogamy] violates so many of the basic ideas of relationships that involve trust and feeling secure and having open communications. I have never had a relationship that I would perceive as a potential partnership where it wasn't monogamous." Bisexuals, it appears, are as monogamous as their lesbian and heterosexual partners. The monogamous bisexual is as comprehensible as the celibate (or monogamous) lesbian or heterosexual.

Heterosexuals and lesbians often fear bisexuals' presumed relationship shifts and nonmonogamy. First, members of this culture operate on a scarcity mentality about closeness and sex. Insular homes and partitioned workplaces leave us chronically isolated, and internalized messages about a single "Mr." or "Ms. Right" leave us frantically searching for and clutching at relationships. Perceived as unwilling to commit themselves to a single relationship (or even a single gender), bisexuals threaten their potential lovers with infidelity—and everyone else with rivalry.

Second, both heterosexuals and lesbians rely on arguments that sexual preference is involuntary and immutable, even biologically determined. Because anyone can be targeted with lesbian/gay oppression, and expelled from the heterosexual community and culture, heterosexuals hold tight to their identity. Bisexuals demonstrate that heterosexuality is neither inherent nor provable, and that one can "suddenly" begin a lesbian or gay relationship. Lesbians, too, cling to their identity for a sense of personal security and community membership. Barbara says: "[Bisexuality] shakes up the mores of both the straight world and the gay and lesbian world because there aren't as many hard set rules. . . . When there are no rules people have to really go into themselves, and [sexuality] becomes a much more introspective process. . . . The overall group isn't as much of a factor. [You have] to come from your own center and take risks." Although the lesbian community has sometimes prescribed political grounds for choosing a lesbian identity, the lesbian and gay rights movement has often relied on the concept of immutable sexual identity as a political strategy. Bisexuals by their very existence sabotage that strategy.

Bisexuals break heterosexual rules about sex roles, sexuality, and closeness with women. Heterosexuals sometimes treat bisexuals as chic, intriguing turn-ons, and at other times as repulsive, deviant turn-offs. Heterosexual medical practitioners commonly treat bisexuals as pathological, victims of "sexual identity disorders,"[13] or simply having "lesbian tendencies."

Bisexuals break lesbian rules, too, about politics, sexuality, and closeness with men. Bisexuals often describe themselves as outsiders in lesbian communities, misunderstood for their identity and afraid of lesbians' rejection. As lesbian culture has gained a set of distinct norms, the status of bisexual women as members or nonmembers has surfaced as a key issue. To create a covert system for identifying one another in an oppressive culture and to provide a feeling of safety and unity within the resulting subculture, lesbians have developed rules for belonging. Unspoken dress codes, politically correct vocabulary, and prescriptions for relationships all hold out the possibility of trust. Bisexuals break the rules, and the penalty is distrust. Lesbian activism created a lesbian community that helped form women's first alternative to compulsory heterosexuality. As lesbian rights are won, however, the rules for membership can begin to relax. Welcome from the lesbian community need no longer depend on any particular identifying characteristics, or even promises of "women lovers only."

Many lesbians blame bisexual women for their supposed ability to pass as heterosexual. Indeed, bisexuals can take advantage of "heterosexual privilege" when they are presumed to be heterosexual, or when they choose visible relationships with men and the associated benefits. Yet, if heterosexual privileges are *rights* belonging to people of all sexual choices, then those who enjoy heterosexual privilege (whether unwittingly or intentionally for personal gain, public safety, or political strategy) do not deserve blame. Any denial of these rights is wrong. Barbara puts it this way: "I feel that choosing a bisexual identity places me more into the gay and lesbian community. . . . The issues that affect gay men and lesbians affect me just as strongly. . . . Politically I have to make a lot of the same choices and put myself out there as much . . . I know I could go somewhere with a man and it would be much easier [for me] to play straight [than for a lesbian]. But that ends up feeling like a joke to me instead of the fact that I have a privilege." Within both the lesbian and the bisexual communities, some choose risky visibility while others choose careful secrecy. Only external and internalized oppression stands in the way of a bisexual— or a lesbian—becoming entirely visible. Coming out can be a contextual decision rather than a moral obligation.

Thus, bisexual women walk a tightrope between the myths and fears of both the heterosexual and lesbian communities. Pressure to identify with one community or the other invalidates bisexuals' deepest sense of themselves. They cope with lesbian oppression without the full support of the lesbian community; they cope with sexism in relationships with men without the full support of the heterosexual community. Even more than lesbian and sexist oppression, the mistreatment of bisexuals is generally trivialized in our culture. In reality, the bisexual experience can be less than the best of both worlds. Bisexuals persist in these choices despite the pain of a path apart from either traditional heterosexual experience or recently developed mores of lesbian culture.

Simultaneously, bisexuals are uniquely situated to serve as knowledgeable ambassadors between heterosexuals and lesbians. Allison:

> I want to [come out] as much as possible so people can know it's a part of what people are. [Still,] I can do a lot for [lesbian rights] by my straight side showing. I can let people hear that somebody like me who has a family thinks that this is o.k. and important. And maybe when their kid says "I'm gay" they won't fall apart. . . . In women's groups . . . sometimes I'll have a whole evening and not say I'm married because that isn't the part of me that I want to talk about or want to be at that point. Two years ago I stopped wearing my wedding ring deliberately. . . because I didn't want . . . the rights nor the bondage . . . just because I had a ring around my finger.

Heterosexuals and lesbians may better understand bisexuals when they realize it is possible for bisexuals to act as excellent allies to members of both communities. For full acceptance of any sexual identity within an awareness of heterosexism and sexism, one needs to assume that any person can be an ally for another: heterosexual for lesbian, lesbian for bisexual, bisexual for heterosexual, etc.

## The Bisexual Community

Distinct bisexual communities have emerged internationally in the last five years. When two researchers on bisexuality searched for bisexual organizations in 1977, they discovered only "embryonic rap groups."[14] Since then, twenty groups have been established across the United States, and a London organization continues to grow after its founding in 1981.[15] In less than two years, the Boston Bisexual Women's Network mushroomed from a support group of six to a mailing list of more than five hundred.

Bisexual organizations are homelands for women who might receive a lukewarm reception in existing lesbian and heterosexual communities. Such organizations support bisexual-identified women once isolated from one another and form a foothold for women stepping toward a bisexual identity. They are without rules for entrance or membership and offer implicit permission to make commitments and transitions without normative constraints. Allison relates how a bisexual women's meeting allowed her to resolve years of internal conflict and feel at home with a bisexual identity. The existence of visible bisexual organizations has undoubtedly helped support an increase in the number of women now identifying themselves as bisexual.

Participants in the bisexual community make a full spectrum of sexual choices: from those who relate exclusively or almost exclusively in heterosexual communities, to those who relate exclusively or almost exclusively in lesbian communities. The 1984 poll of BBWN members confirms this distribution: 3.3 percent described their sexuality as exclusively lesbian, 6.5 percent as "mostly lesbian," 23 percent as more lesbian than heterosexual, 37.7 percent as both equally, 23 percent as more heterosexual than lesbian, 6.5 percent as mostly heterosexual, and none as exclusively heterosexual.[16]

## Implications for the Therapist

Guidelines and suggestions for the therapist are often useful for anyone who wishes to support someone's sexual identity and growth, including friends, lovers, family, co-workers, and co-activists. As more information is generated about the nature of sexual identity and activity, and in particular the bisexual experience, the therapist needs to re-evaluate the theoretical assumptions and content of what she communicates as counselor and educator. First, the therapist must assume that any sexual identity is psychologically and morally acceptable. This can create a safe atmosphere for the client to share her sexual history and current sexual experiences. The therapist is responsible for conveying a clear undertone of support, validating the client's sexual life by asking open-ended questions about her joys and challenges.

Second, the therapist needs to accompany the client through the evolution of her sexual choices. Operating on an assumption that no particular sexual identity is necessarily transient *or* permanent, the therapist can assist the client with a lifelong process rather than a short-term goal. This means assisting the client toward a sense of satisfaction with her history and toward open-minded contemplation of her present and future. Any client exploring her sexual identity and activity needs to look at her feelings about lesbianism, bisexuality, and heterosexuality. After she has discussed each set of feelings and worked to heal past difficulties associated with any particular identity, she can more freely consider her own. The therapist's role is to assist that healing and help the client decide what identity and what relationships are best for her outside of any preconception of the outcome.

Third, the therapist must encourage her client to make deliberate, thoughtful decisions about where, when, and whether to announce her sexual identity. The individual needs to consider each situation anew and not rigidly stay visible or invisible. For example, a client who would hazard her job by coming out at work must carefully weigh the risks and benefits of such a decision.

Fourth, the therapist needs to be aware of the nature of the bisexual experience, including bisexual identity, bisexuals' relationships, and the bisexual community. This understanding will allow the therapist to better support any client contemplating her sexual identity (or someone else's). In addition, this information aids in the understanding of heterosexual and lesbian experience.

Finally, a group therapist needs to encourage members with different sexual identities to talk together about their individual experiences in an atmosphere of respectful confidentiality and trust. Women generally need opportunities to discuss the details of their sexual lives with one another to educate them about the breadth of sexual experience and sexual options, to form a context for their own sexual choices, and to counteract feelings of isolation with their questions about sexuality. Validation among women (and men) of different sexual preferences is rare in a culture of precarious sexual identity and extremely helpful to a client's full pride in her choices.

## Conclusion

This chapter provides preliminary description of the process of identifying as bisexual, what it is like to come out as bisexual, how bisexuals are victimized by lesbian oppression, bisexuals' experiences among heterosexuals and lesbians, how bisexuals perceive their various relationships, the dynamics of the bisexual community, and bisexuals' political beliefs. Bisexuals' lives provide new psychological and social understandings of sexuality and closeness highlighting the mechanics of sexual decision making as potentially self-determined action. Research is needed about all areas of the bisexual experience, including studies of common qualities of bisexuals, therapeutic case studies, and longitudinal studies of bisexuals' relationships. The bisexual experience calls into question traditional definitions of the nature of sexual identity development. Fluid, ambiguous, subversive, multifarious, bisexuality can no longer be ignored.

### NOTES

1. The experiences of bisexual women can often be generalized to those of bisexual men, but generalization should not be assumed. Philip Blumstein and Pepper Schwartz posit some differences between the experiences of bisexual women and bisexual men, "Bisexuality: Some Social Psychological Issues," *The Journal of Social Issues* 33 (Spring 1977): 30–45.

2. Studies of bisexuals are few. Unless specifically documented, statements in this chapter about the lives of bisexual women are based on my observations as counselor, speaker, and workshop leader on bisexuality and as a member of the bisexual community.

3. Names are fictitious.

4. I base this assertion on personal observation, anthropological corroboration, for example, Margaret Mead, "Bisexuality: What's It All About?," *Redbook*, Jan. 1975, 29–31, and projections from what little documentation exists, for example, A. C. Kinsey, W. B. Pomeroy, and C. E. Martin, *Sexual Behavior in the Human Male* (Philadelphia: W. B. Saunders, 1948) and A. C. Kinsey, W. B. Pomeroy, C. E. Martin, and P. H. Gebhard, *Sexual Behavior in the Human Female* (Philadelphia: W. B. Saunders, 1953).

5. See Alan P. Bell and Martin S. Weinberg, *Homosexualities: A Study of Diversity in Women and Men* (New York: Simon and Schuster, 1978).

6. See Mead, "Bisexuality," 31.

7. A. P. MacDonald, "Bisexuality: Some Comments on Research and Theory," *Journal of Homosexuality* 6 (Spring 1981): 21–23.

8. Robyn Ochs, "Survey Results," *Boston Bisexual Women's Network Newsletter* 2 (May-June 1984): 7.

9. The 1984 Supreme Court decision upholding the firing of a bisexual teacher for her lesbian activity demonstrates that bisexuals are not merely half oppressed (*Rowland* vs. *Mad River District, No. 84–532*).

10. Blumstein and Schwartz, "Bisexuality," offer anecdotal observations of bisexually active (versus bisexually identified) individuals. This research predates the development of bisexual communities.

11. See Carla Golden, "Diversity and Variability in Lesbian Identities," 18–34 in this volume.

12. Ochs, "Survey Results," 7.

13. "Wendy Z., Bisexuality in a Psychiatric Setting," *Boston Bisexual Women's Network Newsletter* 2 (May-June 1984): 5.

14. Schwartz and Blumstein, "Bisexuality," 34.

15. Megan Morrison, "Bisexuality: Loving Whom We Choose, Part II," reprinted in *Boston Bisexual Women's Network Newsletter* 2 (Nov.-Dec. 1984): 1–7.

16. Ochs, "Survey Results," 7.

# 4

## *Aging Lesbians:*
## *Observations and Speculations*

BUFFY DUNKER

Thinking about aging in general and aging lesbians in particular, I am aware of an aspect of the theory of relativity: The description of an object under study changes with the position of the viewer, and changes especially if the viewer is in motion. What I write here is affected by my experience of aging and my slight knowledge of other old lesbians. The stereotypes of age that I had when I was forty bear little resemblance to the way I see myself and other old women now. And what can be said about older lesbians now will change greatly in the coming years. This viewer is in motion; the object is not only changing, but it is also largely invisible.

In an article on "Older Women," Matile Poor notes that "relatively few women over sixty-five identify themselves as lesbians." She goes on to estimate from 1977 figures that there were at that time at least 834,000 old lesbians.[1] It's fair to assume that there are a lot more nearly a decade later. Where are they? Today, as younger lesbians are beginning to consolidate their strengths and influence, the presence of older lesbians is sorely needed for role models and mentors, for a source of wisdom and courage, and by their numbers to make all of us more visible, a force to be reckoned with. Many young lesbians need assurance that they can grow into a rich and creative old age not much affected by prejudice. An older lesbian's obvious pride and pleasure in being who she is, politically active or not, can encourage younger ones to have confidence in their futures. A pair of assured, lively, contented old dykes can give the lie to much of the homophobic and ageist propaganda that young lesbians are subjected to.

Most of the observations here are colored by my own experience. Born in the first decade of this century, raised in an upper-middle-class New England family, I married right after college, raised three children, and took part in the average suburban life of the time. After I got a divorce, I taught in a small college preparatory school. When I retired, I got some training to become a feminist therapist and later came out as a lesbian. I'm aware that some of my speculations are not relevant for the large group of working-class and minority old lesbians, many of whom may be lonely and struggling to stay alive well under the poverty line. Recent discoveries in health and nutrition are extending the average life span, now seventy-seven and climbing. Active political groups such as the Older Women's League (OWL) and the Gray Panthers are demanding changes in attitudes and services for old people. But very little is known about the lives and needs of lesbians over sixty-five.

Defining "old" as being more than sixty-five means that all of us older lesbians were born before 1922. We've lived through some tremendous economic, scientific, social, and political changes. Some medical and scientific ones can help make our old age more enjoyable. Recent studies and many books provide us with information and good advice. Other changes have greatly enlarged the scope of our activities and influence. But we are still struggling with the same old oppressions of ageism, sexism, poverty, and racism, and we're still at the bottom of the economic pile.

During their lifetimes our mothers experienced some important changes in their attitudes and beliefs, and these changes strongly affected our development. Their ideas about themselves were of course largely determined by the assumptions of the dominant culture, which was white, male, Anglo-Saxon, and Protestant—much as it is now, although fortunately modified somewhat by eastern and southern European, Jewish, Hispanic, and feminist influences. Our mothers mostly believed that the whole fulfillment of their lives was as helpmate to their husbands and mothers to their children. They understood (with a few lucky exceptions) that sexual desires were natural for a man and that women were asexual. Their strong emotional attachments to their women friends and their adolescent crushes in school and college were normal, without sexual feelings and therefore socially acceptable.[2] Loving friendships between women were not threatening to men, as all power and sexuality were invested in men. A woman who had experienced a deep relationship with another woman was better prepared for the devotion her husband expected, and she had no economic power anyway. "Boston marriages" were not uncommon;[3] for instance, my great-aunt Elizabeth, a teacher and a maiden lady, lived with a woman friend for many years untouched by scandal.

By the early nineteen hundreds more opportunities were opening up for women to become economically independent. Women's colleges were well established, and some universities provided a few women with professional training. More women found they could support themselves, so marriage became less necessary; naturally, male resistance to their independence increased. More disturbing to women's ideas about themselves and threatening to their friendships were the pronouncements of the sexologists (Krafft-Ebing, Freud, Havelock Ellis) that women *were* sexual, and that love between women was abnormal and evil.[4] Close relationships between women became suspect, and the term *lesbian* denoted decadence, inversion, and vice. Those of us who read Radclyffe Hall's *The Well of Loneliness* in the thirties were convinced that loving a woman meant taking on a man's role and would lead to misery and death. Women's feelings about sex during that period were conflicted, to say the least. My aunt Lizzie, also a maiden lady, couldn't understand why anyone would want to read *Gone with the Wind*. "It's disgusting." And my cousin Ruth, in 1981 when she was more than ninety, wrote me, "Hasn't sex gone to the extreme? Certainly when one is married, only a short time is spent sexually, the rest you are busy making marriage work! !"

For those of us who felt "different," the messages we received from our mothers as we were growing up in the nineteen-twenties and thirties were conflicting for us, too. Sex was seldom talked of, if at all, and we knew very little about expressing our sexuality except through marriage. In spite of our feelings of being different, lots of us did marry, usually early, to escape the hazards of promiscuity, getting pregnant, becoming an old maid, or most disturbing in those days, wondering if we were lesbian. Those of us who didn't marry had more resources than our mothers had had to lead independent lives and to understand and take pride in our sexuality, at least to ourselves. Nevertheless, only a few of my 1926 college classmates chose not to get married, and in my narrow experience of close relationships between women at that time, I never heard any of the women referred to as lesbian or homosexual. Besides, many of us didn't understand either the meaning or the derivation of the word *lesbian*, if we had even heard it. Because our strong attraction to women wasn't considered "normal," it wasn't unusual for some of us to develop bad feelings about ourselves. It seemed clear that we had to keep our true feelings secret.

While we were growing up, we were affected by the radicalism, the sexual revolution, and the first of the Red Scares during the nineteen-twenties. During the Great Depression and the New Deal we experienced extremes of deprivation and hope. Along with the sacrifices and awful revelations of human cruelty, World War II brought new jobs for women, new opportunities for independence, and a taste of partial freedom from male dominance. It was a time when some women found they could do very well without men and could recognize their preference for women. At the end of the war, however, there was great social pressure for women to go back to their traditional roles. Only strongly independent lesbians could withstand such prejudice, and not very many were free to come out.

The decade of the fifties was a time when role-playing became an important part of lesbian culture, especially in the bars that appeared in many of the larger cities. In San Francisco, a lesbian publication, *The Ladder*, appeared in 1956, and the Daughters of Bilitis was founded about the same time. But the conservative reaction was strong, and the excesses of the McCarthy era with the persecution of homosexuals frightened many of us into keeping our private lives private.

During the late sixties and early seventies, the power of the women's movement, the slowly growing social acceptance of homosexuality, and the appearance of lesbian and gay communities in some of the big cities made it possible for some older lesbians to come out publicly. That was also a time when quite a number of older women left their marriages. We can assume that many of them were lesbians, because a high percentage of older lesbians have been married previously. Still, a lot of us who had early on accepted and honored our sexuality knew that coming out to others carried too great a risk, socially and economically.

Many older lesbians are now retired, and perhaps some are financially secure enough so that the strong economic reasons for staying hidden aren't so overriding. A recent study shows that it can be psychologically healthy to come out of the closet.[5] The burden of secrecy, deceit, and hypocrisy is heavy. Because we're so old, most of us have lost our parents and even other close relatives and friends whom we felt we had to protect from knowing who we are. So why not come out?

Naturally, the reasons are as diverse as the people involved. It is hard to change at any age, and for old people it often is harder. Old fears and old habits are persistent. We can hope that some lesbian couples find their lives comfortable and satisfying just as they are. And some single ones can take pride in being survivors. Some, like Elsa in *Word Is Out*, who says, "It never occurred to me that it was anybody's business," feel they have a right to their privacy.[6] For many whose relatives and close friends have never known of their secret, the risks are too great, especially the risk of exposing their deception to people who love them as they have always known them. Combined with an older person's usual resistance to change, fear of causing pain to those they love is reason enough to continue in the closet. Because I came out when I was over sixty-five and my job was not at risk, I've had to deal with fewer problems than perhaps most. I came out to my children, grandchildren, friends, and relatives, and their reactions were as varied as their personalities. The lesbian community that welcomed me has provided me with considerably more support and interest than the small part of the older heterosexual community that can't accept me.

It behooves all of us to respect and support any woman's choice to stay where she is. She has had to develop skills to protect her privacy. She has had to deal with feelings of inadequacy and a lot of anger and guilt. She can bear witness to the difficulty of living as one is not, and to the value of self-acceptance.

Old lesbians, out or closeted, have had to develop certain skills and character traits in order to survive, as do other oppressed minorities. First, we've had to support ourselves. In a system where women's earning power is always under pressure and more than a third lower than a man's for similar work and where high salaried positions for women are rare, persistence, skills, and strength to stand up to discrimination are paramount. For lesbians, prejudice and harassment are common, so we've had to develop a degree of solid, stubborn self-confidence and courage. These qualities depend on a clear and pervasive sense of self-worth, with pride in being a woman, a feminist, and a lesbian. We have *had* to be autonomous and in charge of our own lives. These skills are even more necessary for minority women than for the white middle-class women who have provided much of the energy of the women's movement. Many minority women, lesbian or not, have always had to support themselves, and they have had to deal with the double oppression of race and sex.

A lot of older lesbians find themselves with few remaining relatives and no dependents, so self-reliance and ingenuity are required to take care of themselves and deal with loneliness. Some previously married lesbians who had children have lived through that most difficult period of being a single working parent. They've needed great personal strength and constant nurturing power. Not all of us have developed all of these traits in equal measure, but our survival is proof that we have some of them.

In general, old women in our culture get little respect. They are often isolated, patronized, ignored. Most have been married and spent their lives and energies caring for husband and children. As they grew older they find they have lost their main occupation and are ill-equipped to find a new career. Many realize they've received little emotional return for the long years of nurturing others. They've had little experience dealing with the outside world. Some are even afraid to travel alone or to seek other new experiences. Their circle of friends has grown smaller, and because they grew up in a era when good nutrition and exercise weren't emphasized, their health has begun to deteriorate. Few have had the energy and daring to fight against prejudice. Maggie Kuhn of the Gray Panthers is a striking exception—a feisty old woman who makes a lot of noise, insisting on the rights of the old.

The contrast between the situation of the conventional married old woman and the autonomous old lesbian can be enlightening (allowing of course for my prejudices). The lesbian has had to be self-supporting, and the conventional woman has not. The lesbian, especially the lesbian of color, has had to deal with the hazards of oppression, exclusion, and prejudice. The wife has held an honored although secondary position in a society with many heterosexual privileges. The lesbian has had to seek her own friends, lovers, and communities. The wife took her place in the well-established society of couples. The lesbian has been in charge of her own life, making choices of work, recreation, and companions as she wished. The wife has had to please others in most areas; even the kind of meals she prepared and the way she brought up the children had to conform to her husband's wishes.

Many of the disparities will lessen in the future. Today's wives can get jobs and control their lives more freely. The conventional marriage of the nineteen-thirties and forties was firmly under the husband's control, and at the same time the lesbian's life was much more restricted by prejudice than it is now.

One aspect of aging that's hard for many women is the way the body changes. Skin loses its elasticity, and wrinkles, bulges, and flab appear. Hair goes gray or white, and muscles and joints get stiff. The conventional women often accepts the male stereotypes of beauty and youth, and either mourns or fights the change. She can feel bitter, anxious, and self-conscious in the attempt to keep her good looks. Lesbians can reject the male standards. We can appreciate the quality of our own changes as we see what's happening to the faces and figures of the women we love. Our ideas of beauty aren't necessarily subject to male fantasies.

It's still common for women to stick with their husbands in spite of incompatibilities (how many happy, devoted, older married couples do you know?). There are many practical reasons for a woman to stay in an unsatisfactory but protected position. But for lesbians, there is less pressure to stay together if the relationship isn't mutually fulfilling. They can separate (and often become good friends) and perhaps find new partners. Moreover, they can look for younger partners as well as older. An older straight woman seeking a younger male companion is often faced with prejudice, scorn, and rejection; exceptions are rare. Age differences aren't so important for a lesbian, and she may be less fearful of aging and its physical changes. A woman I know who came out at fifty said she felt much more attractive and sexy than she had for years, and she is. The older lesbian is often welcomed where younger ones gather. It's reassuring for them to know that sexual energy doesn't necessarily diminish with age.

Heterosexual women are by definition confined to men for the expression of their sexuality. As they age they usually face an imbalance of sexual interest. Male sexuality seems to be more fragile and more susceptible to the various infirmities of age. After the irregularities and probable discomforts of menopause, women's sexual energy and enjoyment often increase. This can be especially true for a heterosexual woman, now at last free from the anxieties and complications of birth control. But compatibility is threatened. It takes skill and mutual devotion to continue satisfying sexual activity.

No such problem arises for lesbians. We change and develop pretty much according to the same pattern, so our sexuality can be as varied and as satisfying as we want. We've long since discovered the fine nuances of lesbian loving, and they don't diminish with age. Mutuality increases with experience. A lesbian couple who can work through their conflicts and differences can look forward to a good old age together.[7] A young straight friend of mine heard me discussing some of these ideas and said, "What a fine way to grow old!"

Previously married old lesbians have had some special concerns. Most of us married young as we were expected to, right out of school, and had our children while we were still in our twenties. We believed strongly that it was the woman's responsibility to make the marriage a good one. Some of us did well, some did not. Some even tried, at that early date, to combine marriage and a career. There was little social support for leaving marriage. We had to deal with long-established habits of dependency, few marketable and emotionally satisfying skills, diminished income, and a dwindling circle of friends and family. We had had little experience in managing our own lives. We had now to make a living. Some of us faced custody battles, which more often than not were lost.

We turned to women for support and emotional nurturing. We had to accept the loss of heterosexual privileges and face up to the usual homophobic prejudice and exclusion. Instead of (or along with) the problem of coming out to parents, we had to come out to our children.[8] There seems to be significant differences in the needs of life-long lesbians and those who experienced an identity change later in life, especially in the areas of self-confidence and autonomy.[9]

Barbara Macdonald writes in *Look Me in the Eye*, "I never grew old before; never died before. I don't really know how it's done."[10] Old lesbians have few role models, and it's clear that we'll have to fill that function for younger ones. The recent interest in gerontology, fuelled by the fast-growing numbers of the aged, has resulted in a great number of books and periodicals on how to grow old and like it. Most discuss health and nutrition and exercise in great detail and variety. More report on research into housing and recreational needs, always emphasizing what the social services ought to be providing for the old. The chances that our special interests will be addressed are slim. Because we've been in charge of our lives for so long, we can take some of the concerns of aging into our own hands. Such organizations as the Gray Panthers and OWL are politically active and effective in taking responsibility for getting better conditions for themselves. In New York, Senior Action in a Gay Environment (SAGE) has a large lesbian membership. In the Boston area, two women gathered some friends together and started an organization that in a few years grew from twenty-five to more than 150 members and is an active social and support group for lesbians over forty. Another group in Boston is making plans for a nursing home and a shared living project for lesbians and gay men.[11]

"The reason I'm so old is that I haven't died yet," read a quotation in a birthday letter from my grandson to me. The possibilities of enjoying the advantages and privileges of age and at least mitigating its inevitable disadvantages are greater for a woman who has been in charge of her life during most of it. Old lesbians are in a good position for that. We're not likely to have dependents. We're used to making choices, and we've paid our dues. We can choose to take good care of our health, to stay alive, and lively. We've survived in spite of discrimination and oppression. We can ignore the stereotypes and take risks: climb mountains, start a new career, go on bike trips, take cello lessons, become an actor or painter, learn to ski, write a book, adopt a protégé. We can even throw our Puritan consciences out the window and loaf.

We can be peculiar, cranky, and funny, and we can dress as we like. Anyone who has been alive, active, and involved with work and people, always learning and curious and willing to take risks, is likely to continue in that style.

If we are going to live the last part of our lives to the full, it's essential to plan ahead; lesbians younger than sixty-five must be involved in the necessary planning. The usual strategies for enjoying age, with regard to nutrition and health, housing, finances, satisfying work, and family relationships, are much the same for all women. However there are some concerns that are particularly important for lesbians. The first is to find and keep friends, especially younger ones. Isolation and loneliness are dangerous for anyone, but particularly for an old lesbian who may already have lost her partner. The small house in the country is great while one is mobile, but it may be too risky later on. No old person should live out of reach of emergency help. We will have to be creative about new kinds of living arrangements such as congregate housing, shared living, projects with populations of differing age and economic levels. In a rural area, a few old lesbians might find a large house where they could live together for support, protection, and good times.

In dealing with the medical establishment we will have to take the responsibility for seeing that they understand our special needs and strengths. We will have to confront some oppressive regulations, even if it means coming out of the closet. The doctor in charge must know of our wishes, especially about the primary person to be kept informed and included in all important decisions. Many hospitals allow only close relatives in intensive care units. Lovers may find themselves excluded. In the future, social agencies should have special facilities for lesbians, with specially trained personnel. Couples should be able to stay together in nursing homes.

Good legal protection is vital so that a lesbian can be sure that her property goes where she wants it to, and not to others who may feel they have a right to it. It's essential to make a will, including instructions for funeral and other plans. A Living Will can state decisions about extraordinary medical procedures to prolong life. Insurance policies and wills can be specific, drawn up well enough to withstand any protests. We have the right to die as we have lived, with dignity and independence.

Finances are always a problem for old people. Fortunately, social security hasn't been able to discriminate against lesbians yet, but employers often do. Women over sixty find themselves being pressured to take early retirement at a lower pension. They will be among the first to be laid off, too. Because old lesbians aren't likely to have dependents, they can take risks. Even at sixty-five, career changes are possible and challenging. Being self-employed has big advantages along with the risks.

The inevitability of death means that an old lesbian finds her circle of close friends is shrinking, and she has to deal with a lot of losses. Some of us have younger relatives and friends to help keep us in touch with life and our hopes for the future. It's imperative that older lesbians find younger friends. They need us, too. The old crone, the wise woman, the witch have always been valued in many cultures. We can ensure that they are valued here, too.

Looking back now from the nineteen-eighties, it's evident that society's attempts to suppress homosexuals, especially women, have been unremitting, and now and then pretty successful. Our increasing numbers help make us more powerful, but we must be wary of over-confidence. We need to be constantly aware of the deep defensive basis of masculine fear and anger about lesbian independence. Men, naturally, don't want to lose control of those who could provide them with care, comfort, children, and sexual pleasures. Recent conservative and repressive measures are dangerous. All of us, old and young, must work for a world where men can take care of themselves and share the responsibility for bringing up children. And younger lesbians need all the knowledge and encouragement they can get from us survivors.

## NOTES

1. Matile Poor, "Older Lesbians," in *Lesbian Studies: Present and Future*, ed. Margaret Cruikshank (Westbury, N.Y.: Feminist Press, 1982), 165–73.

2. Lillian Faderman, *Surpassing the Love of Men, Romantic Friendship and Love between Women from the Renaissance to the Present* (New York: William Morrow, 1981), 152.

3. Faderman, *Surpassing the Love*, 190–91.

4. Ibid., 297–300, 357.

5. Edna I. Rawlings and Dee L. R. Graham, "Are Closets Healthy?," paper presented at the Association of Women in Psychology Conference, Boston, March 9–11, 1984.

6. Nancy Adair and Casey Adair, *Word Is Out* (San Francisco: New Glide Publications, 1978), 24.

7. Gloria Bailey and Linda J. Davies, "Staying Together, Feeling Alive," paper presented at the Association of Women in Psychology Conference, Boston, March 9–11, 1984.

8. Ruth Baetz, *Lesbian Crossroads* (New York: William Morrow, 1980), 143.

9. Miriam Rosenberg, "Two Contrasting Avenues of Lesbian Identity Development," paper presented at the Association of Women in Psychology Conference, Boston, March 9–11, 1984.

10. Barbara Macdonald, *Look Me in the Eye* (San Francisco: Spinster's Ink, 1983), 19.

11. Elizabeth Wood, "Elderly Shared Living," *Bay Windows* (Boston), March 15, 1984.

# 5

## *Invisibility, Fantasy, and Intimacy: Princess Charming Is Not a Prince*

LEE ZEVY WITH SAHLI A. CAVALLARO

This is the story of an odyssey. A story about lesbian invisibility: how lesbians grow into, maintain, and attempt to undo this invisibility so that they may know themselves and love other women; so that the quest for the princess is reconciled, and intimacy with a real woman and a charmed relationship is attained. To explain the complexity of this process, we chose to combine psychological theory with the telling of one of our stories. Although the details of the story are about Lee Zevy's life, the themes of invisibility and fantasy and the subsequent search for intimacy are common threads that run through the lives of women we both know and the lesbians with whom we work professionally.

### *Childhood: The Development of Invisibility*

In the 1940s when I was growing up, gender-role expectations for boys and girls were pretty strongly delineated. From the beginning, I behaved more like a boy. In nursery school, I was more active, aggressive, and defiant, played more roughly, and took more risks than my older sister and the other girls. They were neater, cleaner, more reserved, and more easily upset. And I would not nap without my football.

Although my behavior was indulged and approved at home, it met with annoyance and censure at the nursery school. My sister, who was two-and-a-half years older, ran interference between the teachers and me, often translating my needs and deeds to them so that my life was manageable. When she left to go to kindergarten, I could not make myself understood and began at two-and-a-half to deceive my teachers and hide my real feelings. Because I already identified with many male characteristics and was often responded to as a boy, I developed what would become lifelong problems. First, I was confronted with the struggle to force me into the behavior of a typical girl. Second, I responded to this struggle by communicating as if I were male, with the behavior, mannerisms, cues, signals, and responses of the boys at school. For example, if someone said to me, "Oh, what a pretty girl you are," and expected a positive response, I would turn away, look at the floor or ceiling, or appear angry. If I was forced to say, "Thank you," I managed to be as ungracious as possible. If, however, they complimented my strength, agility, or intelligence, I would smile. Finally, in my effort to achieve what I saw as the epitome of maleness, I began to lose my ability to communicate emotionally. Because sissies cried, I stopped crying. Because boys play by fair rules, I developed a rigid code of fairness. As I was growing up, most communication between children and adults was explicitly sex-typed, and many adults who found me to be unresponsive to their ideas about feminine dress, colors, games, and toys either broke off communication or became sarcastic and critical. I now understand that the ambiguity of my identity made these adults anxious, and only rarely would one pursue my feelings. I remember one day in kindergarten when I became sick. It was one of the few times that I was quiet in class, and my teacher rewarded me with one of the paper dolls that she was giving to selected good girls that day. Even at that age, I felt outraged. This, my most pronounced memory of sex-role reinforcement, was only one among many, because by the first grade I had managed to narrow my range of emotional expression severely in order to avoid the humiliating possibility of being taken the wrong way. I was well on my way toward invisibility.

### Childhood: The Development of Deceptive Communication

Although the development of lesbian invisibility does not follow a universal path, it usually begins with deceptive communication patterns in early childhood, when children begin to hide real interests from accepted behavior. According to my experience and some of the research, lesbians often seem to identify more with masculine and androgynous traits than with feminine traits.[1] For that reason, most seem to fall into two categories during childhood: those girls who identify with and behave as boys (in dress, speech, and manner) the way I did, and those who identify with boys in the preferences for sports, games, and other boy-favored activities, but who disguise their male sentiments in feminine dress and decorum and thus elicit feminine treatment from others. For the most part, all of these lesbians know their gender identity.[2] Acceptance of the sex-role stereotypes seems totally intolerable for some lesbians, while others can accept some of the roles. Finally, there is a third category of lesbians who as children identify with and look like girls. The issue of being different does not emerge until sometime quite late in adulthood for these women.

Sex is the one area that seems to be related to an almost universal pattern of deception. Sexual expression in childhood is taboo, so children early learn to deceive adults about masturbation, sexual games, fantasies, and thought. The girl who later becomes a lesbian and was attracted to girls at a young age may learn to deceive adults about this, too. Accordingly, many of the lesbians I've known remember that their sexual interests in women occurred at a very early age.[3] At the same time, they also realized that although they liked girls, most girls liked boys, and they were not like most girls. Again, for some lesbians this realization came early; for others, it came in adolescence or adulthood. I, for example, realized that I was different in nursery school when I saw that I was more like boys than like girls.

By the time I was five, I was not only more aware of being different, but I also wanted to be different. My family had just moved into an Irish/Italian working-class neighborhood. The Italian men and boys in that neighborhood seemed to epitomize all of the characteristics of the kind of man I saw as powerful and did not find in the Jewish community into which I was born. In order to be as much like these Italian men as possible, I spoke like them, walked like them, wore high-topped sneakers, and went without a top. The gang I ran with treated me as one of the boys, and once again I was indulged at home and met with increasing scorn at school. Although I was intelligent, charming, and funny, I could not win over adults who found my incongruent behavior peculiar and threatening. Occasionally, therefore, I had to submit to the shame of wearing a party dress, a humiliating experience for an Italian boy who aspired to manhood.

## Adolescence: The Creation of Lesbian Emblems and Deceptive Roles

When I entered adolescence, I encountered even greater risk of exposure, because adolescence is a time when knowing and following the rules of sexual interplay between boys and girls becomes increasingly important. Such rules are based on a communication complex of linguistic, paralinguistic, and nonverbal behavior.[4] When people want to be heard and seen as clearly as possible, they send messages over a tightly braided cable of their own and their partner's communicative intentions and modalities: What is said must be supported by gaze pattern, voice features, body posture and movement, facial expression, turn-taking behavior, and a synchronization of all these with the partner's behavior. When partners are to be deceived or hidden from, one or several channels are used in contradiction.[5] For example, a lie can be delivered successfully behind the screen of a warm, open face. Or a lesbian's sexual preference can be made ambiguous by a clutter of feminine dress and body gestures.

My particular problem in adolescence was to disguise the Italian male I had bred in myself successfully enough so that I could hang out with the girls and not be detected as a fraud by the boys; being seen as either a fraudulent male or fraudulent female would have been devastating. Sex-role invisibility was necessary in order to avoid isolation. I achieved this invisibility in two ways. First, I wore feminine camouflage: makeup, seamed stockings, starched crinolines, and endless curlers. I took on feminine habits; I spoke in deliberate tones and flirted with the boys. This created problems for my Italian male persona, who although now underground always felt as though he were in drag. I could never figure out if I wanted Lennie Nulett because he was a boy or because I craved his leather jacket. The second solution was an even better blind for my sexual identity. My father was a therapist, so I just slipped into his role. I took on the jargon and the technique of objective distancing. This stance of the friend-therapist reserved a unique role for me among my friends and was the perfect cover for my insecurities and inept behavior. I could remain perfectly invisible while analyzing my friends. This solution worked almost too well, because although girls found my relating their boy problems to parental relationships somewhat useful, or at least tolerable, boys hated it entirely. Although my therapist role kept potential girl lovers turned toward their princes, it won no princes or princesses for me, and even a prince would have been better than the growing isolation I felt.

At seventeen, I found my first princess—she wore Fred Braun walking boots and was a woodsy, backpacking woman fearless of being seen as masculine. She was the seducer, and we were at camp, so I labeled the experience a phase and fell totally, romantically in love. To this day, I cannot remember what we actually said to each other. I can only remember events and sensations. The romance lasted fifteen months, and then the reality of a lesbian relationship drove me back to dating men. Like all of us who grew up in the fifties and sixties, I had received the American Dream as gospel. In our minds, the fantasies were reality. One day a prince would come and take care of me, and even if I didn't want a prince, I still wanted to be taken care of. A princess is not a prince, not the kind I had seen in my storybooks and later in the movies, nor the kind my parents had in mind for me. Wasn't it my birthright as a middle-class Jewish girl to be saved by a real prince, one who would care for me forever? Sure, if I lived by the rules for being a princess. Although I didn't want to be a princess (I wanted to be an Italian man who could claim a princess), I still held on to a now-modified fantasy: Perhaps a princess would save *me*. And there I was again, the Italian man in love with women, yet dating men and looking for a prince. This was a very confusing situation.

At this point, I knew I was different. I was no longer merely uneasy about being a man in a girl's suit or a girl in a man's suit. Now I knew what the source of my difference was: I was a lesbian, sexually attracted to women. Now the deceptive communication that I had practiced since childhood took on a frightening new twist. I could either avoid women entirely or assume very sophisticated communication strategies. Such strategies involved my providing cues and signals that would achieve three ends simultaneously: First, I wanted the occasional woman who would be a possible sexual liaison to know I was interested. But second, my communications would have to be ambiguous enough to provide an out in case the woman was not interested. And third, I had to play the heterosexual game with no intention of winning; that is, I had to play the game without really playing, to appear genuine and interested in men for whom they appeared to be — perhaps colleagues and friends, but also potential mates — while still seeming unavailable for sexual liaison with the man who asked. And I needed to look disinterested in women for whom they appeared to be — colleagues and friends, but not potential mates — even though I would have been available to them had they asked. Successful job interviews as well as other public presentations depended on my ability to balance appropriate sex-role behavior against no-nonsense competence. This is a very difficult game for the heterosexual woman to play, but it is even more difficult for lesbians, who must play the game well enough so that everyone remains comfortable, but not *so* well that princess charming, should she happen by, would not recognize a potential love through the heterosexual disguise.

In college, I found a reasonable solution to this problem of being invisible; I was determined to attract the attention of a woman whom I had long suspected as a lesbian. She was a formidable intellectual, always surrounded by a crew of men and women. I bought a copy of *Diana,* a well-known lesbian novel at the time, and made a prominent display of it, knowing that a non-lesbian would be unlikely to show an interest in the book, but that, if she were really a lesbian, this woman would recognize it as an emblem of my identity. It was an effective way to make my introduction but to cover myself if she wasn't interested. Other lesbians I've known have employed similar emblems of their identity. Pinky rings and passing allusions to gay clubs, journals, or musicians are other useful techniques for a novice interested in selective disclosure.

In the art of open flirtation with women, however, I was not as skillful as I was eager. My indifferent flirtations with men were suddenly transformed into focused and directed goals with women. But when I decided at twenty-two to pursue women actively, I faced the old sex-role game. Although the sex had changed, the rules were the same. I was attracted to boyish women but could not sustain the femme role past the flirtation. As a butch, I endured burned fingers while lighting cigarettes, bruises on my face while holding doors, and crushed toes while dancing. I discovered that having straddled both male and female roles in order to avoid growing up in either left me with knowledge about neither. I could not act either truly female or truly male. What I had learned very well was how to be invisible, and I couldn't emerge from this state to make an appearance even to myself, not to speak of those princesses by whom I so desperately wanted to be seen.

### Adulthood: Visibility and Communication

Visibility and acknowledgment between communicating partners involves a synchronized series of cues and responses that are back and forth in nature.[6] Clear communication depends upon intrapersonal as well as interpersonal synchrony among the various communicative channels (linguistic, paralinguistic, and nonverbal). Again, a speaker interested in deceiving while still holding the partner in communication may do so by presenting a message in one channel while contradicting it in another.[7] Thus, a woman interested in making conversation but not in making love with a man may hold him in the verbal channel with the right kind of words but reject him in the nonverbal channel with defensive postures. When this sort of deception is introduced into conversation, the deceiving partner is perceived as ambivalent, indifferent, and tense.[8] In fact, most of my life people have perceived me as angry when I am not. A lesbian is in the paradoxical position of having to be an expert at this sort of deception in order to maintain any social contact at all in a heterosexual society.[9] Indeed, with heterosexual women, a lesbian must successfully accomplish a double deception. If she is totally honest in expressing her feelings toward women (in seeing them as potential sexual partners), she may be correctly read and rejected; if she is dishonest in expressing her feelings, she may be regarded as generally ambivalent and then would be rejected. Thus, she is in the untenable position of having to be dishonest about who she is (I am not a lesbian) but appear earnest about who she is not (I am not a woman interested in heterosexual contact). Her partners are left with wondering who she really is and how to respond to her. Lesbians who develop this stance of invisibility, of being an unreal heterosexual woman by imitating the "correct" norms for female heterosexual behavior, end up experiencing themselves—and being experienced—as a hollow copy intended to be not understood, not believed, and not taken as valid. As I did, many lesbians make and remake this copy in every-day interactions in order to shield themselves from discovery.

Unfortunately, because much of the lesbian's process of making herself into a hollow copy is unconscious, she frequently cannot cease doing it when with a real potential sexual partner (another lesbian). For example, in conversations many lesbians eliminate gender-specific pronouns such as "she" and "her," substituting neutral replacements such as "person," "they," and "someone." Thus, an androgynous description of an evening with a lesbian woman who gave a party for her lover would be: "Well, there was a party in Brooklyn which a friend was giving for someone they know from the place they work." Or, a perfectly opaque explanation to colleagues at her office of why a lesbian is distracted and distressed at work because her lover walked out on her might go: "This weekend I had a disagreement with someone very close to me." Sometimes lesbians describe their attractions to women, even to other lesbians, by saying "She's interesting, I like her energy."

Perhaps the most blatant failure of all is the invisible lesbian come-on by one woman to another, such as the one I recently observed while dining with a friend who was eating cherry pie. An approaching lesbian, having failed to catch my friend with a prolonged, undisguised stare, said to her, "Nice pie you've got there; you know, I like blueberry pie too. It's better hot." It's not easy to extend pie conversation unless you both agree it's a metaphor. Metaphorical communication is a highly sophisticated but risky method used by both lesbians and heterosexuals to conduct flirtations. The difference is that although verbal and non-verbal aspects of heterosexual communication tend to mesh, these two dimensions of lesbian communication are often paradoxical and amount to a contradictory approach/avoidance message. The pie come-on, for example, could be communicated as a sexual metaphor if the linguistic and paralinguistic message were congruent. This is often the case with the clumsy come-ons made by the heterosexual on the prowl. Although the pie reference is not a sophisticated conversational opener, if said seriously, it will be perceived as an earnest come-on if body language and voice tone support the flirtatious intention.

Lesbians' attempts to hide their sexual identity frequently result in overkill: They succeed in hiding most of their intentions from other people. Because identity, goals, needs, and perceptions depend upon feedback from the world about a person, lesbians effectively isolate themselves by not becoming visible. As a consequence, many lesbians become confused about who they are and frequently seek therapy in an attempt to gain clarity. Too often, the confused person a lesbian presents, the interaction strategies she has learned, and the inability to communicate directly are perceived as symptomatic of a more severe psychological disorder.

I never did find out my diagnosis when I went into therapy between the ages of nineteen and twenty-two, but I can well imagine the picture I presented. I did, however, learn something more about invisibility when I was in a predominantly heterosexual therapy group somewhat later. Much to my despair, I learned that my invisibility as a lesbian would be inescapable, not because heterosexuals are against gays or feel that homosexuality is pathological, but because in a straight group, as in the straight world, signals and body cues are heterosexual. When I came out in a straight group, the confusion was even further compounded by my having become visible; men could no longer respond to me as a woman interested in men, and women, even though I was not threatening their sexuality, could not respond to me as another woman who, like themselves, was interested in men. We could, of course, always communicate as people with similar feelings, but that one essential ingredient, a similarity in sexual interest, would always be missing.

## Relationships: Fantasy and Intimacy

What is the likelihood that two women coming from a lifetime of invisibility will succeed in becoming visible to one another? The difficulties are astronomical. First, both women are experts at deceptive communication. As a result, chances are that they have never really communicated on a daily basis about their feelings, thoughts, and ideas. Even if they do succeed in identifying one another as lesbians, they may not succeed in communicating their emotions and wants. Second, each will meet the other with the same confusing preconscious fantasy life: Am I the prince and she the princess? Does she save me, or I her? Maybe we are both princes or princesses? Maybe I should look elsewhere.

After my initial lesbian encounter at seventeen, these problems proved to be of increasing importance during the quick succession of my next four relationships. With each relationship I became more aware that I did not know how to communicate with other lesbians, nor did they with me. I did, however, learn from each person and relationship by accumulating social skills, subculture language, and greater competence in "the life-style" (bars, dances, parties, and friends). I found out that I never wanted to be a wife, nor a husband for that matter. Only after the fourth attempt did I begin to develop systematically a strategy for actually meeting someone with whom I was compatible. But even before acknowledging that I needed such a strategy, I had to let go of any fantasy that a royal love would fall from the sky, and I had to accept the fact that I would have to screen women and start with the aspiring candidates, not the princess-elect. The work side of relationships had thus begun. I found, for example, that reserving a period of time for becoming familiar with a woman was, although novel, useful. Then, if we survived that period (usually six months for me), we might begin the hard labor of becoming intimate.

Intimacy involves the ability to disclose the essential, most inward parts of oneself to another person and have them equally disclose themselves. The potential for intimacy usually is acquired during childhood (if all goes well) and experienced in relationships throughout the course of growing up. If intimate aspects of oneself are withdrawn early in life through deceptive patterns of communication, then intimate relationships cannot be developed until the layers of invisibility are peeled away and the essential person emerges. Therefore, it is possible that lesbians use a series of adult relationships to dissolve, as I did, the protective layers of unintentional deception, each relationship being used to erode one or more of the layers behind which the person has been hidden. As each relationship ends, lesbians examine the ruins for the most durable aspect of themselves, carrying both those parts of them that have weathered the storm whole and those parts that are damaged into the next relationship in order to use the whole parts and to improve the damaged with the repair a new person offers.

Like most individuals coming into gay life from a life of deception and hiding, I believed that I would have what the straight world provides single and married heterosexuals: security, intimacy, love, affection, and friendship. Because there were no models for lesbian relationships other than those following a heterosexual model, I too came to believe that this was the way to have a relationship. Lesbians constantly reinvent the wheel because there is no marriage contract recognized by any community, no common medium through which they can impart wisdom to future generations of lesbians as parents do with children. Because the heterosexual relationship does not offer a prototype that can be used to guide two women interested in developing a primary relationship together, I believe that each lesbian couple must arrive at their own unique solution.

Another source of difficulty is a common, persistent belief that women, particularly feminine women, would not really want another woman. Lesbians like myself, who grew up always wanting women who really wanted men, developed a mistrust for any woman who wanted them; for this reason they frequently fail to make even an initial attempt to form intimate relationships. To this day, it takes me a long time before I trust that another woman whom I care to be with will forgo heterosexual life and put in the kind of work it takes to develop a successful lesbian relationship.

All relationships require daily work—sometimes boring, often routine. Women who come to lesbian relationships having experienced this fact are at a definite advantage. The others, like myself, must be willing to learn through repetition, trial, and error.

In many ways, lesbian relationships have advantages that heterosexual relationships do not. In particular, there is the freedom of not being bound by marriage contracts and the rules and sex roles of heterosexual family life. Even where children are involved, lesbian couples have the advantage of regulating their relationships in unique ways. This very difference, however, seems to create the greatest fear. As women, we have been taught to rely upon mothers and fathers, and then husbands, to provide the regulating structure for our lives. When two women enter into a relationship where both have been taught to rely upon someone else, they often meet the challenge with debilitating anxiety rather than with the search for new solutions. Lesbian relationships seem to work best when there is equality of power, background, and commitment.[10] They do not seem to work when the greatest shared interest is romance and fantasy. Moreover, each woman must give up her idea that a princess will suddenly lift her out of the struggle for visibility and autonomy and replace her mundane bouts with reality with a kingdom not given even to her heterosexual sisters by their princes.

This is not to deny that even I, in my forties and still becoming visible, do not have my occasional flings with fantasy. Allowing my fantasies to join me is part of becoming visible. Every once in a while when life is becoming dull, the Italian man comes out of the closet, puts on his leather jacket, and runs off into the sunset with his princess.

## Clinical Implications

The recent changes in the diagnosis of homosexuality as a pathological condition have brought about a lessening in the stigmatizing of lesbians as sick. Many enlightened therapists began to see past a sexual diagnosis and became interested in helping lesbian clients achieve satisfaction within their chosen life-style. The difficulty lies in the facts that the understanding has not gone deep enough, and lesbians frequently seek out lesbian therapists after failures with non-lesbian therapists because they were unable to make themselves understood and did not have the tools to communicate their feelings. The path to invisibility and deception produces the following traits: incongruent body language, cues, and signals; trouble establishing intimacy; and tremendous anxiety, woodenness, rigidity, or anger about revealing secrets about lesbian identity. Based on these traits, lesbians are often misdiagnosed as narcissistic or borderline personalities. Some have been misdiagnosed as schizophrenic. That is not to say that there are no lesbians who fit these conditions, and whose sexual preference is unrelated to a more profound early difficulty.

The importance of understanding the process of growing up as a lesbian in a heterosexual society is that the therapeutic relationship will, of course, reflect that process. Sexual transference will not be heterosexual and therefore will likely carry more anxiety for both the therapist and client, along with the client's possible incongruent patterns of behavior and communication. The therapeutic relationship is often one of many relationships that a lesbian will use to uncover the various layers of invisibility. Some lesbians feel that they can only accomplish this goal when the therapist shares their experience and reveals her lesbian identity. It is essential that the therapist understand the difficult process of developing a lesbian identity and cope with the differences and possible anxiety of a nonheterosexual transference.

## NOTES

1. Alfred B. Heilbrun, Jr. and Norman L. Thompson, Jr., "Sex-Role Identity and Male and Female Homosexuality," *Sex Roles* 3 (no. 1, 1977): 65–79.

2. Phyllis Katz, "The Development of Female Identity," *Sex Roles* 5 (no. 2, 1979): 155–78.

3. Ellen Fleishman, "Sex Role Acquisition, Parental Behavior and Sexual Orientation: Some Tentative Hypotheses," *Sex Roles* 9 (no. 10, 1983): 105–59.

4. Stanley Duncan, Jr. and Donald Fiske, *Face-To-Face Interaction: Research Methods and Theory,* University of Chicago Law Review (Hillsdale, N.J.: Erlbroun Associates, Publishers, 1977).

5. Bella M. DePaulo, Robert Rosenthal, Carolyn Rieder Green, and Judith Rosenkrantz, "Diagnosing Deceptive and Mixed Messages from Verbal and Nonverbal Cues," *Journal of Experimental Social Psychology* 18 (Sept. 1982): 433–46.

6. Duncan and Fiske, *Face-To-Face Interaction.*

7. DePaulo, et al., "Diagnosing Deceptive and Mixed Messages," 433–46.

8. Howard S. Friedman, "The Interactive Effects of Facial Expressions of Emotion and Verbal Messages in Perceptions of Affective Meaning," *Journal of Experimental Social Psychology* 15 (Sept. 1979): 453–69.

9. Vivienne M. Cass, "Homosexual Identity Formation, A Theoretical Model," *Journal of Homosexuality* 4 (Spring 1979): 219–35.

10. Letitia Anne Peplau, "Research on Homosexual Couples: An Overview," *Journal of Homosexuality* 8 (Winter 1982).

# II

# RELATIONSHIPS

# 6

## Lesbian Sexuality:
## Issues and Developing Theory

MARGARET NICHOLS

I am a Sexually Incorrect lesbian. For years I've hidden it, but now I intend to share my dirty little secret with the world. My favorite sexual fantasies have always been bisexual S/M fantasies, and although for years I refused to tell anyone else in the women's movement about this for fear some Women Against Pornography type would excoriate me for my retrograde thoughts, I've never really tried to repress them—frankly, doing so ruined my sex life—nor have I ever felt terribly guilty about them. On the other hand, I'm not yet prepared to march in the Gay Pride parade in full leather drag carrying a "No Pain, No Gain" banner, and thus the "new wave" of bold young lesbian sexual outlaws considers me hopelessly fainthearted and old-fashioned. I've always harbored a secret love of makeup and dressing up, even during the period in which I never wore any and let the hair on my legs grow; I think it comes from the fact that I was such a failure at dress-up as an adolescent. On the other hand, I am aghast at the thought of calling myself a femme, in the manner of the new lesbian butch-femme liberation movement. As a woman who was married for many years and lived a heterosexual life in which everyone from my mother to my boss to my husband insisted that I be a femme, I must admit that this trend really does baffle me sometimes.

If this is not enough to convince you that I am truly S.I., consider this: I repudiate politically correct lesbian lovemaking. P. C. lesbian lovemaking, for the uninitiated, consists of the following: Two women lie side by side (tops or bottoms are strictly forbidden—lesbians must be non-hierarchical); they touch each other gently and sweetly all over their bodies for several hours (lesbians are not genitally/orgasm oriented, a patriarchal mode). If the women have orgasms at all—and orgasms are only marginally acceptable because, after all, we must be process, rather than goal, oriented—both orgasms must occur at exactly the same time in order to foster true equality and egalitarianism. (I'm not kidding about this orgasm stuff: A "feminist" critique of a paper I published in the journal *Women and Therapy* included the charge that my thinking was "male-identified" because I talked about treating anorgasmic lesbians. The critic charged that orgasms shouldn't be important to lesbians, only to men. I've given up a lot for the lesbian-feminist movement, but this is where I draw the line.)

I think my own struggles with my S. I. nature, the fact that wherever I turned I could find little writing or thought about our sexuality either within the mainstream field of psychology or even within the lesbian-feminist movement, my observations of recent very interesting sexual trends within the lesbian community, and my (somewhat prurient) fascination with gay male sexuality led me eventually to do some theorizing and writing of my own. This essay is best viewed as a work in progress. I am an old-fashioned lesbian feminist from the school of thought that believed that the "personal is political." This concept didn't just mean that housework was oppressive to women. It really had to do with a methodology of political (and I would argue, scientific as well) discovery. The idea was that in any new, unexplored area of human (female) experience, the first stage of research must of necessity be self-exploration, and the next has to be a public sharing of that self-exploration in a forum wherein participants are nonjudgmental and noncritical (critical in the condemning sense of the word) while remaining critical in the Socratic, questioning sense. In my opinion, lesbian sexuality is just such an unexplored field, and so I write here in the spirit of "the personal is political." This work has come from my own personal ruminations about my own sexuality as much as it has come from reading, observations of clients and friends, and ideas of colleagues. I hope what I write can be a springboard for the ideas and self-revelations of others, and that our community can allow now for a nonjudgmental fact-finding stage in our discovery of our own sexuality. We simply do not know enough about lesbian sexuality, or about human sexuality for that matter, to reasonably do anything else right now.

### Lesbian Couples and Lesbian Sex

Some of the most startling information about lesbian sexuality has come from a study by sociologists Philip Blumstein and Pepper Schwartz, published as *American Couples.*[1] These researchers used a large and well-chosen sample and compared heterosexual married, heterosexual unmarried, gay male, and lesbian couples along a number of dimensions including sexuality. They found, for example, that lesbian couples have sex far less frequently than any other type of couple. Gay men have somewhat less sex in their primary relationships than do either type of heterosexual couple; on the other hand, gay males have the highest rates of extramarital sex. This means that lesbians in couple relationships are less sexual as couples and as individuals than anyone else. Only about one-third of lesbians in relationships of two years or longer had sex once a week or more; 47 percent of lesbians in long-term relationships had sex once a month or less. This is in striking contrast, for example, to heterosexual married couples: Two-thirds of these couples had sex once a week or more, and only 15 percent of long-term married couples had sex once a month or less.

Blumstein and Schwartz also report that the lesbians they interviewed preferred nongenital physical contact such as hugging and cuddling to genital sex. However, one-half of lesbians in couples with a low frequency of genital sexual contact said they are dissatisfied with their sexuality. (My guess is that this is the half of the couple that wants sex more than once a month.)

Lesbians in the Blumstein and Schwartz study seem to be more limited in the range of their sexual techniques than are other couples. For example, 61 percent of lesbian couples have oral sex "infrequently or not at all." This finding corroborates similar data from Karla Jay and Allen Young's *The Gay Report.*[2] Lesbians have about the same rates of nonmonogamy as heterosexuals (28 percent report at least one extramarital episode), although they have far less "outside" sex than gay men, for whom nonmonogamy is the norm rather than the exception. But lesbians, like heterosexual women and unlike both gay and straight men, are likely to have affairs rather than just sexual encounters. Moreover, both lesbians and gay men, as contrasted to heterosexual couples, are likely to be open with their partners about their extramarital activity. And lesbians who are nonmonogamous are more likely than gay males and even heterosexual men and women to be, at the same time, dissatisfied with their primary relationships and with sex in their primary relationships. Thus lesbian extramarital activity seems to be qualitatively quite different from heterosexual nonmonogamy, which tends to be furtive and not necessarily related to unhappiness within the primary relationship; and it is different from the nonmonogamy of gay males in that its form is affairs rather than "tricking," and may often be related to dissatisfaction within the primary couple.

And finally, as reported at an eighteen-month follow-up of all couples, lesbian couples had the highest rates of break-up of any couple type. Moreover, the pattern of breakup was that of nonmonogamy (in the form of an affair) followed by the nonmonogamous partner leaving for a new lover.

What are we to make of this? One conclusion, of course, is that lesbians clearly spend more time discussing the political correctness of sex than they spend doing sex. More serious is the fact that these findings fit a very common pattern that I see in my practice and in the community at large: Two women couple, often very shortly after each has de-coupled from a previous relationship, and frequently move in with each other after the briefest of courtships. The women pledge undying love for each other, feel perfectly matched, and enjoy ecstatic lovemaking. Two to four years later, the couple's frequency of sex has dropped off drastically. One partner may complain, but often neither really complains, and usually they claim that the rest of the relationship is "fine." They may rationalize the lack of sex in their relationship with political ideology about genital sex being patriarchal and so forth. They may make a conscious and overt decision to "open up" the relationship, because "monogamy is patriarchal," or nonmonogamy may "just happen." In either case, what ultimately happens is that one partner becomes sexually involved with a new woman, "falls in love" with the new person, and the couple breaks up, with the nonmonogamous partner forming a new couple with the third woman.

What is happening here? I believe that lesbians, like heterosexual women, are essentially sexually repressed. We are at least as repressed as our straight sisters, perhaps even more. We have more sexual conflicts than do men, gay or heterosexual, lower sexual desire, and fewer ways of expressing our sexual needs. Our relationships represent the pairing of two relatively sexually inhibited individuals; thus it is no wonder that the frequency of sex in our relationships is less than in gay male or heterosexual relationships. Inhibited sexual desire is the most common clinical problem of lesbians presenting for sex therapy.[3] Moreover, our sex is less diverse and varied than the sexual techniques of gay males and possibly even of heterosexual couples.

On the other hand, despite our rhetoric about sensuality versus sexuality, sex does matter to us, as individuals and as couples. For most people who are coupled, sex is a significant if not all-consuming part of the relationship. It can be considered for many as part of what holds a relationship together during those periods in which it seems that little else is going well with the partners. Genital, orgasmic sex is indeed important to us, and our sexual inhibitions thus interfere not only with our individual enjoyment of sex, but also with this significant aspect of coupling. When a part of a relationship is missing, the couple is more likely to come undone. And the *way* our couples often become undone, through nonmonogamy and one partner subsequently leaving the relationship for a new lover, is not accidental and is related to our sexual repression. We leave one relationship with an unsatisfactory sex life for a new relationship that promises better sex.

What are the reasons for our relative lack of sexuality, and how are our sexual concerns related to the recent debates in the lesbian feminist movement over sexual issues such as S/M, butch-femme roles, bisexuality, and nonmonogamy? Before exploring the answers to these questions, let me issue some caveats and make clear some of the premises upon which I base my thinking. First, I do not mean to imply that I believe that lesbian relationships dissolve only, or even principally, for sexual reasons. Blumstein and Schwartz feel that the legitimization of marriage is the primary factor involved in relationship longevity. Even though lesbian relationships had the highest dissolution rates at follow-up, the chief difference in couples was between heterosexual married couples on one hand, and all other types of couples on the other. Social sanction seems to be the strongest bond that holds relationships together. Aside from legitimization or lack thereof, surely other factors besides sex lead to the break-up of lesbian relationships. In fact, an alternate way to view the data I gave earlier is to say that the basic problems lesbian couples have is that they couple prematurely, and that the later falling off of sexual desire is a sign that the couple never should have been together in the first place. I mean to point out only that sex is one powerful factor, and a factor that is almost never considered by lesbians themselves as a possible reason for relationship failure. Second, I do not imply that longevity in relationships is always desirable, or that all people should be permanently coupled. Certainly some lesbians will not want to be coupled at all, and others will consider serial monogamy to be preferable to a quasi-married state. But I do not hear many lesbians saying this. What I hear is lesbians professing to want to make their relationships work in a long-term committed way. Because this is what lesbians say they want, it is relevant to examine why they so rarely—more rarely than other couples—get it. My position concerning whether longevity is practical or useful in a relationship is that longevity combined with quality in a couple relationship of any kind is uncommon but attainable, and because so many of us lesbians seem to aspire to that combination, it is worth our while as psychologists and clinicians to figure out how to help our community achieve this goal for those of us who wish it.

There are some premises upon which I base my work, assumptions that I should make explicit for the sake of clarity and honesty. I quite frankly consider the average lesbian and gay male relationship to be generally more advanced than the average heterosexual relationship. In my experience, far too many heterosexual relationships become bogged down in the mire of sex-role conflicts and never transcend these conflicts to a point where both partners see each other as full human beings. I do not mean to imply that lesbian and gay male relationships are without conflict, simply that the conflicts are of a more human, universal, less gender-based order. And they are certainly much less likely to exhibit the vast power differentials that can be found in many heterosexual relationships; what power differentials do exist are most often psychological rather than real, that is, backed up by concrete power in the world such as financial or legal power. I am not saying that heterosexual relationships never transcend gender; surely some do. I only mean that depressingly large numbers of heterosexual re-lationships never get beyond this level to a more authentic and genuine intimacy. They may be perfectly good partnerships on a business or child-rearing level, but not necessarily very intimate or, as C. A. Tripp says, they are not very "finely tuned" relationships.[4] Because of this, I believe that the study of homosexual pairings has great tutorial value for heterosexual relationships: To some extent, we represent what they would face were they not so busy dealing with sex-role conflicts.

Moreover, studying lesbian versus gay male relationships gives us a splendid opportunity to examine the "male principle" and the "female principle" as they are currently culturally defined and as they operate in pair-bonding. That is, gay men represent "unmitigated maleness," both alone and in couples, while lesbians represent "unmitigated fe-maleness." This is indeed a very useful thing; by comparing these two types of couples with each other and with heterosexual couples we can learn a great deal, for it is only by contrast that we discover constancies. It also can be useful to contrast the sexuality found in gay male versus lesbian couples. On the other hand, gay man have more sex, both within their primary relationships and outside, than do les-bians. Their sexual forms are more diverse, more than any other type of couple, they manage to successfully incorporate nonmonogamy into their relationships. Thus in one view gay men have achieved the most advanced state of sexuality within the pair-bonding known to hu-mankind. (I say this despite the knowledge that gay male sexuality has also brought with it sexual excesses with sometimes disastrous results, for example, AIDS, and that AIDS itself has modified gay male sexual behavior as described in Dan Bloom and Michael Shernoff's work.[5] I vehemently disagree, however, with the line of reasoning that says that AIDS was brought about by sexuality. AIDS is caused by a virus, not by sex, and it is important that we not let the tragedy of AIDS reinforce sex-negative homophobic attitudes.) Lesbians, on the other hand, are very good at closeness and intimacy: Our pairings probably contain, in general, more closeness, sharing, and intimate contact than any others. These differences of course correspond to what Carol Gilligan and others have spoken of as differences between connectedness and independence, or expressiveness versus instrumentality.[6] My view is that lesbians and gay men have much to learn from each other and teach each other about sex and relationships. Perhaps, together, we can create relationships with gay men's sexiness and lesbians' connectedness.

### The Sexual Repression of Lesbians

Let us begin by considering, in no particular order, some of the reasons why lesbians might experience greater sexual repression than gay or heterosexual men, and perhaps in some cases even greater inhibition than heterosexual women. Some of the following forces affect lesbians as individual women; some operate in lesbian couples as a particular type of union.

On the simplest level, one thing that accounts for a relatively low frequency of sex in lesbian relationships is that lesbians, by virtue of socialization as women, are less likely to play an active role in requesting sex and are far less likely to pressure a recalcitrant partner. Thus to some extent the low level of sex in lesbian pairings is probably just a result of neither woman asking for it rather than a particular inhibition. As women, we are not only taught to wait for our partner to ask for sex although we may want it; but we are also taught not even to pay attention to our own sexual desires unless or until we are approached by our partner. In a sense, our sexual response is cued to our partner's request in almost Pavlovian terms. Two women together, each primed to respond sexually only to a request from another, may rarely even experience desire, much less engage in sexual activity. And this may all very well be completely unconscious.

Moreover, it is almost certainly true that we are less likely to pressure a reluctant partner to have sex with us, especially compared to men. In fact, we are likely to see sexual pressure as male behavior and thus assaultive and abusive. One of my first sex therapy cases was a couple who had been together for more than ten years and had no sex for the last seven. Remarkably, they had never once had a fight over this, even though for at least several of those years, one partner had been rather upset over the lack of sexuality. One is extremely unlikely to see this pattern in heterosexual, or even gay male, relationships that suffer from low levels of sexual intimacy. In fact, a common clinical issue with such couples is to get the unhappy partner to take some of the pressure off the other partner. We might reflect on the fact that, contrary to our feminist beliefs, perhaps a little pressure is good for a relationship; pressure can simply reflect the desires of one partner rather than be evidence of assaultive behavior.

Another consideration is that sex and love are fused for women in general and lesbians in particular. Sex and love may be even more fused for lesbians, who, again in the absence of male pressure, have no countervailing force attempting to get them to separate the two. When I speak to lesbian lay audiences, some women now bemoan the fact that they can rarely find other lesbians who are interested in purely sexual liaisons; these women find themselves accused of being male-identified for wanting such liaisons. I first got in touch with the power of this fusion when I realized that in all my sexual fantasies, even those involving "stranger sex," invariably I found myself saying, "I love you" as though this declaration were a necessary part of sexual enjoyment. I contrasted this to a gay male friend's sexual fantasies of making love to the image of disembodied penises; we seem at opposite ends of the spectrum of sexual stimulation. As another lesbian therapist I know puts it, "Lesbians can't fuck unless they are married." We are the last of the modern-day romantics, and although in some ways this is charming, it has some untoward effects. For example, it does help to explain our alarmingly brief courtship periods; we are just like the Victorians who married in part to have a legitimate source of sex. It certainly explains why our extramarital liaisons are affairs rather than the less relationship-threatening tricks. But it explains some of our sexual problems within relationships as well. Because sex and love are intertwined for us, our sexual desire is very vulnerable to interference from relationship problems. Few of us can keep the bedroom separate from the rest of our lives as a couple. Moreover, many of us have problems expressing anger. Again, this is because of female socialization to be nice, not to get angry, a deadly combination. In fact, I use lack of fighting in a lesbian relationship as a diagnostic clue to detect low-level sexuality when the partners have not directly told me of this problem, and I am almost never wrong. For us to enjoy sex or simply to feel sexual, our relationship must be going very well indeed. This dynamic can create problems in two ways: First, it is unrealistic to expect couple relationships always to function at a high level, and perhaps more significantly, sexual connection itself can at times improve a faltering relationship.

In addition, we are less "looks-ist" than are men or heterosexual women, another finding confirmed by the *American Couples* study. Often, as a reaction to the way men have defined us only by our looks, we reject ideologically and practically the reliance upon physical attractiveness to form pairings. Unfortunately, what may be good politics may make for bad sex. Human beings, like other animals, do seem to rely at least in part upon visual attractiveness to cue sexual stimulation. To the extent that we feel guilty about that reliance, to the extent to which we avoid cultivating our own physical attractiveness out of the misguided belief that to preen is to be sexist, we detract from our own sexuality. We need surely to redefine physical beauty in our own feminist ways, but we cannot simply reject physical attractiveness and our response to physical beauty as somehow politically incorrect.

Other sources of sexual repression derive from early female sex-role socialization. As women, we already have a built-in acculturated tendency not to recognize our own sexual arousal. From the earliest age, our organs of arousal are hidden from view, less easily seen and less easily stimulated. And the powerful cultural forces that teach us to deny our sexual impulses probably take effect ultimately upon a physiological level. Julia Heiman's classic study is perhaps the best illustration of this.[7] Heiman exposed both female and male subjects to sexually explicit audiotapes at the same time that she had these subjects connected to instruments that measure physiological arousal. She found no differences between men and women in the extent of arousal as recorded by her instrumentation. When she asked her subjects to report on their subjective experience of arousal, however, all male subjects who were physiologically aroused reported feeling aroused, whereas only half of female subjects who were aroused experienced this. It is as if the connection between our crotches and our heads have been severed; we are sexual paraplegics.

In addition to the forces already cited, lesbians may suffer acculturated inhibitions in the form of internalized homophobia. Betty Berzon, a lesbian psychologist who talks about the stage-wise development of lesbian/gay identity, suggests that at one point in its evolution, women who want to love and be loved by other women, but do not want to consider themselves gay, psychologically defend against this identity by eliminating genital sexuality from their female relationships.[8] In other words, women can have loving, close, and intimate relationships with other women but pretend to be straight as long as there is no genital sexual contact. Berzon hypothesizes that lesbians may retain vestiges of these psychological defenses long after they have become unnecessary by virtue of our coming out to ourselves, just as neurotic conflicts are frequently the result of leftover defenses that were once, but are no longer, useful. Her view is worth considering, especially in the light of the almost uncanny resemblance between this description of early woman-to-woman contact and later lesbian relationships with sexual difficulties. She also suggests that gay males, at this early stage, defend against a gay identity by allowing sexual contact without intimacy, and again, this bears a strange resemblance to the intimacy difficulties gay men often experience in later life.

Lesbian sexuality is undoubtedly affected by lesbians' early experience with men. In a culture where an estimated 25 percent of all women will experience some sexual assault by men by age eighteen, surely all women have their sexuality somewhat damaged because of the unfortunate connection of sex with violence and exploitation. But lesbians experience additional troubles. The vast majority of lesbians have had some sexual involvement with men before coming out: More than 90 percent have had sex with men, and one-third have been married.[9] For some lesbians, these sexual relationships have been pleasurable. For others, however, who experience no sexual desire for men but simply had sex in the interests of passing, sex was inauthentic, possibly painful, certainly distasteful. We have no reason to believe that negative conditioning to sexuality automatically disappears when women switch to female partners. Moreover, we are just beginning to explore the incidence and effects of incest upon lesbians as young girls; some studies report a higher incidence of earlier incest among lesbians.[10] Virginia Apuzzo has suggested an interesting theory regarding incest: She suggests that incest may be perpetrated upon young tomboy girls (who are somewhat more likely to grow up to be lesbians, as reported by Bell, Weinberg, and Hammersmith) as a way of punishing them and "keeping them in line."[11]

According to Tripp and others, sexual desire requires a "barrier": some kind of tension, a taboo, a difference of some sort, a power discrepancy, romance, the excitement of newness or the thrill of the chase—some form of disequilibrium.[12] This hypothesis has some important implications for lesbian relationships. First, it helps to explain why our romanticism is a problem. Our romanticism can be seen as a type of barrier to create sexual excitement; that is, we are romantic because it is sexually exciting to be so. The problem is that this appears to be the only acceptable form of tension or barrier we have, and thus the sole method we have for creating sexual excitement. This explains why we must fall in love to be sexual: It is the only thing we allow ourselves to be turned on by. It also explains why our extramarital relationships are affairs rather than tricks: Casual sex doesn't excite us. Moreover, it explains why sex dies in our relationships; when the romantic, or limerant, first stage of our relationships passes, we have no other mechanisms to generate sexual tension. Only falling in love produces sexual desire, so we fall in love again, with a new partner, and the limerance of this new relationship revives our flagging sexuality. Clearly, we need to expand our repertoire so that there are more tensions or barriers available to facilitate sexual desire.

In addition, the barrier theory suggests that, paradoxically, intimacy may hurt sexual desire within a relationship. Lesbian relationships, in part because they are "advanced" relationships, sometimes suffer difficulties of overinvolvement, called *fusion* or *merging*. To some extent, intimacy involves the lessening of differences between partners; certainly it is more difficult to maintain a purely independent sense of self within a very intimate relationship. As intimacy increases and individual differences decrease, so may the very distance, mystery, and unpredictability necessary to maintain sexual tension. The softening or disappearance of individual differences may serve to decrease sexual desire in another, slightly different, way as well. Tripp suggests that one of the functions served by sexual intimacy is that of "importation" of the loved object's characteristics and "exportation" of one's own.[13] One desires another who possesses characteristics that one either feels deficient in or would like to have more of. Sexual contact is a way of feeling that you have incorporated within yourself the desired characteristics of the love-object—importation—at the same time that you export to your partner characteristics of your own that are desired or admired. We can see immediately how this process will tend to happen less frequently as two partners become more similar and thus have less to export to the other. It is a truism within family and marital therapy that the characteristics that attract someone to a partner initially are precisely those that one tries to eradicate later in the relationship. This is another way of saying that differences not only initially attract and are in part responsible for sexual desire, but also make it difficult for people to live together. Paradoxically, it is to some extent true that the more successful we are in obliterating those differences, the more successful we are in creating wonderful roommates (people who can live together easily because they are so alike) but lousy lovers.

Heterosexual relationships exhibit such problems of fusion less often because the partners often have trouble being intimate enough. Those of us who are lesbians need, perhaps more than other couples, to find ways to introduce other types of barriers/tension/difference into our relationships. But as women we are more sexually inhibited and less free to experiment with our sexuality. The result of this bind may be loss of sexual desire.

To find such ways of introducing new barriers, we can look to our gay brothers. By experimenting with new sexual techniques, through the use of sex toys and props, through costume, through S/M (which maximizes differences between partners), by developing sexual rituals with our partners, by introducing tricking into our relationships, we may be able to find other barriers that enhance sexuality once limerance is gone.

### Sexuality and the Contemporary Lesbian Community

What do the issues being debated and acted upon in the lesbian community teach us about our sexuality? First, although I make light of our endless discussions of the "political correctness" of sex, I also recognize the need for these discussions. In fact, for women in general and lesbians specifically, our sexuality is political: It has always been used against us to oppress us.[14] Think of the major issues that feminists have fought over in the last several decades, and it becomes obvious that many of them, such as abortion, birth control, rape, incest, lesbianism itself, and clitorial versus vaginal orgasms, have involved our sexuality. Thus it is essential that we be mindful of the political implications when we talk about sexuality.

Second, the debates that have raged in the lesbian-feminist community over such sexual issues as sadomasochism make more sense if one keeps in mind the concept of a dialectic. This concept suggests that when two political ideas or forces are in apparent contradiction, the answer to which of the dichotomy is correct lies in achieving a higher-order level of thought from which it is apparent that the dichotomous forces are not really in contradiction, but are merely two aspects of the same issue. Let us see if we can view some of the recent politic-sexual differences within our community in just this way.

*S/M versus Women Against Pornography.* First, a summary of the two positions regarding sadomasochistic behavior. The forces against S/M, epitomized by the stance of the group Women Against Pornography as explicated in the book *Against Sado-Masochism*,[15] seem to see polarized role-playing in sex as leading to violence in other parts of the S/M participants' relationship. They believe the roots of S/M to be firmly ensconced in heterosexism and patriarchal modes of domination; they decry the addictive, cult-like aspects of S/M, at least as it seems to be developing among some segments of the lesbian community; and they particularly object to the view, promulgated by some lesbians within groups like Samois and the Lesbian Sex Mafia, that S/M liberation is a political cause comparable to lesbianism or feminism. WAP appears to view the entire emergence of S/M as an issue within the lesbian community as basically retrograde, reactionary, and a symptom of the Reagan eighties.

The viewpoint favoring S/M is best exemplified by the West Coast lesbian group Samois (named from a lesbian-run estate in *The Story of O*) in the book *Coming to Power*.[16] Lesbians who are proponents of S/M practices emphasize the consensual aspects of this relationship and point out that unlike the oppressive power relationships, control in a S/M relationship is really exerted by the "bottom" or masochist. They assert that S/M practices free sexual energy and allow the partners an almost spiritual transcendence of self through "power exchanges," that is, the voluntary giving over or taking of power from one partner to another. More than anything, S/M proponents emphasize the enhancement of sexual experience through S/M, apparently taking the view that as far as sex is concerned, the ends clearly justify the means. "But why do you do it?" asks a rhetorical questioner in "Reasons" from *Coming to Power*. "Because it is erotic" is the answer.

Let us examine this seemingly dichotomous view of lesbian S/M. First, it is clear that the points made in *Against Sado-Masochism* cannot be dismissed simply as puritanical ravings. Any clinician who has worked with clientele who engage in S/M practices knows that S/M can at times have all the worst properties of an addiction. Like drug or alcohol use, or for that matter like some other forms of sexual conduct, S/M behavior can become compulsive, out of control of the participants. People can develop a tolerance for certain pain levels as their thresholds get pushed higher and higher and can, if not careful, get to a point where only dangerous levels of pain excite. Moreover, the S/M movement as it is currently constituted within the lesbian community does have some cult-like aspects, and like all radical or fringe groups, has picked up some borderline personalities along the way. It is also certainly true that for some people sadomasochism can have deep and destructive meanings. A client of mine with a long history of self-destructive and compulsive behaviors that included self-mutilation, drug addiction, and suicidal gestures joined the New York-based Lesbian Sex Mafia group with disastrous results. At one point she told me she had "progressed" to staging "scenes" (pre-arranged encounters that, for her, revolved around being whipped) that no longer were sexual in content and that were so severe that she bore multiple welts for days afterward. Shortly after this, she hanged herself with a rope and came within inches of succeeding in her suicide attempt. Based on my own and others' experiences, I have no trouble believing that some people who engage in S/M do find inequality slipping into other aspects of their relationships, with unfortunate results. Moreover, I admit I find myself agreeing with the WAP group when they object to S/M liberation: I am hard put to see how the proponents of a particular sexual technique can really compare themselves to women, racial minorities, or gay people as a minority (can we next foresee anal sex liberationists or cunnilingus liberationists?). Although S/M enthusiasts understandably feel oppressed because of their preferences, I am inclined to see this as merely a special case of oppression that results from the generally sex-negative views that we all, especially women, hold in this culture. I also admit to being suspicious of anyone who defines herself solely or primarily in terms of her sadomasochism, as do some of the more visible and vocal proponents within the lesbian community. Finally, it is undoubtedly true that some portion of the power of S/M does derive from patriarchal roots. Some of the imagery of S/M is clearly heterosexist in origin; some of the force that makes so many of us sexual masochists is undoubtedly related to our powerless role in society.

But WAP fails to distinguish between the excesses of S/M and the normative practice of S/M. Although we do not know exactly what normative S/M practices are, we can guess that most S/M practiced by lesbians is practiced quietly, perhaps with some embarrassment, behind the closed doors of committed couples' bedrooms. Just as most drug and alcohol users do not become addicts, so it is also probably true that most S/M practitioners do not become compulsive, out-of-control self-destructive users. Among lesbians, there are probably more silk scarves, mild spankings, and fantasy being used than whips and chains, probably more talk than action. On a pragmatic level, the WAP people make the mistake of listening to those for whom S/M has created problems, and ignoring the vast majority for whom it is merely an interesting variation in their sex lives.

The theoretical level is more complex and requires a synthesis of both views and transcendence to the next level of analysis. Let us acknowledge the inherent heterosexism in at least some of the imagery of S/M. Does this mean we must discard and repudiate these practices? I have two objections to assuming that S/M should not be practiced or supported as a sexual variation. One is that I fear that at this point in our culture, so much of female sexuality may be contaminated by heterosexism and patriarchal oppression that if we reject aspects of our sexuality upon this basis we will have little left. I consider this serious because I think the larger issue of the wholesale repression of female sexuality is more important than whether some areas of our sexuality have been contaminated by patriarchal modes. That is, it is more important at this stage in history to support women being sexual, however they are sexual, than to judge which aspects of their sexuality are non-patriarchal and which are male-identified. But beyond that, I object on the basis that we do not yet understand sexuality sufficiently to make pat pronouncements on the origins of various types of sexual interests or drives.

Many alternative explanations of the origins of sadomasochistic sexuality, for example, have nothing to do with patriarchy, or are even positive ways of coping with patriarchy. Tripp points out that on a cross-cultural level, there seems to be little relationship between sadomasochistic or violent sexual practices and violence in the practicing couple. He uses as an illustration a Pacific Island tribe noted for its peace-loving ways and gentle relationships, whose sexual practices include biting one another on the ear until blood is drawn. There appears to be a universality to the fusion of sex and aggression, to the sexiness of power differentials, that is completely unrelated to the aggressiveness/oppressiveness of the practitioners. If this is true, then perhaps heterosexism determines in a somewhat arbitrary way some of the content of S/M erotic fantasies, but not the form itself. One can imagine that the conditioning for S/M eroticism takes place in childhood in ways that might explain this difference in content or form. Bernie Zilbergeld and C. R. Ellison have suggested that, particularly in childhood, sexual arousal is virtually indistinguishable from other arousal states, including physical activity arousal, anger, or fear.[17] This is particularly noticeable in young boys, who have penile erections under many circumstances that could be considered sexual only by great stretches of the imagination, but we have no reason to believe it is not also true of girls. Thus a frightened child, or a child receiving a spanking, may also be experiencing sexual arousal, and it is quite easy to imagine a classically conditioned response to this type of stimuli becoming entrenched at an early age. If this is true, than the root of S/M is the parent-child power differential, and only incidentally the male-female power differential. Even if this is not precisely how S/M becomes conditioned, it is useful to remember how similar physiological arousal states become. If we keep this in mind, it is not hard to see how some people could find pain (a heightened stimulation that increases general body arousal) an enhancement to sexual arousal. In this sense, S/M can be seen as a means of pushing the body's limits rather than unpleasant pain. Most of us can instinctively sense how this might be true. If we have ever engaged in rough sex, if we have ever scratched, clawed, or bitten our lover in moments of passion, if we have ever enjoyed unpleasant stimuli during sexual arousal (e.g., the scene in Rita Mae Brown's *In Her Day* during which the young heroine places an ice cube on her lover's clitoris just before orgasm),[18] then we have used pain for pleasure and can understand this connection. We can see that this aspect of S/M, at any rate, has little or nothing to do with sexism but probably has more to do with the physiology of sexual arousal, an aspect of biological functioning that we are only just recently beginning to understand.

But the aspect of S/M that involves physical pain is only one part of the picture that is disturbing to many feminists. Perhaps more upsetting is the connection between S/M practices and shame and humiliation. Much S/M, at least as practiced by lesbians currently, seems to involve humiliation and subjugation more than it involves actual pain. These aspects of S/M seem more connected to patriarchal conditioning.

This may be so, but it is useful to remember that patriarchy is not the only source of shame for a young girl growing up. Shame is a fairly typical concomitant of certain stages in the development of a moral conscience, or superego in young children. Shame is a concomitant of many types of religious upbringing, particularly religious teachings about sexuality; for example, the Catholic term for masturbation is *self-abuse*, which itself suggests a type of S/M activity. It may be true that many people who practice the types of S/M that involve ritual shaming, humiliation, and subjugation partially rework and psychologically overcome early, frightening experiences of shame, guilt, or domination. And these earlier experiences themselves may have become "sexualized" in childhood through the connection between fear-arousal and sexual-arousal.

Intuitively this explanation makes some sense. In therapy, we recognize the value of ritually acting out old, frightening dramas in our lives; we call it revivification, catharsis and abreaction, psychodrama, and so on. We also recognize the extent to which neurosis itself involves the playing out of ritual scripts and scenes, sometimes from very early childhood. Why should not our sexuality, the origins and functioning of which we understand so poorly, also make use of some of the same kinds of ritual reliving and undoing? If so, we can begin to understand, for example, the observation of an old therapist of mine that it seemed her female clients' S/M fantasies became stronger the more assertive they became in their everyday lives, as though confining their subjugation to the bedroom allowed them to "work it out" there and overcome it. Another therapist commented that a masochistic client avowed that he always felt guilty about sex and had to punish himself afterwards until he figured out that he could punish himself before, get it over with, and then enjoy the sex.

There are four points I want to make about this. First, although it may be true that S/M eroticism is, in part, fueled by sexist power differentials and subjugation of women by men, it is also just as likely to be fueled by sex-negative religious messages or memories of subjugation of children by parents. Second, such eroticism may very well represent, at least for some people, a healthy working out of such early traumas rather than an unhealthy giving in to them. Third, it is quite likely that much of what we find sexually erotic has reached the status of functionally autonomous behavior by the time we reach adulthood. Fantasies and objects that may have become eroticized in adolescence or earlier for whatever psycho/social/sexual reasons—whether to work out conflict, because of familiarity, or however else things become eroticized in the first place—tend, often through repeated masturbation, to become solidly entrenched in our psyches as erotic material long after the relevant precipitating causes have ceased to be salient for us. This explains why humiliation, shame, or pain could be erotic to someone who is no longer religious and is an assertive, feminist adult. It is also likely that such functionally autonomous erotic material is not easily changed once we reach adulthood, and that attempts to eliminate such material from one's sexual repertoire will more likely constrict rather than liberate sexuality.

Fourth, although I have no pretensions to having thoroughly explained sadomasochistic eroticism, I do hope that I have demonstrated that S/M fantasy and behavior, and indeed human sexuality in general, is too complex to defy simplistic analysis, and that attempts to condemn any such type of sexuality in the individuals who practice it result more frequently in sexual constriction than in liberation. If this is so, then the ultimate truth about the S/M controversy within the lesbian community at this point may be that although its roots may be partially in patriarchy and it may carry the danger of excess, it may represent a freeing of our sexuality, an attempt to open up, expand, and embroider our sexual technique and erotic potential, and as such, it may be just what we need right now. Even those lesbians for whom S/M and its variants hold no interest may eventually benefit from the sexual openness that this trend in our community may portend.

*Butch-Femme Roles.* Along with the rise of publicly advocated (as opposed to privately practiced) sadomasochism has come the advocacy of butch-femme roles. The advocacy of such roles appears to be a throwback to the fifties, when heterosexuals and homosexuals alike were busy polarizing men and women (and, more important, masculine and feminine). At first glance, butch-femme lib makes the average feminist's hair stand on end.

But a closer look at butch-femme advocacy shows that it is not so much a throwback to past times as it is a reaction against the lesbian-feminist clone look of the past decade. Most of us know the style: work boots or Frye boots, jeans, work shirt or flannel shirt, man-tailored vest (with or without tie), short hair, no makeup, preferably unshaved legs and underarms, perhaps even facial hair that is emphasized rather than bleached or removed. In an attempt to reject male-defined concepts of women's beauty, many of us ended up looking like teenage boys. Like many other things in our movement, a concept that started out being liberating for many of us ended up being just one more confinement.

In addition, it was sexually boring. Marge Piercy, in the novel *Woman on the Edge of Time*, pictures a feminist society of the future that includes concepts of costume and body adornment, not as means of objectifying one class of people or as ways of physically confining that class (the intent of much of women's fashion throughout history), but as methods of play-acting, variety, and sexual enticement.[19] The butch-femme proponents seem to recognize the importance to sexual desire of physical attractiveness and diversity of physical looks created by costume and adornment.

They also recognize an age-old concept of limerance, that which is popularly known by the truism "opposites attract." C. A. Tripp would characterize this as an aspect of the "import-export" theory of sexual attraction, and it indeed probably has been used historically to promote heterosexual attraction.[20] That is, we can speculate that one of the functions of polarizing gender roles — assigning some personal or physical traits to one sex and others to the other sex — has been to reinforce heterosexual attraction along the lines of the import-export, "opposites attract" principle of sexual attraction. If we are male, for example, and are not permitted to be emotional, tender, nurturing, or "weak," then we may need a stereotypical female to provide us with those traits. If we are stereotypically female, we may need a male to provide us with the strength, emotional control, or aggressiveness not allowed by our role. Along the same lines, lesbians and gay men, although clearly not attracted to the opposite sex, may sometimes be attracted to the opposite sex role. That is, a butch lesbian, one whose gender-role identification has never been with sterotypically feminine interests or traits, may be drawn consistently to a femme lesbian, or one whose gender-role identification has been more traditionally feminine. The butch-femme advocates instinctively recognize this and address it in their rhetoric.

This is a very sensitive topic politically. Lesbian feminists have not wanted to acknowledge that there are some differences within our community in the extent to which women have identified with a traditionally male or female roles, and that lesbians may be attracted to each other on the basis of these differences. We have been afraid to look at these issues, I think because of the heterosexual stereotype of us that we are all divided into butch or femme, and because in our not-too-distant past we ourselves enforced those rigid roles upon ourselves.

The politically correct lesbian feminist line has been that butch-femme roles were essentially imitations of heterosexual culture, and that once we liberated our thinking through gay pride and feminist thought we rejected those roles and discovered that we are really all alike, that there are no roles. There is a good deal of truth to this. Certainly the rigid role-playing in lesbian culture of the past was a caricature of mainstream culture to a great extent, and certainly we are all a good deal more complex than the roles allowed us to be.

On the other hand, it has also probably always been true that there are differences among us in the extent to which we identify with traditionally male or female roles. In Radclyffe Hall's day, these differences were seen as dividing "real" lesbians, those with a male identification, from "imitation" lesbians, those who were more stereotypically feminine. Real and imitation also meant those who were exclusively homosexual (Kinsey 6's) versus those with some heterosexual experiences and impulses (Kinsey 4's and 5's). The two dichotomies were seen as related, and perhaps they are. One still hears echoes of such thinking. In my community throughout the 1970s some gay women maintained that the only real lesbians were born lesbians, meaning those who had an early identification as not female and who had never had attractions to or experiences with men.

The point is that at least for the last fifty or sixty years these differences have existed in the lesbian community, and we have always been a bit baffled and disquieted by them. The butch-femme advocates, it seems to me, are beginning to acknowledge the differences and celebrate, rather than repudiate, them. On the whole, I suspect this is very positive. These women are acknowledging that physical appearance is important to sexuality, that at least sometimes, opposites attract, and that these opposites may be, to an extent, modeled after gender roles, affirming that it is all right to have different tastes and preferences, that we do not need all to act or look alike. They are also saying that it is all right to have different sexual tastes, not just in what or whom one is attracted to, but in what one does in bed: It is all right to prefer an active or passive role, to enjoy making love to or being made love to more. Our community has had a peculiarly ambivalent attitude toward sex roles. On the one hand, the greatest criticism one could make of another woman has been that she is male-identified. On the other hand, we despise the traditionally feminine as male-defined. This has left us very little room to maneuver, and has surely been one of the factors constraining our sexual selves. The butch-femme stance rejects these political limitations and enthusiastically supports diversity regardless of whether a particular behavior seems to be male-defined or patriarchal. I am sure that this has been liberating to many women. I have found it freeing to decide for myself that I like to wear dresses and makeup sometimes and that my lover hates them, and to acknowledge that indeed these apparently gender-linked traits were part of what attracted us to each other in the first place. Lesbians have always privately joked about butch-femme. "She's the butch in that relationship," someone might say jokingly and then look a little guilty, and it is undoubtedly healthy that this troublesome area is beginning to come out of the closet at last.

Indeed, at best the butch-femme position can help us transcend sex roles. It has been symptomatic of our gender conditioning that we always see these differences as gender-linked: The fact that our culture has typically defined a desire to paint one's face as female and a swaggering walk as male does not mean that these are biologically sex-linked traits. At best, we can learn to separate traits and behaviors from gender. Just as I believe that anything women do together sexually is lesbian sex, so it can be true that any behavior a woman engages in can be female behavior. Just as we can define intercourse from a male point of view as vaginal penetration or from a female point of view as penile containment, just as we can define a dildo as a penis substitute or a penis as a dildo substitute, we can redefine traits and characteristics as neither male nor female, but rather human idiosyncratic differences.

The danger of butch-femme, however, is that such redefinition will not take place, but that this trend will simply become a reintroduction of the same tired old sex roles from which we have been trying to escape. This will happen if we begin to see these differences as not merely interesting preferences that perhaps originated in childhood as modeling of gender roles, but as differences that should fit together as cohesive and integrated roles. An example: In my relationship, I am usually the femme in terms of appearance, although this role is by no means rigid, because I enjoy wearing men's jeans as much as I enjoy dresses. In bed my role is less clear. In other areas I am clearly the butch: I can use a hammer or a saw, and my lover cannot. Thus to label me the femme on the basis of differences in our appearance or abilities is misleading, because there exist in our relationship no such rigidified roles as exist in many heterosexual relationships. My fear is that the use of the terms *butch-femme* will inevitably lead to such rigidification and will serve to imprison rather than to liberate us. I already see these trends. I had a client last year who was in a butch support group and who told me that she was feeling confused because she wanted to cry sometimes and "butches aren't supposed to cry." Humans seem sorely tempted to simplify life's complexity, and sex roles are the supreme simplification. I would feel more comfortable with butch-femme if we could find other terms for these contrasts that are less connotative of male-female sex roles. We need to create new terms that represent our striving toward a goal of celebrating difference that is fluid, changeable, and multifaceted, rather than terms evoking the origins of our differences in roles that are static and confining.

*Monogamy versus Nonmonogamy.* As Blumstein and Schwartz point out, lesbian couples handle outside sexual relationships in a unique way. Like their gay male counterparts, lesbians are open with their partners about extramarital sexuality. Like their heterosexual female counterparts, lesbians' outside relationships are affairs, rather than tricking.[21] The combination is deadly. The lesbian-feminist community began debating the issue of monogamy in the mid-1970s, at about the same time, interestingly, that books like *Open Marriage* became popular among heterosexuals. The political rhetoric that developed was that monogamy was a patriarchal form originating from male ownership of women and children, and jealousy was the correspondingly retrogressive emotional concomitant of monogamy. In a matriarchal society, we would not want to own our partners, we would not split sex and love, we would see sex as a natural extension of all loving relationships, and therefore we would have sex with our friends with no consequences to our primary relationships. We then proceeded to put this theory into practice. Many relationships and friendships split up as a result.

It is time we viewed this issue realistically. I have earlier discussed other, not so idealistic motives that might induce a lesbian to engage in extramarital affairs. We need also to consider the possibility that the female tendency to fuse sex and love is not always an idealistic goal but rather a consequence of stereotypic role-conditioning. We are going to have to admit that very few of us are actually capable of negotiating prolonged emotional, sexual affairs with a new lover without damage to our primary relationships. Sex changes things, including friendships, and no matter where jealousy originated, it seems to be pervasive. If we are really interested in preserving, rather than jeopardizing, our primary relationships, we need to reconsider both monogamy as traditionally practiced or nonmonogamy as practiced by gay man. Gay male relationships are nonmonogamous more often than not, frequently without damage to the primary commitment, but the extramarital sexuality is almost always casual (even anonymous), brief, and recreational rather than emotionally intense. Moreover, gay male couples have rules for their nonmonogamy, rules that may seem to limit spontaneity but that surely serve also to limit the potential threat that outside sex poses to the relationship. These rules basically serve to prevent the partners from establishing precisely the kind of outside relationships that lesbians have hoped to achieve: relationships that combine both sex and love. The rules may be explicit or they may be nonverbal and merely understood, but they almost always exist. Most lesbians (as well as heterosexual women) reject this concept of nonmonogamy for the same reasons they reject all casual sex: It seems wrong, distasteful, immoral, and cheap. Many women who do not reject the notion of tricking on theoretical grounds are simply incapable of being turned on by sex without a relationship attached. If this is the case, we may have to live with monogamy until we can change our sexual preferences so that we are less romantic.

In recent years, I see one other interesting alternative, especially among some of the lesbian sex radicals who are experimenting with S/M, butch-femme roles, and other expansions of sexuality. Some women are redefining romance as an erotic game, rather than as ideal love. Instead of attempting to separate sex from romantic love, these women view romantic love as entirely different from the kind of love that is exhibited in a committed primary relationship. This concept, like the concept of tricking, has already been developed by some gay men. In its mildest form, it might involve an acknowledgment of the kind of intimacy that can be present in even a one-time sexual encounter. The gay male erotica writer John Preston writes eloquently of this.[22] Another form of this concept is exemplified by a gay male friend who says that he tries to keep in touch with most of his tricks, even if he only has sex with them once or twice, as part of his friendship network. Yet another acquaintance has explained to me that he and his tricks almost always love one another, but that it is clearly understood from the beginning that there will be no commitment between them that will disturb my acquaintance's primary relationship. And finally, each member of a male couple I know that has been together fifteen years has a boyfriend. These boyfriend relationships themselves have each lasted several years. I am beginning to see women trying to emulate these different forms of relationships.

What new ideas or techniques of handling relationships are involved in these modes of nonmonogamy? First, there is an acknowledgment that the feelings of infatuation that constitute what we call romance are feelings that are totally separate from committed love. In a sense, the gay men and a few lesbians who do this are able to take romance less seriously than others. That is, they see romantic feelings as a variation of sexual feelings and are able to enjoy them without seeing them as a reflection upon their primary relationship. Second, people who negotiate these kinds of nonmonogamous relationships are able to have intimacy that is intense but limited. Third, these individuals (and couples) see the function of a primary relationship as a good deal more circumscribed than do most lesbians (and most heterosexual women). Most people in this culture, and women more than men, are taught to view primary relationships as all or nothing. We expect that our main partners will fulfill all of our intimacy needs as well as sexual needs. We may recognize that we have intimacy needs that must get fulfilled by friends rather than lovers; we may know that we have sexual needs that must get met by people other than our primary lover. It is difficult to comprehend that we might have intimate sexual partners with whom we might want to be intensely involved in a limited way at the same time that we maintain a primary relationship. Our dualistic thinking leads us almost inevitably to compare and choose one or another relationship.

In addition, it takes a great deal of maturity to recognize that the intense passion of the initial stages of such an outside relationship is no indicator of what is to come, and to keep in mind that the apparent perfect fit of such new relationships is an illusion that will pass in time. To negotiate such multiple relationships takes an ability to circumscribe and compartmentalize one's life in a way that most women are unable or unwilling to do.

*Bisexuality.* The lesbian community, like the gay male community, has always been fairly intolerant of bisexuality for some reasons that are understandable. Indeed, the label *bisexual* has frequently been a cover for gay individuals unable to tolerate the homophobia of society and who found the label more acceptable than the homosexual one. Women and men who embraced the label *gay* have been a bit contemptuous and suspicious of those who refused this designation: Bisexuals were seen as people who wanted to have their cake and eat it too, who wanted the freedom to have same-sex sexual activities while retaining heterosexual privilege. Probably many people who called themselves bisexual were attempting to do just that.

But in the last few years our community has witnessed the emergence of a new phenomenon. Ironically, as some of us have evolved as gay individuals we have continued to explore our sexual preferences and, once our gay identities were secure, have found a significant bisexual component. This group of people, who have identified as gay and who later decide that the bisexual designation is more appropriate, are being joined by younger people just coming out, who feel comfortable with gay relationships and a gay identity, but who simply feel that the label *bisexual* describes their feelings more appropriately. Thus a bisexual community, marginal to but connected with the gay community, is now developing, at least in larger urban areas and in academic communities.

It is possible, of course, that some members of this emerging subgroup are merely playing radical chic, identifying as bisexuals with no real intention of ever permanently giving up heterosexual privilege. But my estimation is that many of the people now identifying openly in this way are trying to acknowledge the fact that no matter what their preference (and I know of few people who maintain that they can simply ignore gender or that their attractions are exactly fifty-fifty), their attractions both to men and to women are real and important in their lives.

Why, then, are so many of us threatened by bisexuality? Partly for the reasons I have outlined, but I think for other reasons as well. I cannot speak for men, but I think that many lesbians are threatened because they are afraid that they, too, may need to reopen the issue of their choice of partners. The issue of choice is a sensitive one for lesbian feminists. Many of us would like to believe, on one hand, that we chose to be with women rather than men for reasons that are part emotional and part political, while at the same time we believe that we were always lesbians. It is uncomfortable for us to realize that what is chosen can be unchosen. Particularly in those moments when the heterosexist and homophobic burdens of society press down upon us most severely, it is not necessarily a comfort to feel that our lesbianism may be a product of our own free will. I have a lesbian friend who says, only half-jokingly when pressure and tension mount, "I'm going to find some nice man who will support me and get married." It may be that we have all *chosen* to be lesbians, consciously or unconsciously. For all or most lesbians, sexual preference may be indeed connected to gender role in a quite political way. This hit home for me recently as I read an article in *Ms.* magazine entitled "Two-Career Couples:

How They Do It." I had picked up the article because my lover and I are just such a couple, with a small child to boot, and I thought I could get a few pointers. I was disappointed to find that the gist of the article, entirely about heterosexual families, was that these couples survive, by and large, because the woman still does the bulk of the housework and childcare. Study after study was cited showing that more than two-thirds of such couples are nonegalitarian in work distribution, and that in the one-third that are, husbands leave the wives eventually in depressingly large numbers. I reflected on how unknown this phenomenon is among lesbian couples; whatever problems exist among lesbian couples, nonegalitarianism is rarely one of them. And it struck me again that this aspect of our life-style is not coincidental, not merely a felicitous benefit reaped from our sexual attractions. It is an integral part of our lesbian choice. Many of us, for example, liked sex with men but still chose to be with women because of the quality of relationships with women, but primarily because we were able to attain deep and truly egalitarian relationships with women. Some of us have a highly significant, occasionally even primary, erotic attraction to men but still identify as lesbians for the reasons I have cited, reasons that are personal to be sure, but that are also political inasmuch as they derive from the inherent inequality of many heterosexual relationships. Others of us experience our lesbianism as more unconscious, as a given rather than as a choice. But is this really so? How many of us who experience our sexual identity in this way ("I was always a lesbian, I was always different") remember our earliest lesbian identification, not necessarily as an erotic attraction but rather as dislike of and rebellion against heterosexual female roles. Perhaps those of us who were always lesbians simply blocked off our heterosexual options at such an early age that we no longer remember ever having such options; perhaps we were tomboys who looked around us at the adult war between men and women and said, essentially, "Hell, no, I won't go." Many lesbians who feel they were always lesbian also remember always feeling that they didn't/couldn't/wouldn't fit into the traditional feminine role. For these women, lesbianism is one option that is an alternative to the feminine fate, and thus is a type of political choice, albeit one made unconsciously at a very early age. Incidentally, this is an alternative explanation of Bell, Weinberg, and Hammersmith's data linking adult sexual orientation and nonconforming gender behavior in childhood. These researchers make the very sexist interpretation that the link suggests a genetic explanation for both homosexuality and gender-role behavior.[23] I am clearly suggesting something very different.

The point I am making in relation to bisexuality, however, is that if my theory is even partly accurate it suggests that there is more choice involved in lesbianism than many of us would like to think. If that is the case, it is clear why bisexuality is a threatening phenomenon. To believe that one's sexual identity is a choice does seem to re-open options, a not always comfortable prospect; as a friend once said, "I struggled so long and with so much difficulty to develop a positive gay identity, I don't want to have to reconsider now." Choosing to move from a lesbian to a bisexual or heterosexual life-style involves loss for many women. Women I have counseled who moved from a lesbian identity to a relationship with a man did indeed lose some gay friends as well as their sense of community, activities, and involvements. Finally, the issue of choice implies a moral issue to many. That is, many straight people and some gay people feel that homosexuality is acceptable if it is a given, something unchangeable, preferably genetic, like left-handedness. Gay people who feel this way are able to feel positive about their gayness only by saying, in essence, "I can't help it." Seeing homosexuality as a choice destroys this psychological defense against guilt. Despite these discomforts, we must objectively examine the issue of bisexuality, not only out of fairness to those within our community who are increasingly making a bisexual identification, but also because understanding bisexuality may be critical to understanding the nature of sexual orientation itself. New work on bisexuality suggests, for example, that women may be more bisexual than men, perhaps because our sexual desire is less cued to physical visual stimuli, and that there are many different types of bisexuality.[24] Examining male-female differences in bisexuality and analyzing types of bisexuality (e.g., some bisexuals say that gender doesn't matter, and others describe their relationships with men and women as qualitatively different) can teach us a great deal about sexual and romantic attraction in general.

### The Origins of Lesbian "Erotophobia"

Amber Hollibaugh has coined the term *erotophobia* to describe our reaction to sexuality, and indeed it does sometimes seem that we are afraid of intense sexual desire and passion.[25] One evening while watching our great gay playwright's work about women, men, and sexual passion, *A Streetcar Named Desire*, it struck me that Tennessee Williams had an instinctive sense of the terrible bind in which our society places women regarding their sexuality. Despite the sexual revolution, despite the change in women's sexual behavior, it is still generally true that men encourage women to be sexual and then hold them in complete contempt when they really are and dare to be truly lustful and passionate with whomever they choose. In the worst case, women's sexuality becomes an excuse for sexual assault, just as Blanche Dubois found that her sexual promiscuity both provided an excuse for Stanley Kowalski to rape her and then became the reason why no one believed her story of rape. Think of the stereotypical cry of the rapist who maintains that the victim "really wanted it," or the defense of the child molester or incest perpetrator who claims the child seduced him; and think of the culture that believes these violent men and asks victims to prove their sexual purity as proof of innocence.

Lesbians are women first, and we have been socialized as heterosexual women for at least a portion of our lives. What has been our response to viewing our culture's attitude toward female sexuality? Like other women, our sexuality is contaminated by these conflicting messages: Be sexual/don't be sexual/be a whore/be frigid/be a virgin/be innocent/be experienced/be passionate/be a slut. Our culture allows us only a narrow band of appropriate sexual behaviors, certain techniques practiced within the setting of a committed, loving relationship, and as much as we can and still be lesbians, we obediently comply. More specifically, because our sexual passion has been used as one of the excuses to perpetrate violence—rape, incest—against us, we protect ourselves against this violence in a way that must seem logical to our primitive instincts: by shutting off our sexual desire. We join in blaming the victim—ourselves. As Maryjane Sherfey maintains, we limit what may be a very wild and enormous capacity for sexual pleasure out of a misguided sense of self-protection.[26] Because few of us as lesbians have escaped heterosexual conditioning, we carry this universal female ambivalence toward sex over into our gay lives. And because sexual power has so often been used against us, we try to take power out of our sex, and by doing so make it frequently so ethereal as to be so nonsexual, soft, warm, and cuddly as to eliminate passion.

Tennessee Williams, in the same play in which he portrays the awful price women pay for being sexual, also shows us why women might seek sexual contact despite such strict sanctions. Williams writes that sexual desire is a life force, an affirmation of life, and that sexual women are magnificent as well as tragic. Lesbians, more than heterosexual women, have the opportunity to divorce female sexuality from its heterosexist contest and to transcend male-dominated attempts to control, reduce, and constrain our passion. It is important that lesbians seize our opportunity to open up and expand our sexuality. This is the time for lesbians to explore our passion and the paths down which our sexual desire leads us, and to do this exploration without judgment except when absolutely necessary, when our sexuality is either clearly coercive or clearly self-destructive. Now is the time to affirm that anything that lesbians do sexually really is lesbian sexuality, to affirm all our sexuality as politically correct sex.

## NOTES

1. Philip Blumstein and Pepper Schwarz, *American Couples* (New York: William Morrow, 1983).

2. Karla Jay and Allen Young, *The Gay Report* (New York: Summit Books, 1977).

3. Margaret Nichols, "The Treatment of Inhibited Sexual Desire (ISD) in Lesbian Couples," *Women and Therapy* 1 (Winter 1982): 49–66.

4. C. A. Tripp, *The Homosexual Matrix* (New York: McGraw Hill, 1975).

5. Dan Bloom and Michael Shernoff, "The Impact of AIDS upon the Urban Gay Male Community," paper presented at the Society for the Scientific Study of Sex, San Diego, Sept. 1985.

6. Carol Gilligan, *In a Different Voice: Psychological Theory and Women's Development* (Cambridge: Harvard University Press, 1982).

7. Julia R. Heiman, "The Physiology of Erotica: Women's Sexual Arousal," *Psychology Today* 8 (Nov. 1975): 90–94.

8. Betty Berzon, "Positively Gay," presentation at American Psychological Association Conference, New York, Sept. 1979; Betty Berzon and Robert Leighton, *Positively Gay* (Millbrae, Calif.: Celestial Arts, 1979).

9. Alan P. Bell, Martin S. Weinberg, and Sue K. Hammersmith, *Sexual Preference: Its Development in Men and Women* (Bloomington: Indiana University Press, 1981); Jay and Young, *The Gay Report*.

10. Judith L. Herman, *Father-Daughter Incest* (Cambridge: Harvard University Press, 1982).

11. Virginia Apuzzo, personal communication, Feb. 1984; Bell, Weinberg, and Hammersmith, *Sexual Preference*.

12. Tripp, *The Homosexual Matrix*.

13. Ibid.

14. Ann Snitow, Christine Stansell, and Sandra Thompson, *Powers of Desire: The Politics of Sexuality* (New York: Monthly Review Press, 1984).

15. R. R. Linden, D. R. Pagano, D. Russell, and S. L. Star, *Against Sadomasochism: A Radical Feminist Analysis* (East Palo Alto, Calif.: Frog in the Well, 1982).

16. Samois, *Coming to Power* (Boston: Alyson Press, 1982).

17. Bernie Zilbergeld and C. R. Ellison, "Desire Discrepancy and Arousal Problems in Sex Therapy," in *Principles and Practices of Sex Therapy,* ed. Sandra L. Leiblum and L. Perrin (New York: Guilford Press, 1980).

18. Rita Mae Brown, *In Her Day* (New York: Daughters, 1977).

19. Marge Piercy, *Women on the Edge of Time* (New York: Fawcett, 1981).

20. Tripp, *Homosexual Matrix.*

21. Blumstein and Schwartz, *American Couples.*

22. John Preston, *I Once Had a Master* (Boston: Alyson Publications, 1984).

23. Bell, Weinberg, and Hammersmith, *Sexual Preference.*

24. Fritz Klein and Timothy Wolf, *Bisexualities: Theory and Research* (New York: Haworth Press, 1985); Margaret Nichols and J. Paul, "Some Theoretical Issues Regarding Types of Bisexuality and the Original 'Bipholsia,'" paper presented at the Eastern Regional Council of the Society for the Scientific Study of Sex, Philadelphia, April 1986.

25. Amber Hollibaugh, "The Erotic Voices of Lesbians," *New York Native,* vol. 3, 1983.

26. M. J. Sherfey, "The Evolution and Nature of Female Sexuality in Relation to Psychoanalytic Theory," *Journal of the American Analyatic Association* 14 (1966): 28–128.

# 7

## Barriers to Intimacy: Conflicts over Power, Dependency, and Nurturing in Lesbian Relationships

BEVERLY BURCH

A relationship between two adults that is both loving and sexual always has more elements of mystery than rationality to it. Part of the power of erotic relationships lies in their ability to recreate unconsciously the lost experience of sensuality and safety that each adult once knew, even if only briefly or sporadically, as an infant in the arms of her or his mother. This experience, which is lost to conscious recall, is remembered by the body and evoked in intimate adult contact. In heterosexual relationships, the evocation is more direct and complete for a man than for a woman as he once again loses himself in loving physical contact with a woman. As Dorothy Dinnerstein says, "since the first parent is female, heteroerotic feeling has deeper roots in infancy for men than for women." A woman is one step removed from the intensity: "In the sexual recapitulation of the infant-mother interplay, [the woman] has more of a sense than [the man] does of embodying the powerful mother within herself: a greater part of her than of his reliving of the infant role is vicarious, through the other person."[1]

Only in lesbian relationships do women once again experience this reconnection directly. For many women involvement with another woman is like reclaiming a lost history, an opportunity full of joy promising more fulfilling intimacy. Intimacy becomes a struggle, however, when the threats and injuries of childhood are also reactivated. This triggering of early experience always occurs in adult love affairs, consciously or unconsciously. Because they include such intimate bodily contact, they evoke one's buried primal history.

126

The child's early experience with her or his parents creates some kind of template for future involvements. Because women have provided most of the actual early parenting, the mother-child relationship is especially significant. Some relatively recent theoretical attention to the impact of gender for both parent and child has led the way to a new perspective on women's intrapsychic development.[2] Implications of this work need to be extended to lesbians, focusing on aspects of mother-daughter relationships that have an affect on adult relationships between women.

All relationships must in some way negotiate three major issues: the balance of power, the pulls toward and away from dependency, and the roles involved in nurturing. These issues seem to carry an unusually intense charge in some lesbian relationships; the words themselves occur and recur, thrown back and forth with great feeling as the women fight or retreat from them. The issues look somewhat different from when they occur in heterosexual relationships, differences that highlight women's development and reveal cultural blindspots. We can trace the strength of these issues back to at least two sources: the dynamics of mother-daughter relationships and the devaluation of women and lesbians in this culture.

## Identifying the Issues

*Power.* Many lesbians are acutely attuned to inequalities in power. Some of the reasons for this attunement are easily deduced. Lesbians are often feminists and concerned with women's unequal access to power. Many lesbians recall an early awareness of women's limitation in heterosexual relationships. Some remember making conscious choices against marriage and traditional relationships with men, even if not specifically identifying themselves as lesbian. This early determination not to be subjected to an inferior role is somewhat thwarted, however, by the position of lesbians in the culture. Lesbians lose social and political power through lack of affiliation with men and male power. They have chosen other women—that is, devalued members of society—as partners. They are labeled deviant. Their self-determination is often frustrated in painful ways. Although lesbians sometimes feel more powerful and independent in relationships than heterosexual women do, they lose the narrow access that heterosexual women retain to power in the world.

In therapy, many lesbians express a determination not to be in a less powerful position in a relationship. With some individuals or couples the issue is out in the open: One partner feels her lover holds more power in the relationship and wants this imbalance to change. In other cases, one or both partners defend so well against feelings of powerlessness that the issue is hidden. They may be locked in a subtle but ongoing battle over power, each defending against feeling the other's power. What is often more apparent than the struggle itself is its effects: Their capacity for intimacy is diminished.

Any number of differences may be singled out by the couple as a source of inequality or an imbalance of power. Division of labor, money, or recognition, inequality in emotional vulnerability and felt dependency occur in lesbian relationships as well as in heterosexual ones, although the differences are usually not as extreme as they can be between a woman and a man, and the roles are no longer determined by gender. Differences in race, ethnic background, or class, for example—some way that one has been more privileged than the other—create inequalities difficult to cope with, as do differences in personal qualities or assets such as self-confidence, verbal or physical ability, or success in the world.

The distinction between actual inequalities and felt experiences of powerlessness is a subjective one. Some couples handle differences or inequalities without great difficulty; others are preoccupied with them. Ability to tolerate and work with differences is essential to a relationship's survival. The idea that any difference in power is damaging is not borne out by experience. Behind conflicts about power, envy is often unacknowledged as a component. When differences feel intolerable, the only perceived choices are either giving up on the relationship or constant struggle. What makes these differences feel intolerable, however, is the unconscious fear of power in a woman, a fear that goes back to infancy.

Two clinical examples of lesbian relationships embroiled in power struggles illustrate the problems.

*Kathryn and Paula.* Kathryn and Paula came to therapy because they fought too much: "All the time," according to Paula. Kathryn had several ongoing complaints. Paula was so independent that she wouldn't let Kathryn "in." Paula was more self-assured or at least didn't admit to much insecurity, whereas Kathryn often felt exposed when she tried to talk about her own sense of insecurity or vulnerability. Paula seemed to get her way most of the time.

Kathryn had become defensive and resistant to intimacy with Paula. She was handling the threat of Paula's greater power by controlling the frequency of their contact and by starting fights. She thought she probably ought to leave the relationship.

*Jackie and Pam.* Jackie and Pam had been together two years, but their relationship was on the verge of dissolving when they came to therapy. At thirty-six, Jackie was well-educated, highly successful at work, owned their house, and wanted to settle down. Pam at twenty-five was unsettled, had left college after her second year, and had not found work that suited her. She wanted to be a writer but had lost sight of her goal and now had a low-paying job in a bookstore. Recently she'd had an affair with another woman and had been drinking more than she used to. In therapy she began to articulate that she felt overpowered by Jackie and wasn't sure who she was any more.

With Kathryn and Paula, the power struggle revolved around psychological and emotional differences. Kathryn felt their differences to be unbearable and was tormented by a sense of powerlessness. I'll return to the case of Kathryn and Paula several times in this chapter. With Jackie and Pam, there were many concrete differences such as age, income, education, and success. Pam's experience of powerlessness might have been less disturbing with a man; it might have been perceived as "natural." These differences are ones that many heterosexual relationships rest on. This possibility raises the question of why a woman might feel safer allowing such inequalities to exist with a man than with another woman.

The outcome of therapy for Jackie and Pam was a decision to break up. Pam felt she would never be able to hold her own with Jackie and had to establish her sense of self more strongly before she was ready for a lasting relationship. The inequality between them was striking, yet again in a heterosexual relationship the therapy might have minimized it, and breaking up might not have been seen as a positive outcome for Pam even though it was clear to Pam that she needed to leave. In the actual case the therapist could support Pam's decision and help Jackie to look at her own choice of a partner unequal to herself. Jackie began to see it as protection for her own insecurity, fear of rejection, and fear of being powerless herself in a relationship.

*Dependence.* The struggle with dependence can look different in lesbian relationships. We are more or less familiar with women's struggle against too much dependency on others. That struggle may be primary for women in traditional, socially prescribed roles that define them in relation to other people. There are no prescribed lesbian roles, however, and lesbians are already actively resisting what is prescribed for them as women. Although it is clear that lesbians can also be caught in a cycle of dependency on others, the opposite is just as often true.

A woman who is a lesbian may strongly value independence, even self-sufficiency, as the way out of the traditional constriction of women's lives. Dependency may be feared because it represents identification with the old sense of heterosexual "femininity" that she has rejected. She rejects this identification consciously, because she sees its destructiveness to women's, and her own, integrity. However, there may also be an irrational aspect to her fear; she may feel repelled by things too "feminine," such as passivity, vulnerability, or dependence. This reaction is part of an unconscious fear of woman-ness, an internalization of women's devaluation, a fear of identifying with the devaluation of woman.

A woman who fears or even hates her own woman-ness will project this gynophobia onto her lover and feel further devalued herself by dependency on her. She will probably maintain a safe distance from her and these feelings. Thus her own needs for dependency will be denied; she'll be psychologically isolated, even within a relationship. In the case of Kathryn and Paula, Paula is a woman afraid of dependency on another woman. She controls this fear by controlling her vulnerability. The case of Alicia presents a different example.

*Alicia.* Alicia has a history of short-term relationships, each less than a year and a half. Typically, she falls in love quite intensely, then after a few months becomes disillusioned by her lover and begins to pull away. When her lover tries to hold on or protests her distancing, Alicia is annoyed that her freedom is being questioned. She gets angry and soon leaves the relationship.

Alicia lives very well on her own, earning a good income at nontraditional work. She travels by herself on vacations and is quite capable of entertaining herself. Yet she wishes she could have a relationship that lasted longer. She came to therapy confused, asking whether relationships are really possible. Why do other women always want to "possess" her? She is depressed, and wonders if she should just reconcile herself to being alone.

Alicia is terrified of her own unknown need for dependency and appalled by other women's. As soon as she begins to feel dependent at all on another woman, she backs off, then out of the relationship, never understanding her fears but being controlled by them.

The more traditional woman's issue of overdependency is usually a matter of socialization interwoven with problems in separation and individuation that have never been worked through. As we shall see, establishing an autonomous self, securely independent, is more problematic for girls than for boys. It is no coincidence that sex roles and psychodynamic development both lead girls toward greater dependency and less autonomy.

When one woman is more dependent than the other in a relationship, both are usually conflicted about it. Consciously, the more self-sufficient woman is proud of her autonomy, and both of them may disparage the other's lack of it, that is, her traditionally feminine position. However, internalization of sex-typed values is so powerful that, unconsciously, the self-sufficient one may also fear that she is in fact "masculine"—and the dependent one may feel unconsciously reassured in her role. There is really no stance for either of them to take that is not some kind of threat to her self-image.

*Nurturance.* Another frequent source of conflict in lesbian relationships is who takes care of whom? Women are expected to be the nurturers, especially of men. In a lesbian relationship, that expectation can be revised: At last one doesn't have to be the caretaker and may actually be the nurtured one instead. When both women have that hope and feel freed from the constraints of a caretaking role, there is conflict. Jennifer and Natalie presented an example of this conflict.

*Jennifer and Natalie.* Jennifer and Natalie had been together for eight months. Jennifer was angry and disillusioned about what she thought at first was the relationship she'd always wanted. Whenever she was upset and turned to Natalie, Natalie backed off.

Natalie thought Jennifer was upset too often and expected too much from her. She also felt that whenever she was angry or unhappy and expressed it to Jennifer, Jennifer got angry or hurt in response and the focus shifted to *her* feelings.

Both of them felt wounded and frustrated. Both felt less than hopeful that the other could meet her needs, even though initially each felt the other to be someone who understood and responded to her more fully than anyone else ever had.

Conflict over nurturing manifests itself many ways: a refusal to nurture, a refusal to be nurtured, a demand for constant attention, an insistence on giving more than is wanted, a sense of betrayal at having to ask or specify what one wants. These problems can express conflicts over autonomy versus dependence and may reflect early narcissistic wounds. However, this issue is related specifically to gender also.

Because women are so encumbered with complex, often contradictory, training as nurturers, most women experience some measure of guilt or anxiety about how they do or don't take care of others. Many women find it easier to give than to receive; their self-esteem is inextricably tied into giving. At the same time, resentment or anger may be hidden behind the giving, especially when their own needs are being neglected. Giving may also be a covert attempt to draw attention to one's own needs. A relationship between two women will inevitably stir such conflicts, if for no other reason simply because women are so deeply associated with nurturing. Whatever the old wounds are, they are likely to be reopened.

## Developmental Theory: Women

Like most conflicts, these issues in lesbian relationships may arise from widely differing roots. One explanation will not suffice to explain such complex issues. Adding a gender-based perspective to traditionally understood psychodynamics offers some missing pieces even while it does not provide all the answers. The unique nature of lesbian relationships, that is, that they are formed by two women, directs us to begin by looking at the first female-to-female relationship, mother and daughter together.

The experience of infantile dependency is the basic legacy underlying these issues. Perhaps the greatest difficulty of childhood (also of parenthood!) is the inherent dependency of the child. For so many years, a whole lifetime really, the individual is outgrowing that dependency. Because women are the primary parents, women are the ones on whom much of this dependency is laid. Therefore, it is a woman whom a daughter must leave behind in order to grow up.

The very young child begins life in psychic unity with the mother and slowly develops a sense of self, distinct from the mother, through the process of separation-individuation.[3] Object-relations theory focuses on this process as the centerpiece of development during the first three or four years of life (although it continues throughout a lifetime), a focus that seems more relevant to women's development than the traditional focus on Oedipal conflict. Leaving mother behind and being one's own person is a never-completed task, and it is probably more difficult for women than for men, as we shall see. This perpetual process of moving beyond the mother plays a powerful role in lesbian relationships.

The early developmental stages of separation-individuation do not unfold identically for boys and girls. Two factors distinguish the mother-daughter relationship from the mother-son. First, mothers and daughters have a conscious and unconscious sense of identification. Nancy Chodorow has argued that this identification produces a prolonged period of "oneness and continuity" between them, giving daughters a greater relational capacity than sons.[4] Mothers "hold" daughters in relationship longer. This does not mean mothers provide more support, more nurturing, or in any sense a more positive relationship with daughters than with sons, but simply more psychological relatedness, whether positive or negative. The greater length and strength of this early period also means that separating and individuating are more complicated matters for girls. Daughters generally have a more difficult task in leaving the mother behind, and as adults continue to have issues with ego boundaries, feeling separate and different.

Patriarchal culture places less value on being a woman than a man. For girls and women, this is an ongoing strike against self-esteem, a perpetual narcissistic injury. Ambivalence about being female results — which may be conscious and grappled with or unconscious and acted out in one's life. Jane Flax has pointed out how this ambivalence or even self-hatred disturbs mother-daughter relationships because it is invariably projected onto girl children. Another burden is added to the separation-individuation period for daughters by such projections. Mothers allow daughters both less genuine dependence and less genuine autonomy.[5] They are limited coming and going, so to speak.

This convergence of psychodynamics and sociodynamics creates greater problems for women in autonomy and self-esteem, and in developing a strong separate self. The situation is not entirely negative, however; women's greater capacity for empathy, deep relatedness, and perhaps intuition are also part of this legacy.

The process of separation-individuation is never so complete, for men or women, as to preclude fear of re-engulfment in the original mother-child unity and subsequent loss of self. Margaret Mahler describes this fear as "the defense against the perpetual longing of the human being for reunion with the erstwhile symbiotic mother, a longing that threatens individual entity and identity, and therefore has to be warded off even beyond childhood."[6]

Physical intimacy arouses unconscious wishes to recapture that lost union. For both heterosexual men and lesbians, relationships evoke this longing (and defenses against it) probably more strongly than for gay men and heterosexual women because their relationship includes intimacy with a woman's body once again. Male defenses against engulfment in the mother are established early, however, as part of their developing gender identity. Nancy Chodorow argues that emphasis on differentness and separateness are essential defenses of male identity: "Maleness is more conflictual and problematic [than femaleness]. Underlying, or built into core male gender identity is an early, nonverbal, unconscious, almost somatic sense of primary oneness with the mother, an underlying sense of femaleness that continually . . . challenges and undermines the sense of maleness. . . . [Men] come to emphasize differences, especially in situations that evoke anxiety. . . . Separateness and difference as a component of differentiation become more salient."[7]

Because mothers do not identify themselves with male children to the same extent as they do with female children, they relate to sons as "the other" more than daughters, giving boys further experience with a sense of difference. Boys develop a firmer, albeit partly defensive, sense of a separate self, and the boundary around the self is less fluid, or more rigid. As an adult, a man's defenses against loss of self in intimacy are therefore stronger than a woman's and are fueled by the need to preserve a sense of gender integrity. His defensive strategy provides some boundary to the intimacy in the relationship. For women in lesbian relationships, there is no such built-in boundary. In fact, the boundaries are doubly permeable, more fluid on both sides, and the threat of loss of self may feel greater.

Out of these struggles against early dependency and loss of self, conflicts over power, adult dependency, and nurturance emerge.

### Understanding the Issues Psychodynamically

*Power.* The parent-child relationship is based on such enormous inequality that no other matches it. Boys grow up to have relationships with women that allow them to be the dominant ones: They may avenge themselves quite thoroughly for that early inequality and protect against its repetition in adult life. This is not the case for girls.

Both sexes are left with an unconscious fear of the power of women. Dorothy Dinnerstein says: *"The crucial psychological fact is that all of us, female as well as male, fear the will of woman. Man's dominion over what we think of as the world rests on a terror that we all feel: the terror of sinking back wholly into the helplessness of infancy."*[8]

Men keep this fear in check by establishing and exercising power over women; women do not have such a ready escape. Women's fear is tempered, however, by their ability to identify with their mothers, their positive identification as women. Nevertheless, having a woman lover may arouse unconscious fears of allowing another woman power over oneself again. The experience of the other as powerful can evoke intense feelings: rage, anxiety, envy. In unconscious terms, the lover is guilty by association.

Even when differences between women do not actually represent significant inequality, the differences may evoke feelings of powerlessness. Differences are sometimes resisted per se because they obstruct the wish for merger, they throw one back on oneself and one's own separateness or aloneness.[9] For women, this means being thrown back into the confusion of that troubled passage through separation-individuation, into the anxiety and sense of loss. Differences do not carry the same rewarding function of establishing the girl's gender identity as they do for boys. They signal something to be lost with no compensating sense of gain. This lack of ease with differences means that the other, the different one, is felt to be powerful, while one's own self is felt to be small, weak, and perhaps unloved.

When this other person who is more powerful is also a woman, the inequality will be more terrifying on an unconscious level than if she were a man, according to Dinnerstein. The power of the other must either be overcome or fled. In a lesbian relationship both women may be constantly trying to balance the power. Neither is comfortable for long with feelings of inequality. The struggle over differences and their association with power taps into these deep roots.

To return to the earlier clinical example of Kathryn and Paula, Kathryn experienced herself as less powerful than Paula. Paula's defenses allowed her to appear somewhat invulnerable, but the actual differences between them were not so real as they were for Jackie and Pam, the couple with many inequalities. Nevertheless, Kathryn chafed under fears of losing herself with Paula, of allowing herself to be dominated; in fact, she was quite assertive and generally held her own. Her feeling of powerlessness in relation to Paula was exaggerated, and her sense of self was weak. An open exploration of her fantasies about Paula's power helped her to grasp both the reality and the unreality of her fears and to be able to contain them enough to remain in the relationship rather than flee. As she explored them further, she realized that in a previous relationship with a woman she had felt herself to be the stronger one and was equally uncomfortable with that position. If Dinnerstein is correct, with a man Kathryn might have felt more comfortable being the less powerful one in order to control the fear of powerful women for *both* of them.

How are power struggles to be resolved in a lesbian relationship? A few parameters can be considered by the therapist: How real is the inequality of power and on what is it based? Do the women experience each other as adversaries, and do they actually undermine each other? Who is the intrapsychic adversary? Are the power struggles valuable and constructive or are they destructive? Some power struggles are a way for individuals to define themselves more fully in a relationship, whereas others are perpetual, obsessive, and futile. The question for the client is, Do I need to hold on in the struggle or do I need to get over it? Some battles have an imperative quality, signaling that they are serving another psychological function. Other fights are clearly defining territory and establishing mutual autonomy. Two women who are each willful, self-determined, and independent, for example, will likely have to go through some battles with each other.

A woman's growth into autonomy requires a greater struggle than does a man's. Much of this struggle has occurred in the context of a relationship with her mother, positively or negatively. Being with another woman will no doubt recall the earlier struggle and recreate unresolved parts of it. The relationship may be an impetus to further individuation by highlighting those unresolved issues.

*Dependency.* Adult dependency is intertwined with issues of power: The compulsion to avoid dependency arises from old defenses against that early dependency on a woman. In lesbian relationships there is sometimes a prolonged struggle against dependency on the other. Again, the unconscious association of the lover and the mother in their femaleness intensifies this struggle.

There is another factor as well: A sufficient period of genuine, developmentally necessary, secure dependence as a child seems to be less likely for girls than for boys. Jane Flax and Paula Caplan have both noted that girls are not allowed as much real dependence as infants and toddlers as boys are.[10] The mother's own conflicts about being female are easily projected onto a daughter. Paula Caplan reports research that "mothers are tolerant of baby boys' rituals and requirements at mealtime but insist on quick and unfussy eating by girls. . . . Girls are usually weaned earlier than boys, a practice that seems to be related to a greater comfort in keeping boys dependent on mothers. . . . They are requiring more self-control, more adult and less troublesome behavior on the part of their daughters."[11]

Flax states that girls are given less adequate emotional nurturance during the symbiotic period and later stages of separation-individuation. Both Flax and Caplan have argued that physical nurturance of daughters is especially conflicted. For the heterosexual mother, physical contact is not only potentially laden with forbidden incestuous feelings as it is with sons, but it also touches into homophobic feelings as well. The daughter's early years of dependency are clearly hampered by her mother's conflicts, leaving her deprived and conflicted herself about her female identity and her dependency, especially on women.

Cultural influences give this struggle additional weight. Women are negatively stereotyped as dependent by nature. As they grow older, daughters perceive the devaluation of women when they see their mothers through the eyes of the rest of the family and of the world. Initially the daughter longs to be like her powerful mother; later she learns to dissociate herself from her. She would prefer anything to identifying with her mother—but then she really has no choice. She is a woman, like her. The ambivalence of this identification, simultaneously loving and envying one's mother even while disavowing her, can make an uneasy peace in a lesbian relationship. Each woman has her own conflict of identification as a woman, both her self-love and her self-hate. She may project these contradictions onto her partner; she may keep them deep in her unconscious and cling to the defenses that preserve them there.

A relationship with another woman arouses the pain of this conflict as well as an unconscious wish to relive dependency in a more gratifying way. Avoiding dependency on another woman is a way of fending off both the wish and the conflict. The woman who avoids dependency is just as needy behind her defenses as the one who seems unable to muster any independence. To return to Kathryn and Paula, Paula kept her vulnerability under cover to hide her dependent longings from herself even more than from her lover. She had learned very early to be self-sufficient and to fear exposing any of her needs.

If a woman's ambivalence is great, she may be too conflicted to allow any trace of dependency. This was the problem for Alicia, the woman who left every relationship within a year or so. Alicia's mother had been excessively dependent herself as well as depressed, and her father was emotionally unavailable to the mother or the daughter, leaving Alicia with an impossible choice in relation to her own needs. She didn't want to identify with her unhappy mother, so she developed a rigid stance of self-sufficiency. There had really been no alternative for her, no possibility of getting her needs met because her mother was unavailable and too needy herself. Rather than being helped into a secure autonomy, she had had to be falsely independent at an early age and to identify with her father in some respects. Beneath this self-sufficiency, she felt incredibly weak and vulnerable, although she was unaware of this until she'd been in therapy almost two years—well past her one-year mark.

Alicia scorned her mother's weaknesses. Intimacy with another woman was threatening to her warded-off identification with her mother. If she allowed herself to be dependent on another person, she would feel dangerously close to being like her mother. Because her lovers were also women, she felt more worthless; at the same time her denied needs were stirred by the possibility of finally having another woman attend to her. If she gave up her defenses, she would be flooded with the early feelings of loss, fear, and rage and a terrifying sense of losing herself. Therapy with Alicia gradually brought this to light. She left therapy once, returned, and threatened to leave several more times, but she has stayed and has gained a renewed appreciation of her own struggle. She has strong impulses to flee whenever she feels the terror of dependence on her therapist, but she hopes to be able to handle them and face the difficult work ahead.

*Nurturance.* Ambivalence about nurturance has deep roots. To be fed, held, and tended physically and emotionally is the child's first need. It is the first battleground, too, and again girls seem to suffer deprivation here more than boys. The same conflicts about being female that affect early-stage dependency in mother-daughter relationships determine how a woman will nurture her daughter. Caplan's report that mothers have less tolerance of daughters' fussy eating habits is only one example.

Women's conflicts about nurturance and identificaton as female show most glaringly in the preoccupation with thinness and restrained eating that most adolescent and adult women have.[12] Obsession with food on the one hand and with trying to be thin on the other reflect an impossible, contradictory attempt to nurture oneself while denying the body. The devaluation of women and the fact that women do essentially all the early parenting become so deeply entangled here that they are inseparable.

Girls are raised to forego their own needs to learn to take care of others. They are taught this by their mothers, who have had the same experience as daughters, often by being asked to meet their mother's needs. Paula Caplan describes this process: "Society gives the mothers the task of teaching daughters to be nurturant and self-sacrificing, as they themselves are supposed to be. It is a natural outgrowth of this situation that, as part of her training in responding to the needs of others, the daughter of a lonely and insecure mother will be taught to meet the mother's needs as well. Insofar as the daughter tries to meet those needs, to that extent will her own needs for nurturance go unmet. Thus the daughter grows up feeling inadequately nurtured. When she becomes a mother, she will have unmet needs and may turn to her own daughter, hoping the daughter will meet them."[13] Or the grown daughter may turn to her lover, if her lover is a woman too. It is not surprising, then, that a woman may respond with fear or anger to another woman's expectations that she will take care of her.

In therapy, the issues of caretaking and nurturing can be explored back to their roots, clarifying what are realistic expectations for the present. A woman who doesn't want to nurture or is unable to let herself be nurtured may be fending off desires that feel too over-whelming. If she was the nurturing child to her mother, she may fear any woman's needs and be alienated from her own. She may expect the demands to be endless.

Jennifer and Natalie, the two women who felt unnurtured by each other, came to therapy with intense conflicts about being cared for. Their issues were so intertwined that they were impenetrable at times. Therapy required singling out a number of different threads for each of them. Jennifer had great sensitivity to perceived rejection or neglect. Her early history was a series of wounding experiences at the hands of her parents. Again and again she was shamed over both her physical and emotional needs. Her mother's own wounded narcissism required Jennifer to intuit and tend *her* needs, and the mother could not nurture Jennifer with much empathy. Now Jennifer experienced shame over her neediness and her acute sensitivity. Trying to bring this out in the open was like walking through a minefield, as her rage covered her shame. She believed that her lover, then her therapist, could intuit the wounds, so any failure of perception was probably intended. Her rage and her mistrust came out more and more, and gradually, after much empathy, an awareness that Natalie did not want to humiliate her began to take hold. Jennifer expressed hurt more directly then and could articulate her needs better. Her anger over Natalie's own expectations of emotional attention diminished; she began to tolerate Natalie saying no. In effect, she began to make the distinction unconsciously between Natalie and her mother.

Natalie, on the other hand, had consciously determined not to be trapped into a nurturing role in her adult relationships. She had felt used as a child by her mother, who depended on her for emotional contact, especially after her mother's own mother died when Natalie was six. In the beginning of her relationship with Jennifer, Natalie used her early training as caretaker to stay closely attuned to Jennifer. She resented this role though and rebelled against it by withdrawing, leaving Jennifer feeling betrayed. Natalie was convinced that if she lowered her guard and responded to any of Jennifer's needs, she would be propelled back into the nurturing role with no end in sight. Limiting what she would give frightened her: She expected Jennifer to leave. Instead she became rigid and self-righteous as she defended against Jennifer's demands. On the other hand, she did not assert her own needs very well, giving up easily but resentfully when Jennifer was wounded or angry. Therapy involved many months of going back and forth through these blocks, affirming the anger and fear related to past deprivations and facing the reality that adult relationships do not make up for early losses.

All of these issues are variations on the theme of old fears versus strong attraction. The fears may lie dormant until a woman becomes intimately involved with another woman. The intimacy of lesbian relationships, perhaps more than any other kind of relationship, approaches the intensity of the mother-daughter relationship. The parallel between the mother's body and the lover's body, so powerful unconsciously, is capable of evoking deepest childhood experiences. Fear of re-engulfment in the mother-daughter history can be an unconscious barrier to intimacy. Individually varied early experiences as daughters come to bear forcefully on these more universal issues. And the issues are often intertwined; linkages between conflicts over power, nurturing, and dependence create patterns that are difficult to comprehend.

Traditionally, psychology has presumed lesbian relationships to be pathological per se. When conflicts like the ones I describe show up in clinical cases, the presumption is often made that the woman developed psychosexually into a lesbian precisely because she had such pre-genital conflicts. There is a different way to see these problems, however. Women raised in patriarchal culture inevitably have trouble with issues related to sense of self, and, as we have seen, sense of separateness. It does not seem unlikely that most women would encounter some of these conflicts in an intimate relationship with another woman. Further, a woman's capacity for intensity and intimacy is probably heightened in relationship with another woman, who shares a similar capacity. Simply stated, this shared capacity can heighten the problems as well.

## NOTES

1. Dorothy Dinnerstein, *The Mermaid and the Minotaur: Sexual Arrangements and Human Malaise* (New York: Harper & Row, 1976), 66, 67.

2. See for example, Paula Caplan, *Barriers between Women* (New York: Spectrum Publications, 1981); Nancy Chodorow, *The Reproduction of Mothering: Psychoanalysis and the Sociology of Gender* (Berkeley: University of California Press, 1978) and "Gender, Relation, and Difference in Psychoanalytic Perspective," *The Future of Difference* (Boston: G. K. Hall, 1980); Dinnerstein, *The Mermaid and the Minotaur*; and Jane Flax, "The Conflict between Nurturance and Autonomy in Mother/Daughter Relationships and within Feminism," *Feminist Studies* 4 (Spring 1978): 171–89.

3. Margaret Mahler, *The Psychological Birth of the Human Infant* (New York: Basic Books, 1975).

4. Chodorow, *The Reproduction of Mothering*, 109.

5. Flax, "Conflict between Nurturance and Autonomy," 174 ff.

6. Mahler, *Psychological Birth*, 290.

7. Chodorow, "Gender, Relation, and Difference," 13.

8. Dinnerstein, *The Mermaid and the Minotaur*, 161.

9. Beverly Burch, "Psychological Merger in Lesbian Couples: A Joint Ego Psychological and Systems Approach," *Family Therapy* (Fall 1982): 201; and "Another Perspective on Merger in Lesbian Relationships," in *Handbook of Feminist Therapy: Women's Issues in Psychotherapy*, ed. Lynn Bravo Rosewater and Lenore Walker (New York: Springer, 1985), 100–9.

10. Caplan, *Barriers between Women*, and Flax, "Conflict between Nurturance and Autonomy."

11. Caplan, *Barriers between Women*, 28.

12. Kim Chernin, *The Obsession: Relections on the Tyranny of Slenderness* (New York: Harper & Row, 1981).

13. Caplan, *Barriers between Women*, 17.

# 8

## The Impact of Race and Culture Differences: Challenges to Intimacy in Lesbian Relationships

NORMA GARCIA, CHERYL KENNEDY,
SARAH F. PEARLMAN, AND JULIA PEREZ

This chapter is based on a transcript of a conversation between four women. Two are Puerto Rican, one is Jewish, and one is Irish-American. Three of the women are therapists, and the fourth, Cheryl, works in human services. Cheryl and Julia are lovers and live together with their three daughters. Sarah and Norma have recently become friends. Norma is also Julia's sister.

We hope that conversations like this can bring deeper understanding of the challenges and complexities of interracial relationships, an understanding that will be helpful to women in interracial relationships as friends and lovers, and also to therapists who may be working with women who are struggling with racial and cultural differences in their relationships.

The purpose of the conversation we present here is to discuss issues of race and culture that affect intimacy in lesbian relationships. Being a lesbian can and does offer multiple opportunities and challenges as well as difficulties. As a group we are enormously diverse, our one established similarity being our relationships and sexual choice. As lesbians we can have the opportunity to make contact with women who are different from ourselves in class, age, race, education, ability, and geographical background. While this diversity of experience can be greatly enriching and expanding, changing our thinking and our sense of the world and others, it is by no means a simple or uncomplicated matter.

In particular, interracial relationships confront and challenge our most racist selves, our stereotypes, assumptions, and prejudices toward those who are different. Although one's racist self may be not so much malicious as ignorant or insensitive, a woman who loves another who is racially different can cause particular hurts in the relationship. The white woman can experience pain because of self-consciousness and the shame of her racist ignorance and stereotypic thinking. She knows that at any point she can hurt her lover or friend with her multiple, often unwanted feelings and by what she can say, intended or unintended. The woman of color experiences pain in alternating layers of hurt and rage and knows that at any time the person closest can further open already raw wounds, that the person closest can also be the enemy. The woman of color is capable of hurting and retaliating through cultural insult.

To the extent that there are differences in culture, one's perspective on the world can change. Lack of familiarity with each other's cultural values and habits means that both women can be unpredictable to each other. What is humorous teasing to one woman can be insulting and offensive to the other. What is of concern to one may be nonsense to the other. Differences in attitudes towards money, child-rearing, expression of anger, and other feelings multiply the potential for conflict. What then becomes crucial is ongoing discussion and the deciphering of misunderstandings if the relationship is to remain successful and loving. Yet differences are also fascinating—and erotic and thrilling as each adapts to the other's ways, as a new culture of the particular relationship begins to flower with growing closeness and trust.

An interracial relationship entails a particularly painful struggle made evident during this conversation as the participants themselves confront cultural assumptions and values that lead to misunderstandings and anger. Moving past anger, the participants hope for connection, finally as woman to woman, as individuals clear and unclouded by the social poison that has affected us all. Beyond relationships between individual women is the issue of race and lesbian community, especially in communities like Boston that are deeply affected by antagonisms and separatisms among women of different races. These four women hope that conversations like the following are the beginning of a necessarily long and continuing process.

## The Conversation

*Sarah:* I'm white, Jewish, raised middle-class—actually more complicated than that. We were poor, but our values and assumptions were middle-class—particularly with regard to behavior—conforming to what was acceptable. This was very much my mother's influence, due to her experience as an immigrant child and her intense desire to assimilate and to have her children be acceptable in America. My grandparents had emigrated from Russia, and I had the wonderful opportunity of growing up within a Yiddish immigrant culture before Americanizing really diluted it. My sense of being Jewish—cultural, not religious—is very strong. My family is also biased and prejudiced against people who are not Jewish. There was always this tremendous distrust handed down because of experiences in Russia and during the war. They were and are terribly racist. One irony is that while I was brought up with the idea that Jews were special, there was a solid barrage of messages that being too Jewish wasn't good. Beauty was the American, or rather, WASP look—blonde, blue-eyed, thin—and the less Jewish you looked the better. The word is *shiksa*, and to be told you looked like a shiksa was the ultimate compliment. I early learned that I was not to be loud, that I should not appear cheap, and that my speech had to be free of Jewish intonation. Otherwise I would be kikey—be called a kike. In other words, I was to associate only with Jews, but be a non-Jewish Jew. Again, I see this as coming from my mother's experience, and it was a very misguided effort to protect us, since it also meant a lot of self-hating.

I grew up in a Christian neighborhood and really experienced very little anti-Semitism—or at least did not feel much affected. I had the typical experience of being told I killed Christ, and once, as the only Jew in a summer camp, was treated as something of a curiosity. My worst experience was (in the nineteen-fifties) not being able to find housing in Baltimore until my husband and I figured that we should use first names only. Then we found an apartment. I think I've done a lot of denying of the extent of anti-Semitism and how people feel about Jews, what people actually think of Jews. It's something that can hurt terribly.

I had black playmates when growing up, but in junior high and high school there was really this rule that blacks and whites could socialize in school but not outside. I had fights with my mother over this and thought she was a terrible hypocrite. But my protest was brief, and I was really caught up in dating and being popular; so I was a pretty unconscious kid. Later, in nursing school in New York in a Hispanic section, most of my patients were Puerto Rican. I visited their homes and became friendly with two families, so I had some experience and exposure to people of a culture different from my own.

Afterward, for the entire time I was married, my world was white and mostly Jewish, and I felt very limited and that this was not right. Later in St. Louis I really liked this black woman, and I think we could have become strong friends since there was a lot of mutual respect, but she felt very self-conscious that I was white, and our friendship stayed superficial. I'm in a relationship with a West Indian woman and am becoming friends with Norma. She and I see a lot of each other, so I think that I am just beginning to learn what interracial relationships mean and to take some hard looks at myself.

*Cheryl:* I'm a white working-class woman. I was born here in Cambridge and we lived in the projects until I was going into third grade. Then we moved to the suburbs, which were totally white. In the town I lived in, and on my street, the differences between people were who was Protestant and who was Catholic. I knew two Jewish kids in high school, and they were cousins. And there were three black kids that I knew in school, who were not related but all had the same last name. I remembered as a kid thinking how strange that was.

My mother's side of the family has been in this country for at least four generations. She identifies herself and all of us as American. My father's mother was an immigrant from Ireland; his father's family has been in this country two generations. But her influence caused him to be Irish-American identified. We always did big things on St. Patrick's day. I married, and within my marriage became a hippie and lived in Virginia in a very white world with the other white hippies. I moved back to Boston when I separated from my husband and still traveled in white circles. Came out as a lesbian with another white woman, lived in a group with only white women. Only white-skinned women.

I remember once when walking down the street in Dorchester, an obviously Irish-American man came up to me and made some remark about how it was good to see more of us in the neighborhood. All the busing was going on at the time along with racial trouble in South Boston, so it became less and less important to own any of my Irish heritage and more important not to have racism come near me because I had linked those two together! Irish-Americans are racist, I don't want to be a racist, therefore I totally stopped relating to that part of myself. I also totally stopped relating to my family. That was much more due to my separatist politics than anything else.

And then I met Julia, who I thought was a wonderful woman. Full of life, very caring, lots of energy, and she had a kid. At that time, I had two kids I was responsible for. That she was Puerto Rican was something that I knew in a very shallow way. I had no idea what that meant. I had some consciousness around getting into an interracial relationship, but based on what I know now I would say it was next to nothing, although at the time I probably would've said it was a lot. So that's where I began my relationship with Julia. On the other hand, Julia began her relationship with me with a lot of experience with interracial relationships.

*Norma:* Right. For minority, third-world, black, Hispanic, Puerto Rican women all our relationships are interracial relationships in terms of our contact with the outside world. My first awareness that being Puerto Rican might be bad was in first grade. I remember that my teacher did not like Puerto Ricans, but I did not know what that meant. I'm not too sure that I knew at age five what being Puerto Rican meant. But I knew I was Puerto Rican and she did not like Puerto Ricans, and that made me very quiet in her classroom. I was the first one to go to school from those of my family that were born here. I think I went to school not talking much English. I understood a lot of it, and I may have already started reading. My sister Julia took me to the library as soon as I could learn how to write, at four or five. So I was reading English and I was listening to it and I understood it, but I think I wasn't talking it much. This teacher definitely stopped me from talking at all in the first grade. In the second grade I think that changed for me. Also, I believe it was the first time I had some contact with people who were not in the family. My mother was very protective, because of the environment we grew up in. We lived in a very poor neighborhood in the South Bronx, and I think my mother's concern was that anything could happen outside. She was very frightened for us, which meant I didn't get to play outside, and there were a lot of rules. I didn't get to think, drink, smoke, breathe, anything. If you could think of a "don't do," my mother had it down to a T. I think some of that carries over with me with my son sometimes, but I try not to be protective of him in the way my mother was with me, because the environment he is growing up in is not the same that I grew up in. And so I have to catch myself. Sometimes my anxiety is out of proportion to what's going on in the environment. I think a lot of that anxiety comes from the early anxiety that my mother had about the environment.

I've described my first experiences. The one that stood out more later is the fact that as we were growing up my mother made us not talk Spanish to her anymore, because she saw that would hurt us in school. She would talk to us in Spanish, but we would always respond to her in English. That went on throughout my childhood and by the time I was twelve or thirteen and I wanted to know Spanish, my mother made fun of us speaking Spanish. We sort of lost it as kids and then were trying to gain it back. I think twelve or thirteen was the time when I was trying to gain back my language and my culture. There was more of a sense of my knowing that I was nonwhite, knowing that I was Puerto Rican, knowing that I needed that connection with my language.

I know that Mom was proud. Well, I don't know if she was necessarily proud of being Puerto Rican, I'm not too sure of that. My father was very anti-American, against American politics, American politics in Puerto Rico. His politics helped in defining us, at least for me, in the process of defining myself as being Puerto Rican. That's something that I had to come back to. I define myself as being nonwhite, and as a young person I identified much more strongly with being black. Then I started redefining myself as being a mix, redefining myself as having a lot of different things, of having a different experience of being Puerto Rican. At nineteen, part of that search made me go back to Puerto Rico.

I spent a year in Puerto Rico. I was reclaiming my roots. At the same time, I realized I'm not Puerto Rican like the island Puerto Rican. I'm Puerto Rican in my sense of being *here;* and I realized I was a Puerto Rican-American. My history, my struggle starts here, one of the Puerto Rican-Americans who's here and is not planning to go back to the island, who doesn't have that kind of connection to the island. I have roots and history and culture from there, but that's not where I would wind up. Yet I was being really caught up in wanting the island to be independent and wanting to have Puerto Ricans have control of their own lives. I realized that I did not live there, and I did not have the power to say something about that. But I can tell people here what happens to the island, the conditions of the island, the poverty, the way colonialism has really chewed up and fucked up the people on the island. It is a place that had its own problems, but in a way the Americans have done us in, and the people are exploited economically. I think that's where the roots of my nationalism and my politics are from. I feel growing up in the sixties during the civil rights movement gave me the sense of what it was to be proud of who I was. Through that struggle around class and nationalism came my feminism. So I think I started defining myself as a feminist when I was in my twenties.

*Sarah:* I'm interrupting. We really need to get back to the issue of women and interracial relationships. What I was struck by was both Cheryl and Norma saying that by being women of color, most of your relationships would be interracial —

*Norma:* Yes.

*Sarah:* — and that doesn't happen for a white person who can go her entire life and only know white people.

*Norma:* I think that you're right in pointing that out. That definitely is the case in truth all along.

*Sarah:* What about women friends?

*Norma:* My oldest friends have been Puerto Rican, have been black, have been Jewish, have been everything. The first woman I had feelings toward was this woman named Laura. I was going through my bisexual phase. She was, I would say, basically black, but one of those blacks who's been so mixed throughout their history in this country that they are like, everything? She was Creole and Madagascan and Trinidadian and French. She looked like me. She had long hair and looked like me. And yet there were differences because of her experiences. She was culturally a product of a lot of interracial mixtures. We would have these conversations about cousins of hers who were what she called *passant-blanc,* passing for white for generations. You know that they are your cousins, but you can't talk to them because you don't want to blow their cover of passing for white. We'd have conversations about what that meant to her, what not being able to identify totally as black because of her appearance yet not being able to identify as white. There's no category to even identify with here, in this country particularly, as mixed as she was.

*Cheryl:* You know, one of the things that strikes me is the lack of history of interracial relationships in this country. In general, there is an intense denial that interracial relationships exist. In fact, any racial mix at all and you're black.

*Norma:* One thing I know about our differences is that I had a sense of history and a culture and a connection, even though I was a product of a lot of mixtures of white and African black and Indian, that I had a history and culture which Laura did not have or had lost.

*Julia:* Not lost. Robbed. Assaulted, raped. She didn't lose it, she was robbed of it.

*Sarah:* I guess I'm still concerned we don't seem to be getting to the purpose of this conversation, and I'm wondering —

*Julia:* One of the things I'm feeling right now is that generally these types of conversations create an incredible amount of anger, because I think it's a very privileged kind of thing to say, "Let's sit here and let's get to the fact," when there are two things that happen. One is, you can sit there from a white woman's position and say this is the kind of thing I've run across about interracial relationships and this is how I grew up. But coming from a perspective of a person of color, there is so much pain that's involved in being dehumanized in this society, starting from going to the schools. You know, you walk out your door and it hits you. Sometimes, if you're in an interracial relationship, you don't have to even walk out your door for some kind of racist bullshit to hit you. Even to get in touch with those kinds of situations is hard, you have to kind of touch it a little bit so that you don't start beginning to feel the pain, and then after opening up we have to deal with it once you're gone.

Because I have to be honest and say that the worst form of racism that came at me was not from men, it was not from the whole social structure as it is, because it isn't the whole institution of racism and all that, but from people I trust, loved and cared for and knew: women. Feminists. Who thought that they had it so together on racism, who knew what it was like, who insulted me to my face and didn't know they were doing it. I see it happen in relationships. I've seen it happen in my relationship with Cheryl. It doesn't happen anymore with us because we really worked and struggled, and it's a motherfucker.

To make some kind of sense about what interracial relationships are, to be able to talk about it—even sitting in a room with two white women talking about it, even as close as we are, creates a problem that is not one we bring on but that is imposed on us. I've worked really hard many times not to see Cheryl as a white woman. But I've come home sometimes from a long stretch of work and that's who I see. I see something happening in the street and I come home, and I don't come home to a place where everybody looks like me. So sometimes you need time to sort it out because it's too much pain to be shared with someone you don't really know that well. I go to conferences and I see it happening all the time. White women come and they say, "We're open, let's talk about it, let's get it together, we have an hour." And then you see these women of color sitting around maybe days, days, in stirred up garbage. I'm sitting here and laying down that this is the kind of stuff that really pisses me off. Even thinking about being a kid in this country makes me want to go outside and beat somebody up. Maybe what you need to do is talk and then sort it out, and say, okay what is it we need to do? Okay, we need to talk about relationships with women. But I'll tell you something, some of the most vicious people I've met in this place are women. Because I trust women, I leave myself open to women. I don't leave myself open to men, I don't trust them.

You need two hours just to get down to it. And that's part of the cultural stuff, too. Our cultural stuff says we sit down, we have coffee, we eat, we sit down, we talk, we move . . . and American culture says, okay, we have a schedule, we have a time limit. And we live with that. We live with your culture. I know more about you than you know about me. Even your being Jewish I know more about. I'm sure you don't know about my culture as much as I know about yours, about my customs and about my holidays. Or Cheryl's. Because we have to know to survive. We never can operate in our time frame.

*Sarah:* Time frame?

*Cheryl:* You know, Julia and I stumbled across that early in our relationship. When we would get into discussions about something, and I would want it to be logical, precise, clear, short, stick to the facts, ma'am, and we would be rambling. And I would lose patience. And she would say, "Wait a minute! This is how I talk. This is me. I don't talk like you talk."

*Sarah:* It's true. I try to be direct, get right down to it, make things real clear. But you do a lot of talking wide, you divert and digress, and I have to stay with it. It's different.

*Cheryl:* It is. It's a cultural difference. That's one of the things that I learned. Julia talked about having to define herself better with me. In my ignorance I sat there demanding, absolutely demanding, "Listen, this is taking too long. How come you're off the subject? You're avoiding the issue." That was a good one, right? "You're avoiding the issue, you're not dealing with the situation." It really was not true.

*Julia:* I don't tolerate it, and I won't work on that time frame.

*Cheryl:* So one of the things about being in an interracial relationship is, your home is not a refuge. If you're like Julia and Norma, your home is not a refuge.

*Julia:* Another thing, people who learn how to speak Spanish, they have no concept of what the culture is—they learn the language but never the concept. I've seen women who've had relationships with a woman who speaks another language—they learn the language but they never learn what it means—and sometimes they think they speak the language better than you.

*Norma:* That's what privilege is. Having access to another person's language and thinking that's enough.

*Sarah:* I know I came in here in a rush and said okay, let's get right to it, without thinking through how much pain this would expose, and something that does help me understand is that I translate stuff into my own experience. If somebody said to me, "Okay, let's sit around for an hour and we'll talk about the Holocaust," I would go crazy. What I'm saying is, I've been having to deal with hurt, embarrassment and hurt, when I take in that I've been stupid and insensitive.

*Norma:* Okay, Listen, what I have learned was to adapt like crazy and to blatantly deny. That has even happened with lovers. I adapted.

I think that's the hardest part: looking at lesbian relationships and how we sometimes try to make us one with all those differences. I think some people just bury their heads in the sand rather than deal with them.

*Cheryl:* I remember an article by a black woman—it might have been Audrey Lorde—she was saying how in interracial relationships the woman of color always has to reinvent the pencil. And my reading that and knowing it was true, fundamentally knowing it was true and really wishing it wasn't. Really wishing that that was not something that I brought to my relationship with Julia. But I know that's something I have brought and continue to bring in different ways. Who wants to hear that this is a burden I bring to this relationship by my ignorance and my white skin privilege? There are give and takes in both directions, that's true. For a white woman to enter into an interracial relationship, there are a lot of risks taken. My family cares for Julia. They really care for her. But I know that if I was in a relationship with a white woman, when I go to my mother's house, I would not have some of the tension that I have now when I'm there, that someone is going to say something racist. Racism is no longer on a theoretical level for me. It's a very emotional issue. Even if it doesn't come in my direction, it comes in the direction of my family, Julia and our children, and that makes it a whole different issue for me.

*Julia:* One of the things that happens in the house, too, has to do with when we fight. We may be having a very reasonable argument, but I will not budge. What's behind my not budging is this: I already give so much of myself outside and I have to conform so much, and I have to live according to those rules, that when I'm in the house I don't want to have to do it anymore. So then Cheryl says to me, "Well, what about me?" And I say, "Who cares?" You know, sometimes it comes to the point of, "No, I am not going to do it your way." It may be a very reasonable request, but doing it her way is like everybody else's way out there.

*Cheryl:* And I have to learn to say in those situations, "Wait a minute. We have a commitment to an interracial relationship here. That means that some of that stuff, unfortunately, you have to leave at the door." And it's not enough for you to say to me, "Look, I have to deal with all those people out there and compromise myself, or not be totally who I am or have to deal with people who don't see me as who I am—"

*Julia:* So I don't want to have to deal —

*Cheryl:* —so I don't want to have to do it with you. And I've had to learn to say, "You know what? That is not always acceptable." I can understand what you're saying and I feel really badly that that's true. But on some issues between you and me, I've learned when I have to say, "I'm really sorry that's true. But this is between you and me." And this is one of the things it means to be in an interracial relationship. It means: yes, you do have to come home and face those things again. I hope in not the same insensitive way you face them other places. I hope I've gotten enough education around racism and culture that it won't be to the same extent. It doesn't mean I don't have my slips, it doesn't mean I'm not capable of saying the wrong thing. It doesn't mean I don't feel hurt when I'm confronted with it. I mean I feel like a piece of shit. When I'm confronted by someone I care about saying to me, "Cheryl, listen to what you just said. Think about that. You have enough information to think about that." And I sit there and think about it and it's true and then I think, "Oh God." Getting stuck in that place saying "Oh God" keeps it from moving. Because I was capable of setting up a little dynamic of feeling guilty. Then saying, "You know what? I'm really sorry." Owning it myself, having my own process around it, talking about it with my white women friends, and being able to deal with it. But necessarily working it out with Julia because it's not fair. It's just not fair.

Really, the issues in an interracial relationship are complicated on a day-to-day basis. And with kids, when you have interracial kids in the same household, it is even more complicated.

*Julia:* I knew this white woman who believed that in her previous life she was a Caribbean goddess. What a trip! She was in a relationship mostly with women of color, mostly black women, and she would say that she had this affinity for women of color, and it was because in her previous life she was one.

*Cheryl:* Basically, I felt she thought she was no damn good. The only place she could feel superior to anybody was in a relationship with somebody of color. But what is true is that as white people we are taught racism right from the start. To me, it's like a bag I have. I have this bag of racist thoughts and I can, at any given moment, in anger, when I feel pushed, when I feel fearful, when I feel in any way under stress, I can reach into that bag and pull out something to address that, if one of the feelings I have is directed towards or around a person of color.

*Sarah:* I remember this woman telling me that she had this lineage of family-over-on-the-Mayflower. She said that when she felt at all vulnerable about herself she would think that the other person was Jewish or was working class, and she would think that to get herself to feel better. I've never heard anybody be so out front with something like that. I never dreamed that people would do that so self-consciously. I think that men probably do that with women.

*Cheryl:* I'm sure.

*Sarah:* What I was very aware of, at the beginning of one relationship, was how visible I felt with her. And I was aware of the whole idea of being with a black woman. When we would walk down the street, I felt that it was like wearing placards that said "lesbian." And that was very unsettling. I had such self-consciousness. She and I were able to talk about it some, but it was also very fortunate that I knew other lesbians in interracial relationships who understood.

So anyway, there was this real uncomfortable self-consciousness, not so much in the gay bars, but certainly out on the street. With one of my lovers, I had this delusion. Her family was quite well off. And I had this delusion that with my family, that my being coupled with her might eventually—and this is the classism—make my lesbianism acceptable. She was sort of like everything that my family would've wanted their children to be. This was really delusional thinking. And so, with this black woman, it was like thinking that there it goes— this fantasy. I knew that there was no way my family would accept my being a lesbian if I was with a black woman. Their acceptance was something I would have to give up. I was on my own.

*Cheryl:* You blew it.

*Sarah:* Yeah.

*Cheryl:* Because now you just crossed that line. Ah-ah-ah.

*Sarah:* And I really had to face that.

*Julia:* If you get into a relationship with a white woman, you could probably live any way you choose, you could just come and go as an adult. But it becomes an issue between the two of you if she wants to live somewhere, then you need to think where is this that she wants to move.

*Norma:* Well, when I moved west, the lover I was with found this place in a working-class neighborhood, predominantly white, a southern workingclass neighborhood that if we walked out the door we would pray for our fucking lives.

*Cheryl:* So white women get into relationships with women of color and they say, "Hey, let's go to this restaurant, it's really great." Well, is that restaurant a safe place to go to? Is that bar a safe place to go to? Is that neighborhood a safe place to go to?

Going to beaches is another place. And it really brings a point to me about homophobia versus racism. I feel as a lesbian I can go with a white lesbian lover to any beach. Maybe there'll be some harassment. I don't really fear for my life, or I don't fear for her life. When I was in the relationship with this white woman, we went everywhere. I'm not a very affectionate person in public anyway, but anyone who was cued into the possibility of women together being lesbians would know she and I were, but I felt safe going places.

We go to the beach now, and we have to think, "Is this a safe beach for us?" Last year they beat up a Puerto Rican man at Revere Beach with a fucking tire iron! We don't go to Revere Beach this year. And you know what? That's an easy beach for us to get to. We used to be able to just hop on the train. That's not a risk we're willing to pay for now.

*Julia:* And you could easily go to Revere Beach by yourself.

*Cheryl:* Hey, I could go to Revere Beach in a moment and I'd have no problems.

*Julia:* It was like when we went to western Massachusetts, we were there for two days. I just wanted to see one person who was brown or dark brown or light. I didn't see anybody. And then one day, we went to the movies, and there was this black couple with kids, and I looked at them, and I just grinned at them and wanted to say: "Hi! How are you!" They looked at me like I was odd. Because they probably said, "That woman is very strange, she doesn't know who we are and she's already grinning at us." I felt so glad to see somebody, I mean, you do become self-conscious after a while if you're in a place where you never see anybody who looks like you.

And then I will say, I hate this country, I hate this country, I want to go back to Puerto Rico, that's what I want to do, I hate it, I hate it, I hate it.

*Norma:* You feel like you're in the zoo.

*Cheryl:* Or you get looks. I have got looks from people that are so clearly on their face, "What are you doing with that woman?" Nothing said, but it looks like, you know, you could do better.

*Julia:* In Puerto Rico the situation is you can be all colors, that's the situation. That doesn't mean there isn't racism for them, there is. We have this expression: *Pelo malo o pelo bueno*—"A good hair and a bad hair." That stuff around good hair and bad hair reflects a lot of the internal racism. At the same time, we use *negrita* as an affectionate term. So there's this contradiction in terms of how some of that plays out within the culture.

*Cheryl:* Well, right, I can remember the first time Julia said to me *negrita*. And it was like, "Oh my God!" I did not know what to do. I knew from what she was saying it was affectionate. But there was this feeling that that does not belong to me, this is wrong. She should not use that word to me. And I said, "Wait a minute, how can you do that?" Julia said, "Hey, it has nothing to do with that. It's an affectionate term. It means I care for you. It means honey, sweetheart, it doesn't have to do with color." But to me, it was like, wait a minute, something's really wrong here. And I did not want to accept it. It felt to me that I was overstepping my bounds. I was accepting something I should not accept.

*Sarah:* One of my most alienating experiences was living in a small town where there were very few Jews. Christmas was the most difficult time — the entire town was lights and wreaths and trees . . . it was like living in the middle of a Christmas card. I remember being very, very depressed around that Christmas and a friend said to me, "Maybe you should go out of the house. Why don't you go caroling?"

You know, it was the worst thing that she could've said. It wasn't malicious, just insensitive, out of ignorance.

*Cheryl:* I think with Jews it's really a different experience. Because you're white-skinned, but there's a level where you're no different than I am. So, you get into thinking you have a privilege but —

*Sarah:* You deny it.

*Julia:* You deny it, you absolutely deny that when they come to get us, they'll get you too.

*Sarah:* My level of denial about the way people feel about Jews is unbelievable. I remember watching television and hearing Jews talked about as a different race. I never thought I was a different race.

*Julia:* The reality is here that anybody that they see as different is going to be another race, but you do have privilege.

*Sarah:* What I was taught is that Jews were special and that I shouldn't associate with anybody that wasn't a Jew. And never ever — it was absolutely forbidden that you should ever marry a non-Jew. That was as if in my bones. But on the other hand, half the girls I knew had their noses fixed. Remember we talked about hair? In a Jewish home, you never have a Jewish home without tweezers. Because you get rid of all the hair so you could look more American. Jews are hairy. There were so many messages that we weren't okay the way we were. Everything had to be shaved, plucked, your nose fixed, hair dyed, I'm not kidding, you have no idea of the issue around hair in my family. My mother had facial hair which she bleached. We did all that to be made into a marketable American.

*Julia:* It's a fact that anti-Semitism equaled color. I know that was something I had to struggle with, myself. When I first came here there was this woman who I particularly hated. She happens to be a disgusting human being. She could do anything, she could be any color, she still would be disgusting.

So, the first thing that came up to my head was she was Jewish. And it had to do with the fact that when I was growing up, our immediate oppressors were Jewish.

*Norma:* The landlords?

*Julia:* Right, the landlords.

*Cheryl:* But the only man who gave Julia a job in Florida was a Jewish man.

*Norma:* There was this Italian woman that I met in California whom I liked a lot. Who liked me a lot. She told me that for someone who was Puerto Rican, I was very nice. I was an exception to whatever her rule was. And there was no way to get through to the rule. And she always treated me . . . decently. But I always had to deal with her racism. It was constant.

*Julia:* We were exceptions. That was what it was like to her.

*Norma:* And that has happened to me often. Of being the exception.

*Julia:* You have a conference? You have a woman of color come— she covers the range of women of color. All that color represented in that one woman. [laughter]

*Cheryl:* But talk about built-in stress in a relationship. All the other million stresses you can have between two women, put two women of different cultures and/or different races together, and you have built-in stresses. Add kids to it, and you multiply those stresses by ten.

You know what stress we didn't talk about? That's the stress of I have to be careful who I go to when I have a problem with you. And you have to be careful of who you go to when you have a problem with me.

*Julia:* That's true.

*Cheryl:* I have to know if the person I go to for support is going to be paying attention to any racism they may catch me in, and any racism that they come up with, and be fair in an exchange. Julia has to be careful that it's someone who supports the idea of an interracial relationship, someone who will be honest with her about her role in the particular disagreement and not just come down on me. We have really had to sort out who we go to when we each need to go to someone else, and how carefully we have to make those choices. I would be a liar if I sat here and said there weren't times when in the beginning I wasn't tempted to go to someone I knew would say Julia was wrong. So you have to be careful where you go for support.

*Julia:* When you go for support, you don't know what that particular person's issues are. Race or culture—I've had women say to me, oh God, how can you sleep with a white woman? I lay down and I spread my legs, you know? You do it with a white woman like you do it with any other woman. I used to be invited to places where Cheryl wouldn't be invited. So you know what? I didn't go. Cheryl can't go, I don't go. You know, people say to me, oh, you have no sense of community. Bullshit. My community is my home. That's my community. I carry it with me, you either like it or you don't like it. I'm not going to become a member of some community in Dorchester or Jamaica Plain or Cambridge or anywhere else because you happen to be the same color as me.

*Cheryl:* And yet there's no way that you can go in there knowing enough. I think there's no way a white woman can go into an interracial, intercultural relationship and have enough information. There's no way. Not unless she's already had twenty years with a woman of the same racial and cultural background before. Knowing from my perspective that I'm the one who's going to blow it, I'm the one who's going to learn at Julia's expense. I don't want to do that and yet, that's how it works.

*Sarah:* It makes for a real self-consciousness, which is terrible.

*Cheryl:* Yup.

*Norma:* Because then you can't be yourself with anybody—

*Cheryl:* That's right. It can be every conversation you have, you're preoccupied with "Am I hearing this right? Am I going to say the wrong thing? What's the right thing to say?" You can't be doing all that and still be giving the person that you're with a hundred percent. You know? Already it's an interference before you even open your mouth. If you've gotten to a place where you are so self-conscious, then you're not being there the way you want to be there. Because you're half someplace else.

*Sarah:* That's what beginnings are like.

*Cheryl:* Yeah. That is the beginning. And then the next place is to know, yes, I am going to blow it. Because that's who I am. And I'm going to try my hardest not to do it, to educate myself. Then the next place for me was to feel really sad about the times when I blew it and I would hurt someone I cared about. And there was no way that I could make it different. Because the only other way I could try to make it different would be to take that step back, to become so self-conscious again. You work on paying attention to what's going on, and you work at getting yourself as much of an education as you can get, and then knowing you're going to blow it again, and you really hope you don't, you really hope it's not the most horrendous thing, and you're going to cause people pain. And you cause yourself pain in the process.

*Julia:* There's another issue too that bothers me sometimes in terms of respect. We have to respect each other and then be able to move to hear what people say. Sometimes, I've seen white women who will take all kinds of disrespect and feel that it's okay because it's a woman of color, and "I'm so racist anyway that she has a right to treat me that way."

*Sarah:* That's the liberal guilt.

*Julia:* Right. I'm of the opinion that no one has the right to treat you in a disrespectful manner, no matter who you are. There are some ways that you don't let *anybody* talk to you. And if it's a woman who is white and you're white, and she talks to you that way, you'll say, "Wait a minute. Why are you treating me this way?" "Well, I may have done something that's racist." "That's true, you may have." But you still want within that relationship to be really respected. Lots of times in our relationship I want Cheryl to respect me, so therefore I in turn feel like I must respect her, and what her belief system is. That doesn't mean that I'm going to permit her to do really disgusting things to me. And I don't want her to let me do disgusting things to her.

*Sarah:* A fight I had with one particular lover was over negative remarks about white people—white men. She'd call them white boys. Finally I had to say to her that she couldn't do that because I'm white. She would then say that I didn't understand white man's privilege. I understand white men's privilege, but I couldn't let her do that. One thing that was helpful was that my daughter was in an interracial relationship. It's strange how mothers and daughters get reversed. We talked about this, and she said that she had big fights with her boyfriend because she was white, and he couldn't go around saying that stuff about white people in front of her. This also can happen when the person is angry for other reasons.

*Norma:* You can't use color as name-calling. No matter what direction it goes.

*Julia:* Although it's an easy thing to do.

*Sarah:* I understand what's been done to people of color by white people, but when you're in an interracial relationship you're not free to be out with your anger that way with the other person.

*Cheryl:* I remember what felt to me to be a real risk-taking and turning point for me in terms of that particular struggle. Something happened for Julia; she came in, and she was not wanting to work something out between the two of us because of something that happened outside. I was finally feeling safe enough and strong enough to take the risk to say, "You can't do that here in that way." Before that I wouldn't have taken that risk, I would've taken what Julia had to say. But on this particular issue it was important enough for me to stand there and say, "Wait a minute. I'm real sorry, but you have a commitment to this relationship and that means dealing with me. And I'm really sorry about other stuff that's happened, but what can I say?" And that felt very much like a turning point for me. And a turning point for us, that we could have that kind of conversation.

*Julia:* Places I've been to, the kind of people I've worked with, they say really racist things, and I come back home, and I don't have any place to go with it. You know? And it's not like I can even vent it, and say, "Oh those fucking white assholes." And get really disgusting as I want to get. I'd be letting it out at Cheryl. So then what happens is that some little incident might happen in the house that would be insignificant and I would just blow up. And make it a racial incident. Even if it isn't. Or I sometimes have the feeling of just sort of not wanting to be around any other human being. And sometimes the only human being I want to see is another Puerto Rican. Or I don't want to see anybody. I don't want anything that requires me to think, feel, or react to anything. It's like overkill.

*Cheryl:* Talking about the similarities and differences, I remember when I first began my relationship with Julia, when I heard from some white women that they were very angry with me, that I would be so arrogant as to think that I as a white woman would have *anything* to offer a woman of color. Anything. They were just totally put out that I would think that there was anything that could exist between us where I could also give. That was where I got my initial disapproval. From white women friends.

*Sarah:* I had just the opposite experience. It was racism in its opposite form. Any time I introduced a friend to a black woman, they would tell me how wonderful she was. It's not that I doubted her personableness. It was too fast to get the sense of anybody as wonderful. And it was like their way of saying how—

*Julia:* —accepting they were.

*Sarah:* Initially, I felt very good. Then I thought, this is too weird, this is too repetitive.

*Cheryl:* Now I'm going to say something different. And that is I think interracial relationships are very high and very wonderful. My life feels much more rich than it's ever been before; I have much more understanding not only of Julia and some understanding of her culture, but more understanding of myself. I feel like my daughter's life is much more enriched than my life was.

*Julia:* We are all getting the goodies of learning there are different ways to do different things, learning not to be judgmental, learning to try to pay attention to differences, and the kids are learning that young.

*Cheryl:* We're learning it, but you know, this is the best my life has ever been. With the struggles that there are, this is really the best my life has ever been.

*Julia:* Sarah, your relationships with women of color have been a real catalyst that set you thinking about some of the issues that create the pain.

*Sarah:* I know I felt a lot of things that I didn't like about myself in some relationships. What I have to count on is I think I'm a good person. I may do things I don't mean, do shit, but I have a basic belief in myself. So okay, I feel this, I know this, now what's the next step.

*Julia:* And we all want to be good girls. We all want to be nice girls.

*Cheryl:* But we also need to have these conversations because we do start out wanting to be good, not wanting to have any of that shit fall on us, and already know we have it, and you don't want to hurt somebody else.

*Julia:* You don't want to be called racist.

*Cheryl:* That's right. No one wants to be called racist. There need to be more conversations just among white women about what these things mean to us. What does it mean to have someone call you on your racism? What does it mean to sit there and suddenly realize that you have said something that is at least inappropriate, and at most downright offensive. And you didn't mean it, you didn't mean for it to mean what you said. But in your ignorance you did it, and you can't take your words back because they're there. And how do you deal with that? White women need to come together to talk about that kind of stuff to give ourselves strength. We really need to, we white women, we need to have a lot more conversations about these processes and how we work it out. And take the heat off the individual relationship in those ways too.

# 9

# The Effects of Women's Socialization on Lesbian Couples

SUE VARGO

The past fifteen years have produced a store of theory and research by authors including Carol Gilligan, Jessie Bernard, Cecilia Foxley and others who, inasmuch as the writings represent a departure from traditional psychological thought about women, can be called a "new psychology of women."[1] The strength of these new ideas is that they are based on research and thinking that assumes women to be different from men rather than defective men. However, their weakness from a lesbian point of view is that women and their contexts are largely assumed to be heterosexual. The purpose of this chapter is to see if some of these new ideas about female psychological functioning can explain dynamics of lesbian couples seen in treatment. Specifically, the literature suggests that socialization strongly affects the formation of female identity and shapes relational processes between women and others by influencing women to behave in certain ways. Dynamics between two women in an intimate relationship should be affected by the self-images and relational patterns being influenced by socialization.

Recent thinking about the socialization of women and its psychological implications rests on earlier research about sex-role stereotypes. Well before the writings considered the new psychology of women, the Brovermans' groundbreaking study of mental health workers' clinical judgments demonstrated the existence of gender-identified standards of psychological functioning.[2] This study showed that standards of mental health are influenced by stereotypes of masculinity and femininity. Behaviors judged psychologically healthy for men — competitiveness, assertiveness, aggressiveness — are judged psychologically unhealthy when observed in women. These male behaviors are also the standard for normal adult behavior. Thus, women are caught in a bind: Normal adult behavior is inappropriate because it is seen as male, whereas acting like women—being unassertive, interdependent, and concerned with others' well-being—is by definition unhealthy. In short, women cannot see themselves as both female and healthy at the same time.

Some of the new psychology's discussion of socialization builds on the double bind recognized in the Broverman study by adding the idea that women's socialization, not their intrinsic psychological makeup, is responsible for many behaviors associated with femaleness.[3] If women behave in dependent, unassertive, or other-oriented ways, it may be because they have been socialized to behave in those ways, and not because they are innately dependent, unassertive, and so forth. Combining this idea with the Brovermans' finding about standards of mental health yields the notion that behaviors previously thought to show both femaleness and psychological pathology may be learned behaviors that tell us nothing about femaleness or about psychological health in women.

If previously held notions about women's psychological makeup were distorted by overlooking the process of socialization, how can we understand female psychology as it is affected by socialization? Carol Gilligan's study of women's moral development begins to identify female psychological processes that are a complex interplay of socialization and some real differences from men.[4] Gilligan argues that women have different but equally healthy ways of performing basic psychological tasks. She suggests that women create self-image differently than do men, and that the difference in self-image is then reflected in female interpersonal processes such as conflict resolution.

Are these ideas about how women are socialized, how women's behavior has been judged psychologically and societally, and how all that influences the creation of self-image and relationship, relevant to lesbian couple dynamics, or are they heterosexist? To begin to answer that question, I will look at lesbian identity formation and the effects of socialization on lesbian couples through the new perspectives described, by using as examples couples from my clinical practice to explain familiar lesbian couple dynamics. These couples were having difficulty resolving normal developmental issues that many lesbian couples resolve without the aid of couples' therapy.

## Lesbian Identity Formation

In reviewing what the literature says about women and socialization, one sees a picture emerge of women caught in a conflict between behaving in gender-appropriate ways or being gender inappropriate in the interests of forming a positive self-image.[5] In general, women are taught to be dependent and passive, to seek attention and approval from other people, and to attend to and respond to the needs of others. We are taught that to be other-oriented, unassertive, and caretaking of others is to be appropriately female. We are also taught that self-assertion and a priority of self over others are appropriately male, not female, behaviors. Simultaneously, we experience the one-down status of women in relation to men.[6] We learn that female behavior and characteristics are less valued than their male counterparts and that individuals who behave in female ways, whether they are male or female, behave in culturally devalued ways.

The bind, then, is that to be gender appropriate, women must behave in ways identified with a one-down status; accepting that status makes the development of a positive self-image difficult, if not impossible. Women have had a wide range of responses to this dilemma, all of which have profound consequences on sense of self. Some women accept the definition as one-down and suffer from low self-esteem and depression; some attempt to redefine their position in society by glorifying traditionally female roles. Some women compete with men to be first-class citizens, with varying degrees of success and mixed effects on their self-esteem.

Lesbians do not escape the major themes of female socialization in that as women we are trained to different degrees to be other-oriented, dependent, and passive rather than self-assertive.[7] However, lesbians start at a different point in the process of resolving the conflict between being gender appropriate and having a positive self-image. Lesbians are already being seriously gender inappropriate in their sexual preference for other women. Their positive self-image cannot come only from gender appropriateness—it has to involve a positive valuing of gender inappropriateness if they are to value their lesbianism.[8]

In the process of incorporating lesbianism into self-image, lesbians may suffer from gender confusion and isolation as they experience themselves as having "male" traits, as being "exceptional" women, as being crazy, or at the very least as being different from other women in some fundamental way. How individual lesbians resolve their self-image in terms of seeing themselves as male or female varies immensely in terms of individual psychologies, norms of their immediate community be it heterosexual or gay, and their socioeconomic situations. Lesbians living in feminist and well-supported gay communities may arrive at a more radical vision of self that includes a positive sense of choosing a blend of so-called male and female behaviors for self.[9]

Some of the literature on lesbian couples speaks directly to the issues created by lesbians' struggles to value a gender-inappropriate self in a larger context where women and homosexuality are both devalued. Dorothy Riddle and Barbara Sang write about the stress that lesbian couples experience from homophobia in the workplace.[10] Fears about losing jobs or alienating colleagues because of their homosexuality often have to be dealt with in lesbian couples' relationships. Negativity and doubt about the relationship are inspired by others' homophobia, compounding the internalized homophobia of the couple. Especially where couples lack lesbian support systems, the relationship becomes the only arena in which to resolve doubts and deal with others' disapproval.

Riddle and Sang, and Laura Nemeyer as well, discuss the effects of a negative self-image on intimate relationships.[11] They feel that lesbians have to go through a process of rejecting society's stigmatization of homosexuality, both in terms of others' reactions to them and in terms of their own internalized negative judgments. Failure to work through to an acceptance of one's lesbianism is also the failure to achieve a positive self-image. Riddle and Sang and Nemeyer describe the effects of a negative self-image on intimate relationships as including denial of feelings, denial of the meaning or existence of relationships, and venting of internalized homophobia or misogyny of women partners.

In one couple I saw in treatment, Nancy and Lynn, these dynamics were overt. Nancy repeatedly distanced herself in the relationship, seemed to have problems trusting Lynn, and alternately denied Lynn's positive feelings for her and devalued the relationship. Discussion revealed that although Nancy loved Lynn, she wished that Lynn were a man and eventually said, "I love you, but I can't be a lesbian." Her internal image of lesbianism was so negative that she could not commit herself to Lynn, and she projected her negativity onto Lynn in the form of Lynn's suspected lack of commitment. Lynn's reassurance and promises of commitment or good behavior had no effect, because Nancy was stuck in issues of self-image. Until she could see her involvement with Lynn, and therefore her intimate and sexual self, in a positive way, the couple's dynamics could not change. Couples' interventions aimed at the distance regulation mechanisms within the couple could not alter Lynn's and Nancy's roles as pursuer and distancer. Work on Lynn's and Nancy's relationship could not succeed until Nancy resolved her fears about identifying as lesbian.

A second couple's difficulties show the effects of negative self-image and the destructiveness of homophobia on lesbian relationships that Riddle and Sang describe. Liz complained that Carole wasn't affectionate enough, whereas Carole complained that Liz was over-critical of their relationship, which Liz hid from colleagues at work. Sessions showed that Liz and Carole did not identify as lesbians, and thought that coming out to straight friends or work associates would cost them jobs and friendships. As both women explored and let go of their negative attitudes toward lesbianism, identification as lesbians increased, they sought out other lesbians, and began to come out to friends. Along with these changes came spontaneous displays of af-fection by Carole and a lessening of Liz's criticism of their relationship. Changing their attitudes and behavior about being seen as lesbians brought an increase in feelings for each other and an affirmation of their relationship. As both women built positive lesbian self-images, ambivalence about their relationship lessened and conflict decreased.

## Socialization's Effects on Lesbian Couples

Other researchers and theorists concerned with lesbian couples describe dynamics that relate to ways in which women are socialized. Jo-Ann Krestan and Claudia Bepko discuss the issue of fusion in lesbian re-lationships, defined as the blurring of boundaries between two women such that each identifies with the others' interests as much as with her own.[12] In a fused couple, confusion ensues concerning which person is being threatened or helped by a given circumstance or action, and therefore which person has what kinds of feelings about the situation. Such confusion between two individuals has been seen as indicative of individual pathology, but the occurrence of fusion in a lesbian re-lationship may have to do with the socialization and identity-building processes both women have experienced. If being female has meant attending to others, maintaining a caretaking attitude toward others, and not asserting one's individual needs, as the new literature on women suggests, then two individuals following those rules together may well become involved in a circular process of orienting self toward the other. That two women in a relationship may consider their own and the other's interests in maintaining the relationship could well be the result of successful socialization and not indicative of any individual pathology. Therapeutic work on fusion issues with a lesbian couple will look very different if it is based on an understanding of these dynamics common to women, rather than a hypothesis about the in-dividuals' ego weaknesses or hypotheses about communication patterns in the couple.

Terri and Maggie came to couples' therapy after three years of being together. For each, it was their first relationship with a woman. They had spent the great majority of their time together since they became involved and were now living together. They worked separately, but they knew and socialized with the same friends, knew each others' families, and were as involved as they could be in each others' work lives. When asked about the complaints that brought them to therapy, Terri tended to speak for Maggie and vice versa; it was often difficult to tell who was unhappy about a particular issue. Neither would admit to anger about anything, and neither would make a demand on the other. Problems remained vague and relatively emotionless until we were able to unravel each of their concerns for the other person relative to each issue. It became clear that each woman had an elaborate mental construction of what the other person felt about a given issue and based their own position on trying to take the other person's interests into account.

Terri knew that Maggie felt guilty about not visiting her mother as frequently as her mother wanted, and felt that Maggie wanted support for trying to stay away from her mother. In therapy, Terri presented Maggie's issue with her mother by talking about how much she supported Maggie's independence from her family. This presentation completely masked Terri's affection for Maggie's mother and her own wish to visit Maggie's family. Maggie, of course, received both messages about staying away from and about visiting her mother, and endless conflict ensued whenever plans to visit Maggie's family came up. Because Terri felt that Maggie disliked the visits because of Maggie's uncomfortable relationship with her mother, she tried to limit visits to Maggie's family. Neither of them communicated these constructions to each other, nor did they recognize that they seemed to be acting on the other's behalf rather than on their own.

Both women came from large families with one parent in some way unavailable as a caretaker, and both had had a lot of practice in putting their siblings' interests first. Both had been punished for being assertive and rewarded for sensitivity to others' needs. Both found the process of asserting their needs within the relationship to be awkward, inappropriate, and to feel masculine. Practice at identifying their own interests and negotiating for them brought clarity to their relationship and allowed them to pursue their differing needs. The results were widespread, including the creation of time away from each other and the disappearance of some of their initial complaints upon entering therapy, such as feeling bored and unsexual with each other. Couples' interventions that tried to increase their communication with each other did not succeed until their individual issues with revealing their own needs were resolved.

This case also demonstrates the identity confusion described by Riddle and Sang.[13] They see lesbians as experiencing identity confusion when they adopt "male" traits such as self-assertion in their work and personal lives. Other people's reactions to their violations of sex-role stereotypes are stressful and make assertion harder because they are treated as being inappropriate. Terri and Maggie both found it unsettlingly "male" to be more assertive with each other until they had experimented with assertiveness and found it to be productive, and accepted it as appropriate female behavior through modeling by their therapist and direct discussion of the issue.

### Socialization Reworked

Letitia Ann Peplau and her colleagues did research about the attitudes of lesbians in coupled relationships toward "attachment" and "autonomy," which were posed as two traditionally gender-linked opposites.[14] "Attachment," defined as needs for intimacy, dependence, and orientation toward others was seen as opposing "autonomy," defined as independence, self-assertion, and the drive for self-actualization. The lesbians in the Peplau study did experience a conflict between needs for security and emotional closeness and needs for self-actualization, but the research of Peplau and her group finds that lesbians see these two sets of behaviors not as mutually exclusive ends of a continuum but as necessary parts of a balance to be maintained. Their research subjects' struggle shows that lesbians in the study chose what could be called a more androgynous set of behaviors to meet their own needs for intimacy and autonomy. Peplau's subjects' preference for a balance of intimate and autonomous behaviors suggests a different sense of self. These women had a sense of an autonomous self within the assumption of relationship to others, rather than a self that chose autonomy or intimacy.

Accepting this perspective on self means a different assumption about the source of dysfunction in a lesbian couple. Issues around intimacy and autonomy might be resolved not by lessening one person's attachment or the other's distance in the relationship, but by helping each individual to balance her needs for intimacy and autonomy. Given the socially created link between autonomy and maleness and intimacy and femaleness, individuals might be expected to be acting out imbalance through gender-linked areas of their lives together and to experience a rebalancing of needs for intimacy and autonomy as involving ideas about maleness and femaleness.

Sara and Bonnie came to couples' therapy complaining about conflicts that centered on Sara's "overdependence" on Bonnie. Bonnie's definition of the problem was in fact that Sara was overinvolved in the relationship and depended on her for too much. Sara's complaint, although it was less strongly asserted than Bonnie's, was that Bonnie was distant and rejecting.

In talking about their relationship on a relatively mundane level—who went grocery shopping, cleaned the house, paid the bills, got the car fixed—we discovered that they had a breakdown of labor strikingly reminiscent of traditional heterosexual relationships. As they saw it, Bonnie did all the "masculine" things concerned with bills and cars and other mechanical things, while Sara did all the "feminine" things concerned with creating a home, buying food, and taking care of health issues. Bonnie also advised Sara on how to advance her career, while Sara helped Bonnie understand her feelings. Both women openly appreciated the other's help, but there was also an agreement that what Bonnie knew about was more important than what Sara knew about—an agreement consistent with society's valuing of "male" abilities over "female" abilities. Bonnie's rationality and pragmatic knowledge was seen as more useful and desirable than Sara's emotional skills. They saw the problems between them as resulting from Sara's dependence on Bonnie to help her deal with issues concerning jobs and finances and as focused on Bonnie's resentment and Sara's insecurity. Efforts by both of them to counter this imbalance tended to collapse when Bonnie became unhappy about something, at which point Sara dropped her own agenda and helped Bonnie feel better.

This couple had not reached the balance described in Peplau's research, where each partner pursued a balance between emotional closeness within the relationship and self-actualization in the world. Sara was responsible for closeness, and Bonnie for success in the world. When we began to discuss these responsibilities directly, both women shared resentments about being stuck in these roles, including feelings about being ascribed other gender-appropriate characacteristics (for example, passivity for Sara, stoicism for Bonnie). They redefined their problem as a couple as each having to balance what they called male and female behaviors. Bonnie needed to become more skillful in emotional areas, and Sara more skillful at managing in the world. Sara also needed to be more assertive in the relationship, and Bonnie needed to take Sara into account more when making practical decisions that would affect them both. As they worked at these tasks, Bonnie's insecurity about her emotional capabilities became accessible along with Sara's already acknowledged fears about her practical abilities. Blaming Sara's "overdependence" was replaced by a valuing of each woman's strengths and a lessening of gender-appropriate stereotyping in their serious conversations and their humor.

## A Female Process of Conflict Resolution

The couples' literature and cases I have discussed so far relate to what the new literature says about women and socialization, including women's need to address the devaluation of "female" traits and behaviors and the effects of redefining the range of potential female characteristics to include traditionally male traits. Carol Gilligan's work on the moral development of women moves in another direction.[15] Gilligan suggests that women have a sense of self which, in contrast to male and traditional psychological models of self, is embedded in relationships. Women's self-image comes in part from their relationships with others. Preservation of self and positive self-image involves preservation of relationship. How women handle interpersonal conflict thus involves a different set of psychological priorities than those involved for men. Gilligan feels that in contrast to the typically male mode of conflict resolution, which she describes as the application of moral principles to situations in order to produce right/wrong judgments, women take into account the particular people involved in a situation. Women resolve conflict by assessing the needs and vulnerabilities of the people involved in the conflict and seeking the solution that involves the least damage to individuals and their relationships. A consequence of using the female mode of conflict resolution is that the relationship between the individuals in conflict tends to be preserved, because one or more members take responsibility for the effects of their actions on the other people involved. Choices to resolve conflict are made not just from the viewpoint of an individual woman's needs, but from her efforts to be responsive to others' needs as well. One result is that women's individual needs suffer whenever others involved in the conflict are perceived to be more vulnerable or more in need than self.

Mary Mendola's survey of lesbian couples provides a collection of couples' portraits.[16] Contained in the portraits are accounts of conflict resolutions around a frequently occurring issue for lesbians: sexual monogamy. Mendola's couples all address the issue in some way, but each couple seems to have an ideosyncratic solution to the issue, ranging from sexual monogamy within the couple, to a primary sexual relationship with other relationships acceptable, to an asexual primary relationship. Applying Gilligan's model of women's conflict resolution to these couples' conflicts around sexuality reveals that their solutions follow a pattern. The couples involved seem to have made an assessment of their individual needs and ability to respond to those needs, and evolved a solution that respected both individuals' needs and maintained the relationship—just as Gilligan's model suggests they would do. Understanding how each couple's sexual agreements function is a lot easier if their conflict-resolution process is examined, including their assessments of each other's needs and strengths.

Many lesbian couples come to couples' therapy complaining of an unsatisfactory sexual relationship. Practitioners may interpret lesbians' sexual issues as problems of overattachment, overdependence, inability to express anger or tolerate conflict—in short, as failures of individual women to achieve sexual intimacy.[17] If, however, practitioners accept a different view of what is healthy for women—a view that includes new thinking about the healthiness of relatedness and the positive self-image maintained in relationship—we will make different assumptions about the causes of sexual dysfunction in lesbian couples. It may be true, as the following case illustrates, that sexual dysfunction results from a breakdown in a female process of conflict resolution rather than from individual pathology around sexuality.

Kathy and Diane started couples' therapy to improve their sexual relationship. At the beginning of their three-year-old relationship they were sexually active with each other, but they had been having sex infrequently when they came into therapy. Diane also had had a series of affairs over the last year, all primarily sexual in nature and all tolerated by Kathy. Diane felt extremely guilty about the affairs and furious at Kathy for what she felt was her lack of interest in their sexual relationship. Kathy was hurt by Diane's affairs, but felt she could not object to them unless she was able to resolve her own sexual issues with Diane. Kathy thought it probably was her fault that she and Diane weren't being more sexual, but she had trouble being open with Diane since her affairs had begun. Diane blamed herself for getting involved with other women and driving Kathy away.

At the beginning of therapy, both women clung to their ideas about their individual problems with sexuality. In reconstructing their sexual relationship from the beginning, however, we discovered some things that contradicted their apparent individual issues. Kathy had often been the initiator of sex between them, and Diane had felt pressured to respond. Diane had begun to feel inadequate and criticized by some of Kathy's feedback to her about their lovemaking. Diane got upset enough that Kathy began to back off, feeling that it was easier for her to do without sex than it was for Diane to deal with talking about it. Diane interpreted this as confirmation of her failure as a lover and assumed that Kathy no longer wanted to be sexual with her. Kathy cooperated by assuring Diane that she didn't mind if Diane was too tired, too busy, or too tense to be sexual.

Even though both women were still interested in being lovers, the frequency of their sexual interactions decreased as they each tried to be responsive to the other's needs. Kathy thought that Diane was more insecure about sex than she was, and therefore should be spared any pressure. Diane thought that Kathy was overcritical because of her own insecurity about sex, and that Kathy should be spared having to deal with Diane unless she initiated it. This arrangement eventually backfired when Diane started having affairs. Their beginning conflicts about sex, which had to do with Kathy's aggressiveness and Diane's insecurity, had become completely obscured by their conflict-resolution process; each tried to respect the other's feelings at the expense of her own. Once their assessments of the other's insecurities were shared and refuted, they were able to address the original conflict. Discussion at this point about their individual feelings about sex was useful and produced change, whereas attempts at changing their present-day negotiations around sex in the beginning of couples' work had not been productive. Once their individual insecurities about sex with each other had been discussed, new negotiations about sexuality could begin, and the couples' therapy could focus on building different communication patterns around Kathy's and Diane's feelings.

## Implications for Lesbian Couples

Lesbian couples like those described might have been misdiagnosed as having a variety of individual and relational problems that until recently have been associated with women: low self-esteem, lack of sexual drive, depression, passivity, and fusion. The individual issues of the women involved can be better understood by examining the situation of women in a culture that prescribes various behaviors and at the same time labels them unhealthy. Ideas about female socialization and societal devaluing of women challenge conceptualizations of individual women as lacking normal adult abilities to be assertive or to value self. For many of the women in the couples described, the problem of creating a positive self-image while being appropriately female resulted in problems in achieving intimacy or self-actualization. The literature is heterosexist in stopping short of recognizing the additional complication of being lesbian in a culture that is also homophobic. Lesbians must come to terms with internalized and externally encountered homophobia in the process of creating a positive self-image, as well as in figuring a way out of the double bind that all women face: being female and seen as less healthy psychologically than men. There is much to be learned about how being lesbian affects the development of self-esteem. Some of the research cited in this chapter suggests that lesbians construct self-image differently from heterosexual women.[18] It is possible that the interplay between lesbianism and building self-esteem can make a positive self-image either easier or more difficult to achieve.

Where the literature is most helpful is in identifying women's socialization toward being primarily concerned with other's needs, and how that influences processes like self-image and interpersonal relating. Understanding the direction of socialization and its consequences gives us a context in which to predict normal individual development for heterosexual and lesbian women. Couples practitioners can then envision lesbian development as involving a struggle with learned female behavior concerning relatedness to others and self-image. How women preserve a relationship while addressing their own needs, both in the service of maintaining positive self-image, will affect lesbian relationships in different ways depending on the stages of individual development that each woman has mastered. Lesbian couples in trouble often have members stuck in a developmental stage unrecognized by themselves and unvalidated by an ignorant and unsupportive larger society. Therapeutic work with these couples must involve recognition of the normal developmental processes in lesbians of balancing needs of self and others and the effects on their relationships. Interventions aimed at individual pathology that does not exist, or at couples dynamics that spring from individual crisis, will not succeed. Clinicians must take care to assess how individual crises in lesbian development are affecting a couple and may need to sequence treatment to address individual issues before trying to change the couple's dynamics based on these issues.

Practitioners also need more research into the issues of socialization, self-esteem, and other-relatednesss that produce differences for lesbians. The new literature provides direction for that research; particularly in terms of identifying uniquely female modes of functioning it provides much needed frameworks to organize inquiry and thought. Theoreticians who think about lesbian couples should not dismiss the new literature as only about heterosexuals; neither should they accept it without reflecting on lesbians and our place in society.

## NOTES

This essay is a combination of my thinking and the contributions of workshop participants, to whom I am grateful for their willingness to think along with me.

1. Carol Gilligan, *In a Different Voice: Psychological Theory and Women's Development* (Cambridge: Harvard University Press, 1982); Jessie Bernard, *Women, Wives and Mothers* (Chicago: Aldine, 1975); Cecilia Foxley, *Nonsexist Counseling* (Dubuque, Iowa: Kendell-Hunt, 1979). See also: Mary Ballou and Nancy W. Gabalac, *A Feminist Position on Mental Health* (Springfield, Ill.: Charles C. Thomas, 1985); and Eileen Nickerson, Oliva Espín, Susan Dorn, and Susan Curtiss, *Helping Women* (Washington, D.C.: University Press of America, 1978).

2. I. K. Broverman, D. M. Broverman, F. E. Clarkson, P. S. Rosenkrantz, and S. R. Vogel, "Sex-role Stereotypes and Clinical Judgments of Mental Health," *Journal of Consulting and Clinical Psychology* 34 (Winter 1970): 1–7.

3. Ballou and Gabalac, *A Feminist Position on Mental Health.*

4. Gilligan, *In a Different Voice.*

5. Gilligan, *In a Different Voice*; Bernard, *Women, Wives and Mothers*; Foxley, *Nonsexist Counseling*; Nickerson et al. *Helping Women*; Ballou and Gabalac, *A Feminist Position on Mental Health.*

6. Ballou and Gabalac, *A Feminist Position on Mental Health.*

7. Alan P. Bell and Martin S. Weinberg, *Homosexualities: A Study of Diversity Among Men and Women* (New York: Simon and Schuster, 1978).

8. Susan J. Wolfe and Julian Penelope Stanley, eds., *The Coming Out Stories* (Watertown, Mass.: Penelope Press, 1980).

9. Letitia Anne Peplau, Susan Cochran, Karen Rook, and Christine Pakesky, "Loving Women: Attachment and Autonomy in Lesbian Relationships," *Journal of Social Issues* 34 (Fall 1978): 7–27.

10. Dorothy Riddle and Barbara Sang, "Psychotherapy with Lesbians," *Journal of Social Issues* 34 (Fall 1978): 84–100.

11. Riddle and Sang, "Psychotherapy with Lesbians"; Laura Nemeyer, "Coming Out: Identity Congruence and the Attainment of Adult Female Sexuality," Ph.D. diss., Boston University, 1980.

12. Jo-Ann Krestan and Claudia Bepko, "The Problem of Fusion in the Lesbian Relationship," *Family Process* 19 (Sept. 1980): 277–89.

13. Riddle and Sang, "Psychotherapy with Lesbians."

14. Peplau et al., "Loving Women."

15. Gilligan, *In a Different Voice.*

16. Mary Mendola, *The Mendola Report: A New Look at Gay Couples* (New York: Crown Publishers, 1980).

17. Margaret Nichols, "The Treatment of Inhibited Sexual Desire (ISD) in Lesbian Couples," *Women and Therapy* 1 (Winter 1982): 49–66.

18. Peplau et al., "Loving Women."

# III

# FAMILY

# 10

## Coming Out to Mom: Theoretical Aspects of the Mother-Daughter Process

SHERRY ZITTER

There is something compelling for lesbians about the topic of coming out to mother. Wherever two or more lesbians congregate, sooner or later the conversation turns to coming-out stories, and primary among them is the question of whether one's mother "knows" (about one's lesbian orientation), and what her reaction was, is, or would be if she were to be told.

"A son is yours 'til he finds a wife, but a daughter is yours for the rest of your life." This proverb succinctly describes what many mothers expect of their children. When a mother raises a son, she generally expects to lose him to another woman someday. When she raises a daughter, however, she usually anticipates that even if that daughter marries a man, mother will always be the most important *woman* in her daughter's life. This myth, which runs deep in our culture and our psyche, may be primary in a mother's reaction to her daughter's coming out.

Coming out to one's mother is not just an event, but a process that happens over time and in different contexts. (A mother's acceptance of her daughter's lesbianism to the point of being able to talk about it with others is considered part of a coming-out process as well.) The experience of the mother-daughter relationship changes for each one as the process unfolds, and is affected by where each is in her own process of coming out. It is worth exploring some of the factors that influence the responses of both mother and daughter, as well as ways to help them both survive and grow from the process of coming out.

The issues raised here may be useful for a lesbian to consider in her decision about whether or not to tell her mother and the timing of an initial disclosure. (The dynamics of a lesbian mother/lesbian daughter relationship are not addressed, as they are assumed to be sufficiently distinct to exceed the scope of this discussion.)

As feminists, we have learned that focusing on only one aspect of reality gives a myopic view of the whole. Any event is experienced in at least three contexts: the internal, the interpersonal, and the societal. For lesbians and their mothers to understand and validate their experiences, each of these levels must be explored. Thus, the coming-out process is examined here from intrapsychic, family systems, and sociocultural perspectives.

These theoretical frameworks suggest some commonalities experienced by lesbian daughters and their mothers. However, such factors as ethnicity, age, religion, birth order, and being differently-abled (such as deaf or blind) uniquely affect the coming-out process and may create quite different experiences. Each lesbian's situation is further affected by underlying societal norms and values that so often make coming out to one's mother stressful. It is this societal homophobia that weighs heavily in the decisions of those lesbians who decide not to tell their mothers.

A clear understanding of the dynamics underlying the coming-out process is crucial to helping lesbians develop and maintain a positive sense of self in an often hostile environment. The relationship with one's mother can be seen as paradigmatic to relationships with important others in one's life. Whether or not "mom knows," an understanding of how a lesbian relates to her mother may help her cope with the rest of the world in a more healing and empowering way.

*Intrapsychic Considerations: The Mother's Response*

Why is it that a mother's reaction to her daughter's lesbianism is so often negative? One factor might be the replacement of mother rather than father in what Nancy Chodorow has called the "bisexual triangle."[1] Neither heterosexual nor lesbian girls "replace" their mothers with their fathers at four or five years old (as Sigmund Freud theorized.)[2] Instead, they use the relationship with father to separate from mother, creating an ongoing triangle involving daughter, mother, and father.

When a heterosexual daughter marries a husband, she is in effect replacing her father in this intrapsychic triangle. But what of the lesbian? In some profound way, she is replacing her mother in the triangle, and her mother may experience this as a rejection. Her daughter is not hers "for the rest of her life," but is saying: "I no longer have a closer bond with you than with any other woman."

A daughter's lesbianism can stir up unconscious wishes in mother that have been denied or repressed. Because almost everyone's primary caretaker is a woman, most females in our society are originally woman-identified. As an infant, each of us experienced our original physical intimacy with a woman. Yet we have internalized the societal myth that women cannot be sexually intimate with women. Hence, it could be surmised that a mother's primary attraction to her own mother had to be denied and deeply repressed in order for her to become exclusively heterosexual. It may produce anxiety in a mother for these early memories to be evoked.

A daughter's choice of lesbianism may be experienced unconsciously by mother as a sexual intrusion. A mother might wonder: "If you're attracted to women, what do you feel toward me? And how do I feel about you?" A mother feels a sense of differentness or "not me" in the presence of her male son, which creates a separateness not present with a daughter. A mother tends to experience a daughter as more like herself; ego boundaries are more diffuse. (Some mothers find nursing sexually arousing, an experience that could be scarier to feel toward a female than toward a male baby. Might such mothers experience conflict around nursing their daughters because of internalized homophobia?) The more fluid ego boundaries between a mother and daughter can cause a mother with recent awareness of her daughter's lesbianism to feel confused and uneasy about her own sexual feelings, as well as what she might imagine her daughter's to be.

A daughter's lesbianism can make a mother unconsciously feel jealous: My daughter is nurturing another woman (or women) instead of me. Luise Eichenbaum and Susie Orbach, in their book *Understanding Women*,[3] contend that a daughter's first child is her mother. When a woman has a male child, she experiences him as someone she should nurture, take care of, and teach to be independent. A mother teaches a female child that her task is to nurture others—which the daughter often learns by mothering her own mother. This can occur in a variety of ways, including "parentification" (looking to one's own child to act as one's parent), conforming to the "good little girl" image expected of her, and suppressing any anger toward her mother. Embedded deeply in our psyche is the expectation that it is natural for one's daughter to nurture a man more than she does her mother. If she nurtures another woman in the same way, however, many hostilities or longings can be aroused in her mother.

Compounding this loss of nurturance may be a mother's unconscious resentment in her own relationship of what Chodorow terms
"heterosexual asymmetry."[4] Because women's nurturing capacities are
encouraged in our society while men's are systematically repressed,
there is usually an asymmetry in their abilities to meet each other's
needs. Women cannot expect their emotional needs to be met in a
heterosexual relationship as well as men can. Most mothers, consciously
or unconsciously, teach their daughters not to expect men to meet their
needs. Thus, a mother who realizes that her daughter is having relationships with women—who generally have the potential to meet
emotional needs better than men—may at some level feel jealous or
resentful, as this is something she has never had herself.

Despite the strong negative reactions a mother usually feels at the
point of disclosure, there is potential for her to have many positive
feelings throughout the negotiating process that follows. This is not to
underestimate the overwhelmingly negative response that follows disclosure of lesbianism to a mother. It is rather to highlight how often
initial responses are taken as the only feelings a mother has, now and
forever. As a mother is approached over time by a loving daughter
who respects her need to struggle with the concept of lesbianism, it
may be helpful to keep the more positive aspects of their relationship
in mind. Some of these positive feelings may be unconsciously present
in a mother who is never explicitly told of her daughter's lesbianism,
and thus can more easily respond to the positive aspects of bonding
between women without being forced to deal with her daughter's
sexuality.

At an altruistic level, a mother may feel happy that her daughter
has a greater potential to have her emotional needs met than would
be possible with a man. Many mothers have been socialized to sacrifice
for their children's happiness. They also, at one level, want their daughters to get more than they themselves could get as women. This side
of the ambivalence often takes a while to surface and is one reason
why it is important to view coming out as a process for both mother
and daughter.

There are other positive intrapsychic reactions a mother may have
toward her daughter's lesbianism. When a daughter chooses women
as her primary love objects, she is affirming her mother as valid and
important. Society sees women as unimportant, and a lesbian daughter
is affirming the introjected mother within herself and saying, "You have
value."

Women have been taught to repress their anger, especially their
anger toward men. When a lesbian comes out to her mother, this can

affirm mother's repressed anger toward men (which is partly anger at the lack of options afforded to women) through stating by example another way of life—an option that mother never saw as viable or even existent. Thus, mother's reaction to her daughter's lesbianism may be ambivalent. She may simultaneously feel rejected or abandoned, and yet may feel somehow validated by her daughter's choice of women.

### Intrapsychic Considerations: The Daughter's Response

A lesbian daughter can have both positive and negative reactions to her own coming out to her mother. Some of her fears or guilt can be part of her own internalized homophobia. This often surfaces as self-hatred, either for her lesbianism or displaced onto any number of other issues. Part of a daughter's reaction may be related to the issues to which her mother might react. A daughter could feel unconscious guilt at abandoning her mother (by replacing her in the bisexual triangle), at escaping her mother's fate of heterosexual asymmetry, at failing to live out a basic dream of her mother's (for daughter to be heterosexual like her), and at taking care of another woman better than she is nurturing her own mother.

In addition, knowing that one's mother feels bad or guilty about one's lesbianism is not easy to ignore. A daughter is often unconsciously looking for support or validation from her mother, and a mother's negative reaction may arouse anger, disappointment, shame, or resentment. This can create a cycle in which both mother and daughter are hurt and angered by the insensitivity and lack of understanding that the other has shown toward her feelings.

On the positive side, a lesbian daughter can feel that she is validating womanhood, rejecting the message that dad is better than mom, and escaping from a double bind in which society, via her mother, has put her. Mother has subtly passed on an underlying societal message: "Get your needs met the way I did, be heterosexual. But don't expect men to meet your needs; your needs can only be met well by women." A woman can resolve this double bind in a healthy way by becoming a lesbian and finding a greater potential to have her needs met both on a sexual and an affectional level. She may get, rather than heterosexual asymmetry, a reciprocal nurturance that leads to a greater self-validation and self-worth. Furthermore, the simple act of being honest with one's mother about one's own identity, of refusing to live a lie, increases self-esteem. (This does not imply that coming out to one's mother is the appropriate choice for all lesbians.) A woman who feels greater self-worth is in a better position to help her mother feel more validated as well.

A major theme in coming out to one's mother is the sense of repeating, at a new developmental level, earlier experiences of separation from mother. Every female has had the experience of asserting her autonomy in a society where boys are autonomous and girls are dependent, of forming her identity in a culture where the identity of a women is seen as adjunct to that of a man. As a toddler and again as an adolescent, her developmental progression away from her mother often may have been met by rejection or withdrawal in a subtle form. Coming out may be experienced as reminiscent of these earlier rejections and increasing separations from mother. This process may have both positive and negative components. The pain of rejection may be accompanied by a freeing feeling of greater independence, of having more room to grow as a person separate from one's mother and her wishes and demands. Viewing coming out as a process helps us to remember that a different kind of mother-daughter relationship can be negotiated using the perspective and healing power of time.

*Family Systems Perspective*

Family systems theory examines patterns of interaction among members of a family without assigning linear cause or effect to the observed behavior. Family dynamics can be dramatically altered during the process of coming out.

Coalitions in the family can change when a daughter comes out to her mother. There are often reverberations throughout the family system, regardless of whether others in the family are aware of the lesbianism. Coalitions may either be rigidified in their former positions or undergo abrupt rearrangements. The existence of a "family secret," if the mother cannot share it with her husband, may create tension in the parental subsystem. If daughter and mother, or daughter and father, have had a coalition that excluded the other parent, mother and father may become stronger allies to tell the lesbian there is something "wrong" with her. Alternatively, a split may develop between parents if one accepts the lesbianism with more ease than the other. In a single-parent family in particular, other family members or friends may become triangulated into a tense relationship between mother and daughter.

In many families, a degree of scapegoating occurs. Depending on where she is in the family system, a woman's coming out can either reinforce her role as the scapegoat or can shift this role from another sibling to the lesbian. If she was already in a scapegoat role, then mother (and father) can see her lesbianism as just another example that she is a "bad daughter." If the lesbian has previously been the "good daughter" and another child in the family has been designated as the bad child, there may be a shift in roles. The former scapegoat's relationship with mother may suddenly improve, while lesbian-mother interactions become fraught with increasing tension. Families often have a historical pattern of unique expectations for the oldest or youngest daughter in each generation, and a deviation of this pattern may cause sudden scapegoating or great pressure on the lesbian to conform to what the family expects.

In a family where a father has had an overclose relationship with his daughter, a mother may view her daughter as a rival. Coming out as a lesbian in such a family may actually engender a sense of relief in the lesbian's mother, who might see her daughter as less threatening to her own marital relationship. This perspective could help her to deal better with her daughter's lesbianism. Father, however, may feel quite rejected by his daughter's choice of women as sexual partners. Possibly his own repressed incest fantasies must be given up, as well as feeling a fantasized sexual rejection. This may be a factor in a family where a mother has accepted the lesbianism much more easily than a father. (In view of high incest statistics, we must confront the reality that in many families, a father has had an actual incestuous relationship with his daughter. His reaction to her coming out could then involve anger at her rejection of sexual involvement with him, as well as some guilt at "causing her lesbianism.")

Salvador Minuchin's conceptualization of a continuum of possible boundaries among people is helpful in viewing structural changes in a family.[5] (This systemic concept of boundaries, which describes the relationship between two people, is distinct from the intrapsychic meaning, which indicates the parameters of the self.) At one extreme, a diffuse boundary between two people exists when something that happens to one person feels to another as if it happened to her. From a systems perspective, these two would be enmeshed. (This extreme might be characterized from an intrapsychic viewpoint as fusion or symbiosis.) On the other extreme, a very rigid boundary exists where one person in a family underreacts to major events that happen to another. Along the continuum are many gradations of relationships which are considered functional or nonfunctional to varying degrees. This depends on many factors, including how people experience their relationships, their ethnicity and cultural expectations, and whether the type of boundary interferes with daily functioning.

The boundary between a woman and her mother tends to be more diffuse than between a mother and son. Coming out as a lesbian is one way of defining a clearer boundary with one's mother. A woman who tells her mother, "I am a lesbian" is defining herself as different from her mother. A mother can feel both abandoned and betrayed by not feeling this special relationship anymore. She is giving up the heterosexual daughter she dreamed of and accepting a daughter who is lesbian—a time-consuming process at best. Among what may be given up are dreams of her daughter's marriage, children (her own grandchildren), and easy acceptance into an extended family and society.

By juxtaposing the intrapsychic and systems perspectives, we can see that this major structural change in a family could precipitate a grieving process in a mother similar to the mourning of someone who has died. Some of the typical stages of mourning are usually experienced: denial, guilt, anger, and depression.[6] Mourning a death is a vitally important process for the survivor in order to resolve the grief sufficiently to continue living and growing. However, the type of mourning that involves struggling to accept a fact of life rather than a fact of death has the potential for an even more positive outcome. If this mourning process is allowed to take place, a mother may eventually be able to accept a daughter as a lesbian, opening the way for mother and daughter to establish a different kind of relationship.

For the mothers of most lesbians, this major mourning process happens for the first time when their daughters come out. For differently-abled women, however, this happens for a second time: A mother has already gone through (or more likely is still stuck in) a process of grieving the lack of a "normal," nondisabled child, and now feels a greater gulf and possibility of societal ostracism and pity.

The duration of the mourning process can vary widely. This new separation, this giving up of a former unique relationship, has to be mourned by both mother and daughter. The daughter may also have to mourn the loss of a fantasized mother who could immediately and effortlessly accept her as a lesbian.

### Sociocultural Factors

We have internalized cultural and societal norms at a subtle yet profound level of our beings. The more that a lesbian can understand the impact of society and culture on her own and her mother's feelings about lesbianism, the more informed will be her decision and, if she chooses to tell her mother, the easier will be the coming-out process for them both.

From the perspective of social role theory, part of a mother's role is to teach her daughter how to be a woman. In our society, part of being female is to be heterosexual. Most mothers experience their role in raising their daughters as including the teaching of proper sexual orientation. A mother often feels that her daughter's lesbianism represents the mother's failure to teach the role of womanhood. "Where did I go wrong?"—a response so common as to be stereotypic—encompasses varied reactions of guilt, shame, embarrassment, and a sense of failure. Clearly, one of the social stressors of being a lesbian is the feeling of hurting one's mother by forcing her to contend with the societal stigma of being a "bad mother."

Overall family styles can be challenged as a result of the coming-out process. If the family pattern in the past has been openness, this pattern can be severely strained by knowledge of a daughter's lesbianism. For example, a mother who has always taught her daughter to be proud of saying she is Jewish, even in situations where people dislike Jews, is suddenly faced with a dilemma. She may not want to tell anybody about her daughter's lesbianism. She may think: "I've always been honest and told my daughter not to be ashamed of who she is, and now I don't want people to know about her." It may be quite difficult for a mother to reconcile this contradiction.

Sociologically, lesbians are in the unusual position of belonging to a culture to which their parents do not belong, and indeed find repugnant. Most cultural minorities have a natural socialization network from birth. They learn about coping styles and support networks, primarily unconsciously, from their parents. Lesbians, however, grow up without the role modeling and mentoring that most people take for granted. For a mother to discover, or to become consciously aware, that her daughter belongs to a different culture evokes a powerful "not me" response that can cause her to react as if her daughter were practically a Martian.

The implications of this cultural isolation for Deaf lesbians (over 90 percent of whom have two hearing parents[7]) are profound: There is a double cultural barrier between the Deaf lesbian and her family. (The capitalized "Deaf" is typically used to denote a person identified with the Deaf culture, as opposed to someone who is simply audiologically deaf.) A Deaf lesbian has been socialized by her parents in neither the Deaf nor the lesbian culture, and each of these communities has misconceptions and stereotypes about the other. Unable to find complete understanding in either culture, her relationship with her mother can take on greater importance, even as the barriers to parental acceptance loom larger.

For a woman of color, a negative response from a mother can be particularly poignant. People in minority groups are already oppressed by the outside world. A straight woman of color usually has been able to find support and acceptance within her own family and ethnic group and has felt the double bond with her mother of being a minority woman. A lesbian of color, even when she does not disclose her identity to anyone in her culture, often grows up feeling she does not fit in, that she is unacceptable to the values of her culture. If she comes out, she risks bringing into the open a dual "not me" response from her mother: "You're not [heterosexual] like me; you're something that my whole culture rejects." The minority lesbian may feel even more oppressed within her own family and her own culture, in addition to her constant oppression from the majority culture. A mother of color may not only reject her daughter's sexual preference, but may fear for her daughter's double oppression of ethnicity and sexual orientation.

Oliva Espín has discussed (35–55) how Latina lesbians must embrace three stigmatized identities: woman, lesbian, and ethnic minority. Within the Latina's own culture, lesbianism is strongly stigmatized; she must deal with the reaction that she has "betrayed" her own people by publicizing an identity that Latins believe to bring shame on them and reflect badly on their culture. In Latin culture, where family ties are vitally important, overt rejection is rare, but so is acknowledgment of lesbianism. A Latina lesbian, Espín points out, often must choose between leading a double life within her culture or closing off the possibility of serving the Latin community.

Other minority lesbians, however, have reported that their mothers have had an easier time accepting their lesbianism than they had expected. The mother of a minority lesbian may accept her daughter's coming out more easily than a nonminority mother because of her familiarity with oppression and being an outsider. Her own stigmatization may allow her greater empathy with a daughter who encounters stigma within their shared culture.

Adrienne Rich has said, "Lesbian existence is both the breaking of a taboo and the rejection of a compulsory way of life."[8] Mothers are taught to raise their daughters to be like themselves, and one of the most profound pressures is to be heterosexual, just like mother. Societally, lesbianism is the ultimate rejection of the prescribed female role and the ultimate independence from a man. Whenever a taboo is broken, there is a degree to which the negative societal reaction is internalized, by mother as well as by daughter. There is often a sense of condemnation from society, not only of the lesbian, but also of her family. If a woman is a lesbian, her family—in particular her mother—must have done something wrong. Societal homophobia is internalized by both mother and daughter to create shame and guilt at the lesbian outcome.

In some African tribes, coming out meant literally coming out from the small huts where young girls had to undergo a ritual confinement until the age that they were ready to be married.[9] For some lesbians as well, coming out feels like emerging from a type of confinement; however, mothers are rarely as enthusiastic as those of the African women who come out to be married. Lesbians, by their existence, are challenging societal notions of men as more valuable than women. Lesbian couples provide each other with symmetrical validation by each choosing a woman as her valued partner.

The cultural dichotomy of the virgin and the whore clearly warns us that the consequences of women being sexual are social ostracism and rejection. We learn as women that our sexuality should be hidden, that it is dangerous and shameful. By becoming a lesbian, a woman does the opposite of hiding her sexuality—she reveals it. There is an apt parallel from Deaf culture: Twenty years ago, most Deaf people were taught only to read lips and speak, never to use sign language. Signing would show that they were different. Now there are interpreters at conferences and people signing in public, which proclaims the deafness and in some sense says: "I'm not ashamed to be Deaf—in fact, I'm proud of it, though society may think something is wrong with me." A lesbian, by the mere fact of identifying herself as such, proclaims her sexuality in a similar way. Most of our mothers, raised in a sexually repressed and erotophobic culture, are uncomfortable with any display of sexuality—particularly from women, and most especially a societally unacceptable type of sexuality from their own daughters.

Many lesbians would prefer *not* to proclaim their sexuality by the mere fact of identifying their lesbianism. However, society's tendency is to react to lesbianism as a sexual (behavioral) rather than a socio-cultural identity. This reaction is both a cause and a result of the erotophobia in our society and the difficulty in seeing a woman-identified woman in a sexist society as anything but a sexual aberration. Lesbians, as well as other stigmatized people, contend with the issue of identity spread: One's identity is seen in unidimensional terms. In the eyes of society, a lesbian is only a sexual (and perverted) being, as a Deaf person is only a ("deaf and dumb") person who can't communicate. The cultural benefits in both cultures are neither known or supported.

Most mothers, like many others in the majority culture, don't have a clear idea of what lesbianism is, or are full of some frightening misconceptions. They may think that a lesbian wants to be a man, or has a confused gender identity. Some mothers may think that they themselves don't know any other lesbians, and this serves to perpetuate their fears and myths. A mother may think that lesbians are child molesters, that they are always lonely and mostly do not have long-term, satisfying relationships. She probably also fears the oppression of her daughter, a reality that can be blown out of proportion by ignorance. These myths can tend to keep a mother stuck, unable to be open to the message her daughter is conveying by coming out: "This is an important aspect of my life which I am entrusting to you, and you mean enough to me that I want to risk this sharing."

People tend to assume, when there is no contrary evidence, that everyone they know is heterosexual. Adrienne Rich terms this the "heterosexual assumption."[10] While spouses or dates are often invited to work-related functions, it may be inappropriate or actually dangerous to bring along a lesbian lover—and women who attend a function alone are assumed to be single and heterosexual. In order to be recognized as a lesbian, it is necessary to announce this fact, which is somehow perceived as "flaunting" one's lesbianism or "making a big deal" of it. Thus, there is little opportunity for validation of a lesbian relationship. Colleagues and other associates often provide scant affirmation, even those who may know about one's sexual orientation.

## Some Treatment Considerations

Sometimes a disclosure of lesbianism to a mother can carry with it unconscious expectations of some amount of validation. Total rejection can then be devastating. So often, a lesbian has internalized societal homophobia as self-hatred, and any negative reaction from a mother can intensify the self-deprecation already present. It may be necessary to work through many self-esteem issues before a client can even make an informed choice about whether or not telling her mother is best for her unique situation.

Work with clients can focus on the prerequisites for feeling ready to "come out to mom," as well as exploring whether the motivation for coming out stems from their own inner readiness or from community pressure to do so. What would be the benefits and the liabilities of coming out at this particular point in each of their lives? At what point does a client feel that if her mother rejects her, she will be strong enough to handle that rejection? What past experiences in her relationship with her mother may give her a clue to a likely range of initial reactions from her mother? Is she in a position to get community support, to help her mother work through her negative reactions and homophobia, and to work on nurturing an open communication process between them? At what point in the process might her mother be helped by concrete information, a book, a parents' group?

It is important for therapists to recognize that coming out is a complex and difficult process, and not one which should be pushed upon a client. It is far from the best course of action for every lesbian to take. Honesty between mother and daughter, at the cost of an estrangement, is not always the best decision. Potential gains may not be worth risking possible losses in a relationship with an elderly parent or one who lives halfway around the globe and is rarely seen. However, some lesbians have found that disclosure of this important part of their identity has meant a great deal to a sick or dying parent. It is important to explore whether hesitancy is because of the mother's or the daughter's internalized homophobia (both of which can be valid reasons for rejecting or postponing a decision to come out). A therapist can help a lesbian client explore a range of possible consequences within her particular family. This will help assess whether coming out is a healthy option for each client, and if so, to figure out appropriate timing for her personal and family evolution.

Because adults can easily slip back into children's roles with their parents, particularly around emotionally charged topics, it is especially hard to be rational and calm when coming out to one's mother for the first time. Often clients report that the discussion felt out of control, and that both parties said things they didn't mean. The pattern mothers and daughters often exhibit following disclosure is one where each feels the other is not listening to her, and is consequently unable to listen in return. At a time when communication is desperately needed, it seems to be closed off beyond repair. Such a cycle can escalate without either participant wanting it to, but with each feeling powerless to stop the relationship from deteriorating further.

Anticipating what may happen as a result of coming out can help clients to cope better with the reverberations. One way to help a client anticipate possible scenarios is to use role plays or guided fantasies in group or individual therapy before an initial disclosure to parents. Some have found it easier to "practice" by coming out first to a sibling who is likely to be accepting. If disclosure goes well, this new ally can then lend support and help strategize around dealing with mother. If the event does not go well, the lesbian client will have a chance to review what happened in therapy and work on possible adaptations in her own responses to the situation. Thus, options are broadened to help a client disclose her lesbianism to parents in a healthy, mutually affirming way.

It can be useful for a therapist to view the coming-out process as a reworking of earlier separations from the mother, as are adolescence and other developmental milestones of adult life. As with other separations, clients may feel both positively and negatively toward the prospect of greater differentiation. Therapists can work with both sides of this ambivalence to help lesbian clients work through and feel comfortable with both the repetitive and the new aspects of this experience of separation.

Often, disclosure can be followed by parental hopes for a "cure" and well-meaning offers to pay for therapy. A daughter who is unsure of her lesbianism and looking for external validation may feel her anxieties and ambivalences raised by this reaction. One who is sure of her lesbianism may become enraged at a mother's suggestion of a "cure," and the event of disclosure can end in a full-scale conflict that closes off communication for a time.

Therapists may encounter more than one client in a first session who is unsure of whether she is entering therapy for herself or for her mother. As with other issues, it is vital to let the client know that whatever decision she makes around her sexual orientation is acceptable to the therapist. This will help the client to sort out her own wishes and fears more realistically, rather than simply working to please her mother or her therapist.

Working with a client who is already enraged at her mother necessitates a similarly balanced approach. Empathic connections with such a client will eventually allow her to feel greater ambivalence toward her mother and more empathy with her mother's feelings.

Because of the shifts that occur in a family system following any major change, it can be useful for a therapist to help a lesbian client anticipate some of what could happen in her family if she decides to come out to her mother. It is important to help a client evaluate the quality of the boundary between parent and (adult) child before a disclosure decision. Are mother and daughter enmeshed? Disengaged? What is the lesbian's role in the family now, and how might that change if she were to come out? A lesbian who has played the role of the "good child," counterbalanced by a "bad child" elsewhere in the family, should explore how it could feel to switch roles suddenly and feel like the scapegoat. (In some existential sense, such a shift still leaves the lesbian in the role of a "good daughter," as she has helped to improve the relationship between mother and former scapegoat. This approach may be useful for the therapist as a reframing technique, a way to see a negatively perceived situation in a positive context.)

Although frequently a disclosure to family results in rejection or lessening of contact, there are some instances where a mother who has trouble with her daughter's lesbianism escalates contact following disclosure. This can be the reaction of a mother who is afraid for her daughter, and who hopes to maintain some enmeshment as a way of maintaining control. The fear for her daughter's welfare (which may be partially a fear of losing her daughter to another woman) may justify frequent questioning and contact. This situation, annoying as it may be to a lesbian daughter, can also be viewed as part of a positive process with which a therapist can help. Mother's love and caring can be acknowledged and affirmed, while at the same time a daughter can be helped to state firm limits regarding her independence and frequency of contact.

Helping a lesbian client understand the mourning process can lead to greater empathy for both her mother and herself, because a lesbian needs to mourn the loss of her heterosexual privilege as well. Although the cognitive understanding that the grief process includes denial and anger may not make acceptance of these feelings from one's mother any easier, it can help a lesbian to stay open to different feelings through the passage of time.

For differently-abled women, their mothers' mourning of their lesbianism may be made more complex by their never having successfully completed griefwork around what society views as a handicap. However, the second time around, the differently-abled lesbian has a unique opportunity not available if her mother was mourning a congenital factor. As an infant, she was unable to help her mother deal with her deafness or blindness; in fact, she was unaware of it herself. If she is self-accepting as an adult, a differently-abled lesbian can offer her mother support and encouragement to deal with the realities of her identities that mother has internalized as "bad." She may be able to share some of her own grief or disappointment with her mother— not as a way to say that she wishes she were different, but in order to help her mother experience the range of feelings necessary to successfully work through the grieving process. Whether a mother is invited into therapy or a client talks with her mother outside the therapeutic situation, such a process allows the opportunity for both mother and lesbian daughter to handle both griefs at a new developmental level.

Societal homophobia is internalized by all of us to greater or lesser degrees. However, a lesbian who is in contact with other lesbians in a community has the opportunity to test out and reject many myths with which she has grown up. In all likelihood, her mother has not had similar opportunities. If a mother can discuss some of her fears, her daughter can use the opportunity to help clarify some myths and to reaffirm the love between them. It can help to remember that the mother who appears distancing and rejecting might really be saying "I care about you a lot, and I'm scared for you."

The mother of a lesbian must contend with a strong societal belief that her child-rearing must have been insufficient for this to have happened. Her own guilt and shame influences not only how she reacts to others in the family, but also how a lesbian daughter and her mother feel about themselves and each other. Exploring this issue in therapy can give the lesbian client an important perspective on her own and her mother's coming-out processes.

Crossing cultural barriers is always difficult, and a straight therapist working with a lesbian client is no exception. It is important for a straight therapist to be well informed, to be honest with lesbian clients about her own prejudices, and to obtain supervision from a lesbian therapist if possible.

White lesbian therapists are often in a position of treating lesbians of color, across a different cultural barrier. Therapy with a minority lesbian is more complex in many ways, and it is essential for a therapist to understand the structure of a minority client's family and culture, whether she is white or from a different minority group. Again, it is vital to be open about one's own biases and limitations, and to be supervised by a therapist from the client's own ethnic group when possible.

Therapists can help their lesbian clients—both before and during the coming-out process—to think about their own level of self-esteem, of separation from mother (so rejection will not feel devastating), and about mother's own process of acceptance. The initial disclosure is indeed an event, but it is also the beginning of a process. To be cognizant of where both mother and daughter are in this process can, at best, help them undergo a period of healing to create a different relationship. If healing is not possible between them, then the coming-out process can, at least, result in a feeling of empowerment and wholeness for a lesbian daughter.

*Discussion*

Coming out is a choice. A lesbian can choose not to share this aspect of her life with her mother. A mother can choose not to "come out," to hide her daughter's lesbianism fróm family and neighbors. A bisexual woman can decide to tell her mother about her male lovers and not her female lovers. Coming out to her mother as a bisexual may strengthen her mother's wish (often hoped for with lesbians as well) that she will eventually "find the right man." Lesbians who are able to pass as heterosexual and who decide *not* to come out to their mothers—or those who come out to their mothers, but whose mothers then keep it a secret—can reap the rewards of being viewed as "normal," as well as the problems of living a lie. For a lesbian who is "too butch to pass," a mother often knows at a preconscious level that her daughter is a lesbian. Thus, a mother's level of denial can be quite strong before the coming-out process begins. This may make the process more difficult, or it may make it easier.

Coming out to one's mother is both a behavioral and a self-definitional process on many levels. Intrapsychically, coming out is an alteration of the usual pattern of replacing father with husband in the bisexual triangle; it is a rejection of the frustrations of heterosexual asymmetry; it is an affirmation of womanhood and, in its courageous honesty, an affirmation of oneself.

For a mother, a daughter's coming out may revive her own early same-sex attraction; it may feel like abandonment, rejection, sexual intrusion, or affirmation and validation; it may precipitate a mourning process for the wished-for heterosexual daughter; and it may induce altruistic satisfaction that her daughter has the opportunity for sexual and emotional reciprocity.

From a family systems perspective, coming out often creates a clearer boundary between a mother and daughter, can reinforce or change coalitions or scapegoating, and can challenge a family style. Socioculturally, the coming-out process rejects cultural norms, proclaims a woman's sexuality, and challenges the heterosexual assumption.

As we understand more about the options in the coming-out process for both lesbians and their mothers, we increase the options of creating adult, differentiated mother-daughter relationships. Coming out to one's mother, as an appropriate and well-informed decision, can be a vital and life-affirming developmental task for lesbian adolescence or adulthood.

## NOTES

The author gratefully acknowledges the assistance of Jane Mildred, Carla Golden, and Mark Zitter in clarifying the ideas upon which this chapter is based.

1. Nancy Chodorow, *The Reproduction of Mothering: Psychoanalysis and the Sociology of Gender* (Berkeley: University of California Press, 1978), 191–93.

2. Sigmund Freud, *Some Psychical Consequences of the Anatomical Distinction between the Sexes,* Standard Edition, vol. 19 (London: Hogarth Press, 1925), 243–58.

3. Luise Eichenbaum and Susie Orbach, *Understanding Women: A Feminist Psychoanalytic Approach* (New York: Basic Books, 1982), 57.

4. Chodorow, *The Reproduction of Mothering,* 191–94.

5. Salvador Minuchin, *Families and Family Therapy* (Cambridge: Harvard University Press, 1974), 54.

6. Elizabeth Kubler-Ross, *On Death and Dying* (New York: Macmillan Publishing, 1969).

7. Raymond Trybus, "Sign Language, Power, and Mental Health," in *Sign Language and the Deaf Community,* ed. Charlotte Baker and Robbin Battison (Silver Spring, Md.: National Association of the Deaf, 1980), 207.

8. Adrienne Rich, "Compulsory Heterosexuality and Lesbian Existence," *Signs* 5 (Summer 1980): 631.

9. Fred E. Jandt and James Darsey, "Coming Out as a Communicative Process," in *Gay Speak: Gay Male and Lesbian Communication,* ed. James W. Chesebro (New York: Pilgrim Press, 1981), 23.

10. Rich, "Compulsory Heterosexuality," 631–60.

# 11

## Lesbian Families: Psychosocial Stress and the Family-Building Process

SALLY CRAWFORD

Most literature on the family makes the assumption that the term *family* refers to the heterosexual unit of mother, father, and children, or to the heterosexual single-parent family. This image of the family hangs on tenaciously despite the existence of many lesbian-parent families with special characteristics and needs. Family therapy literature virtually ignores the lesbian family with children, although there has been an increase in material on lesbian couples.

The reasons for this lack of attention are various. Some people still argue that a lesbian-headed family unit is not a family, and that children need to be protected from this life-style. Others insist that lesbian families should be understood and treated clinically exactly as any other family. Both of these arguments are faulty: the first for obvious reasons, and the second because in a well-meaning way it fails to understand and deal with the particular pressures, problems, and issues with which lesbian families must cope in a homophobic culture.

It is also often assumed that a self-identified lesbian will not be a mother if she does not have children before coming out. Although this assumption has been shared until recently by the straight world and the majority of lesbians, within the lesbian community it is dying a rapid death as more and more women make their own decisions about whether or not to have children. While straight peers have struggled to be clear that their decision to bear a child does not result from messages about "compulsory mothering," lesbians have struggled with a different message based on the compulsory childlessness that the mainstream culture has overtly and covertly attempted to impose on women-identified women. It is encouraging that lesbians no longer assume that their life choice precludes mothering.

Any woman choosing to have children must confront both the myths of mothering and a variety of emotional issues evoked by parenting, such as feelings about one's own childhood and family; intense, previously untapped emotional responses that children may elicit, and concerns about changes in one's life structure. The list is long and familiar. In addition, lesbians have other issues to confront: the newer, romantic ideals of raising children within an alternative family, the question of how to start a family, and the inevitable stress in a homophobic culture. Despite the many creative family structures that lesbians have developed to nurture their children, such stressors are an overriding concern in a dominant culture that is troubled by difference.

This chapter considers some of the stressors that lesbian families face. My focus is intended not to portray lesbian parenting in a negative light, nor to imply that traditional families do not have their own problems unique to their structure and role in society. It is intended rather to help lesbians starting families to identify and cope with issues that they might not otherwise anticipate, in spite of their experience with homophobic oppression. Too, the identification of stressors is offered to aid therapists working with lesbian families in the identifying of the many challenges that lesbians face in the process of family building. I will address the relationship of the lesbian family to the outside world, including the dominant culture, the lesbian community, and the family of origin. I will also raise issues to consider within the family, such as the family-planning concerns of individuals and couples and the special issues for co-parents and children. In addition, I identify the locus of responsibility for this oppression and its impact on families in the homophobic cultural context and implicitly highlight the tremendous strength that lesbian mothers have brought and continue to bring to the care of themselves and their children.

The material here is drawn primarily from my clinical work with lesbian couples and families at a public mental health clinic. This population is predominantly white and twenty-five to forty-five years old. There is a wide range of class background and of context for both clients' coming out and their ongoing lives in that they come from both an extremely rural environment, where there is little or no other lesbian contact, and a small city, where there is an active and political lesbian community.

## Individual Concerns

Lesbians choosing to have children have much to consider in assessing their best parenting options: such factors as the status of their relationships, willingness to be a single parent, personal values with regard to pregnancy or adoption, financial resources, options defined by the cultural political climate, and support networks. These issues need to be considered by each individual, including those in couples or extended families planning to parent together.

All women experience some ambivalence about parenthood—in the decision stage and forever after. It is very difficult for lesbians to find a safe place out in the world or within themselves to deal with this ambivalence. The world forces lesbians to justify continually their right to have children and to prove their unqualified competence. As a result, a lesbian may feel that she has to act as if the ambivalence isn't there, lest it be misunderstood. She may need to deny the ambivalence in order to muster the incredible energy that she will need to have or get a child in the first place. The potential lesbian mother needs to create an environment in which there is room for the scary and troubling parts of this process. At the same time, the prospective parent needs to highlight her strengths and to remind herself that lesbians have been good mothers to thousands of children.

The decision to become a parent may arouse feelings of internalized homophobia. Lesbians should not be surprised or ashamed to find themselves grappling with questions such as: Is this natural? Is it okay for lesbians to have kids? Am I hurting my children (especially when they have problems, as all kids do at some time or another)? Is it unfair to bring them into a homophobic world? Am I a woman who is able to be a mother like other women? These old questions are important to take seriously; they are questions that have been answered in positive ways by many lesbian mothers over the years.

In deciding between adoption and alternative insemination, the unique aspects of each choice must be considered. The stress of going through the adoption process can be great. There is no easy answer to the dilemma of whether or not to be "out" to your social worker. The wisdom of this decision depends on agency policies and on the general political climate with regard to alternative families. Because lesbians cannot adopt as a couple, the method often disenfranchises the nonadoptive parent, who becomes invisible during the process. For a couple who has been "out," the going back "in" often required is painful. In addition, the support and dialogue offered to heterosexual couples during the agency's home study may not be available to lesbian couples. They may want to build this process into their family elsewhere.

Often agencies offer special-needs children to single parents, or if the parent is white, children of different cultural backgrounds. It is important to consider the extra demands, money, and energy a special child requires and the various ways in which the parent's life will be affected. For example children with special needs often require the services of agencies and programs that may not recognize or support the family. The potential parents need to evaluate their tolerance for, and skills in, dealing with this type of frustration.

If a child is from another culture and the parents are white, their own racism and the racism in the immediate environment should be examined to assess realistically what positive connections to the child's cultural heritage the parents can offer. The community's and the family of origin's emotional and political views on cross-cultural adoption should also be considered. There will be those who think it is wrong to adopt a cross-cultural child, and those who will deny the significance of the child's ethnic and racial background. Because the issues about one's origins are even more complex in cross-cultural than in other adoptions, the lesbian parents should realistically evaluate the adequacy of the support available to the family.

If the choice is to use alternative insemination, there are other important considerations. If the donor is known, the father's involvement, if any, in the child's life should be worked out in advance in order to anticipate the complexities and maximize the advantages of having an active parent who is not a family member. If the donor is to be unknown, or if there will be no contact between father and child, the parents will need to examine their own values and beliefs about the meaning of this choice to themselves and the child. The parents need to be prepared to explain appropriately to the child the reasons for this choice and to attend to whatever questions and feelings the child has about her or his origins. Some potential issues for the child are elaborated in the section of this chapter on children's concerns. If the parents do not have personal experience with this situation, they may want to talk to peers who do.

The family of origin's possible response to a pregnancy should also be assessed. As with coming out, the family's initial response may not be positive, and the parents may experience another instance where others are not enthusiastic about a joyful event in the parents' lives. This attitude is often hard to accept, particularly in contrast to the celebration of straight peers' and siblings' impending motherhood.

The blended, or step-family, option is not new. Lesbians have formed families in this way for years. What may be new is the conscious decision to become family together and the increased awareness of the importance of validating this unit. The special concerns of step-family formation in general are well documented in the literature on heterosexual step-families. The unique challenges for lesbian parents and their children in this situation are described later in this chapter.

The dilemmas of rearing a child alone require special preparation. The lesbian choosing to parent by herself should read about the single-parent experience and talk to other single parents, straight and gay. Financial strains will be greater, and isolation may be more severe than experienced by lesbian couples or heterosexual single parents. Help, support, and encouragement from family of origin or friends is extremely important. The lesbian will need to ask herself whether she can manage working and child-rearing on her own. What possibilities are there to increase the involvement of caring people in her life? Can she visualize the nitty-gritty: a day at home alone with the flu and a child who feels like being up and about? Both members of a couple must also address those questions, because all parents are potential single parents.

Finances have serious stress implications for the female wage-earner in a discriminatory work force. The income of a single parent or two female parents is often so low that money can be a substantial source of daily stress. Many lesbians, like many others in our society, cannot afford the luxury of taking regular breaks from child-rearing. A potential mother will need to assess her financial resources as well as what she knows about herself and money stress. If she has to deal with a welfare department, there are many accompanying stresses, not the least of which is having a state agency scrutinizing her lesbian family. She will have to consider the impact of this on her life, and her willingness to deal with the intrusion.

Whatever the particulars of any individual's or a couple's situation, realistic planning is the best approach, because it is inherent in the parenting experience for plans to be interrupted and for the unpredictable to reign.

## Isolation

The isolation that lesbian families experience is a most difficult, painful, and hard-to-anticipate problem. Lesbian mothers often feel caught between at least two worlds, and their whole self may not get acknowledged in either place. It often happens that a lesbian gets her major support for the mother part of herself from straight people who cannot understand or relate to the depth of the significance of her lesbianism. At the same time, she may get major support for her lesbian self from the lesbian community, where there is less understanding of the depth of the impact of becoming a mother on her person and life.

This lack of understanding can create some lonely moments and spaces in her life.

Having children pushes a lesbian into regular social contact with the straight world, even if this is not already a part of her life. Children operate "out there" and need parents' ongoing involvement in that part of their lives. Many lesbian parents find that they themselves need straight parents, whose lives are also organized around parenting, for support. However, this need may not be reciprocal, because the straight family often has its own support network of families based on shared friendships and life-styles in the straight world.

Lesbian parents who turn to the lesbian community for support may not find what they need, although this is changing as more lesbians become parents. When the emotional support and interest are there, the structure of the lives of lesbians without children may be different enough on a practical level that little connection over the children is possible.

In some communities, conflict may arise between what the parents feel is right for their children and what the community feels is the correct way to raise children outside of a patriarchal mode. Such political conflicts may be compounded for the parents of a boy.[1] Dealing with this stress takes strength, and the criticism of other lesbians often hurts more than that of the straight world. At best it causes more anxiety. Solutions to life's problems suddenly seem less clear and simple.

Third-world parents may find themselves caught in a particularly complex web of opinions about what is good and bad for children as they attempt to stay connected to two divergent communities. Women of color already know what it means to try to balance their needs and their children's in a straight (third-world) and a lesbian context.[2] They recognize both straight homophobia and the racism of a predominantly white lesbian community.[3] Third-world parents' own sense of alienation and isolation may be compounded by the need to protect children, who must survive both the racism and homophobia to which the family is subjected.

In spite of its occasional past contributions to the isolation of lesbians, the lesbian community is the primary antidote to the alienation of a lesbian family. Lesbian mothers and their children, whenever possible, need contact with other lesbians and lesbian families. The availability of this contact varies widely and is affected by such variables as where the couple lives, the size and diversity of the lesbian community in general, and the degree to which the lesbian couple are out as lesbians. The threat of custody problems has often blocked making these connections, in that looking for support and allowing one's children to see that they are not totally alone with this issue has been known to increase "ammunition" in a custody battle, another ironic twist where healthy adaptations have been treated as aberrant behavior to be punished.

Nonetheless, lesbian families continue to find each other, and the formation of lesbian mothers' support groups as well as the occurrence of informal family get-togethers has done much to help families cope. There may be significant class differences between the lesbian families who find one another, because the lesbian community is more economically diverse than most communities that bond together out of a basic similarity. For this reason, class differences may affect the connection between families just as they universally do between individuals. However, there is already a history of commitment to grappling with these issues in the lesbian community, and as hard as they may be to achieve, resolutions are probably found more often there than in the straight world.

The presence of a lesbian community in general, regardless of the availability of other families, is of significance to the single mother and the parenting couple. It can provide them with a friendship network from which they do not have to hide their family life; it creates social spaces where they can get away from parenting, and, for the couple, not deny their relationship, and it is a continuing reaffirmation of identity for a unit that has to struggle to stay in touch with who they are and what they are doing. Lesbian parents report that an evening with lesbian friends or at a lesbian community event can feel like "coming home" after a day spent dealing with the straight world in their own and their children's lives.

## Invisibility

Family is defined in a certain way in this culture, and although this definition is shifting somewhat, the lesbian two-parent family is not recognized as such. The lesbian family most likely to be recognized as such is the single-parent family, and this recognition, conveniently for the larger culture, skirts the lesbian aspect.

For any single mother or for a couple, the building of family is an extremely important task, and it is a task with certain phases: the establishment of family rules about internal family life and about interaction with the outside world, the definition (spoken or unspoken) of boundaries around the family, and then the introduction of a child into this with the consequent shaking up and reorganizing of it all. Meanwhile, as the parents struggle with all of this and try to help their children feel part of a stable family unit, the world behaves as though they are not a family at all.

Clear boundaries around the heterosexual family are encouraged and respected by the larger system in many significant and little ways. The boundaries around the lesbian family usually are unrecognized, ignored, or reacted to with hostility and negative judgement.[4]

Language is an important aspect of visibility, as are cultural rites of passage. Lesbian families are often unsure how to describe or explain their relationships to the outside world, because there is no culturally acknowledged language for these connections. Furthermore, lesbians are denied cultural rites of passage that mark and celebrate such important life events as when one becomes a couple or a family. Rather than the acknowledgment given the same events in the lives of straight peers, there is often secrecy and anxiety mixed with the feelings of joy and love. There is little sharing of these events and little validation. Lacking this validation in the process of forming a family and experiencing the disqualification of people's denial or discomfort makes family-building a formidable task.

There is also a justifiable sense of insecurity and suspiciousness on the part of any lesbian toward the outside world. Lesbian mothers are always aware of the potential for devastating intrusion that at its worst comes in the threat of a custody case. When lesbians attempt to work out co-parenting arrangements and shared responsibility for the children, they become more visible and run the risk of rejection in their dealings outside the family boundaries; schools, daycare centers, and agencies may refuse to see them or respect them as family. The children, too, become participants in this closing off as day to day they deal with an awareness that their family is different and viewed by the larger culture as "not right," and as they get older and become aware of the need or wish to keep family life secret. The threats inherent in being visible and the consequent secrecy often attached to this anxiety can contribute to a high degree of invisibility. Consequently, the boundaries around a lesbian family may be closed more cautiously in a self-protective stance toward the outside world.[5]

The fact of the invisibility of the lesbian family as a unit gives this closed-system aspect to family boundaries an ironic twist. The cautiously closed nature of the system is maintained by the secret of the lesbianism and the ways in which outsiders often do not know the true nature of the family structure. This fact of self-protectiveness paradoxically leaves the family boundaries excessively permeable and open to forms of intrusion that are largely unheard of in closed-system heterosexual families. When the relationship between the parents is unrecognized, either because they choose to hide it or because others choose to ignore it, then no matter how defined the system may be internally, ex-lovers, ex-husbands, and members of the couple's family of origin can often walk in and out at will, as though the family unit does not exist.

Many lesbians do not feel safe or justified in confronting these intrusions into their families. The invalidation of lesbian relationships inherent in outsider's claims on the space and time of one or both members of a couple make it hard to take self and family seriously as valid, important entities entitled to integrity. Developing this self-validation is an important family-building task.

The critical issue will be learning how to deal constructively with this culture, a task that will not be accomplished overnight. For some lesbians, dealing with cultural forces involves first dealing with their own internalized homophobia. For others, it involves identifying and using effectively the available supports. For still others, it might mean having an ongoing place to deal with the stress, either through a support group or lesbian mothers' group, an informal or formal counseling arrangement, political activity, or simply a strong lesbian friendship network.

There is clearly a need for lesbian parents to make their families solid from within. Although the challenge of this is great, the creativity and strength that lesbians bring to this task enhance not only family members, but also those in the larger culture who choose to learn from them the potential for growth in the appreciation of difference.

## Family of Origin

Becoming a mother or co-parent affects any adult's relationship to the family in which she grew up. As with past "crisis," the announcement that a lesbian is to become a mother may either bring family members closer or distance them more; it may either open dialogue or close it down. Occasionally, the past difficulty of working through the grandparents' (or other family members') concerns at disclosure of their daughter's lesbianism, or the ways in which they have "adapted," may have made positive connections more challenging to achieve. It has been my experience that basic family patterns will not alter significantly around the news of a pregnancy, adoption, or co-parenting arrangement.

However, once there is a grandchild, there tends to be more connection and at least temporarily, more conflict or issues to work out. Grandparents may want to be involved because they feel "concerned" for the child—not surprisingly, this manifests as intrusion. They may also genuinely want to be involved because it is their grandchild—not the way they dreamed of it, but their grandchild nonetheless. A lesbian mother is faced with numerous decisions about the connection to her parents that are more complicated than before because of her children's needs. All lesbians have to assess constantly where and how to take issue with the invalidating behavior that occurs in varying degrees and ways in almost all families. However, a lesbian mother may feel less able or willing to do this when the repercussions will be felt not only by adults, but also by her children. This may operate two ways. Can she give in to exclusion of her lover from family events in the way she might have once, when the children will experience their family as disrupted at an important time? On the other hand, can she freely protest typical invalidating behaviors, such as the assignment of separate beds in the grandparents' home, when the tension evoked will be experienced by the children and cause them anxiety? A lesbian mother needs to assess when to take a stand to maintain her integrity, because she will want to communicate that sense of family and of personal integrity to her children. There will be times, however, when it is right and reasonable to compromise in order to protect the children, just as there will be times when it is important not to compromise in order to protect the children.

When the co-parent's parents are involved as grandparents, the lack of language to describe relationships affects another generation. Both sets of grandparents may share the children's discomfort with explaining the family in a straightforward manner to friends, relatives and neighbors, leaving the lesbian parents caught between denials.

In spite of the obstacles, important relationships and connections regularly happen between the oldest and youngest generation. The lesbian parents' efforts to find the balance between maintaining their integrity and compromising where there is benefit are part of the struggle between a lesbian's need for adult autonomy and her need for these important people in her life. This developmental task differs from that of a straight peer in that the autonomous adult position for a lesbian is stigmatized and often feared by her parents.

Ideally, lesbian mothers and their children will have contact with traditional extended family whenever possible. Children are enriched by connection to grandparents, aunts, uncles, and cousins; for the child in a lesbian family, this is one of the ways in which they are like their peers. For the parents, these extended family members can be an important source of practical and emotional support.

## Couple's Concerns

Lesbian couples who will be raising children together share common concerns regardless of how their family is formed. When the parents come to parenting as a blended (step) family or through a mutual decision to have a child together, the issue of what it means for two females to negotiate the roles of "mother" and co-parent is complex. Both women have had a lifetime of socialization to be mothers, and often both experience a genuine desire to do so, which practically speaking cannot happen all at once. No matter who bears or adopts the child, both females may have their "mother stuff" called forth.

The fact that there is no definition of the role of co-mother as there is of father (a frame of reference even if a man chooses to refute that role) makes the negotiation of roles particularly hard for the co-parent at home and out in the world. No matter how strong her presence and involvement in the family, it is she who bears the brunt of invisibility. It is she who disappears, it is she who is disenfranchised—by the school, by both families of origin, by the outside world, sometimes (even more painfully) by the children or by friends in the lesbian network who do not see her as a parent nor understand the unique pressures of her position in the family. Lesbians are still forging possible models for the potential of this parenting role. The co-parent is clearly of critical importance in the child's life. And there is pain for both partners in the lack of acknowledgment for their joint struggles and joys by the culture at large.

It is hard for either parent to know in advance what the negotiation of parental roles inside the family will evoke in them. The deliberateness with which they engage in this process together may have bearing on how well they will negotiate the difficulties that arise around restructuring a family system if it is a blended family and exploring uncharted water if it is not. Often, for a lesbian couple, this is not done as consciously as it could be, because there are few role models.

In a blended family, the biological mother may not be ready to give up her power, control, and intensity of involvement, especially if she has been a single parent. At the same time, she may show great relief at the idea of not having to do it all alone any more. Often the co-parent is confused by this message and has her own concerns, too, as she experiences possible conflict between wanting to be an "instant parent" and finding that it takes time to bond with the child and adjust to the major transition to parenthood.

In any family formation, the co-parent's bonding process can be impeded by the fact of her nonlegal status.[6] She is often painfully aware that if she and the mother part, she faces a potential double loss because she has no ultimate power over her relationship with the children. This reality (which can be alleviated but not totally allayed by legal contracts)[7] can highlight emotional risks that affect her process of commitment and attachment.

Especially if the women have decided to have the child together, idealistic fantasies about being completely equal, that is, the same, in relation to the child may bring up difficult areas of conflict. These dynamics, should they remain unresolved, provide fertile ground for creation of confusion and divisive behavior on the part of the children. Often this will manifest in the couple's relationship as conflict between the mother and co-parent over the children's behavior and issues of discipline.

When there is some differential between the partners' levels of interest in embarking on this new phase of family life, it must be discussed. If there is a large differential in the level of interest in parenting, it is even more critical for the couple to project into the practical realities of their future together. Although lesbian couples do not have to be bound by traditional parenting roles, a full relationship between a mother and a partner who has chosen not to parent at all can be hard to manage and is clearly without helpful precedents. The couple, whether there is a large differential or not, should share their separate feelings about parenting and their fantasies and expectations of parenting together. A major aspect of this discussion should include how they envision sharing responsibility, including the area of financial responsibility. Lesbian couples have many, and complex, different arrangements for handling money. Whatever their arrangements before the children arrived, shared parenting reopens this issue for most couples. The implications for the relationship of possible alteration of these arrangements make this an extremely important negotiating process.

The couple can also look at stress points in their relationship in general and work with these problem areas to increase the stability of their relationship. When looking at the effect of a child in their lives, they will need specifically to imagine and project the effect on their relationship of such a change, especially with regard to their energy for one another. It is often hard to imagine the deprivation of time and contact in the context of a whole new set of issues and stresses to negotiate. This is true for any family.

Role definition and levels of involvement may be affected by the aging of the children as well. Adolescents who are more conflicted than they were when they were younger about their family being different may attempt to disenfranchise a co-parent who has been very active in their lives. When this occurs, it is critical for the couple to work together to make decisions that maintain the parents' integrity while still respecting the feelings of the adolescent.

It is important to remember that although this process takes its most obvious form in a blended family, it also occurs in homes where two women come to the decision to parent together. In this latter instance it may be unexpected for these concerns to emerge. Couples who have had or have adopted a child together report some surprise at the dilemmas they face related to mother and co-parent roles, both within the home and out in the community.

Whatever final arrangements the couple does make will vary greatly from family to family and will be affected by such variables as the individuality of the women involved, the degree of interest each has in mothering, the age of the children at the time these roles are being developed, and the duration of time the couple has been together. And the process changes continually as the needs of the parents and children change.

The area of role definition in families where both parents are female is an exciting new frontier from which all parents can learn.

### Children's Concerns

Children in a lesbian family will have the same stress of being different. Children do not like to be different, and this homophobic culture forces on the child a series of complicated negotiations with the outside world. No matter what a lesbian mother does to protect her children from ignorance, they will be faced with many decision points in their lives with regard to their family's relationship with the world, starting with "who can know and who can't."

The mother may face many varied reactions from the child over the years to this dilemma, including anger, silence, and anxiety. Some children may be concerned about how much ambivalence or feeling to show the parents out of loyalty and allegiance to family members.

Whatever reaction a lesbian mother gets, she has the task of meeting the children where they are and empathizing with their feelings about what being in a lesbian family means to them. She must help them develop coping strategies and not deny them the reality of their experience. Such a response can require added internal resolve and strength as the mother will recognize the roots of her own, and their, oppression in the world into which they want so badly to fit.

Some parents may experience feelings of guilt about what their children must deal with in this world. It is here that feelings of internalized homophobia on the part of the parents can fuel a dysfunctional response to external oppression; for example, whether these worries interfere with the parents' ability to provide discipline and set clear limits with their children or whether they manifest as anger. No parent, straight or gay, can make up to their children for times of hardship, nor can their children be blamed for their feelings about hardship.

Children who are born as the result of alternative insemination will have their own special concerns. Alternative insemination has been used widely for years by infertile heterosexual couples, and yet for the most part, those children have not been told about the facts of their conception. Lesbians' children conceived by alternative insemination will not be deceived about their origins, and this is as it should be. If the donor is anonymous, however, the children will have to deal with not having a known father. This knowledge, and the issues of fathers in general, is of interest to the children.

Adults adopted as children have made quite clear the importance of knowing their origins, as they actively and persistently search for their biological parents. Their reports of "something missing" in their personal identities are not to be ignored. Not to know or have contact with one's father raises external cultural issues and internal identity issues.

Practically speaking, a woman must ask herself if she can provide her child with the maximum amount of information available in a way that acknowledges its importance. This may mean being quite conscientious and assertive about getting detailed information about the donor's medical history, ethnic background, physical appearance, work-related interests, and, perhaps, reasons for donating sperm.

At an emotional level, the mother must be able to attend over the years to the changing questions and feelings of a child who may not be satisfied to know only about the family that she has provided. There may be questions about the mother's choice as well as questions about the father.

There is no reason why a child without a known father will not grow to a happy, healthy, and productive adulthood, especially if he or she is given the open help and support of his or her parent in dealing with this issue.

An ignorant larger culture will expose children of people in oppressed groups to painful dilemmas and experiences beyond their years. Within the context of the lesbian community, children may experience unrealistic expectations of what they should hear and understand about this world. This may be a manifestation of the occasional lack of familiarity with children, but more important it is an attempt to cope, and help children cope, with oppression. Many children develop a pseudosophistication that appears to make them equal participants, but anxiety is generated by expectations of adult levels of awareness. Children need to be protected from adult-oriented activities and conversations that are not appropriate to their age, both out in the world and within the community. Although this particular problem takes its own form in the lesbian community with aspects unique to the needs of, and the pressure on, this subculture, the general societal pressure on all children to be little grown-ups is the subject of much recent discussion.[8]

These are the primary issues with which, in my experience, the children of lesbians grapple. The issues all overlap with the concerns of many children. Most deal with worries about being different, embarrassment at the "peculiarities" of their parents, difficulties born of being made to grow up too fast, and, in many cases, absent fathers. For the children of lesbians, however, these worries are fueled by the negative judgments of the straight world.

As is the case with the children of many oppressed groups, the mastery of these difficulties develops strengths. The children may bring these strengths to bear on the influence they have on society as adults who appreciate individual difference and respect the wide range of human potential.

## The Responsibility of the Therapist

As lesbian parenthood becomes more common, therapists are more likely to see single lesbians or lesbian couples seeking treatment around issues raised by this possibility. Also, some families may encounter enough difficulty over the process of family-building, especially in a blended family situation, to warrant outside help. When lesbians approach the psychological profession, the response and awareness of the therapist is of critical importance.

The work of being a competent therapist with lesbian families begins long before the family ever comes for treatment. Therapists treating lesbians have the same responsibilities as those engaged in cross-cultural and cross-class treatment: the examination of their own attitudes and values about the specific population before the work begins.[9]

What prejudices, stereotypes, preconceived notions, assumptions, and even fears does she have? Where did she learn them? What does the therapist know about homosexuality and lesbian life-styles? There is much to read on the subject, some of it good, some of it awful, and all of it informative either about lesbians or about the homophobic world in which we live. A lesbian therapist may find that there are leftover issues of internalized homophobia to deal with as she is confronted with a family's problems in therapy. As it occurs, this is an issue for supervision.

This personal work is critical both in the therapy itself and in the relationship with the outside world. Therapists treating lesbian families may occasionally be called upon as advocates to outsiders—schools, courts, and social service agencies—on the behalf of the families. A sincere belief that there is nothing inherently problematic about lesbian parenting makes this task both easier and a trust-building process with a family who may be justifiably suspicious of the psychological profession.

Unless the therapist is fortunate enough to work in a setting known as a safe place for lesbians to come for treatment, there are some general issues around getting a lesbian family into therapy that need to be addressed. Lesbians have historically little cause to trust the psychological establishment, and it often takes a tremendous amount of courage for them to approach a clinic or other out-patient service for help. Often they will not call until it can no longer be avoided, either because a referral source is pressuring or because a state of acute crisis has developed. In either case, the therapist has a potentially tenuous relationship with her new client, and an examination of intake procedures, forms, the agency's general attitude, as well as the sensitivity of workers likely to have first contact is critical. For example, can intake forms be filled out accurately by lesbians with children? Will the form represent, when finished, who is in the home and what their connections are should they choose to state them? Or does the form routinely ask for mother, father, and children with no reference even to "others living in the home"?

If there is an intake meeting of clinicians, is there a listening ear for cases that might be lesbian clients or families (often not stated over the telephone), and are these cases assigned accordingly? If there is a public waiting room, is there a sensitivity, especially in a small community, to the anxiety of a lesbian couple being seen coming into therapy together? How can things be structured between therapist and client to minimize this added stress?

These are just a few of the practical issues to be examined. If a lesbian mother feels the need to hide her sexual identity, the therapist's work and the outcome for the family may be so seriously compromised as to render the treatment ineffective at best and potentially quite damaging.

When the lesbian family is finally in treatment, it may be that the parent(s) will want to investigate the therapist's attitude about homosexuality. This must be responded to in a straightforward and matter-of-fact way. The client has a right to know if she is in a supportive environment. Should this concern not be laid to rest by the therapist's answer, the problem may be the clinician's response. The therapist must look to her own issues first and seek feedback from knowledgeable colleagues.

The assessment of the lesbian family in therapy does not differ significantly from the assessment of any family, but in this instance the therapist needs to develop the ability to view all that is being presented against the backdrop of gay oppression. Although the presenting problem may very well not be directly related to lesbianism, it is probably at least affected by it. The therapist must attend to that with which the family is specifically asking for help, while remaining attentive and alert to the special issues that also inform an understanding of the functioning of this system.

Lesbian families take many forms, and it is extremely important to determine who the members of the system are and how they view their relationships. Assumptions about parenting systems drawn from traditional heterosexual models may cause the therapist to miss important, self-defined extended family in the lesbian community. Although it may be a single parent or a couple who present for counseling, the family may be more complex than the therapist first realizes.

The therapist's exploration of a family's membership serves two critical functions. It identifies what this family's self-image is, how they see and describe themselves. It also allows the therapist to begin to counteract in the therapeutic setting the invalidation of the world. At times, the therapy itself is a rite of passage, often long overdue, a place where the family can be recognized and treated as a family. While respecting the defenses of the extremely closeted lesbian or couple raising children, in general the therapist should overtly support and label the reality of this group of people as a family unit and help them to see the interplay between what they are struggling with and the stage of their developing system. It can be extremely illuminating, affirming, and relieving for the therapist to recognize out loud that it is not a simple task to negotiate such things as adding new members, defining roles with regard to the children, and building a spousal and parental couple simultaneously when the world does not recognize the unit as a family.

And finally, in order to do all of the above, the therapist must examine her own basic notions of family. What does she think constitutes a family? How, and by whom, is family determined? What are her values and beliefs about what a child needs to thrive and grow in the home context? What are the therapist's attitudes about lesbians as mothers? Many lesbian families suffer greatly from the disintegrative effect of not being acknowledged as a family unit, either by omission or by commission. It is critical, therefore, that this validation not be absent in the context of therapy, or the therapist will be working against self and client.

## Conclusion

There have always been, and will continue to be, lesbians who are also mothers. There have always been, and will continue to be, lesbians who are caring, competent, and loving parents of children who will grow to be full human beings with, perhaps, an even greater internalized sense of tolerance, justice, and the full flexibility of human potential than many of their peers.

This reality, the reality of lesbian families, is a reality that is hard won. In a culture that is mother-blaming as well as homophobic, lesbian parents have been the objects of literal and figurative assault and intrusion ever since the dominant culture chose to recognize their existence. The acknowledgment of this existence has been highly selective, however, and most frequently has been invoked to punish. Here the recognition has stopped, as a myriad of invalidating behaviors have been the primary mode of relationship to the lesbian family.

The miracle, like the miracle of the survival of lesbians themselves, is that lesbian families continue to grow, both in potential and in numbers, in the face of a cultural context that is hostile at worst and ignorant at best. This miracle is born of strength and determination.

As more and more lesbians become parents, the responsibility of the psychological community, which has amply participated in this oppression in the past, to provide a healing response to the unique stresses and pressures of lesbian families becomes an incontrovertible fact.

Those lesbian families who seek therapy rarely present initial problems that are directly related to their oppression. They present, like other families, issues of concern in the management of their daily lives and in the functioning of their relationships. Lesbian families are real families, and their presenting problems are real problems. These problems are exacerbated by the homophobia in the culture, but they cannot be resolved or explained away by an exclusive focus on the homophobia in the culture. The therapist who wishes to be helpful must have a respectful understanding of the backdrop of lesbian oppression and its impact of family-building and coupling problems while still primarily attending to that with which the clients have asked for help.

In order to do this, she must truly understand the contexts within which the lesbian family functions, the impact of those contexts on the family's functioning, and purposefully be able to make these understandings available for the use of the family when relevant.

Finally, in the midst of this critical awareness, it is imperative for lesbians and those who wish to support them to remember that being a lesbian parent is as unique in its pains and assets as being a lesbian. There is no satisfying trade-off in life for the integrity inherent in being oneself and the power and strength inherent in achieving this in the face of these odds.

## NOTES

I wish to acknowledge and thank my partner with whom I have experienced, and survived, much of the stress described in this chapter; our children for forcing me to grapple constantly with the complexity of life; my colleagues who have encouraged and supported me in this work; my lesbian clients for courageously sharing their pain and strength; and our lesbian community to whom, with all our individual and collective struggles, I can always "come home."

1. Marny Hall, "Lesbian Families: Cultural and Clinical Issues", *Social Work* 23 (Sept. 1978): 384; Audre Lorde, "Man Child: A Black Lesbian Feminist's Response" in *Conditions: Four* 2 (Winter 1979): 34.

2. Lorde, "Man Child," 35.

3. Lorraine Bethel, "What Chou Mean We, White Girl," *Conditions: Five* 2 (Fall 1979): 86–92; Audre Lorde, Zulma Rivera, Yee Lin, and Barbara Cameron, "I've Been Standing on This Street Corner a Hell of a Long Time," in *Our Right to Love: Lesbian Resource Book*, ed. Ginny Vida (Englewood Cliffs, N.J.: Prentice-Hall, 1978), 222–30.

4. Jo-Ann Krestan and Claudia Bepko, "The Problem of Fusion in the Lesbian Relationship," *Family Process* 19 (Sept. 1980): 278; Sallyann Roth, "Psychotherapy with Lesbian Couples: The Inter-relationships of Individual Issues, Female Socialization and the Social Context," in *Innovations in Psychotherapy with Homosexuals*, ed. Emery Hetrick and Terry Stein (Washington, D.C.: American Psychiatric Press, 1984), 93; Sallyann Roth, "Psychotherapy with Lesbian Couples: Individual Issues, Female Socialization and the Social Context," *Journal of Marital and Family Therapy* 2 (July 1985): 274.

5. Krestan and Bepko, "The Problem of Fusion in the Lesbian Relationship," 278; Roth, "Psychotherapy with Lesbian Couples," 274.

6. Nancy Todor, "Lesbian Couples: Special Issues," in *Positively Gay*, ed. Betty Berzon and Robert Leighton (Millbrae, Calif.: Celestial Arts, 1979), 53.

7. Hayden Curry and Denise Clifford, *A Legal Guide for Lesbian and Gay Couples* (Reading, Mass.: Addison-Wesley, 1980).

8. David Elkind, *The Hurried Child* (Reading, Mass.: Addison-Wesley, 1981).

9. Harry Aponte, "Underorganization in the Poor Family" in *Family Therapy: Theory and Practice,* ed. Philip J. Guerin (New York: Gardner Press, 1976), 432; Hall, "Lesbian Families," 380; Monica McGoldrick, John Pearce, and Joseph Giodano, *Ethnicity and Family Therapy* (New York: Guilford Press, 1982).

# 12

## Child-Rearing Attitudes of Black Lesbian Mothers

MARJORIE HILL

Who is the lesbian mother, and what is unique about her? What is the effect of sexual orientation upon child-rearing attitudes? The lesbian mother has only recently become a focus of psychological investigation, even though one-fifth of lesbians have children.[1] This chapter reports a study that I undertook to examine explicit differences in child-rearing attitudes between lesbian and heterosexual women. Within the comparatively small number of published studies on female homosexuality, the samples tend to be exclusively white, predominantly well-educated, and upwardly mobile. For my study, I used only black subjects in order to raise some questions about the degree of applicability of previous studies. I assume that many of the issues discussed in this research can be generalized to other populations.

The range of parent personalities and attitudes about child-rearing is as broad in lesbian mothers as that found in heterosexual mothers. The principal difference between lesbian mothers and heterosexual mothers is that lesbians present an alternative to the present traditional family structure. The existence of lesbian mothers therefore enables our society to view all social relationships in a new light. For the lesbian mother herself, there are no set guidelines to follow. The universal concerns and problems associated with parenthood, whether as a single parent, as a couple, or as communal parents, may be compounded by being a lesbian. At the same time, having to choose guidelines frees the lesbian mother to make parenting a more creative endeavor.

For people who assume that being a lesbian means rejecting all that is traditionally feminine, particularly motherhood, the lesbian "family" and lesbian mothers are often difficult to conceptualize. Many form unions that mirror traditional family patterns.[2] Some have had children within the framework of a heterosexual relationship (often marriage). Adoption and artificial insemination are the other means that lesbians currently use to become mothers. Adoption agencies have increasingly allowed single women and men to adopt more difficult-to-place, older, or handicapped children, although most agencies prefer married couples.[3] Women who wish to adopt through recognized agencies do not make an issue of their homosexuality, because most agencies consider homosexuality undesirable in a potential parent. An example of this sort of homophobic bias is the decision of the Massachusetts Department of Social Services to take two foster children out of a gay male couple's family in response to public pressure, despite recent research that indicates that young children do not develop "deviant" traits solely as a result of being with gay individuals or gay parents.[4] The problems of children of homosexuals may or may not be specifically linked to the parents' homosexuality.[5] Most women in the lesbian community do not choose adoption, but rather deliberately get pregnant with a friend or by alternative insemination, with or without the "father" of their child realizing that a pregnancy has resulted from the encounter.

The effects on children of being raised within the context of a lesbian household are only recently being examined, and few empirical data are available. Martha Kirkpatrick, Ron Roy, and Catherine Smith base their findings on interviews and a battery of tests conducted with twenty Los Angeles children aged five to twelve.[6] The authors report some problems in these children, but the types of difficulties are the kind typically seen in children of divorced parents: conflicts of loyalties, a guilty concern over the cause of the parents' split-up, and anxiety about whether or not they will face future loss. The children did not form a transsexual self-image or reject gender-appropriate behaviors.

Because so little literature went beyond discussion of custody issues for the lesbian mother and the influence of her life-style on her children, I determined to conduct a study to examine and identify explicit differences in child-rearing attitudes between lesbian and heterosexual women. The investigation was based on the premise that conscious and unconscious factors would have differing effects upon child-rearing. Women who define themselves as lesbians have consciously acknowledged and accepted their homosexuality and would therefore tend to manifest behaviors comparable to those behaviors cited in the current literature as more independent, more candid, resilient, and self-sufficient than their heterosexual counterparts.[7] These attributes, I suspected, would be demonstrated in parenting styles and attitudes. Thus I predicted that:

1. Lesbian mothers would place a higher value on independence and self-sufficiency than heterosexual mothers.
2. Lesbian mothers would demonstrate more tolerance and tend to be more flexible about rules than heterosexual mothers.
3. Lesbians would express a preference for older children because of their more autonomous and independent behavior.
4. Lesbian mothers would be more tolerant of their children's sexuality than traditional mothers.
5. Lesbian mothers would be more candid than traditional mothers.
6. Lesbian mothers would view boys and girls as being more similar than do heterosexual mothers.
7. Lesbian mothers would express more traditionally masculine sex-role expectations from their daughters.
8. Lesbians would tend to interfere more consistently with their children's relationship with their fathers.

## Subjects

A group of twenty-six lesbians and a group of twenty-six heterosexual mothers served as subjects in the study. All of the women were black, and each had at least one child who was between the ages of four and thirteen. Sexual orientation was identified by the women themselves on the initial demographic questionnaire. For the purpose of the study, a lesbian mother was defined as one who acknowledged homosexuality with sexual attraction and interest in women and was the biological mother of at least one child. The women were asked to choose their sexual preference among homosexual, bisexual, and heterosexual orientations. Any woman identifying herself as a bisexual was not included in the study. A total of sixty-three women agreed to participate. Six women identified themselves as bisexual, twenty-six homosexual, twenty-six heterosexual, and five elected not to state sexual preference.

Lesbian subjects ranged in age from 24 to 41 ($X=30.34$), while heterosexual subjects ranged in age from 21 to 41 ($X=29.65$). Thus, there was no significant difference in age between the two groups ($t(50)=.55$, $p>.05$). Lesbian mothers averaged 1.4 children and heterosexual mothers averaged 2.0. Twenty-seven percent (7 mothers) of both samples were single parents living alone with their children. Forty-three percent of the lesbian mothers lived with their lover, while 65 percent of heterosexual mothers lived with boyfriend or husband. Education was predominantly at the high school graduate or associate of arts graduate level for both groups, although the lesbians had more education on the average. Eleven lesbians and twenty heterosexuals were high school graduates, and six lesbians and six heterosexuals were associate of arts graduates. Six lesbians had B.A. degrees, and three had an M.A. degree.

I recruited the women. Because many of them were recruited from two lesbian organizations (Mothers & Co., a black lesbian mothers' discussion group, and Salsa Soul Third World Gay Women, Inc.), I attempted to recruit heterosexual mothers from comparable straight organizations. Several of these mothers were active members in a Headstart parents' group or in Black Women's Collective, a tri-state organization in New England that focuses on consciousness-raising for black women. Subjects themselves also provided additional contacts who participated in the study.

*Method*

I gave to each subject a packet containing an introductory letter, a consent-to-participate form, and five questionnaires. The first of the questionnaires that I developed requested detailed demographic data. The child-rearing practices questionnaire contained 131 items relating to attitudes about punishment, independence, necessity for rules, spouse involvement, and preference for older or younger children. The perceived sex-role questionnaire contrasted mothers' perceptions of boys and girls, explicitly measuring how similar or dissimilar the sexes were viewed. The expected sex-role questionnaire consisted of two sections (boys and girls), on which mothers had to select on a five-point scale the importance of certain attributes important to successful adjustment.[8] Although I collected information on both boys and girls, for the purposes of the study I analyzed only information on the expectations of girls. The final questionnaire I constructed was on sex training. It measured a mother's degree of permissiveness in three areas: information control, modesty, and sex play. I provided a separate sheet for additional comments. Questionnaires were administered in such a manner as to guarantee anonymity and thereby ensure confidentiality. Subjects were apprised of this fact and further informed that total testing time was approximately 1½ hours. Most subjects were given the packets at home, while a few with more flexible work situations chose to receive them at their place of employment. Several of the mothers from the Headstart group filled out the questionnaire in the parents' room. Those subjects who asked about the purpose of the investigation were informed after the interview was completed.

TABLE 1. *t*-Test Values of Hypotheses Under Investigation

| | Lesbian | | Heterosexual | | | Signifi-cance |
| --- | --- | --- | --- | --- | --- | --- |
| | X | sd | X | sd | t Value | Level |
| Promotion of independence | 36.92 | 5.82 | 40.11 | 6.85 | 1.81 | .07 |
| Preference of older vs. younger children | 37.57 | 8.83 | 35.53 | 8.07 | 0.868 | .60 |
| Level of rules used (flexibility) | 34.30 | 6.82 | 38.15 | 4.62 | 2.37 | .02[a] |
| Sex training (overall) | 70.11 | 11.27 | 57.07 | 9.9 | 4.42 | .001[c] |
| Sex training (modesty) | 17.21 | 4.09 | 14.82 | 4.03 | 2.12 | .04[a] |
| Sex training (sex play) | 22.47 | 5.29 | 15.90 | 5.12 | 4.55 | .001[c] |
| Sex training (information control) | 22.51 | 4.02 | 20.02 | 3.94 | 2.26 | .03[a] |
| Motivational distortion | 12.69 | 4.00 | 14.07 | 2.66 | 1.46 | .14 |
| Perceived sex role | 23.15 | 8.53 | 17.15 | 7.98 | 2.62 | .01[b] |
| Expected sex role | 45.5 | 3.04 | 42.03 | 3.73 | 3.25 | .001[c] |
| Alter time | 0.42 | 0.50 | 0.42 | 0.50 | 0 | 1.00 |

[a] Significant at .05 level
[b] Significant at .01 level
[c] Significant at .001 level

## RESULTS

To test the hypotheses of the present study, I used individual *t*-test for independent sample means (Table 1). The first hypothesis, which states lesbian mothers will place a higher value on independence and self-sufficiency than heterosexual mothers, was not supported ($t(50)=1.81$, $p<.05$). Thus, there is no evidence that lesbians would be more likely to foster these attributes in their children than heterosexual women. Similarly, the preference for older children because of the more autonomous and independent behaviors that they manifest was also not supported ($t(50)=0.868$, $p>.05$).

Lesbian mothers were hypothesized to be more tolerant and to demonstrate more flexibility about child-rearing rules. Level of rules of behavior used (factor 2, child-rearing practices questionnaire) evidenced a significant difference between the two groups ($t(50)=2.37$,

$p<.05$) such that heterosexuals demanded adherence to rules more frequently than did the lesbian subjects.

Lesbian mothers as a group demonstrated more tolerance of children's sexuality than did heterosexual mothers ($t(50)=4.42$, $p<.001$). Further analysis of subscale items also yielded statistically significant results. Lesbian mothers evidenced more permissiveness about modesty ($t(50)=2.12$, $p<.05$), about sex play ($t(50)=4.55$, $p<.001$), and greater openness in giving information ($t(50)=2.26$, $p<.05$).

A mother's tendency to be more candid was measured by factor 7 on the child-rearing practices questionnaire. There was no statistically significant difference evidenced in candor between lesbians and heterosexuals ($t(50)=1.46$, $p>.05$).

Compared to heterosexual mothers, lesbian mothers as a group rated their perceptions of boys and girls as being more similar than dissimilar. Thus, the hypothesis that lesbian mothers viewed male and female children as more similar than their heterosexual counterparts was confirmed ($t(50)=2.62$, $p<.01$).

Lesbian mothers did express more traditionally masculine role expectations of their daughters than did heterosexual mothers ($t(50)=3.25$, $p<.001$). There was, however, no significant difference between the groups of mothers in tendency to interfere with their children's relationship with their fathers, with both groups having identical means and standard deviations.

*Interpretation*

Before turning to the specifics of the study, it is important to consider the research context within which it was carried out: the paucity of research on lesbians, and especially on lesbians of color and lesbians in nonstereotypic roles such as motherhood.

Some studies reviewed explicitly stated that the sample was exclusively white, while many did not specify.[9] Alan Bell and Martin Weinberg specifically addressed the poor representation of black gay men and lesbians in the literature, and attempted to rectify this situation in their study.[10]

Furthermore, we must realize that the phenomenology of any given variable may differ for black subjects. Because the issue of race suggests that it may not be possible to generalize comparisons of data based on exclusively or predominantly white groups of lesbians with other racial groups, then the racial homogeneity of the present sample may be of importance either equal to or exceeding orientation. Just as motherhood is complex, so are blackness, femaleness, and gayness. It was beyond the scope of my project to investigate how the women in my study have reconciled these various attributes. Thus it is plausible that some of the variables that I studied may address issues extremely relevant to being black, whereas others may relate to sexual preference.

For example, findings did not support the hypotheses that lesbian mothers would place a higher value on independence and self-sufficiency than heterosexual mothers and that they would also prefer older children because of more autonomous and independent behaviors. These results do not mean that independence is not stressed by gay or straight subjects, but rather that there is no statistically significant difference between the two groups. One interpretation is that independence is quite important to black women, regardless of sexual preference; thus no difference was demonstrated. In fact, Robert Hill points out the self-reliance of black women, which would also encourage and value independence.[11]

Likewise, degree of candor, as studied in the current psychological literature, revealed no significant difference between the two groups. Again, it is possible that openness and candor may be valued similarly by black women as a group, and sexual orientation may be of less consequence. It is also possible that agreement to participate in the study and affinity with the investigator, who is a black woman, may have elicited a similar degree of candor from both lesbian and heterosexual women. In fact, several subjects from both groups agreed to participate because they felt that it was important for black women to work together and be supportive of one another.

It is also possible that my measure of candor did not measure what I wanted. Note, for example, that six heterosexual subjects did not answer the question about what age they began current sex activity, whereas all lesbian subjects answered this question. It is possible that overall candor was not different, but that disclosure around certain subjects (i.e., sex) may be different for the two samples. Mark Freedman also found some indications of more general openness and candor for lesbians in contrast to heterosexuals, a phenomenon that may also have been topic-related.[12]

The hypothesis comparing mothers' flexibility yielded a significant difference between the gay and straight samples. Heterosexual mothers tended to have more rules and be less flexible about transgressions. The lesbians' flexibility can perhaps be understood as an outgrowth of having accepted an alternative life-style and therefore having developed a greater tolerance as individuals, which in turn extended to their roles as mothers. In the process of accepting one's lesbianism, a woman re-examines other kinds of social relationships.[13] The presence of relatively few lesbian family models would suggest that developing and modulating a family system would require relatively more flexibility than adhering to or modifying a more traditional family pattern. Lesbian mothers have to keep in mind they are building new family structures even though they are not sure what the completed form will be.[14] Thus, adaptability and flexibility are indicated strongly.

Not all the lesbians in my sample were "out." Lesbian mothers' acceptance and acknowledgment of their own sexuality suggests that they would have more tolerant attitudes about their children's sexuality. In a more detailed analysis of the components of tolerance, lesbian mothers as a group reported more permissive attitudes about modesty, more openness about sexual information, and more acceptance of sex play than their heterosexual counterparts. For example, lesbian mothers tended not to get overly excited about self-stimulation, but viewed it as a natural phenomenon. Their permissive attitude did not encourage sex play or bombard the child with excessive information, but seemed to facilitate handling these issues in a less rigid, stereotyped fashion. I suspect that identity of sexual preference was a key factor in permissiveness; however, it is possible that level of education may have also had an effect on degree of permissiveness. Thirty-five percent of the lesbian sample had B.A. or M.A. degrees, compared to the heterosexual sample, who had completed at most two years of college education. (These results are comparable to those cited by F. E. Kenyon, who found that in his sample, more lesbians had university educations than heterosexual women).[15] It is, of course, possible that both sexual preference and to some extent education affected mothers' attitudes about sex training.

The hypothesis investigating mothers' perceptions of boys and girls, specifically that lesbian mothers tended to view children as more similar than heterosexual mothers, was confirmed. One explanation could be that lesbian mothers appreciated the androgynous nature of their boys and girls and therefore saw them as less different from one another than did heterosexual mothers. Another possible interpretation could be that lesbian mothers saw boys as being more effeminate and consequently not different from girls; or they saw girls as more masculine and hence not different from boys. The results from the expected sex-role questionnaire yield some insight on these interpretations. Lesbian mothers did express more traditionally masculine role expectations of their daughters. Similarly, the two groups of mothers differed greatly on their support of the Equal Rights Amendment, from which their feelings about women's rights can be inferred. The lesbian mothers supported the ERA twenty-four to two. The heterosexual mothers were more equally divided on this issue, with only fifteen out of twenty-six supporting the ERA. It appears that the lesbian mothers have consistently less traditional ideas relating to the stereotypical feminine role. Maleness is perhaps viewed as less powerful only because femaleness is imbued with the potential to be more powerful.

Political awareness and consciousness, although not explicitly examined in this present study, no doubt have an effect on some of the opinions expressed. More of the gay subjects were affiliated with and recruited from lesbian organizations than straight women from heterosexual organizations. Although some gay women were not members or actively involved, there seemed to be an acknowledgment of the significance of group identity. For example, Mothers and Co. was formed out of a need for a support group that addressed issues specific to these women. In contrast, the Headstart parents' group was formed by Headstart to encourage parents' (primarily mothers') involvement. The clear difference is that if a heterosexual mother elected not to be in the group that I sampled, there are a myriad of other existing bodies to which she could belong and from which she could obtain support. It is possible that not having the option to choose many groups, or specifically selecting a lesbian group, would suggest a more political ideology. Thus, affiliation with a lesbian organization may be a political statement in and of itself. Several studies recruiting lesbians from gay organizations have addressed this issue.[16] Furthermore, there is some suggestion that these particular "types" of lesbians may not be typical of lesbians in general.

There was no significant difference between lesbian and heterosexual mothers in tendency to interfere with their children's relationships with their father. (None of the sample reported not knowing who the father was.) In fact, in response to the question, "Have you done anything to alter the amount of time father sees child?" 58 percent of each group answered no. The remaining 42 percent of heterosexual mothers and 35 percent of lesbian mothers had encouraged the father to see the child more often, while one lesbian mother discouraged the father, and one lesbian mother did not allow the father to see the child. It is interesting that no difference was discerned, especially since 61 percent of the gay women were separated or divorced, compared to only 15 percent of the straight women.

The underlying premise on which my investigation was based was that factors in the realm of consciousness would facilitate parenting, and those indicative of unconscious conflict would interfere or have a negative effect. Fostering independence, flexibility about rules, perceptions of male and female roles, and permissive attitudes regarding sexuality were those variables that related to the conscious domain in my subjects. Under the assumptions of traditional psychology, two other findings would be considered to reflect the "negative" results of the lesbians' unconscious conflicts: their more traditionally masculine role expectations of daughters (resulting from a prolonged masculinity complex, as Freud suggested)[17] and an increased tendency to interfere with the father's relationship with his child (disappointment in father, hostile feeling toward father or father-role, according to Deutsch and Horney)[18] and would be seen as not conducive to the ideal parenting model. I maintain that these may better be viewed as *positive* factors for the child. In our society, it might be extremely helpful for a mother to have more traditionally masculine expectations for her daughter. Similarly, good judgement rather than "unconscious motives" might be the cause of a mother limiting or refusing visitation rights to a child's father.

## Implications of Future Research

The results and implications of the study I have described lend themselves to suggestions for future research. As this book begins to do for the realm of lesbian psychology, the area of female homosexuality needs more research. A closer examination of race, ethnic origin, socioeconomic status, and degree of "out-ness" needs to be addressed to fill the gaps in the literature on the lesbian personality. Attempts to delineate variables, effects, and interactions upon each other (i.e., blackness and gayness) would aid in clarifying the strengths and needs of this population. A replication of this study using white women would perhaps provide some insight on the modulation of race and sexual preference on parenting.

The inclusion of a third group, bisexual mothers, would also provide an interesting replication of this study, particularly in exploring whether bisexual mothers' attitudes would more clearly resemble heterosexual mothers' or lesbian mothers' attitudes about child-rearing.

There is certainly a need for more research on lesbian mothers, not focused on custody cases and legal cases, but rather dealing with child-rearing and issues specific to being a gay mother. When and how should a child be told of his or her mother's sexual preference? What are the positive or problematic effects upon a child of mother's being out in the community or school? What are the effects of secrecy or being in the "closet"? Do children of lesbians have greater options in choosing their sexual orientation and life-style in general?

Another issue not addressed explicitly in my study was the lesbian mother's expectations of her sons. Male children pose a dilemma for gay mothers, and many are concerned about bringing up their sons as well as their daughters in a nonsexist way.[19] It is possible that reflecting upon the similarities or differences in the raising of sons in lesbian households might provide new models or new understanding of the development of sex-role stereotypes in our society. The combined results of such research would be invaluable to educators, parents, and society at large.

## NOTES

1. Alan P. Bell and Martin S. Weinberg, "Homosexualities: A Study of Human Diversity," in *Women and Men* (New York: Simon and Schuster, 1978).

2. Janet S. Chafetz, Patricia Sampson, and Paula Beck, "A Study of Homosexual Women," *Social Work* 19 (Nov.-Dec. 1974): 714–23; Marny Hall, "Lesbian Families: Cultural and Clinical Issues," *Social Work* 23 (Sept.-Oct. 1978): 380–5; Deborah G. Wolf, *The Lesbian Community* (Berkeley: University of California Press, 1979).

3. Dorothy I. Riddle, "Relating to Children: Gays as Role Models," *Journal of Social Issues* 34 (Summer 1978): 38–58.

4. Martha Kirkpatrick, Ron Roy, and Catherine Smith, "A New Look at Lesbian Mothers," *Human Behavior* (1978): 60–1.

5. Ruth N. Weeks, Andre P. Derdeyn, and Margaretha N. Langman, "Two Cases of Children of Homosexuals," *Child Psychiatry and Human Development* 6 (Jan. 1975): 26–32.

6. Kirkpatrick, Roy, and Smith, "A New Look at Lesbian Mothers."

7. Mark Freedman, "Homosexuality Among Women and Psychological Adjustment" (Ph.D. diss. Western Reserve University, 1968), *Dissertation Abstracts* 28, 4294B; June Hopkins, "The Lesbian Personality," *British Journal of Psychiatry* 15 (1969): 1433–36; Norman L. Thompson, Boyd R. McCandless, and Bonnie R. Strickland, "Personal Adjustment of Male and Female Homosexuals," *Journal of Abnormal Psychology* 78 (April 1971): 237–40.

8. I used the "Expected Sex Role" and "Perceived Sex Role" questionnaires, in *Child Rearing Values*, ed. Wallace E. Lambert, Josianne F. Hammers, and Nancy F. Smith (New York: Praeger Publishers, 1979).

9. Virginia Armon, "Some Personality Variables in Overt Female Homosexuals," *Journal of Projective Techniques* 24 (1960): 292–309; Thompson et al., "Personal Adjustment of Male and Female Homosexuals"; Shelomo Osman, "My Stepfather Is a She," *Family Process* 11 (June 1972): 209–18.

10. Bell and Weinberg, "Homosexualities."

11. Robert Hill, *The Strengths of Black Families* (New York: Emerson Hall, 1971).

12. Freedman, "Homosexuality among Women and Psychological Adjustment."

13. Wolf, *The Lesbian Community*.

14. Women in Transition, Inc., *A Feminist Handbook on Separation and Divorce* (New York: Scribner, 1975).

15. F. E. Kenyon, "Studies in Female Homosexuality IV: Social and Psychological Aspects," *British Journal of Psychiatry* 114 (1968): 1337–50.

16. Hopkins, "The Lesbian Personality"; Marvin Siegleman, "Adjustment of Homosexual and Heterosexual Women," *British Journal of Psychiatry* 120 (1972): 477–81.

17. Sigmund Freud, *Femininity*, Standard Edition, vol. 22 (London: Hogarth Press, 1933).

18. Helene Deutsch, "On Female Homosexuality," *Psychoanalytic Quarterly* 1 (1932): 484–510, and "Female Homosexuality," *International Journal of Psychoanalysis* 14 (1933): 34–56; Karen Horney, in *Feminine Psychology*, ed. Harold Kelman (New York: Norton, 1967).

19. Marny Hall, "Lesbian Families: Cultural and Clinical Issues."

# IV

# THERAPIES

# 13

## Internalized Homophobia: Identifying and Treating the Oppressor Within

LIZ MARGOLIES, MARTHA BECKER, AND
KARLA JACKSON-BREWER

In the last fifteen years the gay rights movement increased the awareness of the intensity of social intolerance of homosexual men and
women. A review of the literature reveals numerous articles addressing
this oppression, homophobia, as a social phenomenon, the response
of homosexuals to a prejudiced environment, or homophobic beliefs
of psychotherapists. However, there is a dearth of material concerning
the process by which minority victimization affects internal processes
and sense of self. In our work with lesbian clients, we have been
confronted regularly with the insidious and limiting effects this internalized homophobia has on their lives.

We explore here, for the benefit of clinicians and other readers,
the relationship between the reality of homophobic culture and the
impaired identity of lesbians and gay men. We will not address the
etiology of homosexuality, which we consider a normal variation in
sexual/affectional object choice. We propose both a conceptual model
of, and a treatment approach to, internalized homophobia. The model
provides a structural definition for understanding and identifying
homophobic feelings and behaviors. The treatment approach, developed from classical psychoanalytic thought, offers a reliable set of
clinical tools to facilitate working through these defenses. As an example
of the therapeutic approach, we will discuss the case of one client.

The term *homophobia* was first coined in 1973 by George Weinberg
to describe the irrational fear, hatred, and intolerance of homosexual

229

men and women.[1] We consider the opposite of an intrapsychic homophobia to be a feeling that one's homosexuality is ego-syntonic and integrated into one's whole life.

Homophobia functions on a social plane as well as internally as a defense mechanism. Culturally, it is a belief system that justifies discrimination based on sexual orientation. Gordon Allport claims that the social prejudices develop out of the natural tendency to overgeneralize and oversimplify the complexities of the world. According to Allport, this kind of prejudice is acted out in three stages, each more oppressive than the last: antilocution (offensive language), discrimination, and violence.[2] Homosexuals experience these as name-calling; denial of equal opportunities in the military, adoption proceedings, and employment; and "queer-bashing."

Internally, homophobia is the adoption and acceptance within a lesbian or a gay man of these negative attitudes. The oppressive and prejudiced environment takes root, feeding on histories, issues, and the unique social conditions of each individual. This internal oppressor cannot be identified, re-evaluated, and worked through without first clearly understanding the role of social deviance and the reality of its danger to the individual.

Damien Martin has argued that homosexuals comprise a minority group in this culture because they fit Allport's definition that the group suffers unjustified negative acts from the environment.[3] Allport goes on to identify certain minority group character traits resulting from the group's victimization. The list includes obsessive concern with the group stigma, denial of membership, withdrawal, passivity, aggression against one's own group, and identification with the dominant group (self-hate). These traits, seen in many homosexuals, Jews, blacks, and Hispanics, become the basis of the oppressor within.[4]

Homosexuals have some unique features as a group. Unlike blacks and Jews, for example, homosexuals do not have a group identity from birth, and therefore, the family does not provide the first role model and support system. In addition, blacks and Jews have churches, temples, and social institutions that provide sources of protection not available to homosexuals.[5]

A second critical difference between homosexuals and other minority groups is that the fact of homosexuality is not always visible to others. The lack of visibility permits individuals the option of denying membership publicly. The ability to "pass" means that there will always be a discrepancy between the number of publicly labeled "deviants" and the total number of lesbians and gay men. However, regardless of visibility, most homosexuals are viewed by mainstream society as sexual perverts, criminal, a danger to children, and psychologically disturbed. Alice Moses believes that if an individual is aware of the societal reaction to group members and can identify as one of that minority group, it is likely that the individual will self-label.[6] Kenneth Plummer claims that the consequences of labeling can be the same whether the stigma is socially or self-assigned.[7] A self-labeled lesbian, for example, may be "passing" as a heterosexual, but she often will experience the identical internal reaction of her "out" counterpart. She may fear and expect the public experiences of prejudice, which are overtly or covertly threatening to lesbians in this culture.

In other ways, a hidden lesbian may have a more difficult time. Moses has pointed out that in order to maintain a public impression as a nondeviant, a lesbian must learn how to be extra-sensitive to the common-sense understandings and behaviors of "normal" people. What is taken for granted by the dominant culture must be well rehearsed by the lesbian who desires to pass.[8] The risk of exposure is present daily. The hidden lesbian may also lose sight of the differences between her private and public self. She is isolated from her peers, and she knows always that the acceptance by the approved group is based on a lie. Weinberg claims that the amount of damage to the self caused by such a lie is directly proportional to the amount of self-contempt that motivated the lie.[9] In other words, passing can be motivated either by an accurate perception of a potentially dangerous situation or by internalized homophobia.

Internalized homophobia is expressed in a variety of ways. Some are quite obvious, for example, "I hate myself for being lesbian." The more covert and insidious forms are less easy to identify and are often expressions of unconscious homophobia, and are, in fact, defense mechanisms. If the therapist does not recognize these expressions, feelings, and behaviors, the treatment will have serious limitations. Clearly, no progress can be made unless the therapist has recognized her own internalized homophobia. The following is a beginning list of some of these less-obvious expressions and their underlying defenses.

1. *Fear of discovery.* Although such fear is generated by a need to protect oneself from possible rejection, it is sometimes expressed as the need to protect others from the knowledge of one's own homosexuality. Statements like, "It will kill them," or "We don't talk about my personal life, so there's no need to bring it up," express this fear and exhibit the defense mechanisms of projection and rationalization.

2. *Discomfort with obvious "fags" and "dykes."* The "bull-dyke," as the unembarrassed embodiment of how different lesbians are, evokes public scorn and condemnation that a more "normal-looking" lesbian

believes she doesn't deserve. A lesbian who tries to pass will fear that associating with more obvious homosexual types will give away her true identity. This belief and behavior are examples of the defense mechanism of identification with the aggressor.

3. *Rejection/denigration of all heterosexuals (heterophobia).* This is a homophobic response to reverse discrimination. When a lesbian's homosexuality is ego-syntonic, she doesn't require anyone to share her values and life-style. Projection is the defense at work here.

4. *Feeling superior to heterosexuals.* This form of homophobia is an exaggerated gay pride, a false embracing of differentness. It can be expressed as, "We are better because we have a harder life," or "Our lives are more interesting, freer, more artistic, less encumbered," or "We are better because we don't have to deal with men." These statements are often voiced by the lesbian community when a member decides to relate sexually to a man. These feelings and statements reflect the use of rationalization and reaction formation.

5. *Belief that lesbians are not different from heterosexual women.* This belief rationalizes and minimizes a true difference in an attempt to avoid discrimination (homophobia) from others. It denies the social, political, and sexual context within which lesbian relationships struggle for existence. This can be expressed as "Relationships are all the same, mine just happens to be with another woman," or "What we do in bed doesn't define us." This is rationalization and denial.

6. *An uneasiness with the idea of children being raised in a lesbian home.* This idea is often expressed as "I think artificial insemination is too deviant," or "I believe children need to have a male parent." These statements deny the reality that many children are raised by single mothers, and also demean the validity of the lesbian relationship. It is like saying, "It's okay for me to be a lesbian, but I wouldn't want my daughter to marry one." This employs the defense mechanisms of identification with the aggressor.

7. *Restricting attractions to unavailable women, heterosexuals, or those already partnered.* These attractions, which never lead to a fully committed relationship, are a way of restraining full expression of one's lesbianism. We will elaborate on this in a case presentation. Denial is the defense.

8. *Short-term relationships.* Issues of intimacy, trust, and merging notwithstanding, short-term relationships require less of a commitment to one's lesbianism. Living with a lover involves greater social risks and stigmas than having a casual "dating" relationship. Commitment brings with it decisions about public rituals, for example, Thanksgiving

with the family or the office Christmas party. Rationalization and denial are the defenses.

For homosexuals, internalized homophobia consists of two distinct forces: erotophobia (fear of or discomfort with one's own sexuality) and xenophobia (discomfort with one's strangeness). To live fully as a lesbian is a challenge to be both sexual and different. The weight of these two forces exists within each individual, side by side, playing against each other.

Xenophobia is experienced as a fear of parental and social rejection based on differentness from perceived expectations. As an internal conflict it is grounded within the family. The fear of being unacceptable to one's family, the fear of rejection and expulsion, leads to powerful self-hate. The superego serves as the repository of social/familial rules. Tampering with established patterns is often accompanied by shame, guilt, fear, and anxiety.

It is not necessary to come out to experience xenophobia. It is an internal process based on a projected response. As "weirdos," "freaks," "outlaws," "deviants," and "aliens," lesbians do not fulfill parental dreams, thereby losing the "good girl" status in their parents' or society's eyes, and hence their own self-esteem. Mourning this loss is an important stage in the therapeutic process. The homophobic tendency is either to deny difference, or to deny caring about difference.

Erotophobia, being uncomfortable with forthright sexual expression, is not limited to lesbians or gay men. Ours is a culture dealing with the paradox of pervasive sexual imagery and deep-seated sexual repression. All children are raised with sex guilt. In addition, women have historically equated sex with danger — the fear of unwanted pregnancy, rape, and venereal disease. In the media and popular culture, the openly sexual woman is considered a prostitute, whore, tease, and a "bad girl." Unlike heterosexuals, the lesbian has a total separation of sex from procreation, the one acceptable sexual function. With no courtship rituals or wifely duty to hide behind, lesbian sex is purely for pleasure. One of our society's homophobic distortions is therefore to see the lesbian only as sexual, which exacerbates her internalized erotophobia. When a lesbian comes out to her parents, or even considers doing so, the discussion is often the first family acknowledgment that she is a sexual being. Bringing home a lover reminds or announces to the parents that the two have sex. Love and romance take a back seat to the sexual aspects of the relationship.

Research studies have shown that people with more negative attitudes toward homosexuals express more rigidity and guilt toward their own sexual impulses.[10] They perceive gay men and women as more expressive of sexual impulses. Oppressed minority groups are often seen as more sexual. This may reflect some envy by the dominant group. For example, blacks may be considered hypersexual, Jews sexually exotic, and women insatiable.[11]

Consciousness-raising and political action groups have had major impact in identifying social and institutional forms of homophobia. They contribute to a more positive self-image for group members by placing the oppressive enemy outside the self, validating the feelings and experiences of individuals, breaking down personal isolation, and supporting the alternative life-style.

The more deeply internalized forms of homophobia, those without clear political sources, are rarely reached by these external activities. These untouched forms are often left unnamed, denied, or deemed unacceptable. When feelings are not afforded room for conscious expression, they are repressed and acted out instead. Consequently, when consciousness-raising or radical politics make the homophobia unacceptable, the internal forms become more subtle and insidious. For example, the concept of "political correctness" in the lesbian community has mythologized appropriate feelings and ideas about lesbianism. The subculture, acting as family, replaces the larger social order as an extender of homophobia. The unacceptable impulses and affects then become hidden or distorted. In other words, while the macroculture encourages the lesbian to feel only shame, the subculture pushes an abreactive pride. A rich and full experience of homosexuality must include the opportunity to question, doubt, and explore all aspects of being a lesbian in this culture.

The particular focuses and freedoms of therapy offer greater access to internalized homophobia, with fewer restrictions on expression. The therapeutic milieu and the relationship between client and therapist afford a unique opportunity to search below the social surface of homophobia.

The treatment approach evolves from a contextual understanding of lesbianism and the unique experiences and ego-strengths of each woman. Clients rarely seek therapy to deal with self-labeled internalized homophobia. Their homophobia is most often expressed in conjunction with other issues and remains embedded in a wide range of experiences. A number of studies have attempted to find significant psychological differences between lesbians and heterosexual women. Their results have varied widely; however, the majority of those that used nonclient populations discovered no significant differences in psychopathology and self-esteem.[12] A recent study by Ronald LaTorre and Kristina Wendenberg confirmed a previously tested conclusion that, with the exception of erotic preference, homosexual and heterosexual women possess many of the same psychological characteristics.[13] While studies of the limiting and deleterious effects of internalized homophobia have not been conducted, it is assumed that the homosexual burden of living in a hostile environment would produce some discernible differences between lesbian and heterosexual psychological profiles. This, then, needs to be the primary variable in developing a distinct treatment methodology for lesbians and gay men.

Internalized homophobia functions as a defense mechanism resulting from the ego's struggle between rules and desires. Rather than a single entity, internalized homophobia is comprised of a constellation of defense methods. Allowing for individual variations, the cluster usually includes rationalization, denial, projection, and identification with the aggressor. Similarly, Freud cited introjection, or identification, and projection as the tools employed to deal with unacceptable homosexual impulses and labeled them neurotic mechanisms.[14] It is the therapist's role to facilitate the differentiation between the pathological uses of these defense strategies and the healthy functions. When is the homophobia based on irrational, unfounded, or obsolete fears, and when is it a management defense the ego employs to cope with a hostile or ego-alien environment? Concurrently, therapeutic intervention must include an evaluation of the internal price of the defense, for example, the hiding, lack of intimacy, and sexual rigidity.

Anna Freud explained defense mechanisms as the techniques the ego makes use of to protect itself against unendurable or painful ideas, drives, and affects.[15] Anxiety can be in the form of objective anxiety, superego anxiety, and id anxiety. The ego struggles to ward off both unacceptable drives and the affects associated with the prohibited impulses.

Objective anxiety is developmentally a precursor to a child's superego. It is the internal representative of outside powers, a "forepain" that governs the ego's behavior. The anticipation of suffering that may be inflicted on the child by outside agents has ramifications, whether or not the expected punishment always or ever actually takes place. In adulthood, objective anxiety is the reality of an internalized homophobic culture.

In homophobia, id anxiety is triggered by homosexual sex (erotophobia), and the superego anxiety is a result of social deviance (xenophobia). Sexual impulses enter consciousness and seek gratification. Developmentally, once the ego is separated from the id, it views these demands more hostilely. The ego fears the superego, setting up an ideal standard demanding degrees of sexual renunciation. Whether it is the dread of the outside world, or dread of the superego, it is the anxiety that sets the defenses in motion. The political lesbian has an additional form of superego anxiety. A second ideal standard of adamant pride in one's lesbianism causes new anxieties for the ego.

The ego also wards off affects associated with the prohibited impulses. Whereas impulse gratification is always something pleasurable, affects may be either pleasurable or painful. The tendency to resist an affect may be greatest when it is distressing. With homophobia, the pain, longing, and mourning associated with living an unacceptable life-style become defended against.

After the therapist and client recognize the homophobia, the primary treatment goal is to reconcile the conflicting pulls between sexual impulses and shame or guilt. The ego must learn to gratify the id without recriminations from the superego. The internal battle needs to be exposed and a truce drawn up. A secondary goal is to help clients experience their sexual choices as ego-syntonic. Neither denying nor clinging to a lesbian identity allows for the fullest range of choices concerning living in this culture as a free sexual being. This involves observing and working through homophobic beliefs, feelings, and behaviors.

This treatment approach is fluid enough to allow for compatability with a range of therapeutic styles. These strategies will be most effective with clients with more intact egos. The approach, based on therapeutic work at a cognitive level, has its limitations in applicability for borderline and psychotic disturbances. Those patients are less able to make use of the relationship with the therapist or to develop intimate romantic partnerships with members of either sex.

Objective anxiety can be revealed by the exposing and exploring of conscious and unconscious fantasies. The cognitive structures of the client's ego are engaged to re-examine the old fears. The present-day accuracy of the homophobic fantasies is evaluated for signs of exaggeration, crudeness, distortion, and obsolescence. The therapist at this stage can question whether realistic difficulties are being used as a cover for other, more deep-seated fears and anxieties.

Id and superego anxiety are tapped by focusing discussion in therapy on the client's erotophobia and xenophobia. Therapists should encourage clients to deal with their families' responses to their lesbianism, whether real or imagined. They should direct discussion also to the resistances to forthright sexual expression. Therapy is the passage back into consciousness of the superego demands and the distorted or prohibited id impulses.

Finally, therapists should help create room in their egos for both the affects associated with the prohibited impulses and the more conscious feelings associated with choosing to live an alternative life-style. Clients need to discover and express discomfort, doubt, mourning, and fear, as well as pride and delight. It is a myth of lesbian politics that the healthy lesbian does not have these feelings. Such dogma encourages the twisting or denying of feelings that are appropriate to living a minority-group existence in a hostile environment. A by-product of this phase of treatment is often outwardly directed anger. As self-directed anger, shame, and identification with the oppressor are expressed and released, clients are more able to see the cultural expressions of homophobia and feel a righteous anger and indignation.

The role of the therapist in this work is crucial. The transference relationship can be examined in terms of projected fears and criticisms. What feelings or behaviors does the client perceive as unacceptable to the therapist? How does this vary if the therapist is heterosexual or homosexual? A positive working relationship can be the client's first building block of a support system. Clients internalize the acceptance of the therapist, an acceptance that acknowledges sexuality, differentness, fears, doubts, and pride. This internalization can facilitate fuller expressions of lesbianism in the outside world by reducing projection of unfounded, negative attitudes.

Therapists also serve as role models. Although it is certainly controversial to consider coming out to clients, Morin and Garfinkle have suggested that a crucial experience in changing homophobic attitudes is close personal interaction with gays of similar social status.[16] A successful, proud, competent lesbian therapist can pass this possibility on to her clients. Although some lesbian therapists are not in a position to be out in their jobs, they need to question if or how their own homophobia may play a role in that decision. Similarly, the choice of when or if to come out to clients needs to be examined in terms of individual treatment issues. Too often, therapists' internalized homophobia contaminates this treatment rationale. The internalized homophobia of both lesbian and heterosexual therapists will have transferencial counter consequences.

Rand, Graham, and Rawlings cite research that shows that the most significant role of the lesbian community is to validate members' self-esteem.[17] Their own study confirmed that psychological health is positively correlated with appropriate and selective self-disclosure, as well as frequency of contact with a lesbian community. Therefore, it becomes incumbent upon therapists to support and encourage client participation in lesbian groupings, with referrals to community resources when necessary.

A case example will illustrate the issues and techniques. Karen, twenty-six, is from a white, lower-middle-class family. She is the second oldest of six children. Her parents were divorced when she was seventeen. Her relationship with her father had always been positive and nurturing, whereas that with her mother was distant, critical, and conflicted. Karen moved to New York to be closer to her older sister. This sister, always considered the "bad girl" in the family, was living at that time with her lesbian lover. Although her older sister was often in trouble, Karen was her father's proclaimed favorite.

At the time that Karen entered therapy, she stated that she wanted to deal with career and family issues. She had just spent the summer going back and forth between her mother's and father's homes and was feeling torn and confused. Her professional aspirations were in music; however, she had spent her two years in New York as a daycare teacher and was feeling unfulfilled. During this first session, Karen also stated confusion about her sexuality. Karen did not identify herself as gay, straight, or bisexual, although she had never had a relationship with a man. She had been sexually involved with one woman throughout high school and two women during college. Since coming to New York, Karen had had a crush on a woman already in a lesbian relationship, followed by a futile courtship with a woman who was "confused" about her sexual orientation. As treatment began, Karen was "in love" with her married supervisor.

After six months of individual therapy, it was suggested that her treatment be supplemented by weekly group sessions. After several weeks in group, and in the context of telling another story, she inadvertently revealed that she had been sexual with a woman. She reported in her next individual session,

> I left the group and all the next day I couldn't believe that I told them. I walked down the street and heard myself saying over and over, I can't be gay, I can't be gay. I just can't handle how people react to it, how my father would react to it. . . . I asked myself if I could have my wish, what would it be: to be straight or feel good about being gay? And I chose being straight. . . . Instantly, I responded to myself, but I *am* gay. As I looked up, I saw two straight women come out of the store in front of me. They were talking to each other about make-up and I said to myself, I'm not straight, I'm not one of them. . . . I feel so much shame for how I felt about Mary. Guilt and shame. Even *she* told me I wasn't gay, that we'd both outgrow it. . . . I look at both my lovers and they're

married now. And I look at me and I say, Where am I? . . . I know I feel less shame when I love someone who doesn't love me back. It's not as real.

In Karen's case, the xenophobia was a more potent force than her erotophobia, although the two always operate in tandem. During the course of treatment, she examined her various fantasies of how her lesbianism would literally kill her father. Through this process Karen was able to understand how she had always felt pressure to be the "good girl" to compensate for the pain her sister's behavior inflicted on the father. This resulted in a release of previously internalized anger at her sister.

Building from the support and acceptance she experienced within the therapeutic relationship, Karen was encouraged to explore what it meant to her that she was not what her father hoped she would be. Although she was still passing as the good girl, she was not heterosexual and never wanted to have children for her father to grandfather. Her hiding permitted him to continue his expectations, although Karen always knew his perceptions were based on a lie. Karen cried and mourned for the loss of the imaginary perfect relationship with her father.

Finally, Karen had to deal with the fact that she was different in the context of the larger world. She was soft-spoken and dressed in dark conservative clothes. She had never liked attention drawn to her, never strived to be noticed or unique. In a classically xenophobic style, she aspired to sameness. She discovered and expressed through therapy the fears and discomfort that surrounded her choice of an alternative life-style.

Karen's erotophobia was expressed in a variety of ways. She could make love to her partners but had difficulty allowing them to reciprocate. Similarly, her attraction to unavailable women, for example, a nun, allowed her the romantic component of a relationship without the sexual commitment to lesbianism. Therapy brought these issues to light and connected them with her internalized homophobia. During this period, Karen began dating a woman. Within the context of this relationship, she experimented with her sexuality and was freed to experience sexual pleasure. Positive feelings about herself and her relationship helped Karen develop some of what may be called "gay pride." Identifying more as a lesbian, she began to feel some righteous anger and indignation at the ways she and her lover were treated. This was an acknowledgement of the homophobic culture.

Although Karen may be unusual in her degree of psychological health, the potential success of treatment methodology is not exceptional. The application of the concepts of erotophobia and xenophobia has proven to be both direct and efficient in working through internalized homophobia. Results have been achieved with a variety of clients and clinical styles.

Because homophobia is a reflection of the way in which society views homosexuality, the nature of homophobia may change over time with society's changing attitudes toward sex and difference. Other areas for further investigation include an exploration of how internalized homophobia is both different from and similar to other internalized oppressions and the interactions of multiple internalized oppressions. This chapter provides a possible framework for future examination.

## NOTES

1. George Weinberg, *Society and the Healthy Homosexual* (New York: Anchor/Doubleday, 1973).

2. Gordon Allport, *The Nature of Prejudice* (Garden City, N.Y.: Doubleday, 1958).

3. Damien Martin, "The Minority Question," *Et Cetera* 39 (Winter 1982): 22–42.

4. Allport, *The Nature of Prejudice.*

5. Damien Martin, "Learning to Hide: The Socialization of Gay and Lesbian Patients," in *Annals of the American Society of Adolescent Psychiatry* (Chicago: University of Chicago Press, 1982).

6. Alice Moses, *Identity Management in Lesbian Women* (New York: Praeger Publishers, 1978).

7. Kenneth Plummer, *Sexual Stigma: An Interactionist Account* (London: Routledge & Kegan Paul, 1975).

8. Moses, *Identity Management in Lesbian Women.*

9. Weinberg, *Society and the Healthy Homosexual.*

10. Stephen F. Morin and Ellen M. Garfinkle, "Male Homophobia," *Journal of Social Issues* 34 (Winter 1978): 29–47.

11. Gail Pheterson, "Heterosexism: A Costly Privilege," paper presented at the meeting of the Voordracht voor de Vereininging van Sexuologie, Utrecht, Holland, May 1982.

12. Virginia Armon, "Some Personality Variables in Overt Female Homosexuality," *Journal of Projective Techniques* 24 (1960): 225–52; Ralph A. Gundlach and Bernard Riess, "Self and Sexual Identity in the Female: A Study of Female Homosexuals," *New Directions in Mental Health* (New York: Grune & Stratton, 1968); and Norman L. Thompson, Jr., Boyd McCandless, and Bonnie McCandless, "Personal Adjustment of Male and Female Homosexuals and Heterosexuals," *Journal of Abnormal Psychology* 78 (Spring 1982): 237–40.

13. Ronald A. LaTorre and Kristina Wendenburg, "Psychological Characteristics of Bisexual, Heterosexual, and Homosexual Women," *Journal of Homosexuality* 9 (Fall 1983): 87–99.

14. Sigmund Freud, "Some Neurotic Mechanisms in Jealousy, Paranoia and Homosexuality," in *The Complete Psychological Works of Sigmund Freud* (London: Hogarth Press and the Institute of Psychoanalysis, 1953).

15. Anna Freud, *The Ego and the Mechanism of the Defense* (New York: International Universities Press, 1966).

16. Morin and Garfinkle, "Male Homophobia."

17. C. Rand, Dee Graham, and Edna Rawlings, "Psychological Health and Factors the Court Seeks to Control in Lesbian Mother Custody Trials," *Journal of Homosexuality* 8 (Fall 1982): 27–39.

# 14

## Doing Sex Therapy with Lesbians: Bending a Heterosexual Paradigm To Fit a Gay Life-style

MARGARET NICHOLS

One of the important accomplishments of the women's movement in the last fifteen years has been the uncovering of aspects of female sexuality previously never discussed publicly. Feminists have been at the forefront of bringing a host of sexual issues out of the closet: abortion, rape, incest, clitoral orgasms, and lesbianism. Ironically, we have also occasionally helped keep an issue hidden. Through our own fear, embarrassment, and stereotypes, we have kept the problem of lesbian sexual dysfunction under wraps. Nancy Todor, in her article "Sexual Problems of Lesbians," writes that no one took her seriously when she was working on the subject: Lesbians themselves refused to acknowledge that sexual problems exist for our community.[1] I myself have also been criticized by other lesbians for discussing or writing about lesbian sexual dysfunction. Within the women's community, there seems to be great resistance to the concept of defining any aspect of lesbian sexual practice as a problem. As witness to that, I note that since my article on "The Treatment of Inhibited Sexual Desire" in 1982 there have been only a few published articles on lesbian sexual difficulties until JoAnn Loulan's *Lesbian Sex.*[2]

But the silence and taboos within the lesbian community regarding lesbian sexuality and lesbian sexual problems are not only manifestations of puritanism or fanaticism. There are some good reasons to be cautious about defining, explaining, or treating lesbian sexual dysfunction. Historically, female sexuality has been defined by male standards and heterosexual norms and has thus been a source of oppression

242

rather than help.[3] This oppression has in fact sometimes taken the form of defining our sexual problems for us, as when, in the 1800s, the presence of sexual passion or masturbation in women was defined as a problem. More recently, the absence of a vaginal orgasm (or more recently yet, a G-spot orgasm) was defined as a problem. We do indeed need to be exceedingly careful of who defines our dysfunction for what reasons and by what criterion, lest that definition becomes a judgment levied for purposes of social control. Thus a thoughtful and politically sensitive sex therapist must consider labels of dysfunction, malfunction, or illness carefully.

To complicate matters, we also know that female sexuality, whether for environmental or biologic reasons, appears to take different forms from male sexuality, and that lesbian sexuality, representing female-female pairings, shows some unique manifestations. For example, Lillian Faderman, in her book on "romantic friendships" between women through the nineteenth century, emphatically demonstrated the existence of lesbian marriages completely devoid of genital sexuality.[4] Philip Blumstein and Pepper Schwartz found lesbian couples in the 1970s and 80s to have less genital sex than any other form of pairing.[5]

From the point of view of a sex therapist, what does one make of this? Does this mean that inhibited sexual desire is endemic to the lesbian community? Or does it mean, as C. A. Tripp has suggested, that it is normative behavior for a lesbian couple to cease genital sexual activity after a few years?[6] It is important that we clear our minds of heterosexist/male models as we proceed in defining lesbian sexuality and dysfunction. Yet to do this leaves us essentially without adequate models; we must make our own.

Let me give an example: a lesbian couple, together for twenty-two years, whom I saw for sex therapy. The initial complaint was that all sexual activity between them had ceased for the last year and had been infrequent for many years previously. Upon detailed questioning, the problem became defined. Betty, named by both women as the less sexual of the two, enjoyed nongenital sexual activity and was quite happy to engage in sensual activity as well as to make love genitally to Agnes, her partner; however, she rarely desired to have Agnes make love genitally to her. That is, she rarely desired or required that she herself have an orgasm as part of lovemaking, although she was perfectly happy to accommodate Agnes in that regard. Agnes, however, could not accept this. Her definition of sex included orgasm, and by this definition, Betty rarely wanted sex. Over the years, Agnes had stopped making overtures to Betty because it seemed that Betty didn't want sex, that is, the entity defined as an event in which both women tried for and achieved orgasms. When Agnes and Betty were helped to accept their differences,they were able to re-label sex as an event during which Agnes would probably strive to reach orgasm and Betty probably would not. Their sex life promptly began to thrive.

Unfortunately, in the process of developing new models of sexuality we cannot rely much upon the mainstream field of sex therapy. Although the medical terminology used within the sex therapy field creates an aura of objectivity, as if the entities described as "dysfunctions" were real illnesses with material causes, in fact everything about sex therapy is quite subjective and biased. Consider, for example, the designation of "premature ejaculation" or "inhibited sexual desire," implying knowledge that the individual's sexual desire is really present but blocked or somehow repressed.

The sex therapy field is not only subjective, but it is also biased heterosexually. Heterosexual sex and relationships are not so much taken as the norm as they are unconsciously assumed to be the only kind of sex and relationships to exist. For example, the labeling of sexual dysfunction revolves around heterosexual intercourse. Many dysfunctions seem to have, as their connecting characteristic, the quality that they make intercourse difficult if not impossible: that is, premature ejaculation (defined by William Masters and Virginia Johnson as the inability to sustain erection without ejaculation within the vagina for a certain length of time) or erectile dysfunction in males, or vaginismus or dyspareunia (painful intercourse) in females.[7] Gay or lesbian lovemaking techniques are ignored within the framework of the field. Thus difficulties with anal sex are nowhere defined or discussed within the mainstream literature, despite the fact that they are probably the most common presenting problems shown by gay males in sex therapy. Sexual techniques such as S/M, the use of rubber or leather, or involvement with urine or feces, commonly seen as sexual enhancers by gay men, are labeled "paraphilias" by traditional sex therapists. Oral sex problems, among the most common complaints of lesbians seeking sex therapy, are absent from the literature on dysfunction, as are problems concomitant with the "your turn, my turn" sex that is perhaps more typical of lesbians than any other group. Similarly, the use of dildos and vibrators, an integral part of lovemaking for at least a minority of lesbians, is rarely discussed as anything more than an occasional sexual enhancer.

I am going to suggest some new models for sex therapy with lesbians. My approach will be best understood by those who have at least some familiarity with the work of Masters and Johnson and Helen Singer Kaplan,[8] I would strongly recommend reading these experts and obtaining supervision from an experienced sex therapist before attempting independent sex therapy. My therapeutic approaches are based primarily on my experiences with white middle- and working-class East Coast lesbians from the mid-seventies until the present. Recognizing this time frame is important, because lesbian sexuality is changing. We talk now at conferences about redefining the clitoris[9] or about "safe sex" techniques for lesbians.[10] We are proud to see ourselves as sexual beings at the same time that we are expanding our sexual techniques and practices. Thus sexual problems and solutions defined in the eighties may not be relevant by 1990.

## The Role of the Therapist in Sex Therapy

Typically, the role of the therapist in sex therapy has been to be active and directive but a bit authoritarian and distant. One sex therapist I know even advocates wearing a white lab coat if in medical school or hospital settings, and many routinely call their customers "patients" and require that customers call them "doctor." These distancing and hierarchy techniques have been recommended to enhance the authority of the therapist and increase the likelihood that therapeutic directives will be followed. Most lesbian therapists working within the lesbian community will find this authoritarian stance impractical, even if it does not conflict with their own values. I have found that an active and directive stance is essential within sex therapy: A good deal of sex therapy is behavioral, utilizing homework assignments and so on, and there is little that would require a nondirective stance such as analysis of transference. On the other hand, I have found it impossible to be distant.

Lesbian communities tend to be so incestuous and enmeshed that I, like most lesbian therapists, find boundary-setting to be difficult. Furthermore, an authoritarian stance would turn off most of my clients, who value egalitarianism and distrust hierarchy, even in a therapeutic relationship. Few of my clients would be willing to call me "Dr. Nichols," even if I wanted them to.

Most therapists function as role models for their clients at least some of the time. I find this is particularly true within the lesbian community. Lesbians, like other members of oppressed minorities, hunger for positive images and models; therapists become prime objects for this appetite. Indeed, the combination of the interweaving of most lesbian communities and this fierce need for role models makes the open lesbian therapist both more accessible and visible (and thus more scrutinized) than most therapists, and also more revered. I find myself considered much more than a therapist: a combination shaman/wise woman/witch/bad mother/good mother. It is a peculiar and rarely discussed position to be in, yet it has particular importance for lesbian sex therapists. Given the generally sex-negative attitudes women hold, and given the sexual rigidity of the lesbian community as evidenced by the rhetoric of "politically correct sex," lesbian sex therapists need to model sex-positive attitudes. I have found this often means giving explicit messages about the inappropriateness of the concept of political correctness as applied to personal sexuality. It also may mean giving permission to consider sex as not very important, as well as giving permission to enjoy a wide variety of sexual styles. It means succumbing neither to the sterotypes that heterosexuals have had of our sexuality nor to the stereotypes that we have perpetuated about ourselves. Pat Califia illustrated these extremes articulately when she once joked, "If I have a sexual problem and I go to a straight health care provider, he will treat me 'knowing' that as a lesbian I always use a dildo, always have one-night stands, always engage in unusual sexual practices, and always am promiscuous. If I go to a lesbian health care provider, she will treat me 'knowing' that as a lesbian I never use a dildo, never have one-night stands, never engage in unusual sexual practices, and never am promiscuous."[11]

### Common Sexual Problems Found in Lesbian Popluations

Within the mainstream field of sex therapy, most practitioners have categorized sexual functioning/dysfunction by using either the four-stage model of the sexual response cycle developed by Masters and Johnson or Kaplan's three-stage model. While in the past I also have attempted to conceptualize gay and lesbian problems within the framework of these models and found Kaplan's model to be the best because it is more encompassing, I now feel that there are so many sexual problems found among lesbians that really don't fit into either of these essentially biology-based schemas that I don't attempt to categorize lesbian dysfunction into response cycle patterns. One of the newer ways of looking at sexual dysfunction in general is through the technique of *script analysis*. Script analysis sees dysfunction in individuals or couples as primarily the result of faulty sequences of behavior— scripts—that individuals or couples play out repetitively and usually unconsciously. Script analysis with heterosexual couples often becomes analysis of how men and women in couples play out sexist roles, and this is not applicable to lesbian couples. The concept itself, however, of looking at dysfunctional sequences of behavior is much more productive in categorizing and assessing lesbian dysfunction than the four-stage or three-stage models. For example, the case of Betty and Agnes could not easily be defined by either Masters and Johnson or Kaplan. Although at first this couple presented as a case of inhibited sexual desire, this designation (from Kaplan's schema) is inadequate to describe these women's problems. On the other hand, their problems could easily be characterized by clarifying the two conflicting scripts that resulted in a repetitive "couple script" that was so maladaptive that eventually the couple ceased playing the game at all.

Lesbians do sometimes suffer from some of the more well-known and easily labeled female sexual dysfunctions, including primary anorgasmia (the complete inability to experience orgasism). I have found lesbians to be less likely to manifest primary anorgasmia and more likely to exhibit a form of secondary anorgasmia (the ability to orgasm through self-stimulation but not through lovemaking with another person). Therapists sometimes see general arousal deficits, but I have never seen a case of vaginismus or dyspareunia. I suspect that this is simply because if penetration is problematic or uncomfortable for a lesbian she simply eliminates penetration from her sexual repertoire.

Low desire, inhibited sexual desire, and desire discrepancy problems in couples are probably the most common presenting problems of lesbians who seek sex therapy.[12] One encounters individual lesbians who complain of lack of interest in sex. Far more common is that general sexual uninterest or sexual inhibitions surface in ongoing relationships only after the limerance phase of the relationship has passed. As Blumstein and Schwartz and Tripp have observed, it is common to find extraordinarily low levels of genital sexual contact among lesbians in couple relationships, and even to find relationships in which sexual contact has completely ceased despite an otherwise apparently harmonious relationship.[13]

As clinicians, do we counsel lesbians to accept this situation and reject as patriarchal their internalized standards of genital sexuality? Or do we assume that low levels of sexual contact are "abnormal"? I have tended to take a perhaps traditional view: I do not meddle in relationships where neither partner has complained, but if there are complaints of low desire or frequency, I assume that this situation is dysfunctional and attempt treatment. I contrast this, for example, with my approach if a lesbian complains of a lack of multiple orgasms. In such a case I would point out that only 18 percent of women experience multiple orgasm, and would counsel the individual to consider changing her standards of sexuality.

When confronted with low sexual frequency in lesbian couples, I generally attempt differential diagnosis with regard to the following possible diagnoses: 1.) sexual inhibition problems in one member of the partnership, including history of assault or incest; 2.) extraordinarily high sexual desire on the part of one partner; 3.) relationship problems surfacing via the sexual relationship; 4.) sexual script problems, for example, the case presented earlier; 5.) sexual frequency problems that are the secondary result of another sexual problem such as an oral sex phobia; 6.) sexual frequency problems as a result of simple boredom and the need for sexual enhancement in a long-term relationship.

Other sexual problems experienced by lesbians do not fit easily within a four-stage or three-stage framework. For example, aversion to oral sex is an extremely common complaint. Most typically, a couple will seek help because one member has this aversion, and the partner feels strongly that oral sex must be a part of lovemaking. Sex therapists are unlikely to encounter couples in which both partners are aversive, or both agree to exclude cunnilingus from their sexual repertoire.

Sexual difficulty experienced by some lesbians in the past was common enough so that the subculture developed a name for it: being a "stone butch." Until the advent of the lesbian-feminist movement, and even now among working-class and third-world lesbian communities, it was customary for lesbians to choose either a male or female role in relationships. Some of the women who acted out the male role denied their femaleness to the extent that they would not allow their partners to touch or make love to their bodies. When I practiced in a working-class, poor community farther from a large urban setting, a number of women who fit this description came for treatment, usually because of complaints from their lovers. It is becoming less and less common a phenomenon.

This does not mean, however, that so-called role-playing or expectations about roles never affect lesbian sexuality. One sees couples in which one or both partners feel constrained always to be either the aggressor or the recipient of sexual advances. One woman, Enid, sought therapy because she was unable to tolerate sexually assertive partners and began to see this as a problem in that in all her relationships lovers complained of this rigidity. In another case, Lisa was unhappy because her lover, Andrea, refused ever to be sexually assertive; Lisa wanted to "be seduced" at least occasionally. It is worth noting, by the way, that the roles lesbians fall into sexually do not necessarily correlate with either stereotypic appearance or interest; that is, the partner with the short hair and workshirts, the partner who loves to play softball, may also be the partner who cannot be or prefers not to be sexually aggressive.

The impact of lesbian-feminism has produced another almost opposite kind of sexual role problem. That is, the ethic of egalitarianism when translated to politically correct sex has meant that many lesbians feel that it is unacceptable for partners to have different sexual tastes, especially if these tastes appear to correspond to what are thought of as male-female differences. For example, Barbara and Susan complained of low sexual frequency in their relationship. Upon further analysis, it appeared that the couple's sexual disinterest stemmed from Barbara's preferring to be the more active partner in sexual encounters and Susan's preference to be less active, more the recipient. Neither partner, however, felt that this was "okay"; both feared that this differentiation might lead to role-playing or power differentials in nonsexual aspects of the partnership. Consequently, both constrained their sexual impulses, and sex had become ritualistic and stultifying. It is partly in recognition of this diversity of sexual proclivity that the lesbian butch-femme liberation movement has arisen.

These problems are examples of script problems: sexual difficulties that arise from differing, conflictual, or covert sets of expectations about how sex should be among partners. Although script problems can exist in any type of couple, there are some types of script problems— overavoidance of role-playing, for example—that seem largely idiosyncratic to the lesbian community. Some script problems have to do with differences over the newly emerging S/M, or sadomasochism, movement in the lesbian community, or differences involving the issue of nonmonogamy. One lesbian in a relationship may have strong S/M proclivities while her partner's sexual script calls for sex always to be gentle. In another case, one woman may find the idea of nonmonogamous relationships to be repugnant, while the other cannot function, sexually or otherwise, in a relationship unless it is monogamous.

Lesbian S/M and lesbian nonmonogamy are worth discussing a bit further, for not all the sexual problems attendant to these two issues are script, or expectation, problems. Sadomasochistic sexual practices, although undoubtedly not entirely new to all lesbians, are newly *defended* by a community that in the past was not only relatively sexually repressed, but which also severely judged sexuality on the basis of political correctness. Because the lesbian community has been so repressed sexually, with sexual techniques confined to those the S/M advocates call "vanilla sex," the S/M movement caught on like wildfire. In the early 1980s no lesbian conference was complete without a S/M workshop, no rap group survived without discussing S/M, no couple could not at least consider S/M or its impact on the community. Although the overall repercussions of this movement have been productive and beneficial to lesbians, some problems do exist. Not all people are stable enough to use a sexual enhancement tool like S/M in a healthy way: Clinically, lesbian therapists have been seeing some women who really hurt each other through S/M practices, and some women who become compulsively addicted to S/M and push themselves on to potentially self-destructive levels of pain.

It might be said that the S/M controversy took the place in the early 1980s that in the seventies had been filled by the nonmonogamy controversy. Nonmonogamy is no longer so much debated among lesbians. Many, perhaps most, lesbians aspire to a monogamous ideal in relationships, while a significant minority espouse an ethic of nonmonogamy. (This is very different from what one finds among heterosexuals, where few people would view nonmonogamy as a principled decision.) Most lesbians who attempt to succeed in committed relationships at the same time as they practice nonmonogamy do so in a way almost guaranteed to destroy the primary relationship. Lesbians, unlike many heterosexuals and unlike gay men, have affairs rather than casual sex when they are nonmonogamous.[14] Indeed, they are likely to have these affairs with close friends who are intimately entwined in their lives and the lives of their committed partners, and they are usually open about these affairs, not just to their partners but often to the whole community. These situations can be disastrous. When lesbian couples desire nonmonogamy, I try to help them develop clear rules and guidelines to protect the primary relationship and minimize the potentially destructive jealousy such affairs can generate.

The final set of problems one encounters in sex therapy with lesbians is the most difficult to describe and is exemplified by the example I cited earlier, of Betty and Agnes. Given the sex-negative way in which most of us are raised, given our difficulty communicating with partners over sex, it is not unusual that we suffer in our relationships from clashes between individual sexual scripts where those scripts are private, perhaps ill-defined even to the individual, and rarely or never discussed between the partners.

### The Assessment of Sex Therapy Problems

The key in assessment of sex therapy problems is specificity. Even when lesbian couples come to treatment asking for help with sexual issues (and most do not, but will instead present with more general relationship problems), they really are not actually prepared to talk about sex. It is critical that the clinician be calm, matter-of-fact, and explicit about sex, even in the face of giggles, shuffling feet, red faces, and averted eyes. When couples come to me for relationship counseling, I ask questions, both in a personal interview and on a written questionnaire, about frequency and quality of sexual interaction and about the existence of any sexual problems. If sexual problems emerge, I can then discuss with the couple their interest in working on these problems and *when*. Many lesbian couples who experience sexual difficulties as only one of a number of relationship problems prefer to wait until later in treatment to deal with these issues, and often it is just as well to wait until other conflicts have been resolved.

When couples come to treatment asking for sex therapy, or when a couple with other relationship issues decides it is time to deal with their sexual trouble, it is best to get as much specific detail about the situation as quickly as possible. In the first interview, I seek the following information:

1. What is the problem in exact terms? Not "we don't have sex very often," but "we only have sex once a month and I would like it twice a week"; not "our sex life isn't as exciting as I would like it to be," but "I would like her to go down on me and she won't."

2. What is the history of this problem? When did it start and what were the circumstances; has it been chronic, periodic, acute? Most critically, is this a problem either woman has experienced before, either alone or with other partners?

3. What other attempts have the couple made to solve this problem? How did they work? This tells me what interventions to avoid as well as giving me some idea of what behavior has maintained the problem, because attempts to solve a problem often turn out to worsen the situation.

4. Along the same lines, what are the individuals' own assessments of the problem? Often couples have a very good idea of how problems started, what caused them. They know how they got into the mess they are in, they just don't know how to get out. Even if I think the assessments are out of line, this question at least gives me information about the belief systems I need to cope with in devising my strategies. If a client feels her problems are the result of early childhood conflicts and I privately disagree, I know I have to frame my intervention in terms of solving childhood conflicts in order to make it acceptable to the client.

5. Why did the couple seek help now, as opposed to last week, last month, last year? This is a crucial question, because most couples will struggle along with sexual conflicts for long periods of time without seeking therapy. The answer can give some good prognostic information. For example, when the couple has come because one partner has finally threatened to leave unless their sex life improves dramatically, therapy will be more difficult than if, as one couple said to me recently, they are coming to therapy because the rest of the relationship was going so smoothly that both partners felt they could look non-defensively at sexual problems that had existed for several years.

6. I try to get in the first session a detailed description of the last time the couple made love. When was it, what were the circumstances, who approached whom, how did the situation progress, how did both partners feel? If it seems relevant and is not obvious from the partners' narrative, I will ask specific questions about sexual techniques used. In gathering this information, as with other information obtained from the couple, it is important to note the degree of discrepancy in both women's reports of the same situations.

After my first joint assessment session, I typically schedule an individual session with each partner. There are three purposes for this: 1.) I obtain a general impression of each woman as an individual, separate from her coupled state; 2.) I cross-check information given in the presence of the partner to see how synchronous or discrepant data are when given alone or with the partner. I also give each partner, alone, the opportunity to say anything that is relevant that she might not want to say in front of her partner, and I do this primarily to find out if there are any secrets, such as an affair, that might affect the course of therapy; 3.) I gather a detailed individual sexual history. Included in this history are data about earliest sexual experience, both lesbian and heterosexual; sexual abuse or trauma; masturbation and fantasy experiences; and sex-positive or sex-negative messages received in childhood and adolescence. I pay particular attention to heterosexual experiences and to the coming-out history. I have found that early negative heterosexual experiences (very common among lesbians who often had sex with men in order to "fake" heterosexuality, rather than from desire) and a difficult and conflict-laden history of coming to terms with lesbianism affect later sexuality, years after both types of events have been cognitively and intellectually understood and processed.

By this time, I have a reasonable assessment of the problem and have devised intervention strategies. In formulating my view, I think in terms of the cause of the problem, the factors that maintain the conflict, and intervention techniques, but do not assume that the last are necessarily related to the first or even necessarily to the second. Some of the questions that may serve as guidelines for me are: Is this primarily a couple problem or a difficulty caused by one member of the partnership? If it is a couple problem, how much is the sexual problem separate from other relationship issues and how much is it a symptomatic result of other problems? To what extent can the sexual problem be approached without addressing other individual or relationship issues? To what extent can the sexual problem be solved behaviorally, without addressing root causes at all? For example, Rita and Mary asked for sex therapy because they had had sex together only twice in the past year. During the assessment process, it was learned that Mary had never had sexual difficulties in prior relationships, but that Rita had always found herself unable to experience desire after about six months in a relationship, and that the thought of being the sexual aggressor in an encounter was almost repulsive to her. Moreover, she had a history of sexual molestation as a child, extremely sex-negative early messages, and a very difficult time accepting her lesbianism. I decided that the problem really resided in Rita, not Mary, but that Mary was needed almost as a sexual surrogate for sex therapy. Rita herself viewed her sexual issues as resulting form her early childhood molestation. I decided she was probably correct, but that she was not emotionally prepared to unearth and discuss these experiences. Moreover, Mary would probably not be willing to wait a long time for their sex life to improve. Therefore, I opted for a strategy that included a couple of sessions alone with Rita so that she could superficially discuss her early experiences and then a course of fairly traditional, behaviorally oriented sensate focus experiences.

One final tool I use for assessment, in fact, is the sensate focus exercises themselves. Often by the second conjoint session, I give a homework assignment of sensate focus (described later) to see how the couple reacts. Their reaction in the session, but especially how they carry out or fail to carry out the exercise, gives me a final, very complete picture of the extent and severity of their problems.

So far, I have been talking exclusively of couples, because by far most lesbians request therapy for sexual difficulties in the context of a couple relationship. Generally I will not attempt therapy only with one member of a couple, unless after assessment I determine that individual therapy is the preferred mode. If asked, I will treat single lesbians for sexual dysfunction. This is often more difficult because many problems simply cannot be treated in the absence of a partner with whom to try out new sexual ways of being, homework exercises, and so on. To date, I have not considered the use of sexual surrogates with lesbians.

## The Causes of Sexual Dysfunction in Lesbians

In general, many of the same root forces that shape sexual dysfunction among heterosexual women and heterosexual and gay men operate for lesbians as well: performance anxiety, anxiety caused by guilt about sex, depression, classical conditioning paradigms, relationship issues, and so on. Medical conditions are perhaps even more rare as the causes of lesbian sexual problems than is true for heterosexual women, because with heterosexual women these medical causes are usually tied to dyspareunia, a complaint rare among gay women.

Some causal factors of sexual unhappiness are special to the lesbian population. Virtually all lesbians have had heterosexual experience[15] and much of this has been quite negative sexual experience associated with no pleasure, with inauthenticity, even with a sense of being exploited. This early conditioning can remain as part of a lesbian's sexual response—the concepts of functional autonomy and classical conditioning are quite important here—long after she relates only to women and cognitively views sex quite positively. Early anti-gay attitudes, similarly, can linger long after a gay woman has come out. Further, many lesbians denied their sexual orientation to themselves for extended periods of time by repressing their sexual (but not emotional) attraction to women. Again, the tendency to repress sexual desire may remain despite a heartfelt wish to be sexually active. Finally, the lesbian may learn to reject one whole set of sexual standards—that of the heterosexual society she grew up in—only to assimilate a new set of sexual imperatives from the lesbian community. She may no longer believe her sexual fantasies about women are "bad"; now she may feel that the sexual fantasies she has about men are politically incorrect, or at least dissonant with her gay identity.

## Therapeutic Tools

For a complete discussion of sex therapy techniques, I refer the reader to existing texts in the field, especially Masters and Johnson, Kaplan, and Leiblum and Pervin.[16] Briefly, here are some principles I have found useful:

1. When possible, I go from the simple to the complex, rather than the other way around. In other words, I will often try a simple

intervention—information-giving or support and acceptance, for example—before I assume that more complex maneuvers are necessary. In particular, I will frequently use behavioral techniques even if I suspect a behavioral approach will be too simple to work.

2. Along the same lines, I frequently use sensate focus as a partly diagnostic, partly therapeutic technique. I employ the Masters and Johnson technique that uses a series of gradually more sexual pleasuring exercises. I will frame the sensate focus homework in a win/win way: "Either you will find this a positive experience, and that will be helpful, or else you will experience negative thoughts and attitudes and that will help us pinpoint your problem."

3. I try to encourage a ban on sex within the relationship for the duration of therapy, and especially a ban on outside affairs for the time of therapy, but, as discussed earlier, I do not do this in an authoritarian way. I often say something like, "Of course, I can't tell you what to do, but . . ." and then elaborate in a straightforward manner all the reasons why the bans would be productive and advisable. Clients usually get the point. I also, like other sex therapists, rely heavily upon homework assignments and take a similar stance regarding homework assignments as I do with bans.

4. Many of my techniques are behavioral and include systematic desensitization procedures (for example, I find *in vivo* desensitization to be the therapy of choice for lesbians with oral sex phobias), sensate focus, guided imagery, and fantasy. At times I also use hypnosis for its value with imagery, fantasy, and visualization rather than for purposes of direct suggestion.

5. I will see couples or individuals for sex therapy, although it is usually preferable to see couples. Couple counseling is a useful way to approach sex therapy because, first, many sexual problems really are or have become couple rather than individual problems. Second, even when one determines that a sexual problem belongs to an individual rather than to the couple, the partner can often be used as a sexual surrogate, or, in other words, an undemanding and sensitive partner who will help her partner carry out behavioral exercises.

It is in most instances more difficult to treat individuals who do not have a partner, even if the sexual problem really does belong to them. There are some behavioral methods that simply don't work without a partner. I rely upon guided imagery and fantasy exercises with the understanding that the client may need eventually to come back for additional help when coupled.

To help lesbians I have occasionally used groups specifically designed to deal with sexual problems. Although it is difficult to assemble such a group, I find these sex groups to be incredibly powerful tools for women who are inhibited, experience low desire, or have orgasm problems. Lonnie Garfield Barbach's books are indispensable for this type of group work.[17]

6. Bibliotherapy is an invaluable tool, particularly when dealing with sexual problems that are rooted in homophobia. In a sense, bibliotherapy is an alternative to a group and provides much the same thing: not simply information, but validation from other women. In addition, erotic books can be useful in therapy as methods of helping women become more sexual and to discover previously unknown aspects of their sexuality.

### Enhancement of Sexuality

Just as the line between dysfunction and preference is blurred in the area of sexuality, so is the line between sex therapy and sexual enhancement. I believe that not only is it a legitimate function for sex therapists to serve as sexual enhancers for lesbians, particularly those in long-term relationships, but I also think it is a necessary function. If, as I believe, problems with sexuality are a leading cause of deterioration of lesbian relationships, it is critical that as therapists we play a role helping gay women renew and revive flagging sexuality.

It seems clear at this point, both from the work of sex researchers and from common experience, that few couples sustain the height of sexual passion that is the hallmark of the initial limerance phase of a relationship.[18] It may be one of the great paradoxes of relationships, in fact, that the more one loves and is comfortable with one's partner, the less automatic and jolting is sexual desire. Gay men compensate for this loss of lust in the primary relationship by tricking: casual or anonymous sex with outside partners that serves as a sexual outlet but theoretically does not threaten the committed relationship. Lesbians, more than any other kind of couple, seem to suffer from the loss of limerance: Their frequency of sex becomes lowest of all couples, and if they do turn to outside sex, it is usually an affair rather than tricking, and usually that can have negative effects upon the primary relationship. What are we to do about this situation? It appears to me that lesbian couples need to turn more energy to enhancing and revitalizing sex within the primary relationship.

Of course an alternative to this is for lesbians to learn to trick. This seems in theory a fine idea to me, but I think it may take several new generations of lesbians to make it work. I know few women who really are turned on by casual sex, fewer still who can keep the sexual relationship really casual. Tricking, anonymous sex, fuck buddies—all concepts indulged in by gay men for years (at least until AIDS became a threat)—all seem like lovely ideas to me, but impractical, at least for the majority of lesbians at the current time.

It is more realistic for us to develop methods of enhancing sexuality within our primary relationships. Here we can borrow methods from heterosexual couples (through the literature on sexual enhancement within the sexology field) and from gay men. Briefly, I see three key elements: time, build-up, and variety.

Time is the difficulty I encounter most frequently. Our culture promotes the concept of instant sexual turn-on. Most of us assume that sexual desire comes automatically in a relationship: Just as one gets hungry automatically, signalling a time to eat, so will we become lustful automatically, signalling an opportunity to have sex. In the limerance phase of a new relationship, this seems to be so. But, unfortunately, in an ongoing relationship sexual desire is usually not so automatic, nor is it so capable of conquering and overcoming fatigue, tension, or normal preoccupation with everyday affairs. And yet the typical couple assumes their sexuality will continue to function in an automatic fashion, and they consign the role of sexuality in the relationship to something that should occur, without planning, attention, or forethought, at the end of the day just before falling asleep. For most long-term couples, this method of handling sexuality is ineffective. We pay less attention to our sex lives than we do to maintaining friendships, to planning meals, to physical exercise. It goes against the grain of all we have learned and all our cultural expectations to place this kind of priority upon sex, and it is particuarly grating to us to plan for sex; it feels mechanical to us. But our sex lives suffer from the myth of spontaneity. As I mentioned earlier, I find one of the most positive benefits of assigning the sensate focus exercises to dysfunctional couples is that it forces them to set aside time to be alone without distractions, in a sensuous, physical way. Many couples will need to develop this concept of planned time alone together in order to preserve or bolster a faltering sex life.

Related to this concept of time is the idea of build-up. Just as desire between two people who have been together for some time is not automatic, it is also not so easy in a long-term relationship to move from one state of consciousness, the one in which we conduct our everyday lives, to the state of consciousness in which we can feel physically relaxed, sensual, passionate. Most people, when not in a state of limerance or another high arousal state, need decompression time, and many women need build-up time. In other words, most of us need a transition period, a time when we take a bath, sit quietly and listen to music, have a glass of wine, and so on, so as to move from the attentional state required for work or taking care of daily business to a sexual state. And many women, in particular, need also to "simmer" sexually long before they actually become sexual: to think about sex during the day, have fantasies, anticipate pleasure and excitement, to build up their sexual desire before the actual encounter with the lover. I have found one of the strongest correlates of strength of sexual desire in women to be the frequency with which they think about sex. Very sexual women tend to think about or fantasize sexually many times during the day, and they tend to assess newly met people almost automatically on a sexual level. In other words, they view the world in more sexual terms, and they keep sex more in the forefront of their minds: They "simmer" themselves. Other ways for couples to build up tension and sexual excitement are to make sexual jokes or innuendos with each other, to touch each other sexually frequently even when there is no chance of continuing the touch to a sexual liaison, to talk about sex with each other frequently, and so on. This can help also to develop a sense of sex as play. Many women may think of sex as intimacy, sharing, or in other similar, serious ways; few women see sex as play, fun, and lightness. Developing a sense of sex as play is crucial if women are to participate in the third method of enhancing sex: increasing variety.

Michel Foucault said, in one of the last interviews before he died, "for centuries people have always spoken about desire, and never about pleasure. 'We have to liberate our desire,' they say. No! We have to create new pleasure. And then maybe desire will follow." It will be helpful to many lesbian couples to spend some energy introducing new pleasure, variety, and innovation in a playful way into their sex lives. This can include the use of toys or props, everything from dildos and vibrators, lotions, and ice cubes, to cucumbers, feathers, silk scarves, to wrist and ankle cuffs and paddles. It can also include the use of mood-enhancers like music, candles, lighting, romantic dinners or settings. It can include dress-up, new places, or atmospheres. Variety might mean introducing simple or elaborate fantasies, simply recounted to each other or acted out: One couple told me they acted out a fantasy *in vivo* of meeting in a bar as though they were strangers. Written or visual erotica can help many couples enhance their sex lives: stories told to each other, "talking dirty" to each other, and so on. Some couples will want to develop and encourage fetishes: the playful use of leather, rubber, articles of clothing. Others will find it exciting to experiment with less usual, kinky techniques such as S/M, bondage, use of urine, and so on. It is not important whether the variety introduced is very innovative, creative, or far out, only whether it is novel to the couple. It may even be less important whether the innovation works than that the couple tried it: Many an experiment with a new technique or toy has resulted in both partners dissolving into laughter at the absurdity of what they are trying and then proceeding to have wonderful sex together. In some ways, what I am saying about sexual enhancement all amounts to the same thing: Making sex more rewarding for ongoing couples means making sex more of a priority, and making sex more of a priority means thinking about it more, talking about it more, and setting aside more sensual, physical time together.

In some ways, lesbian sexuality needs to get more "male" in its orientation, with more emphasis on sex itself and perhaps less on romance. Trends in the lesbian community suggest that this is happening, and I see these trends as, on the whole, extremely healthy. The therapist working with lesbians on their sexuality, whether to help solve sexual problems or to enhance a stagnant sexual relationship, plays a role not only with her or his clients, but also within the community at large. If our attitudes are sex-positive, sex-expanding, and playful, we model for the community a vision toward which we all can strive.

## NOTES

1. Nancy Todor, "Sexual Problems of Lesbians," in *Our Right to Love: Lesbian Resource Book*, ed. Ginny Vida (Englewood Cliffs, N.J.: Prentice-Hall 1978).

2. Margaret Nichols, "The Treatment of Inhibited Sexual Desire (ISD) in Lesbian Couples," *Women and Therapy* 1 (Winter 1982): 49–66; JoAnn Loulan, *Lesbian Sex* (San Francisco: Spinster's Ink, 1985); Gail Kaplow, "Making Sex Better, a Therapist's Thoughts," *Sojourner* 10 (Aug. 1985).

3. Ann Snitow, Christine Stansell, and Sandra Thompson, eds., *Powers of Desire: The Politics of Sexuality* (New York: Monthly Review Press, 1984).

4. Lillian Faderman, *Surpassing the Love of Men: Romantic Friendship and Love between Women from the Renaissance to the Present* (New York: William Morrow, 1981).

5. Philip Blumstein and Pepper Schwarz, *American Couples* (New York: William Morrow, 1983).

6. C. A. Tripp, *The Homosexual Matrix* (New York: McGraw Hill, 1975).

7. William H. Masters and Virginia Johnson, *Human Sexual Inadequacy* (New York: McGraw Hill, 1975).

8. Helen Singer Kaplan, *The New Sex Therapy: Active Treatment of Sexual Dysfunction* (New York: Brunner/Mazel, 1974).

9. Federation of Feminist Women's Health Centers, eds., *A New View of a Woman's Body* (New York: Simon and Schuster, 1981).

10. B. Starrett and Pat Califia, "Lesbian Sexuality," panel presentation, National Gay Health Conference, New York, June 1984.

11. Starrett and Califia, "Lesbian Sexuality."

12. Nichols, "The Treatment of Inhibited Sexual Desire."

13. Blumstein and Schwartz, *American Couples*; Tripp, *The Homosexual Matrix*.

14. Blumstein and Schwartz, *American Couples*.

15. Karla Jay and Allen Young, *The Gay Report* (New York: Summit Books, 1977); Masters and Johnson, *Human Sexual Inadequacy*; Kaplan, *The New Sex Therapy*.

16. Sandra R. Leiblum and L. Pervin, *Principles and Practices of Sex Therapy* (New York: Guilford Press, 1980).

17. Lonnie Garfield Barbach, *For Yourself* (New York: Doubleday, 1975); Barbach, *For Each Other* (New York: Doubleday, 1982).

18. Dorothy Tennov, *Love and Limerance* (New York: Stein and Day, 1979).

# 15

## The Persephone Complex:
## Incest Dynamics and the Lesbian Preference

EILEEN STARZECPYZEL

### TO PERSEPHONE

Persephone, Persephone,
  lost in the cold hell of a black sky,
Aloneness shines in her eyes, curiously touching,
  sharp as a bright star reaching me from a great distance.
She is an orphan set apart from her sister constellations,
  with only the dimmest trace of a twinkle.
Like watching blue-white stars on a soft night in a high sky,
  I wonder what she is like.
Is she a burning soul,
  a cold blue light, a magic mystery?
Perhaps if I put my yellow ladder against the sky,
  I can climb up to Persephone,
And we will talk about stars and hell,
  and how to find love in such dichotomies.

E. Starzecpyzel[1]

The myth of Persephone, vulnerable victim and powerful survivor, can be an important allegorical symbol of the incest dynamic as it relates to lesbianism. My approach to incest incorporates this symbol in a framework of object relations psychology that offers a lesbian supportive perspective toward treatment of the adult incest survivor.

I use Persephone, a figure of power and mystery that speaks of men's fascination and women's endurance of historic incestuous rape, for the first time, as far as I know, to represent the powerful incest

261

survivor. Because of her unique separateness from the mother, which is part of the incest dynamic and which is unusual in the psychosocial development of girls, the incest survivor is freer to make flexible and creative choices in her life.

Nancy Chodorow's work on the matrisexual bond is brought to its logical conclusion—one that Freud hinted at in his works.[2] All women experience love of another woman in the mother-daughter dyad, while most reject lesbianism because of cultural taboos and the overwhelming intensity of the mother-daughter relationship. But because an incest survivor has lived outside the rules since childhood, and because her unique psychological distance from her mother gives her unusual independence, she has the freedom to revert to the matrisexual bond that others must forego.

Because all women today live in an androcentric culture that demeans and diminishes so-called female values, I contend that the lesbian choice is in many cases the most healthy and empowered choice for the modern woman—incest not withstanding. Why are incest survivors most likely to be able to make that choice while the more traditionally bound, "normally" raised female is less likely to make the lesbian choice? In attempting to answer this question, I will draw from four years of private practice with approximately fifty individuals, in group or individual therapy, of whom about 70 percent consider themselves to be lesbian. I have integrated all the information from clients with my own experience as a lesbian survivor of father-daughter incest and with insights from extensive therapy and professional education.

I will confine this chapter to the dynamics of father-daughter incest and will define incest here as a sexualized interchange of indefinite duration that happens between a father, or significant other father figure, and a child in a family. This does not include siblings or relatives unless they are heavily invested with paternal authority. When the incest is covert (as in cases of intrusive voyeurism, sexually colored ridicule of a child, and sexually motivated exposure), it does not involve physical contact. However, the dynamic is always sexual misuse, both of authoritative power and of the legitimate need for closeness, over a child who is unable to resist.

I propose that:

1. All incest creates lifelong trauma for the survivors, but incest survivors have unique strengths that help them to heal strongly, with the help of incest-oriented therapy.

2. Father-daughter incest alters the family dynamics and the significant early object relations of the child/victim.

3. Damage to the mother-daughter bond, which always occurs following the seductive interest in the child by the father, may be a significant contributing factor in the development of lesbianism as a sexual preference in the adult father-daughter incest survivor. Karen Meiselman cites an incidence of 30 percent lesbianism in her small sample of twenty-three.[3] I observe in my practice that virtually all of the lesbian father-daughter incest survivors reveal an intense longing for a nurturing, positive relationship with a woman, which I see as a distinctly separate issue from the survivor's anger at and difficulties with men.

4. When the terrible trauma of incest is healed in therapy, this "victim" can emerge, like Persephone, resurrected with life and power that, because of inadequate separation from the mother, most women are never able to attain.

I draw from Chodorow's work on the significance of mothering for daughters and Freud's view of the pre-Oedipal bond between mother and daughter as longer lasting (one to five years) than for boys and as distinctly sexual[4] to support and develop my theory of this characteristic post-incest syndrome. The Persephone complex is thus presented here as the most significant personality factor resulting from father-daughter incest and its resolution as the most important therapeutic objective, regardless of later sexual identity.

## *Object Relations: Normal Family Development*

Psychologists consider object relations as an internalized perception of the individual that incorporates the separate mental representations of the self and the other [object]. An individual is affected profoundly by the inner world in which she senses herself in relation to others, and develops her inner self-perceptions from the kinds of parental interactions she has experienced in childhood, especially during the early developmental ages of one through three.[5] Normal object relations develop through a series of stages that the individual passes through. Each of the stages (from normal autism, symbiosis, separation, rapprochment, individuation, to object constancy)[6] provide the individual with a growing sense of herself as good and bad, loved and independent, separate but not alone in a world where people can be trusted to be more or less good and constant in her life. This ability to see oneself as connected to other people who can be trusted and to feel wholeness in oneself and others is critical if a person is to have a healthy, normal start in life.

Nancy Chodorow presents a theory that fundamentally states that girls and boys grow up differently and relate differently because both sexes are mothered by women, a thought earlier introduced in Freud's "Theory of Female Sexuality."[7] Because the child's first intense emotional/libidinal love object is a woman, it is the smell and feel of a woman to which both sexes are primally drawn, and according to Freud, feel the first sexual attraction.[8]

For boys, the first love object is therefore of the opposite sex; whereas for girls, the first love object is of the same sex.

Freud went on to struggle with the question of why girls would pull away from the same-sex attraction with their mother to develop an "inferior," passive heterosexual attachment to men. Chodorow contends that, indeed, women do *not* give up their primary attachment to their mothers, but add secondary heterosexual attachments to men later in life primarily because of internal and external taboos against lesbianism and the deep ambivalence of this first love.[9] Chodorow contends that in heterosexual relationships women recreate the primary mother bond by the intense attachment to their children, and particularly daughters, rather than with their husband or lover. Because a man's masculinity is tied into his being unemotional and therefore less connected than a woman often wants, a mother is inclined to see her child/daughter as a reflection of her own mother in order to bring the emotional connectedness to her life that she is missing with her husband. This provides for the intense pre-Oedipal bond Freud refers to in his "Theory of Female Sexuality."[10] Because it occurs so early in the little girl's development, this primary emotional/sexual bond with woman/mother precedes and underlies sexual attachments to men later in life and constitutes a continuing pre-Oedipal link into a woman's adult life. For lesbians, this underlying link with a woman remains or later becomes sexually charged.

A woman's relationship with her sons is different from that with her daughters and produces significant personality differences in her male child; this phenomenon has its analogue in incest survivor psychology. A mother knows that her son, having a penis, will grow up to be more like his father than like her. Under the influence of powerful cultural and patriarchal pressure, the mother subconsciously relinquishes the boy to his father, who must teach him manhood. At the same time, her relationship to her son takes on strong Oedipal (sexual) overtones, because she begins to relate to him as a sexual "other" or "little man," while her own husband remains distant and absent from her daily life, as is customary in this culture.[11] This new, sexually charged interaction with the mother frightens the boy, who gives up the emotional link with his mother in favor of masculine identity and power. Until he gains a wife/mother substitute later in life, he loses the warmth with mother that girls retain.

I hypothesize that the early loss of mothering, or severance of pre-Oedipal connectedness to mother, not only happens to boys in normal development, but also happens to a girl who has been victimized by father-daughter incest. It creates for the boy and the incested girl an unsatisfied longing for mother. Loss of and longing for the early sexual pre-Oedipal bond with mother may be a significant factor in the development of the choice of women as sexual objects for both a man and a lesbian who has been a victim of incest with her father.

### Demeter and Persephone: The Incest Myth

A useful model of the incest dilemma, which clarifies the developmental elements of object relations in incest dynamics, can be drawn from the myth of Demeter and Persephone.[12] It poignantly presents the treatment issues with regard to providing a corrective emotional, cognitive, and behavioral experience—the heart of the healing matrix—for the incest survivor.

The story tells us of the mythological goddess, Demeter, whose daughter is violently abducted by her uncle, Hades. Persephone, child and sexual slave, is then held in the underworld with the permission of her father, Zeus. Torn from her mother, raped by her uncle, Persephone is seen crying and mourning for her mother—inconsolable over the loss of her mother and the violence she has suffered. Although Hades eventually returns her to Demeter, Persephone is never again young and carefree. She is irrevocably marked by her experience and tricked into returning to Hades seasonally, thereby creating winter on earth. But because of her familiarity with death, Persephone remains a powerful and mysterious figure in mythology. And because her tragedy stems from incest, Persephone resurrected is a symbol of the powerful incest survivor; she is one who has dealt with death and loss, and whose separateness is a source of creative and individual power in the world.

The child, Persephone, experiences herself as torn from her mother and sexually bartered with the collusion of her father. As the stolen child, she suffers intense pain and longing for her mother, while at the same time her mother anguishes, as does one who is robbed of her child. This myth parallels the incest dynamic (both for mother and child) and the therapeutic dilemma for incest survivors, while it also offers the image of the powerful Persephone "reborn" as the model of healing for all incest survivors.

Like Persephone, we experience ourselves as motherless, as irrevocably marked by the incest trauma, as curiously powerful and mysterious, older and wiser than our contemporaries, but also as women who feel different and emotionally alone because of the double wounds of maternal loss and paternal seduction. We have never felt young because of the early blows we suffered, and only through healing can we reclaim our right to the playfulness we never enjoyed. The memory of daddy, abuser and lover, is the Hades to which we must compulsively return in memory and unreasonable guilt until we can claim our own power to let go and move on to the powerful image of Persephone returned.

### Demeter and Zeus: Patriarchal Incest Dyad

In father-daughter incest, the father initiates incest consciously or subconsciously by appropriating his daughter as his "special" child, his possession. This often occurs while the child is still quite young, during the separation-individuation phase of development (between the ages of one to three). In some cases, the man's wish for a little girl of his own is acted out by marrying a woman who is so subservient that his "ownership" of the child is guaranteed even before the child is born. "In many cases, the father is actively keeping the mother from having a relationship with the child."[13]

The father carries an unwhole perception of himself; he sees himself primarily as either all good or all bad, and he needs another person to carry the unwanted half of himself. If he is sadistic, he needs first his wife and later his child/victim to carry the unwanted bad projection of himself and to punish and humiliate for "being bad"—so that he can continue to feel good. More commonly, the father feels bad and needy inside and cannot nurture himself. He therefore needs to pull in another person (at first the wife and later the child) to be the good stabilizer, whom he sees as existing to make him feel good.

In this kind of powerful way, the father begins to draw the child into his own projection, and the child (being sensitive to the unspoken messages of her needed parents) begins to act out the message she is being given—that she is especially bad/ugly/seductive or good/caring/pretty.

This projective dynamic is set in motion by father's special inclusion of his daughter on walks and business trips, for example, and his clear preference of her over her mother (which sets up competition and division between mother and daughter). The child is induced through clear although often quite subtle parental persuasion to be what her father wants, which confirms the father's illusion that his child really wants him sexually. The mother and the rest of the family begin to relate to this child as if the projected labels really were the child's whole personality. Thus the child is taught to behave according to her belief that she is only what others tell her she is; in this way she is prohibited from developing a whole personality.

This dynamic, initiated by the father but complied with by the mother, is used to devalue the mother and keep the child from being close to her, while it teaches the daughter to be "better than" or apart from her mother. It splits mother and daughter totally. Because the daughter carries the projection of intentionality of the sexualized behavior, none of the family is aware of how this has been set up by the needy, but too powerful, "head of the household."

The specialness of the father-daughter dyad causes the mother, who already feels disenfranchised by the imbalance of power in this severely patriarchal relationship, to feel, like Demeter, that her daughter has been stolen from her. Although Demeter in the myth is a more powerful figure who actively saves her child, this mother sees herself as powerless and ineffective against the seduction; in effect, she surrenders her child to the patriarch.

Ironically enough, before this paternal disruption of the mother-daughter bond begins and the mother's conscious or subconscious surrender is in process, the mother may attach special significance to her daughter and feel a great connectedness to her. She may experience a strong desire to have an ideal relationship with her, much as she might have felt a strong desire to have an ideal relationship with her own mother.[14] She, too, needs her daughter to fill needs of her own, although not usually sexual needs.

The incest pattern of intense father-daughter bonding is a betrayal by the father of his wife and causes her acute shame, rage, and helplessness, which may for the most part be denied and projected. This mother is trapped by the cultural attitude that proclaims the man as the head of the household, and she is not able to step out of this powerless position to understand fully how she has invalidated her power and lost her child.

The mother then adapts to the loss of her child and the concomitant loss of control by taking the blame or projecting it. Because the experience of powerlessness undoubtedly must be exacerbated by events of the mother's own childhood, the mother feels unable to protect her child from the powerful other, her husband. To further the tragedy, the mother often adapts by coming to perceive her child as bad, different, or unlovable as a defense against the loss and feelings of powerlessness. By the mechanism of projective identification, which is exemplified in the father's inducement of sexually interpreted behavior in his daughter, the mother's own sense of badness is carried by the child and denied by the mother, and her rage at herself and her husband is tragically and characteristically displaced onto the child.

The father is always solely responsible and culpable for his betrayal of his wife through the rupturing of the mother-daughter bond, and of his child through the seductive and sexual abuse. The mother, victimized by her husband, must nevertheless bear the responsibility for the surrender of her child to her husband's dominance. Acknowledgment that the mother's actions and feelings hurt her child gives the incested survivor the opportunity to externalize her feelings of anger and helplessness as well as shame and loss at the appropriate object, rather than displacing them all onto the father. For the father, the incest is and should be a lifelong guilt. Psychology around this indicates that, as with the criminal mentality, the incest offender must progress towards *feeling* guilty and making reparation in his life for his offenses.

Likewise, the mother must carry appropriate blame for her true failures, although never for the incest itself. An important part of healing for the incest survivor is to apportion blame in this way to the appropriate parental figure. Survivors' literature supports the idea of placing appropriate blame on appropriate people.[15] The survivor is then left with her own responsibility to work through the feelings and distorted perceptions that hinder her present life as a result of the failures of her parents.

### Persephone: The Incest Survivor

The father's appropriation of his daughter from the tight primary emotional bond with her mother is a pre-incest dynamic. In an object relations developmental schema, this co-opting usually occurs during the symbiotic and the rapprochement periods, which overlap the girl's pre-Oedipal phase. Because of disruption of the mother bond, which precedes the actual incest, there is always damage to the child at early developmental levels, even if the incest occurs much later in the girl's life, for example, in adolescence.[16]

For the child, what results is a sense of being unconnected to and stolen from her mother—the feeling of being a motherless child. Like Persephone, the daughter has a profound sense of being unwanted, unloved, and unprotected. Because the mother feels powerless, enraged at her husband, and unable to keep her daughter for herself, she projects this sense of overwhelming badness to her child.

Such verbal labels as "selfish," "lazy," "tramp," "different," "unpopular," and "crazy," coupled with behavioral patterns of emotional distance, favoritism of another child, or physical abuse, communicate to the child that she is bad and unlovable in the most profound way possible. Furthermore, the enactment, or threat of enactment, of the Oedipal wish to win daddy convinces the child that she is witch-like and evil for hurting mommy this way. Oedipal sexual awarenesses, issues of competition—either too much or too little—and a grandiose sense of power are thereafter much more conscious for the incest survivor than for other women.

The negative communication from mother results in a distortion of the healthy primary maternal bond, which instead becomes a negative bond to the mother and has its analogue in the negative transference we see from such a person in therapy. In cases where such a negative bond exists, there is often so little of a positive connection to the mother that the child has made early promises to herself never to be like her mother, and indeed is induced to do so because of her identification as being different from mother and being "daddy's girl." For children with this clear sense of negativity in relation to their mother, the damage to the mother bond is easy to see for both client and therapist. This kind of mother-daughter relationship, with powerful negative bonds that substitute for positive connections to the mother, is what I refer to as the Persephone complex in cases of father-daughter incest.

For some children there exists, however, a pseudopositive bond between mother and daughter. Such a child does have a way to connect positively with her mother and thus feel loved and accepted by her: She must sacrifice herself to her mother's well-being by mothering her mother, either physically, emotionally, or in a co-mothering role in the family, while she also forms a bond with her around their shared suffering. In this way, the child can achieve a conditional, positive mother-bond experience.

She becomes the so-called good girl, and when her situation is coupled with father-daughter incest, it involves great denial of reality and misuse of the child for the mother's own needs. As an adult, the child will feel tied to her mother and unable to criticize her and will struggle to maintain the co-bond of suffering in her present life that she established in her early relationship with her mother. She will deny the rage and loss created when she was not allowed to be herself and was forced into a role that invalidated her individuality. The pseudopositive link is a defense that protects the survivor from the experience of loss she has had with her mother.

As long as the survivor maintains this kind of link with her mother, she will not think of herself as motherless—the core issue in the Persephone complex. But during the course of therapy, many incest survivors relinquish this defense and uncover the loss of their mother that resulted from the extremely conditional acceptance to which they had to adapt. What is then revealed is the underlying longing for the mother who was lost so long ago and the accompanying feelings appropriate to the real abandonment. The loss of the mother may become more conscious to the client as she allows herself to perceive and enjoy the nurturing of the therapist as a transference object.

### The Incest Complex: Mother Bond Damage, Father Bond Substitution

If we recall for a moment Chodorow's theory on the role of gender in the formation of personality differences in men and women, we see that boys grow up differently from girls because they experience an earlier end to the pre-Oedipal attachment to their mothers and an earlier resolution of the Oedipal conflict that involves the necessity of identifying with their fathers if they are to avoid "castration."[17] In pulling away from their mothers, boys form a father-son bond that encourages the development of masculine identity that has as its basis being "unlike" a woman, that is, mother.[18] At maturation, boys go on to seek another woman to fill in the gaps created by mother's loss.

When little girls are stolen from their mothers by father in psychological/sexual incest, they experience an atypical severance of the pre-Oedipal mother-daughter bond that is needed for a girl's secure development. The father forces the girl, through the powerful means of his seduction, into a tight father-daughter bond that replaces the mother-daughter relationship. This replacement bond causes the child to develop an identity that has as its root being "unlike" mother, similar to the boy's psychosexual development. Furthermore, I suggest that the exclusivity of the father-daughter bond, which devalues and minimizes mother, may induce the child to form greater psychological distance from her mother than is experienced by most other girls. Then, like her counterpart, the traditionally heterosexualized male, she can utilize the primary sexualized response to a woman.

The establishment of a rejective father-daughter bond ruptures the pre-Oedipal mother bond and directly affects the incest survivor's early object relations because she is forced to bond with her father to the exclusion of her mother. Because the dynamic occurs so early in the child's development, during the crucial years from birth through age five, the father's seductive interest and bonding interrupts one of the progressive stages in the psychological development of ego and object constancy. This damage to the pre-Oedipal bond and the early introduction of active paternal seduction forces Oedipal attention to be an early event for this child, regardless of the onset of actual physical incest. The activation of the Oedipal triangle, caused by the father's pitting the child against the mother and granting the child specialness in her relationship with him, brings on a similarity to the developmental issues that a boy faces: early loss of the pre-Oedipal mother, strong inducement to bond with father, strong inclination to identify with the father as the new acceptable mother substitute, introduction of Oedipal issues earlier in the child's development that have the threat or reality of consummation, and for lesbians, a reversion to the original sexualized attraction to the mother object with eventual displacement onto a suitable lesbian later in life.

For the female child in an incestuous situation, the reality of Oedipal interest and its resulting lack of safety in being able to express the normal part of developmental desire for her father, does not bring on a fear of castration (since she is already "castrated") but rather a fear of body damage and intense ambivalence toward, as well as fear of, the mother and her power.[19] On one hand, the child has been forced by the incestuous loss of her mother to desire and need her father more than most girls do; and on the other hand, the desire for father (because it involves an active sexual element) is equated subconsciously with annihilation by her mother. For lesbians, at least, it seems that this subconscious fear of mother's rage, this open encouragement to bond with the father, and the underlying strength of the sexualized attraction to and love of the lost mother, all form a powerful inducement to utilize the primary sexualized response to women that is an inherent part of the female experience.

This relationship with the father can protect the child from the damage of primary psychological loss of her mother, as Kohut has proposed in his *Analysis of the Self*,[20] because it often stabilizes the child and offers her a positive experience in many ways. Incest survivors, for example, often have been encouraged to develop their talents or excel in life. But such success sets her up for the ironic and tragic betrayal experience of having a greater parental connection and sense of being important to the same one who sooner or later sexually abuses her.

Paternal appropriation of the child is covert and shields her from primary maternal loss, but the actual sexual interaction is a second and concrete blow to the child's ego, which most often becomes the focus of the recognized narcissistic injury occurring after the first and more crucial wound in the loss of the mother. The loss of the mother (because it is earlier) is hard to pinpoint in specific ways for the client until she allows it to emerge in her consciousness. But the loss of the father leaves the child with a very conscious sense of futility and betrayal, shame, incontrovertible badness, powerlessness, and rage.

The concrete damage of sexual contact with the father will sometimes be denied, because it is the last support and defense against real psychological abandonment. Depending on the age at which the actual incest begins, it creates a second level of developmental damage to the incest survivor, which overlies the loss of the mother bond attachment. Depending on the circumstances, the actual incest activity (versus the preliminary seductive attention) may overlap with the pre-Oedipal phase or may occur later in latency or pubescence. If the incest activity occurs later in the child's life, she has some years of "precarious" stability (because of the bond with her father) on which to build ego strength, which gives her a good amount of capabilities in the therapeutic struggle. It is important for the therapist not to underestimate the strength of these clients (because that has been a major mistake of many traditional psychologists), while at the same time maintaining absolute respect for the feelings of fragility such orphan abuse creates for the victims.

The loss of the mother is, in itself, a devastating narcissistic wound to the girl—one that humiliates her in the most profound sense because her whole being is seen as unlike and unloved by her mother. This humiliating sense of maternal rejection and the concomitant need and longing to connect with her mother is coupled with the defensive effort to control the pain and rage that result. The pain, and the defenses against it, provide the core disorder in incest survivors and is what I refer to as mother-bond damage—the matrix of the Persephone complex.

The sense of rejection by the mother may be so early, because of the earliness of the father's intrusive disruption of the mother bond, that the client may be aware only of her rejection of mother as a worthy object to identify with, and she may be more conscious of having never wanted to be like her mother. She may enter therapy "hating" women and identifying primarily with men, which is quite a challenge to the female therapist, whose best response is empathizing with the pain beneath the defense. These hateful negative bonds with the survivor's mother must be worked through in therapy. But they give a survivor the powerful advantage of being more separate from her mother than many women, and she is therefore often freer to make creative choices to shape her life—an empowering perspective most male or male-identified therapists miss, because traditional male definitions of females do not include true female empowerment. She often has so much determination to heal and make a better life for herself that her chances for improvement are particularly strong despite the damage to her personality.

### Lesbian Preference: Persephone Resurrected

It is this very separateness that gives an incest survivor the empowerment to heal, and to heal with a richness and diversity that allows her the flexibility to look beyond cultural restrictions in the life solutions she creates. For this reason, lesbian life choices may be more visible in incest survivors because the survivor's freedom leads her more easily to the choice of a woman who can provide the best and most fulfilling relationship for her. In our culture, the most empowered woman is the woman who does not need to please men; in this sense the lesbian incest survivor truly embodies the figure of Persephone, the mysterious and powerful.

In my work with lesbians who have suffered father-daughter incest, I have isolated and observed five core issues that occur with significant frequency in almost all of my clients; that is, that every lesbian incest survivor I have worked with is conscious of at least three of the five issues presented here. Repeatedly seeing this in my work has prompted me to suggest that there is a significant correlation between these factors and lesbian preference. The core issues that I see in the overwhelming majority of incested lesbians are identification with the father, protectiveness toward the mother, rejection of the mother, intense longing for the mother, and feelings of abandonment by the lost mother.

It seems that a turning away from identification with the mother and a preference for identifying with the father is sometimes an important factor in the formation of lesbian sexual identity. Despite the sexual abuse, it frequently occurs that the relationship with the father was the most available to the child. As a result, the child is inclined to value the power of masculinity (i.e., father) as the healthier model of adaptation. In a culture that reinforces androcentric values and then denies them to women, this personal choice becomes a healthy alternative to traditional passive female identity. This variable has been present in about 80 percent of the cases that I have seen. On the other hand, lesbians who seem more identified with their mother (or sometimes a grandmother), describe their fathers as having practically no redeeming qualities to idealize. I believe that in these cases the father identification is submerged in the bad father/good mother splitting that was necessary as a result of this. As repair of the splitting progresses, the lesbian client's perceptions more clearly align with this model.

In virtually all of the incested lesbians I have seen, there has been a strong sense of having been the mother's protector (although many report having been frustrated in that role). It may be that the wish to protect mother is one of the few positive ways the child can relate to her, especially in the pseudopositive bonding, and this becomes exaggerated beyond the norm. But even in negative situations the incest is usually seen as protecting the mother from loss of the father, that is, "keeping the family together."

In many incested lesbians (about 80 to 90 percent), I have noticed a strong conscious rejection of the mother and her model of femininity, along with negative bonds as they are played out in the negative resistance patterns in therapy. As the child comes to accept feelings of badness, negative bonds (such as the distance mentioned earlier) become a substitute for a positive relationship with the mother. Working through the negative bonds is a necessary separation process for the client.

For the majority of lesbians I have worked with, there has been a conscious awareness of intense longing for mother, which is manifested through sexual desires for women and conscious wishes for the nurturing and holding of which they have never received enough. In a small percentage of these cases (approximately 5 percent), clients who were closer to the subconscious processes indicated that they felt some subtle seduction on the part of their mothers. It is uncertain if this was actual mother-initiated interaction or if the feelings of sexuality were not more of a projection of the client's own sexual pre-Oedipal feelings onto her mother. It is possible that feelings of seduction in the mother-daughter interaction, except for physical maternal incest, may have more to do with sexualization of closeness and tenderness by the child, who has been conditioned to make this association by the incest and who has been deprived of nurturing in the mother-child relationship. It is also possible that what these clients experienced were denied feelings of homosexuality in the mother that were projected onto the client.

Many of the clients I have seen have a conscious awareness of feelings of abandonment (emotional and sometimes physical) by the mother. More subtle feelings of abandonment occur when the child has experienced conditional acceptance by the mother for caretaking and co-suffering roles. Conscious feelings of abandonment occur in roughly 50 to 60 percent of the clients I have treated. Such abandonment was a real factor in the lives of these clients. Hence, the repair work involves real mourning for what never was and never can be replaced, with additional positive bonding to the mother substitute/ therapist, whom the client can more adequately internalize.

## The Persephone Complex: Treatment Objectives

In clinical work with incested clients, five key issues seem to emerge as therapeutic treatment goals. These issues, of mistrust and isolation, fear of closeness, ambivalence over mother, control and humiliation, and sexual intimacy, are areas in which the therapist hopes to provide a corrective emotional experience and assistance in healing.

The primary issue for any incest survivor is lack of trust. Her mental and physical boundaries were violated, not just from the sexual assault(s), but also from earlier childhood experiences that taught her that the world was not safe. Because of the father's psychological appropriation of his daughter for himself, the development of maternal object relatedness for the young child is disturbed and replaced by the incestuous father bond. Before the onset of incest, the father served as a secondary maternal figure, and his betrayal of this role by initiating sexuality in the relationship, combined with the preceding loss or betrayal by the mother, is the final event that convinces the child that she cannot trust anyone to care sincerely about her. This inability to feel safe with others, either intimately or in the world, creates a profound sense of emotional isolation, even if she has adaptively learned to be the "queen of the prom." The internal loneliness of the incest survivor is the most painful aspect of her life and the one which, when brought out and talked about in therapy, gives her a powerful motivation to change.

Because of the inability to trust someone else, or to let someone be important to her, a survivor frequently uses defensive detachment, numbing-out or disassociation, suicidal ideation, self-mutilation, and false self-identity as adaptations that preserve for her the greatest autonomy and dignity in the face of massive abandonment and misuse. Such defenses also cover the underlying feeling of impotent rage at both father and mother, and ironically it takes trust to express rage.

Mother-bond damage, with or without the Persephone complex, is the primary damage in incest. Through the healing effects of the transference, the therapist must establish repair of the mother-bond damage as the integral part of her therapy.

In the transference, a client will often detach from the therapist or others when she feels threatened by closeness. She will mutilate or hurt herself to protect herself and the "mother"/therapist from her rage and bring her out of numbness, and present herself in a way that will attempt to please or provoke the therapist as transference object but will hide her true self. The therapist must be aware of these tendencies and observe and interpret them in order to help the client understand her own fearful reactions. It is also important for the therapist not to be manipulated by such acting out of rage and powerlessness, and to encourage the client actively to talk about the feelings that these behaviors are demonstrating.

Learning to express feelings in words is a form of mastery and control the client must learn. An incest survivor is afraid to talk about her rage, her envy of others, her powerful manipulations to control the significant people in her life (including the therapist), her angry alienation from even those who genuinely care about her, and her tendency to sexualize relationships (which frightens her because she feels dirty and like her father when this happens). When the therapist can provide a corrective experience involving acceptance of the hated aspect of the self, the client will be able to separate from this powerful negative bond/relationship with her mother. To do this, the therapist must first adequately work through the same feelings of rage, jealousy, powerlessness, sexualizing, and alienation in herself so that she can accept them in her client.

Because of the lack of trust, the incested client has a handicapping fear of closeness. In her life and in the transference, she protects herself from feelings of rage, abandonment, and humiliation by acting out her perceptions about intimacy and loving as they relate to her childhood predicament. Particularly disturbing for most incest survivors is the fear that closeness with someone will result in sexual interaction, either intrusion from the other or by the self. Closeness and sexuality were never differentiated in the incest survivor's home, and this association in adult life causes the survivor to defend against closeness constantly or to sexualize closeness constantly in an effort to deal with this threatening feeling of extreme danger. It is of utmost importance that the therapist talk about closeness, including its learned association with sexuality, as normal for incest survivors and to find a way to tell the client that she is only wanting to be close when this happens. The therapist must never become a part of the seductive projection, because this would confirm for the client her distorted belief that all intimacy must be obtained by sex and barter, rather than the real qualities she possesses.

Particularly for a lesbian survivor of incest, therapy must involve working through the strong ambivalence about her mother. Because of the child's feelings of rejection by her mother, she must deal with a wish to reject, punish, and humiliate the mother whom she also needed and loved. This core conflict is reflected in the transference and also in love relationships of the client, which will sabotage her adult life. She feels extremely needy on one hand, and humiliated by what seems to be her "weakness" with lovers (mother) on the other. At the same time, she is intensely enraged by the humiliation of neediness in the face of inadequate response, and she subconsciously wants never to need another woman again.

For many therapists, there is a fear that extreme neediness in a client will become a demand for help so great that they will feel smothered and drained. This countertransference reaction to neediness must be carefully controlled, because the therapist must provide a corrective experience for the client who has often been given the message from mother: "You need too much and you are disgusting." To provide a corrective experience for the incest survivor, therefore, therapists must handle their own aversions to neediness in themselves and others by strengthening their boundaries around giving in the face of intense transferential neediness. They must learn eventually to validate their right to give what they can, but not to give beyond their limits.

Issues around control are also central to the incest survivor's psychology. Perfectionism, various forms of food control (obesity, anorexia, bulimia), money issues, and excessive striving for success or achievement are defenses against the humiliation of not having had control over parents whom she once needed and by whom she was hurt.

The incest survivor also has a need to control closeness in order to protect herself and others from the surfacing of sexual feelings that are strongly associated with closeness. Rather than fear of fusion, control may indicate fear of badness (sexuality) in the incest survivor, who wants very much to be "good" and has little structure in which to conceptualize goodness.

Lack of trust and the need to control closeness lead the survivor to an emotional isolation that is reinforced by her feelings that she should have controlled the incest and sometimes the pleasure associated with the incest. She feels guilty for not having done so, and that what happened to her was so bad that she is apart from the rest of humankind. She feels alien to other people and that the normal world, with joy and sufficiency in life for others, does not belong to her.

Without control, and around issues of closeness, the client believes she will be humiliated. A client's reaction to humiliation is defense and rage. Eventually, the rage must be re-experienced and worked through. For lesbian clients, the rage at mother is usually more defended against than it is for heterosexual clients, because lesbians consider themselves woman-centered, and efforts to be politically correct may hinder free expression of anger at mother. The therapist must enlighten and encourage her lesbian client about not carrying all the anger inside herself and to let the anger at both parents exist, because she was hurt by both parents.

All of the preceding issues play into the fear of sexuality, which is very common after incest for lesbian and heterosexual women alike. For an incest survivor, sex is never just sex, and it is rare to experience pleasure, good feelings, and the vulnerability of orgasm. Instead, sex becomes the focus of difficulties with trust and a struggle to believe that letting someone be close will not result in humiliation, degradation, betrayal, and rejection, as well as recapitulation of the original feelings of powerlessness and badness. In an effort not to repeat the trauma around mother's lack of connection and father's sexual abuse, the survivor uses sex to control against feelings of badness and powerlessness that are intensified in sex for her. She may at times try to overcome these fears by being extremely withdrawn and at other times will try to give in to the "whorish" feeling by letting herself go. Both behaviors are attempts to cope with the double messages she was given about sexuality.

In reaction to fear of sexuality, lesbian incest survivors experience a variety of symptoms ranging from physical numbness, lack of clitoral sensations, a sense of unreality, spaciness, disassociation from their bodies, and unwanted thoughts that distract them from the sexual experience. There is also the phenomenon that Meiselman refers to as "specificity,"[21] or the client's belief, confirmed by some of her experiences, that if only she could be touched in the "right spot" or be in the "right" circumstances, she could be orgasmic. This projection of inadequacy onto the lover protects the incest survivor from the underlying sexual issues and controls the amount of sexual intimacy she experiences. It also allows the survivor to put bad feelings associated with sex and incest onto the lover, while protecting her own self-esteem.

The incested woman was invariably told that she must be good or nonsexual while she was constantly reinforced for behaving badly or sexually. This kind of double bind was impossible to cope with, so the child developed patterns of behavior to manage the situation in which she was placed and that she finds re-created in her adult sexual relationships: asexuality, hypersexuality, and conditional sexuality, which may be experienced separately or alternately by the same individual at different times.

Much of the sexual difficulty comes with the strong associations of badness that incest induced around enjoying pleasure, even if only the pleasure of attention. These associations often make the incest survivor overvigilant against unwilled sexual responses in herself. She is paranoid about seeing a sexual response to herself in others, and because of the overvigilance, frequently notices this and focuses on it. She is unable to mitigate the sexual response with other significant qualifiers and tends to feel as if she has done something bad to elicit this and to withdraw consequently. The opposite reaction, with over-sexual response to the stimulus, is an adaptation to the original trauma which involves feeling helpless against the overwhelming parent and reflects the child's original choice to go with the overriding parental will rather than to fight it.

Underneath, she often feels as if her behavior is offensive and intrusive to herself and others. This is an exaggeration of her sexual power and part of the incest projection that she is so sexually powerful. It is also an inability to accommodate to the reality of present adult sexual variables and a defense against the disorganizing impact of the childhood sexual trauma on the developing ego. Because of the early sexualized attention of the father and the intrusive sexual action later on, the child develops a schema that is consolidated and stabilized by the constant environmental influence of a sexually overstimulating family relationship.[22] The representation of sex, because of this environmental influence, becomes generalized into concepts of closeness, caring, attention, intrusion, lack of control, humiliation, and badness. The therapist may help the client differentiate sex from these various other feelings so that the whole general schema of sexual overstimulation will not be triggered by a look or gesture that the client interprets as sexual and responds to in her conditioned way. This separation of sex from the whole conditioned response is also one of the most difficult aspects of the therapeutic work, both because of the power of the sexual bond and because of the embarrassment attached to talking about sex for both client and therapist.

It is important that the therapist not respond sexually to such a client, because the client will interpret that as a re-creation of her old power/omnipotence over daddy, as an indication of her badness or witchiness in inducing sexual responses in someone (daddy), or as a symbol of her specialness with the therapist. Such interpretations can initiate a negative grandiose reaction that hinders the development of true therapeutic intimacy. Because' of these core issues, it is best that the therapist restrain all physical contact with this type of client (because it is very late in therapeutic healing before the client can differentiate between safe closeness and sexual intrusiveness). This issue is so central to the psychology of incest that a therapist is most ethical if she regards the client as one whose sense of safety *depends* on clear nonsexual messages and boundaries and makes a policy of only giving that physical affection within ethical limits that the client requests.

Learning to trust with a therapist is like learning to love in a safe family. It lays the groundwork for a client who can then learn to trust in a sexual way with an appropriate partner, after she has internalized that it is safe to come out of her head, be real, and exist in her body again. Perhaps the most central issue, and the highest achievement a client can accomplish as a result of therapy, is the kind of sexual trust and intimacy that involves awareness, sensitivity, openness, and a whole relationship between herself and another. In this way, a full experience of trust, including eventual sexual trust, can open the door for a joy, a playfulness, and a richness of living that has been denied this woman all her life.

### Conclusion: The Power of Persephone

I have attempted to reinterpret developmental dynamics for lesbian survivors of father-daughter incest. I have presented a theory (drawn from the work of Freud, Chodorow, Slipp, and Kohut) that suggests that incested lesbians, because of the seductive paternal bond, develop an intense father bond to replace the ruptured maternal liaison that occurs in incest dynamics. This father-daughter bond stimulates the reversion of the girl's sexual energy to the first love, the mother object, which the girl re-creates in lesbianism as an adult.

The primary wound of incest is the loss of the mother bond, which is damaged severely by the father's sexual appropriation and misuse of the child. But in lesbians, this loss of the mother gives the girl the advantage of more separateness from the mother, which allows her a measure of personal power and creative flexibility in choosing more freely the appropriate personal relationship that best meets her needs.

I have brought out the original dynamic between mother and daughter as a specifically sexual bond—one that Freud referred to quite clearly. Freud's theory of the innate bisexuality of all women underscores the fact that, for women at least, the first sexual bond is for the same sex, not the opposite sex. This fundamentally homosexual model is an innate part of the psychology of women and the most important aspect of lesbian adaptation after father-daughter incest. Because of a woman's psychology, it may be that we need to rethink lesbian adaptation after father-daughter incest, not as adjustment to the pathology, but as healthy reversion to the original matrisexual model that is a normal part of female psychology and a normal dynamic in the psychological development of males.

In the myth, Persephone is condemned to return to Hades and her abuser each year, bringing winter to earth. Incest has hidden beneath the ice of denial for all of history, it seems. But Persephone returns as a powerful figure in the myth, and it is in breaking the pattern of denial (the secret the client was told never to tell) that we begin to see Persephone emerge victorious. By understanding incest, the client and the therapist can begin to nurture the unfolding of Persephone—this woman with an abundance of strength and power, anger and healing, love and creativity, to share with a world that she gradually comes to understand is for her, too.

## NOTES

1. After the poem "Persephone," by Edna St. Vincent Millay.

2. Nancy Chodorow, *The Reproduction of Mothering: Psychoanalysis and the Sociology of Gender* (Berkeley: University of California Press, 1978).

3. Karin C. Meiselman, *Incest* (San Francisco: Jossey-Bass Publishers, 1981), 245.

4. Chodorow, *The Reproduction of Mothering*; Sigmund Freud, *Collected Papers of Sigmund Freud*, vol. 5, "Theory of Female Sexuality" (London: Hogarth Press, 1956): 264–70.

5. Samuel Slipp, *Object Relations: A Dynamic Bridge between Individual and Family Treatment* (New York: Jason Aronson, 1984), 5–7.

6. Althea J. Horner, *Object Relations and the Developing Ego in Therapy* (New York: Jason Aronson, 1984): 25–36.

7. Chodorow, *The Reproduction of Mothering*, 92–110; Freud, "Theory of Female Sexuality," 7.

8. Freud, "Theory of Female Sexuality," 270.

9. Chodorow, *The Reproduction of Mothering*, 127, 200, 203.

10. Freud, "Theory of Female Sexuality," 263–64.

11. Chodorow, *The Reproduction of Mothering*, 127.

12. Michael Grant, *Myths of the Greeks and Romans* (New York: Mentor Books, 1962), 126–28.

13. Elizabeth Stark, "The Unspeakable Family Secret," *Psychology Today*, May 1984, p. 42, reference to David Finkelher's work at the Family Violence Research Program at the University of New Hampshire: The development of a theory of early allocation is supported in part by Finkelher's observations, by case material, and by direct observation in my own family.

14. Chodorow, *The Reproduction of Mothering*, 201, 204.

15. Justice E. Harmony, "Are Mothers to Blame?" *For Crying Out Loud*, vol. 1, issue 2, Aug. 1984 (Boston: Incest Resources).

16. Stark, "Unspeakable Family Secret," 44; the author's allusion to the sexual relationship beginning very subtly, and to the aggressor's "obsession" with the child raises this idea of very early paternal intrusion into the mother-daughter relationship. This affirms clinical observations of individual client accounts, and with some family work I did with a father-daughter dyad, where it was clearly evident that the father still retained a highly cathected attitude towards his daughter, and the client reported her mother's story of his near obsession with his little girl after her birth.

17. Chodorow, *The Reproduction of Mothering*, 127.

18. Ibid., 176.

19. Freud, "Theory of Female Sexuality," 263.

20. Heinz Kohut, *The Analysis of the Self* (New York: International Universities Press, 1956), 66.

21. Meiselman, *Incest*, 236.

22. Horner, *Object Relations*, 10.

# 16

## Lesbian Alcoholism: Etiology, Treatment, and Recovery

LEE K. NICOLOFF AND
ELOISE A. STIGLITZ

In recent years, advances of the women's and the lesbian and gay rights movements have encouraged increased self-understanding and esteem among lesbians, at the same time providing energy for positive self-examination and self-help rather than self-blame. Improved understanding of the lesbian experience has resulted in greater cognizance of both strengths and vulnerabilities within this community. Few would dispute the fact that alcohol abuse and alcoholism are significant problems for the lesbian population. These problems appear to be more severe for lesbians than for heterosexual women or for the heterosexual community at large.[1]

For example, when Marcel Saghir and his colleagues compared a nonclinical sample of fifty-seven lesbians and a group of forty-three unmarried heterosexual women, they found that 35 percent of the lesbians revealed a history of drinking that the researchers judged to be excessive or alcoholic, compared with only 5 percent of the heterosexual women. Collins Lewis and his colleagues, in a reanalysis of these data, reached a similar conclusion (that the rate of alcoholism and alcohol abuse was higher within the lesbian sample), but believed that 33 percent of the lesbians exhibited heavy drinking or questionable alcoholism versus 7 percent of the controls, and that 28 percent of the lesbians were alcoholic versus 5 percent of the heterosexual women.[2] An appreciation of some of the problems of defining and measuring alcohol abuse and alcoholism as well as of the difficulties of representative sampling from the lesbian population, prompts caution in reliance upon these particular figures. More research is needed. However, the data support the opinion that lesbians constitute a unique, at-risk population with regard to alcohol abuse and alcoholism.

## ETIOLOGY

Where one seeks an explanation for the high incidence of alcoholism among lesbians depends partly on the conceptual model applied. Although the medical model, which views alcoholism as a disease much like diabetes, has compelling explanatory advantages, it alone does not explain differences in rates of alcoholism among different social groups in other than genetic terms. No evidence exists that would suggest a difference among lesbians in the incidence of genetic characteristics predisposing them to alcoholism.[3] Even if such evidence did exist, strict application of the medical model would divert attention from social, economic, and cultural influences in alcohol and drug use.

It has been noted that women and other low-status groups are particularly vulnerable to inappropriate applications of the medical model.[4] The problems of these groups are frequently interpreted as biologically based, and appropriate solutions are seen to require handling by "experts" who may actually understand little about the experience of the patient. There is a vital need not only to focus on the individual difficulties of lesbian alcohol abusers, but also on chemical dependency as a problem within the lesbian community and on lesbian substance abuse as a public issue as well. The following discussion of the etiology of lesbian alcoholism will therefore include discussions of individual psychological factors, social factors, and cultural/political factors.

### Individual Psychological Factors

Although a number of writers have discussed social and cultural influences upon lesbian alcohol and drug abusers,[5] only one published study has attempted to investigate the personal psychological dynamics of lesbian alcohol abusers. Through intensive interviews with ten lesbian alcohol abusers, Deborah Diamond and Sharon Wilsnack studied the roles of four possible motivations in the drinking behavior of lesbians: the gratification of dependency needs, achievement of enhanced feelings of power in relationships, relief from the stress of sex-role conflicts, and improvement of self-esteem.[6] Through qualitative analysis of the content of their interviews with these ten women, the authors concluded that all of them drank in response to dependency needs.

However, they found little direct evidence that drinking led to gratification of these needs. Instead, drinking seemed to be associated with increased power-related behaviors such as assertiveness, sexual advances, and verbal or physical aggression.

One interpretation that Diamond and Wilsnack offer for this finding is that feelings of enhanced power provide compensation for unresolved feelings of dependency. They suggest that, as a group, lesbians may accept their dependency needs less readily than heterosexual women, and drinking may help them overcome these feelings. With regard to sex-role influences, Diamond and Wilsnack note that the behavioral changes reported with drinking were predominantly in the traditional masculine direction, for example, greater aggressiveness, activity, and dominance. They suggest that these women might be using alcohol in an instrumental way in order to reduce sex-role conflict. The authors propose a possible discrepancy between perceived and desired sex-role attributes—the most valued self-image being in a more masculine direction. Drinking might make it easier for these women to shift their self-perceptions and behavior in that direction. With regard to self-esteem, lesbians in the study reported a lack of self-confidence while sober, along with a positive change in self-esteem while drinking. A majority of them also reported, however, that drinking often increased feelings of depression.

## Social Factors

A simple way to describe social factors in the etiology of lesbian alcoholism is to say that the lesbian subculture supports drinking. Some have referred to alcoholism as a community addiction; individuals manifest it, but the community supports it. Celinda Cantu suggests that within the lesbian community, the bars provide a co-alcoholic network. (A co-alcoholic is someone who is as dependent on the alcoholic as the alcoholic is on drinking.)[7] A number of authors have noted that within the community, drinking and drunkenness are considered normal rather than deviant behavior.[8]

While the relationship between drinking and socializing is a common thread running through American culture, this emphasis is exacerbated within the lesbian subculture because of limited social options and the lack of alcohol-free alternatives.

## Cultural/Political Factors

Lillene Fifield refers to alcohol abuse as a manifestation of what she calls "oppression sickness"—a malady that afflicts all minority groups that have been victims of systematic and ongoing oppression. Its symptoms include feelings of alienation, despair, low self-esteem, self-destructive behavior, and drug and alcohol abuse.[9] Society's hatred becomes internalized as self-hatred. Abby Willowroot, a lesbian and a recovering alcoholic, states that, "It is believed that alcoholism is a disease. I disagree; I think that our culture is the disease and alcoholism is a symptom of that disease. . . . This culture is designed to keep us barefoot, pregnant, and loaded."[10]

Several writers who view alcoholism and drug addiction from a political perspective have suggested that rather than talking about lesbians abusing alcohol and drugs, we should be talking about lesbians being abused by these substances — which are tools of our oppressors.[11] They believe that on a political level, minority groups are forced into addiction. Drugs and alcohol are provided in order to keep people under control. Addiction takes away the focus and power of minority individuals and communities, keeping them ineffective in the world. The job of the oppressor becomes easier when individuals engage in self-destructive behavior and render themselves powerless. It therefore becomes the responsibility of the individual lesbians, as well as the lesbian community as a whole, to keep themselves from being controlled. Essential to this process are both belief and understanding that change is possible, and a commitment to directing fear and anger constructively outward, rather than toward the self and one's loved ones.

Cantu, a Chicana lesbian and recovering alcoholic, describes her message to other Chicanas about alcohol thus: "It kills us quicker and takes away our culture much more than any racist act can do and that we are not supposed to survive. And I say survive. If they are going to get us, let them get us sober; we will leave a much more visible trail."[12]

In general, alcoholism among lesbians may be considered a multiply determined disease, influenced by biological, psychological, social, cultural, and political factors. These etiological factors in turn determine what issues are important to address in treatment.


TREATMENT

*Special Treatment Needs*

Etiological influences in lesbian alcoholism clearly have a bearing on the treatment process. Some views of etiology, such as the cultural/political perspective, suggest that lesbians have different treatment needs than other alcoholics. Other perspectives, such as the psychological view, offer less clarity regarding the necessity of specialized treatment for lesbians. A controversy exists within the alcohol treatment field about the necessity of specialized treatment for any subpopulation of alcoholics. A commonl· held attitude is that alcoholics are more alike than different, and th   an emphasis on special needs distracts from the treatment of alcoł  ِ٠sm as the primary disease.[13] No doubt lesbians do have common issues with all alcoholics, particularly women alcoholics. However, in addition to their common concerns, lesbians have unique concerns as well that relate not only to their experiences of alienation and isolation within an oppressive society, but also to their unique life-styles, family configurations, and friendship networks.

Potential differences in the treatment needs of lesbians compared to heterosexual women are suggested by differences in the age and educational level of lesbians entering treatment, by differences in the avenues of their entry into treatment, and by differences in their attitudes toward treatment. In her investigation of the treatment needs of lesbians and gay men in the Los Angeles area, Fifield discovered that lesbians in her sample tended to enter treatment at a younger age than heterosexual women.[14] In addition, while they were likely to be underemployed, the lesbians were more educated. The youth of these women entering treatment, however, does not imply that their disease was less advanced. Saghir and his colleagues offer evidence that lesbians, compared to heterosexual women, may in fact enter treatment at more advanced stages of alcoholism, as indicated by a higher incidence of serious difficulties which they have encountered as a result of their drinking.[15] Lesbians also appear to have stronger feelings of mistrust in social service agencies than do heterosexual women.

Not surprisingly, although they manifest alcoholism in greater proportion than does the general population, smaller proportions of lesbians present themselves at agencies.[16] Agency policy has a major impact on this phenomena. Policy not only determines the philosophy of treatment, allocation of monies, the hiring of staff, and the specific services rendered, but also who will use and benefit from the services. Linda Beckman and Katherine Kocel suggest that several conditions are necessary in order for a client to use a service: She must see that she has a problem, be willing to alleviate it by going to an agency, see the particular agency as helpful, and be able to transform her need into action.[17] For lesbians, who may approach agencies with more misgivings than other potential clients, perceptions of a particular agency as helpful will be influenced by staff composition (number of women, lesbians, and recovering lesbian alcoholics), types of services available (women's groups, lesbian groups, and child care), and by the philosophy of the agency conveyed in outreach activities. In the absence of a conscious effort to do otherwise, an agency may easily inadvertently limit lesbian participation in its services.

We have noted several unique treatment concerns for lesbians, which can be addressed through agency attention to special services, staff composition, and outreach. Yet other options include the provision of "separate" treatment facilities for lesbians. Although the value of all women's treatment facilities has been fairly well documented,[18] too few lesbian treatment facilities exist to provide comparative data. Fifield evaluated one lesbian alcohol program and concluded that important components of the treatment process for lesbian alcoholics included the following: a safe supportive environment in which to interact with peers, an understanding of societal oppression and discrimination as it affects and is internalized by lesbians, and the freedom to focus on the issue of sexual orientation and how it relates to alcoholism. These goals can only be achieved, Fifield contends, in a separate treatment facility for lesbians.[19]

In contrast, some have argued that an "integrated" program (by gender, sexual orientation, and other characteristics) offers a richness of experience, maintains a proper focus on alcoholism as the primary disease, and facilitates adjustment to the real world after treatment. Regardless of what services might be considered ideal, however, most communities lack the sufficient financial resources and clientele to make totally separate services for lesbians feasible. Wherever practical, separate treatment facilities for lesbian alcoholics offer significant advantages. Where such programs are not workable, special services for lesbian alcoholics within women's and mixed-gender treatment facilities offer important benefits.

Lesbian-oriented services within larger programs are uncommon at present. Sexist and heterosexist values often color administrative attitudes regarding treatment, resulting in an underestimation of the importance of addressing the special needs of women and lesbians. Similar difficulties are experienced by members of racial and ethnic minorities and economically disadvantaged groups. It has already been noted that lesbians tend to underutilize treatment facilities. This tendency, combined with the low visibility of closeted lesbians within treatment facilities, makes it easier for administrators to excuse their policies and priorities. On the other hand, if an agency becomes known for serving lesbians, administrators commonly fear that heterosexual clients, and worse yet, funding sources, will withdraw their support from the agency. In programs in which the philosophy of treatment, staff composition and training, and programming and outreach activities fail to address the needs of lesbian clientele adequately, several problems frequently arise during the course of treatment.

## Working with the Issues

Once in treatment, lesbian clients are likely to encounter a series of obstacles that must be negotiated successfully in order to maximize treatment effectiveness. Issues of concern include coming out in the treatment setting, involvement of a significant other and of an extended "family" of friends in the therapeutic process, and inclusion of the family of origin in treatment.

An initial dilemma for a lesbian in treatment in an integrated setting involves whether or not to come out. A decision to remain closeted may perpetuate dishonest patterns of communication that have developed during her drinking and may prevent the exploration and resolution of significant issues influencing her recovery. Throughout treatment, she will need to maintain an extra layer of defenses, which will in turn function as an obstacle to progress. On the other hand, a decision to come out may be met with nonacceptance or outright rejection by fellow clients or staff members. The mere discussion of her sexual orientation may be viewed inaccurately as irrelevant or as a means of avoiding the "real" issue of her alcoholism. Similarly, knowledge of her sexual orientation may encourage misinterpretation of her behavior. For instance, she may be perceived as "coming on" when she attempts to make contact with other women.

In addition to difficulties arising in working relationships with staff and peers, problems also may arise over who should be included in treatment. The inclusion of significant others and family members in the treatment process of alcoholics has been viewed increasingly as desirable, if not essential, for recovery. The dissimilar relationship patterns of lesbians, compared to heterosexual women and men, challenge the flexibility and sensitivity of traditional alcohol treatment staff. Too often, agency staff are insensitive to the complexity of lesbian relationships and automatically bring the family of origin into treatment or refuse to see same-sex couples for counseling. Alcoholism is no less a "family disease" for a lesbian than for any other alcoholic. The family simply looks different. The dynamics of co-dependency may differ from those of many heterosexual women in the sense that the typical lesbian co-alcoholic is not bound to her lover by a paycheck, children, or social convention. However, her commitment to the relationship or place in the community may bind her to her lover; she also may experience a need to be needed or wish to deny her own alcoholism. An exploration of these and other co-dependency issues with the lesbian couple in treatment is critical. Too often though, the partner is excluded, whether purposefully or inadvertently.

For similar reasons, it is important that the extended family of friends of the lesbian alcoholic enter this process. In the absence of a socially and legally defined nuclear family, this supportive network is important to her self-definition, self-esteem, and day-to-day functioning. The role of the social network in enabling drinking has already been discussed. Family members are in a position either to enable drinking or to support sobriety. With education, not only will they be able to bolster the alcoholic during and after treatment, but they also will become an informed part of the lesbian community, contributing to changes in norms within the subculture.

Inclusion of the family of origin in treatment may be constructive or destructive and must be considered on a case-by-case basis. The client herself is probably in the best position to make a judgement about this. If she has not been open with her parents and siblings about her sexual preference, coming out to them at this time may distract her from the primary focus, the treatment of her alcoholism. If she already has come out to her family members, they may not have accepted her sexuality and may maintain cold and hostile attitudes. Parents will not look at their daughter's drinking if they are too focused on her sexuality. They may blame her alcoholism on her sexuality, or even take responsibility upon themselves for this double affliction.[20] Any of these responses will detract from, rather than contribute to, successful recovery.

The special needs and concerns that arise in the treatment of lesbian alcoholics point to the need for more education for alcohol counselors and administrators regarding these issues. Alcohol treatment professionals must be made more aware of the concerns of lesbian alcoholics as a special population. They must develop a better understanding of sociocultural factors that affect lesbians and their drinking, and of lesbian life-styles and relationship patterns. Heterosexist values and homophobic behaviors must be uncovered in policy decisions, staff composition, programming, outreach activities, and the counseling process itself, toward an end of creating a trustworthy environment in which lesbian alcoholics can work toward recovery.

## RECOVERY

Once an alcohol rehabilitation program is completed, the newly sober alcoholic needs support from the community to which she returns.

Alcoholics Anonymous is a prominent resource in this regard. Although some lesbians are uncomfortable with sexist and heterosexist attitudes that they encounter in AA meetings, others are able to put these feelings aside and to benefit from what AA offers. In addition to traditional AA, other types of AA may be available such as lesbian, gay, and women's meetings. In some areas, however, such meetings are actively discouraged by regional General Services Organizations and the AA membership. In the Los Angeles area, a separate organization for lesbians and gay men, Alcoholics Together, was founded on AA principles.

Other networks can support recovery: lesbian, gay, or women's after-care groups sponsored by treatment facilities or recovery groups created within the community. Unresolved issues relating to dependency, power, sex-roles, and self-esteem can be worked on within the group setting, and new ways of dealing with problems developed. Individual and couples counseling, and skill development groups such as assertiveness training may also be helpful.

## CONCLUSION

Jon Weinberg has suggested that alcoholics need better coping mechanisms than the general population does because nonalcoholics can choose to drink in order to cope.[21] Likewise, lesbians may need to be better adjusted than heterosexuals in order to deal effectively with the impacts of sexism and heterosexism in their day-to-day lives. The recovering lesbian alcoholic, then, needs a lot of help from professionals, friends, and her community in order to maintain and continue her progress. Educational and political work within the lesbian community can help to develop this support. Dialogue between the lesbian community and treatment facilities offers the potential for changes in attitude, policy, and services. Recovering alcoholics are in a position to initiate new lesbian, gay, and women's AA meetings; to advocate the support of such meetings within regional AA General Service Organizations; and to work toward the acceptance of open lesbians within more traditional meetings. In addition, the creation of alcohol-free alternatives for socializing is a necessity. Flexibility, determination, and patience will be required to make these changes. Fortunately, the strength of the lesbian community and its commitment to health and mutual support seem to be growing.

## NOTES

1. Marcel T. Saghir, Eli Robins, Bonnie Walbran, and Kathye A. Gentry, "Homosexuality, IV: Psychiatric Disorders and Disability in the Female Homo-

sexual," *American Journal of Psychiatry* 127 (Feb. 1970): 147–54; Collins E. Lewis, Marcel T. Saghir, and Eli Robins, "Drinking Patterns in Homosexual and Heterosexual Women," *Journal of Clinical Psychiatry* 43 (Dec. 1982): 277–79; David W. Swanson, S. Dale Loomis, Robert Lukesh, Robert Cronin, and Jackson A. Smith, "Clinical Features of the Female Homosexual Patient: A Comparison with the Heterosexual Patient," *Journal of Nervous and Mental Disorders* 155 (Feb. 1972): 119–24; and Lillene H. Fifield, *On My Way to Nowhere: Alienated, Isolated, Drunk: Gay Alcohol Abuse and an Evaluation of Alcoholism, An Analysis of Services for the Los Angeles Gay Community* (Los Angeles: Gay Community Services Center, 1975).

2. Lewis, Saghir, and Robins, "Drinking Patterns."

3. Ibid.

4. Jeanne C. Marsh, "Public Issues and Private Problems: Women and Drug Use," *Journal of Social Issues* 38 (Spring 1982): 153–65.

5. Jeffrey M. Brandsma and E. Mansell Pattison, "Homosexuality and Alcoholism" in *Encyclopedic Handbook of Alcoholism*, ed. E. Mansell Pattison and Edward Kaufman (New York: Gardner Press, 1982), 736–41; Fifield, *On My Way*; Brenda Weathers, *Alcoholism and the Lesbian Community* (Washington, D.C.: Gay Council on Drinking Behavior, 1976); and Peter M. Nardi, "Alcohol Treatment and the Non-Traditional 'Family' Structures of Gays and Lesbians," *Journal of Alcohol and Drug Education* 27 (Winter 1982): 83–89.

6. Deborah L. Diamond and Sharon C. Wilsnack, "Alcohol Abuse among Lesbians: A Descriptive Study," *Journal of Homosexuality* 4 (Winter 1978): 123–42.

7. Celinda Cantu, "In Sobriety You Get Life," in *Out from Under: Sober Dykes and Our Friends*, ed. Jean Swallow (San Francisco: Spinster's Ink, 1983), 84–92.

8. Diamond and Wilsnack, "Alcohol Abuse among Lesbians"; Marcel T. Saghir and Eli Robins, *Male and Female Homosexuality* (Baltimore: Williams and Williams, 1973); and Weathers, *Alcoholism and the Lesbian Community*.

9. Fifield, *On My Way*.

10. Abby Willowroot, "Creativity, Politics and Sobriety" in *Out from Under: Sober Dykes and Our Friends*, ed. Jean Swallow (San Francisco: Spinster's Ink, 1983), 123–24.

11. Celinda Cantu, "In Sobriety"; Suzanne Balcer, "Recovery Is Power in the Now," in *Out from Under: Sober Dykes and Our Friends*, ed. Jean Swallow (San Francisco: Spinster's Ink, 1983), 79–83; and Willowroot, "Creativity, Politics and Sobriety."

12. Cantu, "In Sobriety."

13. William E. Bittle, "Alcoholics Anonymous and the Gay Alcoholic," *Journal of Homosexuality* 7 (Summer 1982): 81–88.

14. Fifield, *On My Way*.

15. Saghir et al., "Homosexuality, IV."

16. Weathers, *Alcoholism and the Lesbian Community*.

17. Linda J. Beckman and Katherine M. Kocel, "The Treatment-Delivery System and Alcohol Abuse in Women: Social Policy Implications," *Journal of Social Issues* 38 (Spring 1982): 139–51.

18. Joan Volpe, "How Women Recover: Experience and Research Observations," *Alcohol Health and Research World* 7 (Winter 1982): 28–39.

19. Fifield, *On My Way.*

20. Nardi, "Alcohol Treatment."

21. Jon Weinberg, "Counseling Recovering Alcoholics," *Social Work* 18 (July-Aug. 1973): 84–93.

# 17

## Lesbians, Weight, and Eating: New Analyses and Perspectives

LAURA S. BROWN

Disorders and dysfunctions related to food intake and body image are among the most common aspects of women's lives in late twentieth-century North America. Getting and staying thin seems to be a national preoccupation and pastime for women in ways that it is not for men.[1] In a comprehensive review of the literature on women, weight, and eating, Judith Rodin and her colleagues have commented that there is little difference between the attitudes toward food and body image found in so-called "normal," nondisordered women and those of women with identified eating disorders. Rodin has also noted how such a pervasive syndrome of eating-disordered cognitions is not present in men, who lack overt pathology with regard to eating and weight.[2] Persons diagnosed as having eating disorders tend overwhelmingly to be women. Women of every age, class, race, and sexual orientation are bombarded regularly with messages from various aspects of the culture regarding the value of adherence to a standard of bodily appearance that emphasizes that one can never be too thin. Thriving industries exist by playing on women's fears about body size, selling everything from exercise classes to foods altered chemically to be low in calories to a myriad of best-selling diet books, each with a different "expert" telling women how to lose weight.

It would seem that lesbians would be as likely as heterosexual women to be affected by these cultural attitudes toward weight and eating. Lesbians are socialized in families where general cultural attitudes and values regarding fat and eating are operative. Lesbians, for the most part, live and work in a world where these norms and their correctness are often taken for granted. It might seem, therefore, that concerns for lesbians regarding eating disorders would resemble those of heterosexual women, and that rates of eating disorders in lesbians would be proportionate to the percentage of lesbians among the population of women. Lesbians also have higher rates of at least one problem, alcoholism,[3] that many believe raises the risk of developing bulimia, an eating disorder.[4] This would lead to an informed speculation that lesbians might have higher rates of eating disorders than heterosexual women, given the greater number of women with high-risk histories in the lesbian population.

However, the reverse seems to be the case. That is, lesbians appear to make up a smaller percentage of women with eating disorders than of women in general. Most of the women with eating disorders who are described in the literature are either clearly defined as heterosexual, or their sexual orientation has not been a focus of inquiry. My personal communication with researchers in the area of eating disorders has also yielded some consensus that lesbians are highly under-represented among bulimic women presenting for treatment or research studies.[5] In the lesbian community, the question has been raised regarding the appropriateness of defining obesity as pathology; consequently, fat lesbians may experience some social or political support (or pressure) for defining their body size and eating styles as normative variations rather than disordered eating styles. Lesbians appear to be over-represented among fat activists, that is, people who define fatness as a normative variation and the stigmatization of fat people as political oppression.[6] However, there is no evidence that there are more fat lesbians than heterosexual women; rather, evidence is that fat may be construed differently by some lesbians than by most heterosexual women. Judith Rodin reports that she planned to collect information on the sexual orientation of her female subjects in a study being conducted as this chapter was being written.[7] However, there is no clear empirical data to explain the apparent absence of lesbians from the ranks of women with eating disorders. Although some of this could be attributable to the invisibility of lesbians among the female population, it seems that even those researchers and clinicians who attend to their subjects' or clients' sexual orientations discover fewer lesbians among women with eating disorders.

Given the near absence of empirical data about rates of eating disorders in lesbians, I will focus primarily on presenting some feminist therapy theoretical issues regarding eating disorders and focus on concerns relating to lesbian clients who present with problems of eating disorders, body image disturbance, or dissatisfaction about body size.

Although these three types of problems are often assumed to be synergistic, they can and do manifest in each other's absence, and, for theoretical reasons, may need to be addressed separately in therapy.[8]

Nomenclature is an important theoretical issue in the development of a conceptual framework. The power of naming as a technique for reshaping cognition has been commented on by a variety of lesbian-feminist theorists.[9] The naming of certain behaviors as disordered has powerful implications of deviance and dysfunction. However Rodin's data very strongly support a perspective that the behaviors that are commonly defined by the term *eating disordered* are continuous with a range of behaviors that are normative and often considered normal in women. Bulimic and non-bulimic women, for instance, apparently experience similar amounts of body image disortion and distress over body size. The difference appears to be in the strategies by which the distress is actively expressed.[10] Bingeing and purging are considered disordered, whereas chronic dieting is perceived as normal, if narcissistic.

Very few North American white women have never been on a diet. It is common for women to report a long history of dieting, often beginning in middle childhood.[11] Popular diets have included those with life-threatening regimens such as the protein-sparing fast and the Cambridge diet. Another popular diet, the Beverly Hills diet, prescribed attitudes and behaviors that mimicked anorexia nervosa and bulimia. Popular women's magazines almost always have one diet plan in each issue. Fear of fat and the pursuit of thinness at almost any cost are prescribed by medical experts and the popular media.

I agree with Rodin's conclusion that behaviors that fall within the purview of the eating disorders are so normative in women as to generate the risk for the development of such a problem in all women. Because almost any woman might correctly be found to have an eating disorder at some time in her history, I find the term *eating disorder* overinclusive and unnecessarily stigmatizing of normative behaviors. Although I can and do see the extreme destructive potential for women in certain of these attitudes and behaviors, I would prefer not to use the label *eating disorder* to describe them until certain theoretical questions are elucidated more fully. These questions pertain to issues of high rates of disorders among women within a misogynist cultural context. A lesbian and woman-centered psychology avoids stripping context from behavior. Consequently, I will refrain from general use of the term *eating disorders* in the remainder of this chapter and will instead refer to specific kinds of behaviors, for example, distortions of body image, fear of fat, and inaccurate self-feeding.

My working hypothesis regarding the high rates of these behaviors has been described elsewhere.[12] I have developed the following series of rules about food intake and body size that I believe women are required to adhere to; it is my theory that distortions of body image, fear of fat, and inaccurate strategies of self-feeding in women result from the conflict between adherence to these rules and strivings for health.

1. Small is beautiful. When women are small they occupy less space, are less visible, and utilize less resources. Women who are small in body are likely to have less of those aspects of the female body that are mediated biologically, for example, breasts, hip pads, and fat on belly and thighs. Consequently, they look more like men and less like women.[13] Women are valued culturally by their adherence to this rule, although the precise dimensions of correct smallness have varied across time according to the whims of various social control agents.[14]

2. Weakness of body is valued. Women's physical weakness helps to keep in place patriarchal norms of male dominance of women.[15] In consequence of this rule, women who have identifiable and developed musculature will be stigmatized as unfeminine.

3. Women are forbidden to nurture themselves in a straightforward or ego-syntonic manner. Women are, however, specifically enjoined to attend to the nurturance of others. Because self-nurturance is almost inevitable for human beings, women's self-nurturing behavior should thus be done in ways that induce shame or guilt and that stigmatize the woman in question. Eating and feeding oneself as forms of self-nurturing are particularly to be avoided, because they bring a woman into danger of breaking rules 1 and 2. However, because eating and feeding oneself are also primary means of self-nurturance for humans, the processes constantly bring women into violation of this rule and are sources of shame and guilt for women.

4. Women are forbidden to act powerfully in overt and ego-syntonic ways. This rule subsumes the first three and extends to cover behaviors beyond the range of food and body size. It underscores and strengthens the first three rules.

5. Women are valued only when they adhere unfailingly to the first four rules. Fat women are, by definition, not valuable, are shameful and stigmatized, and ought to feel guilty about their size, their visibility, and their eating. However, any woman runs the risk of breaking any of these rules at any time, because patriarchal cultural standards of fat and thin can be highly unstable and changeable. In consequence, even though a woman intends to follow the first four rules, she is always in danger of having her efforts negated by forces not within her control.

A woman must thus be constantly fearful and vigilant, guard how she eats, punish herself for rule violation, and fear fat in herself and in other women at all times.

In examining the cumulative impact on women of such hypothesized rules, one can see how distortions of body image, self-punitive relationships with food, and ambivalent relationships with the body appear normative for women in North American culture. How better to be vigilant constantly and fearful of one's own fat than to have a continual distortion of one's own body image as fatter than life? How more effectively can women punish themselves for eating than to interrupt the pleasure of the process with diets, restrictions, vomiting, laxatives, and fasts? The penalties imposed on women who break these rules are very high. Fat women are stigmatized and shunned, stereotyped as "stupid," "ugly," and "pigs." Assumptions are made about fat women's sexuality, with stereotypes of fat women being fearful of sex and using their fat as protection against intimacy. Fat women are made into a sexual fetish, with those attracted to them defined as perverted. Fat women are discriminated against in a wide range of settings. On the job, in college admissions, in the availability (or lack thereof) of comfortable, attractive, and affordable clothing, in medical treatment and in psychotherapy, fat women are told that they are bad, wrong, and out of control. Fat women are told that their size and their eating habits are the problem, and that changing their body size and orientation to food will make them nondeviant and nonpathological.[16] Although research data now strongly suggest that body size is determined primarily through genetics and not by behavior, and that efforts to lose weight may in fact lead to greater weight gain over time,[17] women are encouraged to change and reduce what they eat. Because any woman can be culturally defined as fat at any time, women are rewarded for engaging in strenuous efforts to be thin. The cliché of the woman perpetually on a diet mirrors the belief that only self-deprivation stands between any woman and the stigma of fatness.

A careful reader may at this point begin to detect parallels between attitudes toward fat women and attitudes toward lesbians. There is a sixth rule for women in the patriarchy that states that women are forbidden to love other women, because that would lead them to love and value themselves, and perhaps to break the other rules. A lesbian is stigmatized and devalued by patriarchal culture, as is a fat woman. Discrimination against lesbians, like discrimination against fat women, is considered acceptable by many segments of American society. Like fat women, lesbians are told that they are the problem, and that their lives would be better if they would change their orientations. Like fat women, lesbians violate the rules by being visible or powerful as lesbians.

My clinical observation is that homophobia and "fat oppression" (oppression caused by negative attitudes toward fat) can and do intersect in very particular ways in the lives of lesbians. It is within these points of intersection that it may be possible to make coherent sense of the anecdotal information available about lesbians' struggles with food and body image. My reasoning is as follows.

Lesbians and fat women are both valued negatively and stigmatized in patriarchal culture. Fear of being fat/being perceived as fat and fear of being a lesbian/being perceived as a lesbian are used by the institutions of patriarchal culture as means of controlling women socially. All women will internalize homophobia and hatred of fat during their socialization in patriarchal culture.

Lesbians are at risk from fat oppression in different ways than are heterosexual women. A lesbian's own internalized homophobia is likely to determine the degree to which she fat-oppresses herself. Specifically, I hypothesize that the more a lesbian has examined and worked through her internalized homophobia, the less at risk she is to be affected by the rules that govern fat oppression. The more a lesbian shames and stigmatizes herself for her lesbianism, the more likely it is that she will also actively fat-oppress herself. Once having successfully begun to challenge the rule against loving women in a patriarchal and misogynist context, a woman may be more likely not to impose other such rules on herself, for example, conventions about attractiveness, size, and strength. Conversely, a lesbian who has a high degree of internalized homophobia is likely to be at very high risk for engaging in behaviors that will be emotionally or physically damaging in an attempt to appear to be adhering to the rules. Keeping the rules about size, strength, attractiveness, and eating may become more important if a lesbian is homophobically self-hating. The fear of falling under suspicion for her size is added to the fear of her lesbianism.

My clinical experience with women who have problems related to food and body size, as well as that of other therapists specializing in this area who are interested in questions of sexual orientation, seems to offer anecdotal confirmation for this theory. Highly closeted lesbians may never reveal their sexual orientation if seeking treatment for bulimia, thus maintaining the illusion that few lesbians have this problem, or they might avoid seeking treatment from lesbian and non-homophobic heterosexual feminist therapists, who comprise the sample of colleagues from which my anecdotal information is drawn. Those self-identified bulimic lesbians whom I and my colleagues see appear to

be more overtly homophobic, as well as more psychologically dysfunctional in other ways, than bulimic heterosexual women or non-
bulimic lesbians. More bulimic lesbians seem also to be alcoholic or
otherwise chemically dependent than heterosexual bulimic women
whom I and my colleagues see in our practices.

Lesbian fat activists, a non-client population, seem to be women
who are comfortable with their lesbianism. My lesbian clients who are
fat, although not necessarily activists, seem generally unconcerned about
their weight and are for the most part physically active women who
perceive themselves as healthy and attractive. I have noticed a relationship between healing from homophobia and reduction of negative
self-concept where weight is concerned. For example, a lesbian client
who entered therapy from a position of great internalized homophobia
could not comfortably say the word "lesbian" and avoided associating
with other lesbians. Her weight was greater than average for her height,
although within the norms for women in her family; she consciously
perceived her fat as one of the indicators of her lesbianism and her
undesirability as a person. Therapy focused on issues of internalized
homophobia as it affected self-concept and interpersonal functioning.
However, a side effect of the therapy was that as this woman came to
embrace her lesbianism in a more positive manner, she also began to
perceive herself as attractive at her current weight. She changed her
hairdo so that her face, which she had previously stigmatized as looking
fat, and had tried to hide with her hair, would be more visible. She
also purchased clothing in the bright colors that she had always liked
but had avoided buying for fear of bringing attention to her "fat,
unattractive" body. She took up exercise, which she had loved as a
girl but abandoned after puberty as her body assumed its (apparently)
genetically determined larger size. She became active in the lesbian
community and often commented in therapy sessions about her amaze-
ment that there were so many attractive women who were also fat.
Her relationship with food also changed; she began to be more careful
about what she put into her body, and paid better attention to foods
that left her feeling uncomfortable and off center, rather than simply
to caloric content.

Such anecdotal and clinical observations must be made cautiously
because the empirical data are sparse. The trends that I and my colleagues have observed clinically when we consciously attend to the
relationship between homophobia and fat oppression are suggestive.
They point to some directions that lesbians as therapists, and therapists
who work with lesbians, may wish to consider in working with lesbian
clients around issues of food, eating, and body image and size.

It is essential for therapists to examine internalized myths of fat oppression as we apply them to ourselves and our clients. Do we, for instance, assume that fat women are fat because they are eating in an out-of-control manner? Do we assume that women who are not fat are not concerned with their weight and are eating in ways that are healthy and functional simply because the result is one of normal size? Do we accept the ego-dystonic nature of a woman's fat as proof of the need to lose weight, or do we ask the same questions that are now asked about so-called ego-dystonic homosexuality as a diagnosis? Do we secretly envy women with bulimia because "they can eat as much as they want and it never shows"? Do we fat-oppress ourselves by shaming ourselves about our own pleasure in food or by engaging in self-punitive actions such as compulsive dieting? Do we fat-oppress fat women by assuming that they want suggestions about diets, or by telling them "I feel fat, too"—pretending empathy with the real-world aspects of discrimination against fat women by virtue of our own participation in the process of fat oppression? When we hear lesbians derided as fat and ugly, do we protest that "we're not all fat," or do we examine carefully the relationship between the devaluation of fat women and the devaluation of lesbians? Until and unless the therapist examines and changes her own internalized fat oppression, she is likely to fat-oppress her clients, in either overt or covert manners.

In re-examining our fat-oppressive norms, we must also make the personal connections to our internalized homophobia and from there, to the misogyny that lies at the basis of them both. A woman who nurtures herself with food, and who does so without guilt, shame, and self-hate has challenged a very basic message given women against feeling worthy of love and sustenance.[18] A lesbian who loves herself and her love of other women and does so without guilt, shame, and self-hate breaks another such rule, that of compulsory heterosexuality.[19] A woman who is spending time and energy on her own pleasure by feeding herself lovingly, by using the resources available to her, by taking as much space as her body grows into, is as clearly revolutionary as is the woman who loves, values, and commits her energies to the love of women. It is quite natural and healthy for women to rebel against the woman-hatred inherent in both fat oppression and homophobia. So-called "eating-disordered" women are the most obvious casualties of that battle. The struggle to be able to stay thin enough while still eating enough to satisfy hunger is often manifested in the alternating bouts of bingeing, purging, and laxative abuse found in bulimia, or in the swings between compulsive stuffing and compulsive dieting found in other women who feel too fat.

An interesting literary portrait that makes the connection between coming out as a lesbian and coming out loving food and one's body is found in the character of Beth in Marge Piercy's novel, *Small Changes*.[20] Beth leaves her battering husband, stops eating the meat she hates, and finds freedom and pleasure in her new chosen diet. As she grows more comfortable in her body and more trusting of it, she grows into an awareness of her love for women and into a lesbian relationship. Her foil in the book, Miriam, is marked by a combination of male identification, compulsory heterosexuality, and extreme internalized fat oppression. She is ashamed of her appetite and love of food as well as of her lush, large body. Piercy shows how Beth grows more fully into herself, loving her body, determining what gives her pleasure and loving women, while Miriam becomes more alienated and estranged from herself and her needs and simultaneously more ashamed of her eating and body size, all the while giving men the power to determine her value for her. Although this particular example comes from fiction, it could as easily be a case example from my client load or that of my feminist-therapy colleagues, both lesbian and heterosexual. This is not to imply that lesbianism is a magical cure for problems with weight and eating. Rather, it is to suggest strongly that perceiving problems with weight and eating in women as possible manifestations of sexist oppression can be linked to perceiving problems with lesbianism as manifestations of homophobic oppression.

With this theoretical analysis, I have come to an understanding of a variety of food and body-related problems that lesbian clients may present in ways that will not reinforce either sexism, homophobia, or fat oppression (which I analyze as a variant of sexism). In the case of bulimic lesbian clients, this means that treatment focuses simultaneously on the obvious problem of bingeing and purging, as well as on the woman's attitude toward her lesbianism and her gender. With fat lesbians whose size is ego-dystonic, I attempt to work on the connections between homophobia and fat oppression. My experience has been that self-hating fat women of all sexual orientations have difficulty with the notion that they, too, have the right to eat food and enjoy it and so may eat furtively and not pay attention either to quality of taste or nutrition. With fat lesbians who are also dealing with manifestations of their internalized homophobia, there is often, in addition to these common deficits in self-nurturing, the strongly held internal sense that lesbians don't deserve the best in life, for example, good quality self-nurturing. Just as confronting internalized homophobia may in part require a therapist to reframe lesbian differences as positive rather than negative, so fat women can be reconceptualized as having taken power by taking space, being visible, and violating the rule against feeding oneself.

A lesbian psychology of women and eating can identify the signs of misogyny and fat oppression in their guise as eating disorders. Recent research by Marie Root and Pat Fallon suggests that most women with eating disorders are also survivors of sexual abuse or domestic violence; these authors ask us to see bulimia as a form of coping distorted through the lens of violence against women.[21]

An important clinical step is to avoid accidentally colluding with patriarchal rules by keeping them clearly in mind. One vulnerable area is that of the concept of appropriate uses of food for self-nurturing. My clinical experience, as well as anecdotal data from other therapists, suggests strongly that most women who struggle with food have some awareness that feeding themselves is indeed a form of self-nurturance. They know that food can function as friend, support, soother, companion, and entertainment. However they are in conflict about this relationship with food, because it breaks the rules so thoroughly. Unfortunately, even feminist-identified writers have become part of the problem. Susie Orbach, for instance, has identified appropriate and inappropriate uses of food, enjoining her readers to eat only in response to hunger for food and not in response to other hungers for nurturance.[22]

This new, "feminist" set of rules regarding food (it's okay to eat, but only when you're *really* hungry) has led to new ways for women to feel guilty about feeding themselves. This analysis assumes (incorrectly) that women will have equal access to other means of safe self-nurturance (or could if only they took themselves to therapy and learned how to nurture themselves in more symbolic and appropriate manners) and burdens women with a new sense of inadequacy. This may place a particular burden on lesbians, whose self-nurturing skills are often challenged to their limits simply by dealing with the assaults against integrity engendered by life in a patriarchal society, and who are faced with the additional complication of coping with the stigma associated with their lesbianism. By attending to the subtle signs of patriarchal rules contained even in some feminist approaches to food and eating, it may become possible to develop a perspective on self-nurturance that acknowledges lesbian reality more completely. In my own clinical practice, this develops into exploring strategies for making food a better self-nurturing device. For instance, I may ask clients to attend to the specificity of what they want to eat and facilitate giving permission to eat highly satisfying foods in their most tasty and attractive form. I simultaneously will work with a client to develop other self-nurturing alternatives that are easily and cheaply available, and that have equally good potential for satisfaction of emotional and physical hungers. Seeing eating as an equally good strategy for self-nurturing rather than a desperate last resort makes it easier to choose eating when it's an accurate response to what is wanted. Supporting a lesbian client in acknowledging the drains on her internal resources created by daily life in the patriarchy can create greater awareness of the need for self-nurturance, and less shame regarding the depth of that need.

Therapists working with lesbian clients who have concerns about their size must acknowledge to their clients the issues they face in dealing with the double stigma of lesbianism and fatness. It is vital to draw the relationship clearly early in the process of therapy and to empower the client to examine how her own internalized homophobia may have rendered her more vulnerable to fat oppression. This is not an approach that blames the victim. Rather, it clarifies how one form of oppression may create greater vulnerability to the effects of other forms of oppression. The context in which being a fat lesbian is a problem is an essential element in identifying whose problem it really is, that of society or that of the fat lesbian.

On careful examination, what often emerges is the lesbian client's fear that by being fat she is falling into negative stereotypes about lesbians and is carrying the burden of proving to society in general that lesbians can be as attractive as heterosexual women. In addition, a fat lesbian is likely to have been fat-oppressed by other lesbians, but to have accepted that fat oppression as being a reflection of acceptable norms and values. Empowering a fat lesbian in her awareness that such standards of attractiveness are not immutable truths, but rather reflections of patriarchal values regarding women, can often be a first step in such a woman's increased assertiveness and comfort in interpersonal and sexual settings, and in confronting the fat-oppressive behaviors of other lesbians in those settings.

It is highly unlikely that in the 1980s a lesbian therapist would respond to a request from a lesbian client for help in changing sexual orientation by agreeing to that goal for therapy. Rather, it is more likely that such a therapist would work with her client to uncover and heal from internalized homophobia. A lesbian therapist would probably not use terms such as *abnormal* or *deviant* to refer to lesbianism. To develop a woman- and lesbian-centered perspective on weight, eating, and body image in psychotherapy, similar perspectives are necessary regarding the value of normative variance. The following guidelines are suggested for therapists who seek to incorporate a non-fat-oppressive perspective into their work with women.

Removing the concepts and terms *overweight* and *overeating* from your vocabulary is a starting point. These terms imply the presence of one correct norm, rather than a range of normative variations. One study found that people could have vastly different caloric intakes, ranging from 1,600 to 4,700 calories daily, while maintaining a stable weight.[23] Genetic heritage plays a large part in the weight and fat distribution in any woman's body. No woman is over her own weight; she is the weight that she is at any given time. This perspective focuses on developing a standard of comfort and healthy function, with a concurrent de-emphasis on attaining a particular number on a scale. Similarly, attempts to predetermine a correct amount of food and to label the intake of more as overeating denies the great variability between individual women regarding what amounts of food are comfortable to eat, as well as sustaining to health. Attempts to control intake and to reduce weight artificially to below a body's natural set-point are highly likely to meet with failure and to be counterproductive to attempts to change or regulate body size over time; the body will intervene to increase appetite and weight until the set-point is again achieved. William Bennett and Joel Gurin's popular book, *The Dieter's Dilemma,* reviews the literature on set-point theory and examines the implications for interference with metabolic homeostatic mechanisms inherent in dieting.[24]

At this point in the discussion, the question is nearly always raised regarding the relationship between obesity and ill health. Available data strongly suggest that it is only at the extremes of obesity that health risks are present, and that the same level of health risk is contained in the extremes of thinness as well.[25] Vivian Mayer's review of the literature further suggests that health problems may be a function of stresses upon the body from large and frequent weight changes, for example, loss followed by gain in the endless cycle familiar to most women on diets. Many of the tactics used by women to maintain low weights, such as highly restricting intake, vomiting, laxative abuse, or compulsive overexercising, carry significantly higher health risks than simply being fat does.[26] Specific medical concerns such as diabetes do carry different risks related to body size and food intake, and these should be explored carefully in collaboration with a client's primary health care provider if such concerns exist.

It is also useful to give up the notion that it is an appropriate goal for therapy to stop having self-feeding as a strategy for self-nurturing. It is more in tune with a woman-centered perspective to acknowledge that food is legal, available, and can work well when consciously chosen for self-nurturance when other coping techniques may not be available.

It may prove to be counterproductive to ban food on the grounds of inappropriateness unless and until a woman has access to other self-nurturing techniques that are as available and work as well.

It is also important not to identify any particular strategy for feeding oneself as being better or more correct than others until a range of such strategies is available. It appears that to forbid a strategy may carry the meta-message that forbids feeding oneself as well. Thus, although a client may present with a goal of stopping her bingeing, it may be more useful to work first on developing other means of self-feeding while giving support for eating, enjoying food, and knowing what tastes are wanted at a particular time. Rather than agreeing to forbid the binge, it is useful to examine what the binge eating is about, for example, an attempt to eat and still follow the patriarchal rules about women and eating at the same time, and to aid the client in reframing bingeing as one of many strategies for food intake rather than an inherently bad behavior. It may be helpful to develop a hierarchy of strategies of self-feeding on which bingeing is a low-priority choice, for example, and to work concurrently on techniques for giving permission to break the rules against taking space and nurturance for oneself. I have, on occasion, had clients bring food into therapy sessions and have them practice eating in a self-nurturing way with support from me, when necessary, to confront the shame and fear they feel while feeding themselves.

It is important to focus therapy on ending behaviors that are self-oppressive and have the potential for harm. Reframing fat-oppressive thoughts, not throwing up or taking laxatives at the end of a binge, learning to obtain and prepare food that is pleasurable rather than punishingly uninteresting, are all examples of therapy goals that do not collude with fat-oppressive norms. Of particular consequence here is challenging the notion that food can constitute an addictive substance. On the one hand, it is true that many women experience themselves as addicted and out of control in relationship to food; on the other, it seems apparent that women learn to label their desires for food as bad and uncontrollable. A relationship with food can be described as having an addictive component, and thus a woman is relieved of some of her responsibility for breaking the rules, although the rules are left intact and in force. Reframing this perspective in therapy requires seeing the strategies for self-feeding, rather than the use of food for self-nurturance per se, as the problem. Twelve-step addiction recovery programs are very popular in many parts of the lesbian community as I write this chapter, and the model has been applied to food as an addiction. My argument with such an approach is with the identification of the food as the problem. Because one must continue to eat in order to sustain life (not the case with alcohol, drugs, gambling, and other targets for recovery in twelve-step programs), there are problems inherent in describing food as a dangerous addictive substance.

Finally, in working with women around issues of food and body, it is essential to examine how the issue of personal power is entwined in their struggles. For women to heal from fat oppression is for them to acknowledge and be overt regarding their ability to have impact on themselves and on others. With lesbian clients, the recapture of overt personal power via the examination of issues of food and body often leads to anger and grief regarding their oppression as lesbians, and then to further empowerment to change that oppression as well. The therapist working with lesbian clients on such concerns must acknowledge how ingrained internalized homophobia may be, and thus how frightening it can seem to some lesbians who are also fat-oppressed to cease keeping themselves in line with such oppression. Validating the sense of personal risk that some lesbians may experience from feeling too good about themselves can be a step toward giving permission to take that risk. One client has commented to me, apropos of this issue, that she fears that if she continues to increase her positive feelings about herself as a lesbian she will be unable to stay in the closet and may have to leave her work as a teacher. Because the risks to many lesbians of being out are quite real in terms of job loss and threats to housing and child custody, a therapist working with lesbians healing from both fat oppression and homophobia must have a clear vision of the alternatives available for expressing a newly empowered self, as well as the not always visible risks of maintaining internalized oppression.

Issues of eating and body size may be a problem for any lesbian, but not necessarily for fat lesbians. Because of the inroads made in some sectors of the lesbian separatist and lesbian feminist communities by lesbian fat activists, the level of awareness regarding fat oppression tends to be somewhat higher in those settings. Thus the problems usually faced by a fat woman because of the fat-oppressive attitudes and behaviors of her significant others may be less likely to be present for some fat lesbians. Consequently, it is important to obtain a complete history of eating issues and body concerns from *all* women. Bulimic women in particular risk being unidentified by therapists who are inattentive to issues of eating and body, because as a group these women tend to be normal weight and, for lesbians, the stigma attached to being bulimic seems to be intensified by the sheer lack of information about the actual numbers of lesbians with bulimia (just as lesbians in the past would not be out to therapists who assumed them to be heterosexual and who never asked, thus intensifying the lesbians' sense of self as deviant and alone). Because the medical complications associated with bulimia are severe, it is particularly important that identification and intervention occur as early as possible. Women with a history of anorexia may also not be immediately identifiable unless they are actively anorexic and underweight. Such women may continue to have significant struggles with food, distortion of body image, and vulnerability to anorexic behavior under stress.

In the final analysis, working with women around issues of food intake and body size is simply the work of teaching women to love themselves as women, in women's bodies, and with women's needs. For lesbian therapists and lesbian clients, that task is both easier and more difficult. By being woman-oriented in our affections and emotional and sexual energies, we have made an initial step toward loving women. Because that step is stigmatized and punished in patriarchal culture, we may be ambivalent and conflicted about having made it. Thus we will find ourselves weaving the connections between fat oppression and the hatred of women, between the stigma associated with fat and the stigma associated with loving women, between the penalties for loving ourselves by feeding ourselves well and loving ourselves by loving women. For lesbians, to address the one completely requires that the other be confronted as well.

## NOTES

1. C. P. Herman and J. Polivy, "Anxiety, Restraint and Eating Behavior," *Journal of Abnormal Psychology* 84 (June 1975): 666–72; and A. C. Nielsen, *Who's Dieting and Why* (Chicago: A. C. Nielsen, 1979).

2. Judith Rodin, Lisa Silberstein, and Ruth Striegel-Moore, "Woman and Weight: A Normative Discontent," *Nebraska Symposium on Motivation* (Lincoln: University of Nebraska Press, 1985), 267–304.

3. Jean Swallow, ed., *Out from Under: Sober Dykes and Our Friends* (San Francisco: Spinster's Ink, 1983).

4. Maria P. P. Root and M. Pat Fallon, "Victimization Experiences as a Factor in the Development of Bulimia," unpublished manuscript.

5. Personal communications with Victoria Vetere, Maria P. P. Root, and M. Pat Fallon, 1982–86.

6. Lisa Schoenfielder and Barb Wieser, eds., *Shadow on a Tightrope: Writings by Women on Fat Oppression* (Iowa City: Aunt Lute Press, 1983).

7. Personal communication with Judith Rodin, August 1984.

8. This theoretical perspective may strike some readers as overly political. I add this caution after reading comments by two anonymous reviewers who had difficulty with a perspective on these issues that clearly integrated a

political perspective into the practice of psychotherapy and that supported the views of the lesbian fat activist movement. One reviewer, in fact, commented that I must be a lesbian fat activist myself (although I am neither fat enough to qualify for acceptance in those groups nor ever have been a fat activist; I simply happen to support the politics of fat activism), indicating, I suppose, a belief that only a member of the group could espouse such views. Feminist therapists have traditionally integrated political analyses into the process of assessment and psychotherapy. This chapter will be no exception to that standard. Feminist canons of scholarship are not always those of traditional science; that difference may also be apparent here.

9. Mary Daly, *Pure Lust: Elemental Feminist Philosophy* (Boston: Beacon Press, 1984); Mary Daly, *Gyn/Ecology: The Metaethics of Radical Feminism* (Boston: Beacon Press, 1978); and Adrienne Rich, *On Lies, Secrets, and Silences* (New York: W. W. Norton, 1979).

10. Rodin et al., "Women and Weight."

11. Schoenfielder and Wieser, *Shadow on a Tightrope.*

12. Laura S. Brown, "Women, Weight, and Power: Feminist Theoretical and Therapeutic Issues," *Women and Therapy* 4 (Summer 1985): 61–72.

13. Kim Chernin, *The Obsession: Reflections on the Tyranny of Slenderness* (New York: Harper Colophon Books, 1981).

14. Lois W. Banner, *American Beauty: A Social History through Two Centuries of the American Idea, Ideal, and Image of the Beautiful Woman* (New York: Alfred A. Knopf, 1983), and Susan Brownmiller, *Femininity* (New York: Simon and Schuster, 1984).

15. Audrea Dworkin, *Right-wing Women* (New York: Perigee Books, 1983).

16. Schoenfielder and Wieser, *Shadow on a Tightrope.*

17. Rodin et al., "Women and Weight."

18. Geneen Roth, *Feeding the Hungry Heart: The Experience of Compulsive Eating* (New York: New American Library, 1982).

19. Rich, *On Lies, Secrets.*

20. Marge Piercy, *Small Changes* (New York: Doubleday, 1973).

21. Root and Fallon, "Victimization Experiences."

22. Susie Orbach, *Fat Is a Feminist Issue* (New York: Paddington Press, 1978).

23. G. A. Rose and R. T. Williams, "Metabolic Studies on Large and Small Eaters," *British Journal of Nutrition* 15, no. 1 (1961): 1–9.

24. William Bennett and Joel Gurin, *The Dieter's Dilemma* (New York: Basic Books, 1982).

25. Ancel Keys, "Overweight, Obesity, Coronary Heart Disease and Mortality," *Nutrition Review* 38 (Sept. 1980): 297–307.

26. Vivian Mayer, in Schoenfielder and Wieser, *Shadow on a Tightrope.*

# V

# COMMUNITY

# 18

## The Saga of Continuing Clash in Lesbian Community, or Will an Army of Ex-Lovers Fail?

SARAH F. PEARLMAN

The need to belong or feel a part of a particular group is a deeply human urge. For lesbians, it has special importance, for a sense of community helps to establish and maintain lesbian identity, gives one a sense of belonging somewhere, and provides the affirmation and acceptance that is missing in the larger culture. This sense of community helps make bearable the rejection and contempt present in the larger world.

At times, however, the lesbian community is not a haven. Instead of being accepted and supported, lesbians find themselves rejected, alienated, or in conflict with their peers. My interest is the exploration of these conflicts and the ways in which women react when personal feelings are tapped or political differences result in differing points of view. My goal in this chapter is to deepen understanding of the rifts and tensions apparent in many lesbian groups through looking at some of the roots of these conflicts—sociological, political, historical, and psychological.

Although I focus on problems in community building, I want to emphasize that lesbians love their lives as lesbians and their women-centered communities with the special pride and joy that is part of being authentically oneself. Thus, pride, joyfulness, camaraderie, and solidarity are as much a part of lesbian communities as are tensions and conflicts.

It is also important to note that there is no one history of twentieth-century American lesbianism. Accounts differ according to one's per-

313

ceptions, one's experience of events, and the particular community. My
own account is based on being part of, and in contact with, a number
of lesbian feminist communities since the early 1970s on the East Coast
and in one major city in the Midwest.

## Sociopolitical Sources of Conflict

The cost of the lesbian choice is high and provides fertile ground for
anger and conflict. Invisibility, pretense, and concealment produce
stresses and feelings of vulnerability beyond those of people whose
relationships and sexual desires are considered normal. Most lesbians
live with fear that exposure will lead to loss of jobs and income. Many
fear loss of their children through custody awarded to fathers, or
through emotional estrangement as the children react to their mother's
difference. Few lesbians have the authentic acceptance and affirmation
of their family of origin. Some lead half-lives of lies and omissions,
hoping that this will maintain some sense of family and home. Still
others endure tense and emotionally distant family situations.

These losses of acceptability, security, and connection combined
with isolation from both family and the larger culture create an intense
need to experience oneself as part of a larger group, to have some
sense of belonging through relationships, alternative families, friendship networks, and social and political organizations. Thus, community-
as-connection provides definition, acceptance, and inclusion; it offers
sources for social life, political activity, friendships, lovers, places to
go, and other types of assistance. It is these needs that make community
profoundly powerful.

Lesbian communities are typically defined by geography and composed of groups or networks who are connected through social and
political activity. In small towns or universities, there may be a sense
of one large community; in larger cities, there may be many communities. The center of community can be one or more bars or coffee
houses, a women's center, a social organization, self-help or discussion
groups, or an occasional dance or musical event. Thus, community is
not a fixed entity, but rather a sense of connection or "groupness,"
defined and maintained by extended affiliations and frequent or even
periodic contact. Community can also be more myth than reality when
there is limited contact because of severe estrangements between community members.

In fact, the myth of community can itself be a source of conflict.
When needs are intense and expectations of community are high,
idealized notions may go beyond what any group of individuals can

realistically provide—especially a group that is beleaguered and lacking in resources. Dependency upon community is also heightened by isolation from and discomfort in the larger homophobic culture. The world of the lesbian community is a small one, and social compression creates a claustrophobic sense of limitation and confinement. No matter how much support and sustenance the community does offer, it cannot replace what has been lost. Thus, members often experience feelings of bitterness and disenchantment over what the community has not and cannot provide, including the experience of "normalcy," which exists for those who conform to the values of the dominant culture.

Communities also bear the weight of traumas, hurts, and jealousies as break-ups and exchanges of lovers create ex-lovers, single lesbians, and new partnerships. Friendships between lesbians are often intense and erotically charged so that minor disappointments can be experienced as if one's friend were a rejecting lover. Tensions also exist between single and coupled lesbians and between one's friends and one's lover, because a relationship often reduces social availability. The wonder of lesbian community is not that problematic conflicts exist, but rather that communities remain cohesive, friendships weather hard times, and ex-lovers become friends. Social events too are often joyous occasions characterized by excitement, affection, gaiety, elation, and a wonderful sense of belonging and oneness.

However, stresses remain and an additional burden on lesbian communities is the self-hating of internalized homophobia. If a woman has ambivalent feelings about herself as a lesbian, she may also have ambivalent feelings about the worth of other lesbians. Frustration, rage, and bitterness toward one's condition may be turned outward toward the community of similar, inferiorized, and powerless others. Certainly, hating other lesbians is safer than turning one's rage toward the dominant group, which is less accessible and a great deal more threatening. Such feelings can also provide a sense of the little power any oppressed individual has in oppressing someone as powerless as herself. Thus, within-group conflict contains and deflects the impulse toward aggressive action inherent in frustration and rage, a convenient dynamic for any dominant group.

Another factor that can create conflict is the intense demand for sameness, for a common and collective identity that is typical of many communities. This demand for sameness can clash with the drive toward individual identity—that is, the wish to be one's own person and make independent choices. Susan Krieger describes this demand for sameness as "mirroring," that is, the expectation that others will be a mirror image of oneself.[1] This demand for sameness in lesbian communities makes differences uncomfortable and suspect, as if dissimilarity could erode cohesiveness. The contradiction is that lesbians happen to be a remarkably diverse group. What lesbians share, aside from gender, is a decision to act on a preference, the preference to relate both emotionally and sexually to women. All the rest can be differences—race, ethnicity, class, politics, education, work, living styles, bisexual inclination, role identity, differences in sexual/political coming-out, sexual behavior, early or late awareness of attraction to women. What is special to lesbians (and gay men) as an oppressed group is that there is an attempt to create bonding and community without a shared historical and cultural experience (unlike other oppressed groups, blacks or Jews, for example), and in spite of enormous diversity. That both community and lesbian culture have been achieved, including a sense of lesbian history, tradition, and humor, is no small accomplishment.

The women's movement added substantially to community cohesiveness in terms of political beliefs and activity. It also drew lines between politicized and nonpoliticized lesbians and created new arenas for dispute in its initial denial of difference and its insistence on political sameness.

## Historical-Political Sources of Conflict

Before the women's liberation movement, lesbian friendship networks and communities were primarily social and bar-oriented, although there was increasing interest and political activity directed toward attaining civil rights. In pre-movement communities, strict social norms—that is, those based on relationship, dress, and role (butch/femme)—had prevailed with frequent belittling of those lesbians who did not conform. The second wave of feminism added new sources of conflict to what were really newly politicized lesbian communities. It also generated a massive coming-out of previously heterosexual women.

Feminism in the late sixties and early seventies was white, middle-class, and composed primarily of heterosexual women with Marxist and New Left backgrounds who were emerging out of civil rights and anti-war activism.[2] The involvement of lesbians quickly increased as the early women's movement offered opportunities for political activism and social change beyond that of the primarily gay male organizations. Feminist political activity gave lesbians places to meet outside of the bars through consciousness-raising groups, women's centers, and services such as rape crisis and women's health centers. Radical feminist inquiry, in addition, provided lesbians with a means for political analysis and a new revolutionary consciousness of lesbian oppression.

Feminism gave lesbianism a female-oriented political movement and a political understanding of the basis of their persecution. The analysis suggested that, for women, the choice to relate emotionally/ sexually to women and to make their primary relationships with women is basic to one's freedom. Lesbianism, it was argued, was far from being unnatural, pathological, or sinful; it had been stigmatized and made deliberately taboo through a variety of interconnecting institutionalized ideologies—religious, psychological, medical, and legal.

As lesbians, women move beyond the control of men (at least individual men) sexually, reproductively, emotionally, and as domestic and child-care workers. Thus, lesbianism not only means an actual loss to men of women as commodities, but also arouses psychologically primitive fears of exclusion and loss that may underlie the male compulsion to dominate and control.

Because the control of women is basic to patriarchy, heterosexuality must be mandatory and enforced, and lesbianism penalized. Lesbians must be kept invisible (exception: pornography), or if they are visible, their choice must be defined as sick and leading to the most tragic of lives. Otherwise, lesbians may suggest to other women what independence and autonomy might look like. Lesbians might also evoke mutinous attractions or hint that women can be nurtured in relationships, given the prevalence of emotional deprivation and abuse in heterosexual relationships.

The stigma of lesbianism can also be used by the patriarchy to frighten women into subordinate, dependent behaviors through what Shulamith Firestone calls the lesbian as buffer.[3] Any woman who seems strong, athletic, competent, and assertive, or who has intense friendships with other women, can always be called a dyke to intimidate her back into line and force her to prove femininity and heterosexuality.

If feminism gave lesbianism a more revolutionary political movement, lesbians may have returned more of a favor than was originally wanted. Less dependent upon male affirmation and emotional and economic support than heterosexual women, lesbians were freer to evaluate critically heterosexuality, male behavior, and biological maleness. Lesbians could see that heterosexual relationships were frequently heterosexist, patronizing, and demeaning to women, and there developed a growing wariness and impatience with those heterosexual women who too quickly rose to the defense of men.

Straight feminists began to find lesbians embarrassing, and concern grew that the women's movement would be stigmatized by a lesbian presence. Could the lavender menace play in Peoria? In answering the question, the movement split across gay/straight lines—the first of many splits—and the stage was set for lesbian separatism and the lesbian nation. Women-identified women began to insist that the true revolutionary feminist was a lesbian, that the nonfeminist lesbian was unenlightened, and that women could personally and politically develop only in the absence of men. The new lesbian politics declared that lesbians should give energy to lesbians only, should withdraw from relationships with men (including their male children) and from women who continued to relate sexually to men. A new idealized lesbian emerged, and a set of new, remarkably similar rules took hold in politicized communities across the country. This new correctness resembled the old social or role correctness, except that it was now supported and made true by political philosophy. The result was that sameness was politicized.

Few white women, straight or lesbian, noticed that feminist analysis did not consider issues relevant to women of color. Women of color had yet to describe their own experience and confront feminism with its inherent racism and classism. Denial of difference also made it difficult to notice that lesbians were not all alike, and that differences along ethnic, class, and educational lines did exist. Leftover prejudices and stereotypes also existed with perhaps the ingrained cultural habit of generalizing particular experiences to all. These issues, then submerged, led to later confrontations and challenges.

Feminism had changed the context for coming-out. In the seventies, lesbians came out in an environment in which there was the potential of political support and pride, whereas pre-movement lesbians had come out with little support or notion of pride in communities that emphasized sex and sexual attraction and an eroticism often tied to dress and roles. Many of the new, previously heterosexual, radical lesbians had based their choice as much on politics as on sexual interest in other women. These radical lesbian feminists, still reeling perhaps from an oppressive male sexuality, from objectification and unequal and frequently abusive relationships, constructed a less sexual lesbianism. In the highly charged atmosphere of a rape crisis center or a battered women's shelter, it was not difficult to develop a hatred of male physical and sexual aggressiveness. Sexuality became suspect and along with it the distinctive eroticism of lesbian culture. A new, correct sexuality became one more source of future difference and antagonism.

Thus, feminism beyond the idyll of its sisterly beginnings, its idealizations and sense of oneness, began to prescribe a purity of analysis, philosophy, and behaviors. There was now a political right and a political wrong, a correct and an incorrect lesbian-feminist line with trashing and exclusion of those who differed.

Yet differences were also emerging. Political divisions of liberal versus radical versus socialist were becoming more apparent and less reconcilable. Assertions and challenges regarding racial, class, and ethnic differences, while creating new comfort and pride based on older and more primary identities, added to community fragmentation. Communities had also increasingly polarized around a variety of issues including separatism, transsexualism, S/M sexuality, pornography, monogamy, drug and alcohol use, and affiliation with gay male or lesbian-feminist groups. While the content or the subject of these particular controversies differed, the reactions and behaviors across communities were remarkably the same: rigidity and intensity of feelings and opinions, inability to discuss or accept differences, absolutes of right and wrong, exclusion and rejection of those who differed. Such characteristics can be signs that more is at stake than is psychologically conscious. And so we turn to the psychological roots of conflict.

### Psychological Sources of Conflict in Lesbian Communities

> . . . women together is a work
> nothing in civilization has made simple.[4]

There is no question that women have a long history of intense and loving but also problematic relationships with each other. Groups in particular are a curious example, because they seem to evoke such powerful feelings and reactions. Women join groups—social, political, professional, or therapeutic—for multiple reasons including wanting to belong somewhere, wishing to meet friends, and wanting to find a lover. If these needs have primacy over the purpose or goal of the group, disappointment can result in undermining behaviors or departure. In addition, initial group formation stirs feelings and wishes for collective identity or a sense of oneness, so that beginning groups are often charged with magical expectations and unrealistic hopes of what will be experienced or achieved. Any differences that then emerge disturb these wishes and lead to anger and quick disenchantment.

Once a group is past the formation stage, a more established, less tentative sense of groupness occurs. At this second stage, issues of power and differences between group members may emerge and become primary so that meetings and interactions are often filled with unspoken tensions and resentments. Again, different members may depart and some undermining of the group may occur, so unless there is a functioning core of people, group life can be remarkably short.

What is especially curious is the struggle within women's groups to ensure the equalizing of power as part of a collective process. While the equalizing of power is an important part of feminist theory and practice, the original intention was to ensure that decision making be shared among group members, that all members have near equal say or influence, and that male hierarchal structures be avoided. However, what frequently happens is that the collective process becomes primary, while group effectiveness and purpose become increasingly secondary and are often willingly sacrificed by group members.

Collective process was never intended to disqualify leadership or expertise. However, misuse of process can mask undermining behaviors that serve to level or equalize power, leadership, and expertise in groups of women. Underneath this leveling struggle are feelings and fears of inadequacy, envy, competitiveness, and anger evoked by differences, and differences in abilities among group members. An unspoken group agreement can be that its members would rather be the same and equal rather than effective. For those women who openly disagree, the outcome is often the decision to leave, or to be expelled.

A second curious example involves community controversies and polarizations. What seems important is the intensity, the purism, and the dogmatism of the controversial stand so that polarizing lines are drawn with extreme judgment and exclusion of those who differ. What becomes primary is the *stand* with its accompanying sense of rightness and righteousness along with the demand for agreement and the personalizing of disagreement. What becomes split off and secondary are the consequences or outcome such as community fragmentation, estrangements, and withdrawal of community members. Also lost in the compulsiveness of the stand are the priorities for concern as lesbians, women, and people in America of the late 1980s.

To help explain these curiosities or dilemmas in lesbian community, there are a number of women theorists who have looked at the early mother-daughter relationship and its impact on later relationships and behaviors. Many of their ideas are being extended to lesbian relationships on issues such as fusion, dependency, power, nurturance, sexuality, and difficulty with differences and separateness (see Beverly Burch, Margaret Nichols, and Sue Vargo in this volume). Their theoretical speculations may also have relevance in understanding conflict among extended relationships, that is, lesbian community.

The first of these theorists, Dorothy Dinnerstein, describes how power or authority in women is problematic for both women and men in that it evokes feelings and fears connected to our earliest experiences with an all-powerful mother.[5] It was this woman who had the power to love and gratify, or to deprive and hurt at a time of our most extreme helplessness and dependency—during infancy and childhood. It was this woman who was the first person to whom we all as infants and children first submitted. She, too, was the first person against whom we rebelled and thus began our beginning assertions of individuality. These interactions took place also before language and thought, and thus the ability to articulate feelings. This gives later adult feelings that may be connected to these infant feelings and interactions a wordless power and intensity unaffected by the modifying impact of language. To Dinnerstein, female power is associated and connected with danger.

Women do fear power, both in themselves and in other women. Women fear power in other women because it evokes their own feelings of inadequacy, envy, and anger. Women fear power in themselves, in part due to fears of alienating or losing others. Ruth Moulton attempts to explain these particular feelings as being based in maternal ambivalence, envy, and competitiveness towards daughters' independence and achievement.[6] To the extent that one's mother competed, envied, and discouraged achievement (overtly or disguised), the daughter will later avoid competition, will fear envy and disapproval, and will feel vulnerable to angry retaliation on the part of other women.

Differences can also be experienced as unequalizing or power differences. Burch in her therapy work with lesbian couples (described in this volume) has observed that differences between two women are often looked at as a problem of inequality, and that one's sense of powerlessness in relation to another woman seems to be experienced as unbearable.

The theories of Nancy Chodorow have begun to have enormous influence on the deciphering of conflicts and difficulties in lesbian relationships. Chodorow states that women share an experience of being mothered by a same-sex parent who typically believes and expects a high degree of sameness and responsivity in daughters, with resulting confusions around identity and boundaries.[7] Differences and moves toward independence and autonomy are then often experienced by mothers as rejection, betrayal, and denial of their own worth based on their life choices, and they react in turn with rejection and emotional withdrawal. Independence and difference can also be perceived as threatening to mothers who have built a half-conscious security around the notion of eventual dependence on daughters.

While this blurring of self and other enhances the qualities of empathy, nurturance, and ability for intimacy in adult women, a typical growing-up experience for women has been that sameness and responsivity to others is reinforced, while autonomy, separateness, and differences are discouraged. Separateness and difference then become associated with rejection, withdrawal, threat to emotional safety, and possible relationship loss that continue into adult life and adult relationships. Certainly, this is part of the problematic fusion so many lesbian couples experience. An additional fact is that by becoming "different" as lesbians, women do lose their relationship with their mothers.

Another theorist, Jane Flax, speculates that women are raised by mothers who are more intensely conflicted in their relationships to daughters compared to sons.[8] She points out that mothers carry a damaged sense of personal worth because of female inferiority under patriarchy, and may be devaluing of daughters as well as homophobic regarding physical contact. Flax believes too that mothers may be less responsive to daughters' needs because the needs of daughters can evoke memory or recognition of their own unmet needs in relation to their mothers as well as to male partners in adult life. This conflicted responsivity can leave daughters with a sense of inadequate nurturance and means that women as adults may tend to seek emotional reparation in later relationships to make up for the bonding and closeness not received from mothers. This sense of inadequate nurturance may explain the intensity of relationships with women, and Flax emphasizes that unresolved longings for one's mother "fill intimate female relationships with extraordinary power to damage and gratify."[9]

In addition, female devaluation, lack of nurture, and a socialization that continuously discourages competence and mastery leave women with a wounded or flawed sense of self. This impedes healthy competition and taking risks and creates the tendency to compare oneself unfavorably, to feel others have attributes one cannot attain, and to relinquish trying and withdraw. It also contributes to protective behaviors that defend against all possible criticism and feelings of inadequacy and wrongness. This too makes argument and difference difficult.

Flax also suggests that the idyll of the early women's movement (applicable to lesbian community) may have aroused feelings and longings for oneness, sameness, nurture, and belonging that never could have been fulfilled. When the fantasy of oneness is disturbed through recognition of difference, leftover feelings of rage and betrayal from the early mother-daughter relationship can be evoked. To Flax, the women's movement has never fully recovered from the discovery of differences, nor have lesbian communities.[10]

To this notion of betrayal and rage, Artemis March adds her suggestion that the original betrayal in the mother-daughter relationship may be the heterosexual mother's preference for a mate of a different sex.[11] Karen Fite and Nikola Trumbo extend this issue of maternal betrayal by describing common experiences of mother's inaccessibility because of sickness, depression, and alcoholism, mother's subservience to fathers, preference toward sons, and keeping daughters in homes characterized by paternal physical, sexual, and verbal abuse.[12]

Dorothy Dinnerstein also suggests that women may have difficulty with same sex solidarity because of two developmental factors or experiences.[13] One is that although boys achieve independence from mothers, in part through identification with fathers and establishing solidarity with men, women lack this particular developmental experience. Daughters, instead, struggle with independence from a same sex parent, so that same sex solidarity has no part in assisting with autonomy. The second developmental factor is that when daughters do attempt more independence from their mothers, they may utilize idealizing fathers and devaluing mothers, a kind of splitting so that fathers get assigned the good and mothers, the bad (congruent with societal devaluing). Dinnerstein suggests that for women to achieve solidarity with other women, splitting must be tempered, and ambivalence and mixed feelings must be able to be tolerated.

A last point is the observation that women tend to be extremely dyadic in terms of relationship patterns. Most women can readily recall experiencing or being part of exclusionary interactions as children or adolescents, that is, where one girl or another is excluded or expelled from a clique or a threesome, thereby reducing it to a twosome. Fite and Trumbo speculate that these exclusionary behaviors may be rooted in the dyadic socialization common to women (the original mother-daughter pair), as well as expression of anger toward one's mother, along with an attempt to feel powerful, included, special, and loved through the rejection of another.[14] Whatever the psychological source, it is as if some old powerful psychological drama based on dyadic bonding, exclusion, and one person's holding of all of the bad is being re-enacted.

From these observations and speculations, we can perhaps begin to construct a theory to account for the conflictual aspects of relationships between women based on fear of female power and female difference and the splitting and betraying aspects of the mother-daughter relationship, and to build on an interconnected group of ideas that can explain what seems to be a rage-in-waiting between women, a too-ready hypercriticalness, an immediate reaction to disappointment or difference perceived as betrayal or abandonment, and a response reflex to be placed or displaced on another woman.

Crucial also is that these speculations not place all blame or attribute total personality outcome to mothers, a too painfully familiar assumption within traditional psychology. Whoever has the role of first and primary caretaker must have profound impact. However, it is important to remember that mothers do mother under incredibly debilitating circumstances including overwork, exhaustion, poverty, emotional deprivation, and abuse. The idea is perhaps neither to idealize or condemn, but to recognize the endurance and strength that go into mothering, to understand the personal limitations of one's mother, and that she too has been socialized under patriarchy and is a victim of it.

*New Challenges*

The theories I have discussed primarily describe preverbal experience and the psychological unconscious. It is questionable what one can do about preverbal interactions and the unconscious, except perhaps to speculate about it consciously and become aware of one's own personal behaviors as signs that more than what is conscious may be in operation. What does seem important to consider is that there may be some early psychological confusions around sameness and closeness, and separateness, difference, and rejection. There may also be unresolved feelings connected to women such as fear of authority, power and dependency, a vulnerability to experiencing certain actions as betrayal, and a susceptibility to feelings of rage when those actions or interactions involve another woman. In addition, events during early life and the position of women in society can lead to a sense of self as flawed that makes self-protection paramount. This affects relationships and behaviors and can further result in treating women who disagree or disappoint, or choose to think differently as if they were indeed an abandoning or betraying ex-lover.

Equally important are the multiple social reasons for antagonism between women, which encumber relationship and solidarity and prevent the formation of a full social movement. These reasons relate to oppression as women and as lesbians, the dynamics within lesbian communities, the diversity of lesbians (particularly class and economic differences), and living in a fairly stressful society. In actuality, we live in an extremely destructive and pathological society that makes both living and keeping down personal neuroticness a struggle.

The politicalization of lesbian consciousness was an extraordinary gift. The politicalization of sameness was less of a gift and instead forced polarizations and a political purism that ignored diversity, personal timing, and the right to individual choice. Concealed under that purism are also those who behave irresponsibly and unthinkingly in terms of a common or community good, who waste time on the detail and lose sight of the whole, and who act out the personal under the political. The result is that the true enemy is forgotten as enemies are made of one another As the persecution of lesbians increases, as poverty among women accelerates, as abortion remains under threat and custody of children is jeopardized, some reordering of priorities and some hard looks at self may be necessary. There is some responsibility here.

Lesbians do need each other, but not so desperately at this time. The reality is that although consensus may be impossible, it is through differences that we learn from each other. Conversely, conviction and the unswerving stand also jar thought, stir imagination, and create new passions crucial to maintaining vitality in any movement. What remains unfortunate is that lesbian communities lack a tradition of those mediating forums or structures that contain and resolve community tensions and conflicts. Until such forums exist, responsibility must remain personal instead of collective.

## NOTES

1. Susan Kreiger, *The Mirror Dance: Identity in a Woman's Community* (Philadelphia: Temple University Press, 1983).

2. Sara Evans, *Personal Politics* (New York: Vintage Books, 1979).

3. Shulamith Firestone, *The Dialectic of Sex: The Case for Feminist Revolution* (New York: Bantam Books, 1971).

4. Adrienne Rich, "Twenty-one Love Poems, No. XIX," in *The Dream of a Common Language* (New York: W. W. Norton, 1978), 35.

5. Dorothy Dinnerstein, *The Mermaid and the Minotaur: Sexual Arrangements and Human Malaise* (New York: Harper & Row, 1976).

6. Ruth Moulton, "The Effect of the Mother on the Success of the Daughter," *Journal of Contemporary Psychoanalysis* 21 (April 1985).

7. Nancy Chodorow, *The Reproduction of Mothering: Psychoanalysis and the Sociology of Gender* (Berkeley: University of California Press, 1978).

8. Jane Flax, "The Conflict between Nurturance and Autonomy in Mother-Daughter Relationships and within Feminism," in *Women and Mental Health*, ed. Elizabeth Howell and Marjorie Bayes (New York: Basic Books, 1981), 66.

9. Flax, "The Conflict between Nurturance and Autonomy," 60.

10. Ibid., 66.

11. Artemis March, "Betrayal and Rage: Early Dynamics in the Mother-Daughter Relationship," paper delivered at the Association of Women in Psychology Conference on *Lesbian Psychologies*, Boston, March 1984.

12. Karen Fite and Nikola Trumbo, "Betrayals among Women: Barriers to a Common Language," *Lesbian Ethics* 1 (Fall 1984): 76.

13. Dinnerstein, *The Mermaid and the Minotaur.*

14. Fite and Trumbo, "Betrayals among Women," 83.

# 19

## Mediation for Lesbians

BONNIE J. ENGELHARDT AND
KATHERINE TRIANTAFILLOU

Before we began to work together, we had dealt individually with the legal and emotional ramifications of lesbians separating from each other in painful and often financially debilitating ways. Given today's legal system and the realities of lesbian relationships, we began to see the need for a multidisciplinary approach as we grappled with these problems in professional isolation. What began as a dialogue between us because of our unique relationships to the Boston lesbian community grew into a business relationship called "Gay Mediation."

We created our mediation service to address a growing need for lesbians and gay men to have an alternative process for resolving disputes. One of us, Engelhardt, a licensed independent clinical social worker, has had twenty years of experience as a social worker/therapist, now specializing in couple counseling and sex therapy in the lesbian and gay community. The other, Triantafillou, is a family law practitioner and civil rights attorney who has represented lesbians facing such legal issues as divorce, custody, buying and selling of houses, starting businesses, and making wills and contracts.

We will focus in this chapter on our work over the past decade with lesbian couples and groups. We will present part of this chapter in the form of a dialogue, much as we presented it to an audience of psychotherapists at a conference on issues in the psychology of women.

We will consider the following questions the most relevant to understanding the process of mediation between and among lesbians: What is "lesbian mediation" from a psychological and emotional viewpoint? What personality characteristics are helpful for or detrimental to a mediator? What is the process between therapist and lawyer? Who is responsible for the outcome? Are we equal or two bosses?

Our mediation service grew out of the political context of a generally homophobic legal system that pits gay couples and groups against each other in a highly charged hostile environment. This advocacy system costs a lot in time and resources and potentially jeopardizes people's lives beyond the issue in conflict, such as job loss and custody disputes arising from public acknowledgment of lesbianism.

The goal of lesbian mediation is to provide a forum for couples and organizations to define or redefine their relationship, deal with the emotional issues involved, and formulate workable legal contracts. All the parties in a dispute agree to three to six one-and-one-half hour sessions; at the end of this process, the parties sign a contract reflecting the agreements made during the sessions.

One of the reasons this process is so important is that courts are unable to deal with conflicts between lesbians without "punishing" the participants for their homosexuality. Hence, gay people do not generally have access to courts without the attendant fear of being found out. A lesbian mediation service is unique because it provides an additional level of safety for the participants. It also serves as a forum to validate, psychically and socially, the changes that relationships undergo. Because lesbians cannot marry, they cannot divorce institutionally, unlike heterosexual couples who can go into court immediately to redress their relationship grievance in fairly direct and simple ways. A lesbian in conflict must deny her relationship and create a legal action based on something else, for example, home ownership or a landlord-tenant problem. Some gay women have been known to use criminal laws such as conversion or trespassing to deal with disputes over property.

Another area of intensity for divorcing lesbians is the issue of child visits between the divorced lesbian and her ex-lover. To attempt to deal with this problem in heterosexual courts is to invite serious legal problems with an ex-husband, not to mention the difficulty of fashioning a complaint.

Another example of the unique use of mediation is between groups of lesbians who have formed business relationships with each other. We use "business" advisedly, because we have found that the business partnerships that couples and threesomes form usually have highly emotional underpinnings. (The collective wishing to provide services at low cost to women is an example of such a partnership, as is the lover/business partner wishing to work in a nonhierarchical atmosphere while providing an alternative service to other lesbians.) The problems in these partnerships might be resolved in heterosexual courts, but not without expense and danger. The most publicized example, of course, is Marilyn Barnett's suit against Billie Jean King.[1]

Although lesbians approach business and personal relationships with as much romanticism as do heterosexuals, an additional component of the romanticism is political correctness. Hence, groups form not to make money but to help other women. Problems arise when partners discover intense reactions to differences in class background and race that were not evident in the beginnings, or the limerance phase, of the relationship. (*Limerance* is the word coined by the psychologist Dorothy Tennov in her book *Love and Limerance* to mean the state of being in love.) Mediation *before* groups organize gives partners a forum to explore possible pitfalls with both a therapist and lawyer present to challenge and translate romantic notions into working contracts.

We must also distinguish mediation from arbitration. Mediation is a voluntary process in which the participants discuss the conflicts or issues between them and arrive at a self-directed solution with the aid of a facilitator. Arbitration involves all parties submitting a claim to an arbitrator, who hears evidence and renders a decision much as a judge would in a court of law.

In addition to the actual mediation service, we are also interested in developing models for lesbian feminist lawyers, therapists, and judges to create alternative dispute resolution techniques. Our dialogue begins with an analysis of characteristics of a mediator that have been compiled from our subjective experience as mediators; they should be used as indicators to determine whether a person is likely to enjoy this kind of work and be effective at it.

BJE: To me, these are the characteristics most important in enhancing the enjoyment of the role of mediator: that the person has the ability to do creative contracting; enjoys the role of director; is extroverted and can use humor; strives to be clear and open about her own values; is able to allow others to set rules of fairness; can tolerate intense emotional expressions and can create an atmosphere of safety; is able to develop structure but is prepared for spontaneity; is comfortable with "wheeling and dealing"; is aware of her own blaming behavior; and is able to work in collaboration with another discipline.

These ten characteristics seem essential to our lesbian mediation process; if someone is uncomfortable with many of these criteria, she might consider using arbitration or another form of mediation practice that would allow for more control. Let me go into more detail about these ten criteria.

1. Creative contracting: Some therapists sign written contracts with their clients concerning the practical aspects of the therapist/client relationship: missed sessions, fee responsibilities, vacations, and so forth. Other professionals look a little blank when one uses the word "contracting." I probably enjoy this mediation process because I came from training and experience in contracting with couples and groups that included contracting on practical issues as well as emotional focuses; for example, "This group will provide a safe place for you to ventilate your feelings if you strive to be completely honest with yourself and us." Being able to ask pointed questions, "What do you want right now?" and "How are you going to get that from her?" is a useful skill; liking the give and take of contracting increases the effectiveness of the role.

2. Enjoying the role of director and the process of orchestration: One has to appreciate the balance between directing and controlling, that is, being sure that things are moving in one direction, or happening so clearly that everyone can see the orchestration.

3. A degree of extroversion: I can't really find a better word than extroversion here. A true, full extrovert probably cannot be a good mediator because it's not really her show. On the other hand, if one is not able to be a bit extroverted and really get in there, then the process is slowed down.

4. Being clear about values: There is no way that as mediators we can keep our values or our biases out of the process, but it is always useful when we own up to our biases with the individuals we are working with, trying to be clear that what's good for us may or may not be good for each person.

5. Being able to let others set up their own rules of fairness: This one is difficult for me, because I usually judge what's fair in terms of my own values. Even though I felt concern that a couple of contracts were not fair, the subjective experience of the individuals involved was that the contract was fair. That is the goal of mediation as we find it: to arrive at a contract that all parties consider equitable. Sometimes we really have to struggle with our own ideas about fairness, equality, and values that we've inculcated in ourselves or have had as part of our professions.

This is not to say we do not interject our opinions of fairness to keep the issue alive. If a client were to say that she felt a particular arrangement was comfortable for her but I felt she was not getting a good deal, I would be very assertive in trying to get her to defend her view of the contract. For example, we would try to get her to say more about why she doesn't want half of the house. I might say, "What's wrong with the situation so that you don't deserve half?" This prodding helps to achieve equity. (That is a little different from deciding somewhere along the way to stop the process because it doesn't feel fair to us.) It's my responsibility to interject my own opinion, to help people get to their *own* feelings about what's fair.

6. Not being afraid of anger; that is, allowing anger and rudeness: Some feminists have commented that rudeness is antithetical to feminist theory and female behavior. But if we didn't allow rudeness during the mediation process, we would get nowhere. It is an acceptable form of behavior when you feel finished with your relationship with someone. We have to be semicomfortable with the idea that people are going to be rude and relatively insensitive to the other person's feelings in the process: expressing anger, rudeness, or fighting. Many people use the mediating process to end a relationship, which can clearly involve fighting. That doesn't necessarily mean physical fighting, but the situation is often very tense, with a considerable amount of clash.

People who have not talked or who have not shared emotional feelings for quite some time are often not willing to do so in the space and time that's allowed in mediation. They are generally not immediately open to the process of sharing hurt feelings with a person they believe has really damaged them. The mediator's responsibility is to help them get out enough emotions in a cathartic way so that they can at least go on with the process. One has to enjoy digging into people's emotions; some people, including therapists, find this difficult to sustain if the feelings are intense.

7. Being able to develop structure: There are various approaches to the use of structure in therapy and wide differences in the experience of trained therapists. In mediation, we have a minimum of three hour-and-a-half sessions, and the entire process is very structured. We know some therapists who don't work well with that kind of time constraint. They feel pressure to get things done and see the process as regimented and legalistic. Liking or not liking structure would make a difference in one's decision to be a mediator. However, one must have room for spontaneity. We've never had one mediation that was ever like any other. Unexpected things are always happening, and appropriately so for change to actually occur.

8. Being comfortable with the "wheeling and dealing": Sometimes it feels like a Perry Mason kind of atmosphere, with three or four people in the room, each with a different agenda, and Katherine and I in the corner privately conferring about how we can get out of this

emotional mess, how we can get to the facts. There is something in the process that feels a little dramatic, sometimes a little bigger than life. I think lawyers wheel and deal much more often than therapists. Being able to operate in a process way, more openly and more dramatically, was a new experience for me.

9. Being aware of one's own blame behavior: This process can bring out blame behavior in everyone. Katherine and I have to be repeatedly careful not to say to each other, "Well, things would have been fine if only that person hadn't done that," or feeling that the need for mediation is the result of one person's bad behavior, rather than understanding that the *process* of mediation is the focus.

10. Being able to collaborate: Collaboration between a therapist and lawyer requires respect and willingness to use *all* of each other's skills, not just the ones we feel ourselves to be lacking. We must be both lawyer and therapist in our mediator role: fulfilling and completing all of the processes for both.

*KT:* In addition to the characteristics Bonnie mentioned, lawyers should have these characteristics for working as a mediator: a willingness to take risks with the legal community; a belief in establishing a new form of conflict resolution or a distaste for the advocacy system; no fear of feelings or dealing with feelings—their own or others; some experience in therapy themselves; some experience in grass-roots feminist groups.

Basically, Bonnie and I started mediating because quite often I would get called from both sides of a conflict. Ten years ago there weren't as many women lawyers in private practice in the Boston area. One lover would call up, and I would hear her story and make an appointment. On the next person's call I would have to say, "Well, I think I've heard this story before, hold on, I can't represent you." As an attorney, I am governed by a "conflict of interest" rule about representing two sides of the same conflict.[2]

Another reality of the legal system is that courts are filled with an enormous amount of negative energy. When I first started practicing there were very few days when I wouldn't come back from court and cry just because of the psychic battering that both my clients and I (I was working with battered women at the time) would experience. The third factor that led us to mediation was a commitment to the lesbian feminist community. I wanted to create a new form of conflict resolution that was less damaging to women and more in tune with my political beliefs. In my opinion there is no such thing as a feminist attorney. I think the words *feminist attorney* are mutually exclusive. Feminism is a belief system based in part on the efficacy of the "feeling process."

As a therapist, Bonnie really has a lot more room for creativity in that process. If you are an attorney, you must be an advocate that manipulates, denies, or misnames feelings, when and if they are present. I wanted more from myself and more from the feminist community in the way we solve problems. We don't need more women attorneys thinking, talking, and feeling like men. With that background, I finally called Bonnie and said I was beginning to feel like a therapist because many of my clients didn't have exclusively legal problems, and their emotional blocks were standing in the way of the decision-making process — people have to cope with enormous feelings in these situations, and they don't know where or how to vent them. No amount of good lawyering was helping, especially in a homophobic legal setting.

Lawyers are generally not trained to deal with feelings at all. Having been through both singles and couples therapy, I am familiar with the process, and I am comfortable with therapeutic language. I was also very determined at the beginning of my practice to create a holistic environment in which to work and not to distance myself from my own feelings. Particularly when I was working with battered women in divorce situations, I would try to get the women to recognize their feelings about the battering in order to mobilize them to undergo the legal process so that they could agree to specific terms in the divorce agreement. Therapists looking for lawyers with whom to do mediation must realize that there is nothing in a lawyer's training that teaches us how to mediate or arbitrate disputes. Lawyers are basically trained to advocate. There is right and wrong depending on who pays you. You know case law, and there is a way and style of talking and being in a courtroom that is very different from what a therapist does. I could not walk into court and say, "Well, your honor, she needs to rant and rave and process her rage before she'll agree to visitation or to that amount of support"; I must translate the language of the therapeutic process into a context and language that is very concrete.

*BJE:* We do not know of any place that is teaching what we do; there is definitely a need for lesbian feminist mediation training. In divorce mediation training, one learns very specific things that are endemic to heterosexual divorce, not something that would necessarily help lesbians. Family therapy training was most useful to me in this experience; it deals with the issues of roles people assume, not blaming one person, but understanding the process and dealing with it. Systems theory, an understanding of how things happen and where and when, and being able to draw maps about how things happen, is also useful. Many times we have to pull people back to get them to notice how they are feeling and how their position affects what they are saying.

They need to be cognitively aware of the differences in power, ability, skill, and access. Sometimes it has been very useful to take people's emotions and put them on a map to show where they stand in relation to one another.

Couples and group therapy training have also provided the kind of training that I fall back on in doing mediation. There are some new "contracting" books that I feel are useful, but they alone are not enough to prepare one to mediate.

There is also a need for more lesbian feminist arbitration. We have talked with women from California and New York who were trying to set up arbitration boards that were appropriate for lesbian feminists taking the role and responsibility for being arbitrators. This is an entirely new and exciting development.

*KT:* Another important aspect of the type of mediation we do involves legal and personal issues of money, trust, and responsibility.

*BJE:* Mediation is a co-therapy situation in many ways, but it differs in that Katherine and I represent different disciplines. I think things work well between us because we have a full friend relationship as well as a professional relationship. When Katherine and I have looked at other lawyers or therapists to do this work with, we ran into some difficulty. Working together in this volatile situation, each of us has to have 100 percent trust that the other is going to do her own job, and I'm going to do 100 percent of my job plus part of her job as well. There is a real need to be fully there in the hour and a half, fully trusting and respecting the differences between us, our disciplines and our personalities. You have to work with someone whose work *you trust completely,* because you can't be spending time worrying about your own relationship in this process. There is too much going on. Of course there are times when Katherine and I disagree. I may say, "Wait a minute, that sounds off the wall," or Katherine says to me, "You are really getting into your therapist role."

*KT:* I don't say it quite that way, it's more like "Bonnie, lay off, you're being an idiot . . . ."

*BJE:* As in any co-therapy situation, after we leave the first session, we will argue about who the people are, whether we like the way they do things, and whether we think that their position is fair. If mediators cannot be brutally honest with each other, they cannot keep the relationship as clean as necessary to be effective. We trust that even though Katherine might hate one of the people in the room, she will write a good contract for that person. Even though I really might not get along with a person or be able to stand her idea of fairness, I am able to bring out her feelings and help her deal with taking care of herself.

I consider myself 100 percent responsible for the emotional activity of what's going on and 50 percent responsible for the contract. Katherine considers herself 50 percent responsible for the emotional work and 100 percent responsible for the contract.

*KT:* The setting of fees is also one of the difficulties we see as important in this interdisciplinary approach to mediation. Our base rate in 1984 was approximately $400 minimum, which includes the contract and covers the four-and-one-half hours of time we spend in session, as well as some time spent outside the session.

*BJE:* My experience of setting fees as a therapist is different from Katherine's as a lawyer. We had to work out a system that covered the clients' need to have a lawyer and a therapist and still not be so financially out of bounds that they would feel they would be better off hiring two lawyers. We struggled with offering a sliding scale fee. For our purposes, we decided to set a fixed amount, making it clear that that amount is sometimes more, sometimes less than what we make in the rest of our work. It has not been cost efficient for us to do mediation; both of us tend to make half of our usual hourly rate.

There have been difficulties because I feel that Katherine does more work than I do after the session's end. The therapist shows up for a meeting, emotes, relates, and then goes home. That's when the lawyer starts her work. Katherine writes the contract; she goes through several drafts. She has to be present during all of the sessions and then do homework afterward.

*KT:* We also see money as the big issue in terms of people's willingness and ability to pay. We talk about the fee the first thing, and usually half the money is up front. A structure concern for me is that I cannot split fees with a non-lawyer, so they pay half to Bonnie and half to me, not to both of us. If additional documents have to be drafted, such as a deed or a promissory note, we negotiate the cost when the matter comes up.

We also spend a lot of time talking on the telephone to figure out what our feelings are, what they think is fair, and what we think is the next step.

*BJE:* Also, for some people, our price is too high. There are two different values at odds with each other for those people who feel that their only next choice is to go to court and spend even more money. In the spectrum of litigation expenses $200 for each is not very expensive.

*KT:* Sometimes I'm asked why I got into this work. Unlike the women's health movement, we in the legal profession have tinkered with words but we have not focused on empowering women. We have not changed the nature of the advocacy system nor the patriarchal concepts underlying that advocacy. I believe the existing models of legal analysis severely limit the nonviolent or nonpatriarchal resolution of conflict. I also believe that the process harms both the female participant and advocate, and the results do nothing to empower women.

The usual legal forum simply doesn't offer the participants an opportunity to discharge feelings constructively and does not allow anyone to reach catharsis. Because resolutions are imposed from an ostensible authority (the judge), the participants, through a go-between (lawyer), never let go of the conflict and rarely take responsibility for their actions. People seldom feel good about the process. The rage that clients often feel toward the wrongdoer is transferred onto the system, the judge, the lawyer, and the costs.

*BJE:* This system also perpetuates the "victim mentality" and leaves our community cluttered with unresolved relationships.

*KT:* I can always write a contract and to a certain extent get what I want in a contract, but I want my clients to feel better about the process, not abused or manipulated.

*BJE:* I often work with women who are unable to get an agreement about anything. They go through many hours of emotionally draining experiences that result in nothing legally enforceable. It's been a very important, empowering experience to help women feel connected to their "awful" feelings and still realize that the process of the mediation was a good one for the relationship, especially when they end with something legally binding and that covers their financial interests, something that they often could not get from standard couples therapy.

Clinicians have asked me why we limit the process to a fixed number of sessions, no matter what. My experience has been, as with all short-term therapy, that if the participants know how much time they have to deal with an issue, they get organized and deal with it. That philosophy works here. I give myself room several times to say to people, "Well, we are about a third of the way through, do you feel that you have done a third of the emotional work?" Or when we are near the end, to say "we expect that by the end of the second session everyone is really clear about the wording of this contract." We do not wait for that until the third session, because in our experience wording is where all the emotions come together. We have found it best to have people do their homework, to come back with written words they feel represent them concretely. By the end of the first session we try to give to each a draft of where we are and what has been accomplished. Declaring in what areas we are in agreement early is helpful, and we try to get them in writing early to feel that we are starting out from agreements.

I've learned a lot about creative financing from Katherine, especially the process of rethinking something in terms of how one deals with money and how to translate it into contracts. It was not a part of my training as a therapist and certainly not for me as a woman in the world to learn how to refinance things. There are different kinds of legal information that can affect different emotional processes. We've dealt with battering situations as well as with real estate, property, a car, a house. Today, if a couple wants to break up the relationship, and they are not speaking to each other, what can they do?

We are also dealing with what is really missing in terms of our larger lesbian feminist community and our experience as women: the ability to negotiate for what we want.

*KT:* It is my experience that lesbians are really invested in being politically correct and feeling correct. One example comes to mind: two or three women who have bought a house with the political ideal of no "ownership" — no boss. They are buying to give everybody a cheap apartment, or a shared living arrangement to have an ideal space to grow. When it gets down to mediation and renegotiating about it, they are still saying these politically correct words and not really getting to, "Well, I'm really furious because it was my money we used for the down payment," or "I paid the taxes," or "You did work but I didn't get such-and-such." There are a lot of hidden issues around what is called capital contributions and what goes into buying property.

*BJE:* It's a question of how to value those things we feel very emotional about. Some things of value to lesbian feminists may not be valued by the broader community. Consequently, we need to learn to put a financial value on something for which we want to negotiate. We come to the point of saying, "What is your bottom line?" "What will make you feel OK?" Women say, "Oh, I can't do that, that's so arbitrary." But that's what we are here for, an arbitrary feeling about what would be *all right for you.* That can be a new way to think for women concerning their values. We seem to be more stuck on the idea that things have a right or wrong value, or that things have an absolute value, rather than things that are valuable to me, based on my experience with them. In mediation, we deal with emotions, and how to place monetary values and negotiate for ourselves.

*KT:* People will call us when they are interested in mediation, or are referred from another therapist, or present a problem where it seems appropriate to ask if they would be interested in having us mediate. When they say they really don't want to go to court, they really don't want to sue, they just want to get out of a situation and find a solution, I'll present mediation as a possibility.

In the very first mediation session, after we define what we are there to do and what we are not there to do (Bonnie is not a couples therapist for them, and I'm not a lawyer for either one of them), we try to determine what the facts and issues are. What is going on? What property needs to be split up? Also, what additional information do I need about the house, the car, whatever? Does the home or car need to be refinanced? Can they get refinancing to buy someone out? Where are the deed and other documents?

Bonnie and I usually confer after the first session and try to figure out if we both have the same opinion about what we think the issues are, and what we think the hard issues are or are not going to be. Here's the stumbling block, or here's the way to get around this issue. When Bonnie sees something going on with emotional issues, she may want to know if something is possible legally. Is it possible in the spectrum of the world of law as opposed to the world of feeling? The second session is usually when people get the most emotional, the most violent in terms of their feelings. "No, I am not signing over the house because you get your way all the time." "You went off with my best friend, and I'm not going to give you the Holly Near records too."

*BJE:* That sounds like a joke, but we discovered that often the hardest issues are the smaller ones. Bigger issues had already been discussed. People discuss houses more than clothes, clothes more than records. Record albums have wrecked many a second session. After suggesting buying duplicates, I even came to the point once of going and getting one of my records off the shelf saying, "Look, this is fine, now we have two records." It is so ironic, the small but important issues that people latch onto emotionally. "This was my record . . . ." "No, it was not, it was my record, and I'm not leaving this relationship without this record." It seems the little points are the ones that people get emotionally invested in, and the larger issues have been thought through and ventilated more.

I think another important issue that I've discovered in couples therapy as well as mediation is that there is a great lack of ability in the lesbian feminist community to know how to negotiate or contract. That's probably true for women in general. I've been most impressed by feminists who are very capable of analyzing and understanding why they don't have what they want, but they lack the ability to *negotiate* and stand up for what they want. This is a level of skill that is generally lacking in our clients.

*KT:* By the third session, I will have drafted the final contract. Everyone gets her own copy. We go over the points that are definitely agreed upon. Bonnie usually keeps lists of what we have and have not agreed on—she's really good with lists. Sometimes I will put alternatives to unresolved questions in different paragraphs using wording reflective of the different points of view.

*BJE:* We arrive by the end of the second session with all of the alternatives we are considering. We may have six alternatives, and we would have all six of them in writing. Then we can eliminate the ones that are intolerable, ranking them in terms of which can even be considered. What else can be changed now? I try to keep in mind the questions anyone has any emotional difficulties about, as well as the ones they are not so dead set on. Someone might be thinking differently about an issue, so perhaps at the end I may need to say, "Well, you said you could sort of think about this. Could you just for a minute do that?" I try to keep in mind how invested people are in the process as we go along, because those last minutes are ticking away. "OK, we are halfway through the last session, we have to sign this in one-half hour. And we must get to what your bottom line is. You must know, right now, how you feel about this. There are no alternatives."

People have to choose among written alternatives in the final draft contract. It's not all right for anyone to come up with new alternatives at the final session unless that was agreed upon earlier. By the end of the second session, we try to have in writing all the possible alternatives. Nothing new should happen at the third session. One ought not to start anything new in the termination process of therapy, and if you start something new in the third session of mediation, you've lost it. Then you are into a whole new process. Clients could say, "It's easy, I just want to change this little thing," and fail to realize that this "one little thing" may have a big impact on the other person and the process.

It is because partners have consented to the fixed number of sessions at the beginning that lesbian feminist mediation works. It would not work if we said, "You have to do this because we want you to." It only works because partners want to be finished with this issue in their own lives and because they feel that they are getting something for what they are giving up.

What ultimately brings lesbians to mediation is the dilemma of having unfinished and unresolved relationships that inhibit them from moving on in their own growth as a person in a relationship or a partner in a business concern. Gaining freedom to remove money, time, and emotional investment is a highly motivating force to complete the mediation process. Resolution occurs most frequently when a lawsuit is the next step and when the mediation process allows each member to express herself powerfully and personally by the use of "facts" and "feelings."

We don't tell people they need resolution. We offer resolution to those who don't quite know how to figure out emotionally and practically that they want it. Our model is similar to what would be covered in a conflict resolution workshop, because we get agreement from the beginning that the partners are ready to get rid of this problem emotionally. Because most people don't know how to do that, they feel their only alternative is to go to court. We seldom see people who feel that if they just went to therapy things would be better. They have exhausted all the other options when we see them. Most lesbians, in our experience, would prefer not to go to court, not to have their names in the ledger, not to go through all the stuff that goes along with going to court. This is a good incentive to get a contract that feels fair.

*KT:* If someone gets in touch with me about wanting to sue, I'll try to find out at what stage they are, and perhaps send them some information about lesbian mediation. I may ask, "Are you interested in mediating this issue before you tell me too much?" I don't want to get myself out of the ability, ethically, to mediate the issue; I don't want them to tell me too much about the facts, just where they are in internal process. Someone might say, "I really don't want to sue. I want to know my rights but I don't want to go to court."

*BJE:* I do think, though, that in every situation we have seen, the next step would be a lawsuit. We are talking about large amounts of money or property, or about investments in a relationship for a long period of time. So far, none of our clients have ended up in court. I can imagine being in a situation, however, where the process might not work. That involves our definition of success and failure. We have had a situation that we felt was a failure because we didn't like the process. We didn't feel that people were being fair and honest. We did as much as we could and repeatedly struggled with the issue as a group. It just didn't end up feeling good to Katherine and me. Although we might count that as a failure, the participants felt very relieved that they were out of the situation and were not going to have to deal with it in court, and they didn't *expect* to feel good. I think they felt we were being idealistic in expecting them to feel better.

*KT:* It is important to remember the distinction between mediation and arbitration. Mediation as we define it is a process to resolve a property matter, or to resolve a relationship. It is a process whereby both people can come to an agreement that is enforceable, that they can live with, and that they feel good about. Everybody finishes feeling better about the process. It is less expensive than hiring separate attorneys; it is expected that some emotional catharsis will happen as a result of the process.[3]

It is becoming very trendy in the legal system to "mediate," and there are a lot of divorce mediation centers or probation centers or probation departments that offer mediation. I would, however, be very hesitant about letting lesbians go into these mediation centers and court clinics. I think what they call mediation differs very much from what we call mediation, primarily because of the institutionalized power disparity in heterosexual relationships, how they are perceived, and how it is handled by the mediator.

Arbitration is just like going to court, except that each person submits a claim to an arbitrator, who basically acts like a judge who doesn't necessarily apply judicial concepts or legal concepts all of the time. Arbitrators listen to one side, then listen to the other side, and then they render a decision based on their perception of fairness. The parties have agreed to be bound by the arbitrator's decision. Arbitration is governed by state statutes. There is an Arbitration Act, a national arbitration association, and a particular way of resolving disputes according to rules that are enforceable in court.

We prefer the mediation model because it allows the participants a vehicle to decathect from a painful situation. It also serves the goal of empowering participants to solve their own problems and learn skills that may be useful to them in the future.

## NOTES

1. In 1981, Marilyn Barnett sued tennis star Billie Jean King alleging that their seven-year lesbian relationship entitled Barnett to King's Malibu home and half of King's earnings from professional tennis. Barnett—King's former secretary and lover—did not prevail, but the suit and King's acknowledgment of the affair generated enormous controversy and media attention.

2. This is not a problem unique to the lesbian community. Since 1983 there has been considerable activity throughout the country regarding the use of mediation or other alternative dispute resolution techniques. Many insurance companies have instituted alternative dispute resolution (ADR) programs to expedite the resolution of insurance claims arising out of automobile accidents. The American Bar Association Special Committee on Dispute Resolution lists thirty-seven organizations that have newsletters covering the subject of ADR. Several states have enacted or are considering mandatory ADR programs designed to divert disputants away from costly and time-consuming litigation.

Massachusetts has recently enacted a "mediator privilege" law designed to protect the secrecy of the mediation process if the matter ends in court at a later date. Bar associations and family mediation associations have promulgated new rules of ethics to deal with the role of attorney/mediators.

Thus, mediation may not be as risky professionally for lawyers as it once was. However, institutions are still grappling with what it means to be a mediator, which ethical rules govern mediators, what training is required, where institutionalization perverts the voluntary basis of mediation, and in what circumstances mediation should *not* be used.

For a continuing update on bibliographical information on ADR, readers should contact the American Bar Association Special Committee on Dispute Resolution, 1800 M St. NW, Washington, D.C. 20036, and the American Arbitration Association, 150 W. 51st St., New York, NY 10020. For a feminist perspective, contact the National Center on Women and Family Law, 799 Broadway, Room 402, New York, NY 10003, and the NOW Legal Defense Fund, 132 W. 43rd St., New York, NY 10036.

3. Useful sources of information on mediation include: O. J. Coogler, *Structured Mediation in Divorce Settlement* (Lexington, Mass.: D. C. Heath, 1978); Hayden Curry and Dennis Clifford, *A Legal Guide for Lesbian and Gay Couples* (Reading, Mass.: Addison-Wesley, 1980); Ann Lusas Diamond and Madeleine Simborg, "Divorce Mediation's Strengths . . . and Weaknesses," *California Lawyer* 37 (July 1984); Gilbert R. Egle, "Divorce Mediation: An Innovative Approach to Family Dispute Resolution," *Land and Water Law Review* 18 (Fall 1983); John A. Fiske, "An Enthralling Introduction to Divorce Mediation," *Boston Bar Journal* 25 (Dec. 1981): 15; Gary Friedman and Margaret Anderson, "Divorce Mediation Strengths . . . and Weaknesses," *California Lawyer* 36 (July 1983); John M. Haynes, "Divorce Mediator: A New Role," *Social Work* 23 (Jan. 1978): 5; John M. Haynes, *Divorce Mediation: A Practical Guide for Therapists and Counselors* (New York: Springer Publishing, 1981); Richard G. Hoffman, "Resolving Domestic Relations Cases: The Conference Method vs. the Courtroom Method," *Boston Bar Journal* 22 (Dec. 1978): 5; Howard Irving, "Diluting the Damage of Divorce," *The Boston Globe*, 8 Aug. 1983; Harry Finkelstein Keshet and Kristine M. Rosenthal, "Fathering after Marital Separation," *Social Work* 23 (Jan. 1978): 11; Robert H. Mnookin and Lewis Kornhauser, "Bargaining in the Shadow of the Law: The Case of Divorce," *The Yale Law Journal* 88 (April 1979): 950; Joanna M. Mole, "A New Approach to Conciliation," *Family Law* 23 (July 1983); Opinion of the Association of the Bar of the City of New York Committee on Professional and Judicial Ethics, "Attorneys—Mediation," *The Family Law Reporter* 7 (13 Oct. 1981): 3097; Linda J. Silberman, "Professional Responsibility Problems of Divorce Mediation," *The Family Law Reporter* 7 (17 Feb. 1981): 4001; Janet Maleson Spencer and Joseph P. Zammit, "Mediation-Arbitration: A Proposal for Private Resolution of Disputes between Divorced or Separated Parents," *Duke Law Journal* 1976 (Dec. 1976): 911; Janet Miller Wiseman and John A. Fiske, "A Lawyer-Therapist Team as Mediator in a Marital Crisis," *Social Work* 25 (Nov. 1980): 442; Morris

H. Wolff, "Family Conciliation: Draft Rules for the Settlement of Family Disputes," *Family Law* 21 (Jan. 1983): 213–38; and Zena D. Zumera, "Mediation as Alternative to Litigation in Divorce," *Michigan Bar Journal* 62 (June 1983): 434–40.

# 20

## *Beyond Community:*
## *Politics and Spirituality*

My grandparents were immigrants from Italy, brave and proud. I spent most of my early life convinced by the dominant culture that Italian-Americans were either ruthless gangsters or ignorant "grease-balls." As soon as I could, I ran as far and as fast as I could from the community into which I was born. Some of the motivation to run came from internalized hatred of Italians. Some was a survival response to the crushing sexism and homophobia of the Italian-American community. But part of the motivation came from inside knowledge of the potentially and often actually crippling effects a strong community has on dissenters, progressives, and visionaries.

Although I later reclaimed much of value in my Italian heritage, throughout my years of participation in the antimilitarist, feminist, and antinuclear movements, I have retained my childhood skepticism toward the glories of community living. I want to pass this skepticism on to others. Once we get clear about what communities are, I think we'll see that developing lesbian communities would undermine the strength of our feminist politics. If as lesbians we hope to renew our commitment to social change and replenish our energies for the long struggle that lies before us, it isn't communities we need, but rather the conscious addition of a spiritual dimension to our politics.

People use the term *lesbian community* without a clear sense of what they are talking about. It is one of the many unexamined and misunderstood concepts in our common vocabulary. And all unexamined concepts that are misunderstood lead to confusion, misdirected energies, and pain.

To understand this concept, it would be helpful to use ethnic and racial communities as our models rather than spiritual or utopian ones, because the vast majority of lesbians are in no position to choose the renunciation from the world entailed by joining spiritual and utopian communities. If ethnic and racial communities are our models, we can define a community as a group of people living in the same geographic area, sharing customs, beliefs, values, and language, who are bound to one another by traditions, norms, and institutions of mutual support and reciprocal obligation.[1] Given this definition, the common use of the term *lesbian community* is often completely inappropriate. To the extent that lesbians live in different neighborhoods, speak different languages, have different customs, beliefs and values—and most important, to the extent that they are *not* bound to one another by norms and institutions of mutual support and reciprocal obligation, they do not form communities. What we call the Boston-Cambridge lesbian community, for example, is really a set of intersecting friendship networks and lesbian enclaves, where *enclave* is defined as a minority culture group living within a larger group.

Often neighbors, even if they share the same language and customs, live quite independently of one another. It is ongoing, day-to-day positive interaction that transforms neighborhoods into communities. This interaction is structured by traditions, norms, and institutions of mutual support and reciprocal obligation. Traditions and norms include the sharing of news, gossip, meals, and child care; gifts and loans of money; sharing housing with people temporarily displaced or financially burdened; giving and receiving emotional, financial, and practical help around significant events such as childbirth, sickness, marriage, divorce, and death. Community institutions may include schools, banks, health care services, retailers, religious organizations, and social clubs. These institutions are community based to the extent that they are owned or controlled by community members *and* rely on the community's patronage and good will for their survival.

There are good material reasons why lesbians have not developed these conditions for creating communities: We have neither the numbers, the geographic proximity, nor the money to support many institutions. Women's bookstores, for example, may be owned and staffed by lesbians and may stock a tantalizing selection of lesbian writings, but they could not survive without selling to nonlesbians and selling materials by nonlesbians. There are a few bars, publications, and presses exclusively or almost exclusively for lesbians, but as institutions they are the exception rather than the rule. Even when lesbians in big cities choose to live in the same area, they do not have the capital to set up neighborhood stores, social clubs, health centers, and so forth. For the most part, lesbians are dependent on institutions serving the wider women's and gay "communities," and even straight society.

Even if we overcame these material obstacles, we would still face structural ones. A significant difference between ethnic or racial communities and lesbian groups is that the traditions and norms we develop come almost exclusively from friendship networks. Friendships, whether or not they are based on sexual intimacy, are often unstable bonds. I do not by any means think that this is more true for lesbians than for anyone else. But heterosexuals have a structural advantage in developing community norms and traditions: the existence of formally recognized blood and kinship ties. Blood ties are indissoluble: You can't divorce your family members, even if you hate their guts. Kinship ties can be socially reinforced. As a result, in ethnic communities one learns early that loyalty and obligation do not have to rest on friendship or approval.

As a child I was expected to respect family members, across class lines, regardless of their individual characteristics. We considered ourselves entitled to financial and emotional support without question, even when our behavior was questionable. Personal feuds were not *allowed* to continue for very long. I remember the time my father hadn't spoken to his uncle for several months. My mother and aunt simply announced that we were all having dinner on Palm Sunday, and they would shake hands in front of all of us before dinner. We expected and were expected to be in close contact our whole lives. This perspective made it imperative to try to see each other's point of view and learn to get along with one another. Where our differences were irreconcilable, they were often set aside, as in the case of my father and uncle, for the sake of the family. In part, this was because *not* meeting a family obligation would usually entail community retribution. This situation contrasts sharply with most lesbian associations, which are based almost entirely on positive personal feelings — an insufficient foundation for long-term stability.

Two kinds of lesbian groups that tend to avoid this difficulty are self-help organizations based on specific conditions or oppressions and organizations based on common work. Once again, these conditions are usually based on larger ones. In the former category, for example, both Overeaters Anonymous (OA) and Alcoholics Anonymous (AA) have lesbian chapters in the Boston-Cambridge area. Both of them provide ongoing support and create reciprocal obligations among their members. They foster tolerance of members' idiosyncracies and differences for the sake of enabling them to free themselves from addiction. People who do the same work, like members of a family, often believe they will be in close contact for the rest of their lives. Unions and professional associations often engender reciprocal obligations among their members.

During my academic career I was a member of the Midwest branch of the Society for Women in Philosophy (SWIP). It is a model of the values and virtue of sisterhood. In SWIP, more established members write hiring, promotion, and tenure support letters for less established members. During meetings no one has to shout to be heard, but we care about each other enough not to be polite or timid when we disagree. Even when we disagree, we come to one another's defense when the seriousness and value of our work is questioned by male philosophers. Personal feuds are expected to be settled, and are mediated by other members when they are not. For feminists and lesbian feminists harassed by the arrogance, ignorance, and intractability of patriarchical academia, SWIP provides an intellectual community that is essential to its members' survival and integrity.

But although organizations based on specific conditions and those based on common work foster strong bonds, the *kinds* of support they offer members are necessarily limited by their functions. For example, it is not SWIP's business to help its members face the end of significant relationships, although friends within the organization often do this for each other. So these types of organizations are vital to lesbian survival in a homophobic world, but in and of themselves they do not constitute the basis for full-fledged communities.

There are a few historical examples of friendship networks arising from these and other kinds of organizations that are strong and flexible enough to create full-fledged communities among their members. But because lesbians lack numbers, money, kinship structures, and sufficient separate, ongoing institutions to serve them, these communities rarely survive more than one generation—if even that long.

The conditions that prevent lesbians from establishing communities are historically contingent, and it is possible that they could be overcome. But I believe the goal of creating lesbian communities is not politically desirable. It rests on a misconception of the nature of politics, as well as a misconception of who we are. Politics is essentially about power—the power people have to control the conditions under which they live. Communities bring their members three important political benefits. I believe lesbians can obtain the first two benefits by other means, and that the third, far from being a benefit to us, would undermine our movement.

The first benefit of a community is that to the extent that institutions are truly community based, they are necessarily responsive to the needs of those they serve. That providers of services essential to one's well-being are responsive to one's criticisms and requests certainly gives a person more control over the conditions under which she lives. But as we have seen, lesbians do not have the resources to create all our own institutions. What we can do is continue to struggle for quality services from the institutions we need, whether they be health care centers or hardware stores.

A second benefit of a community is that the more we are a visible, publicly identifiable group, the more our claim to be recognized and protected legally is legitimized. Without visibility there can be no legitimacy to political struggle on behalf of particular groups. But notice the limited nature of this benefit. It is related primarily to civil rights protection for lesbians as a group. This is unquestionably important, but as feminists we want a lot more than legal rights; we want the end of patriarchy. Furthermore, we can achieve visibility without the ghettoization intrinsic to establishing communities, by continuing our work as lobbyists, special interest organizations, and caucuses within organizations. Our quest for visibility is also better served by the courage of individuals and groups of lesbians who openly identify themselves as lesbians and challenge homophobia where they live and work.

The third benefit that a community may provide its members is a strong sense of self-identity. Common wisdom from at least Marx onward has it that a group cannot organize on its own behalf without a conscious sense of self-identity. Lesbians do need a sense of self-identity, but not just the kind fostered by communities. Communities are based on the similarities among their members. In communities of oppressed people, it becomes even more important that members be similar; it seems to make clear the boundaries between those who are with us and those who are against us. And the more society tells us that what we are is perverted and despicable, the more important it will seem that when we are among "our own kind" we should not be criticized. In communities of oppressed people, difference is often perceived as betrayal, especially when it involves contact with or similarity to the oppressors. Paradoxically, the demand for uncritical acceptance leads to *more* rather than less interpersonal criticism. It leads to lesbians policing one another's behavior.

Community policing is familiar to me from my childhood. When I was growing up, I was told if I valued my Italian heritage I would not want to live outside my parents' home until I was married. The suggestion that Christopher Columbus was not the first European to come to this continent was considered proof of mental instability. As a university professor, I was told by local feminists that if I valued working-class women I would not have such a bourgeois, "apolitical" job. Once I had my hair permed. You can imagine what I was told then. Fortunately for me, I never wanted to wear skirts or dresses.

I am not suggesting that lesbians stop living in enclaves and making autonomous, lesbian-only spaces. We need spaces in which we are the norm in order to reconstruct our identities in a positive sense. But the fact that a space contains only lesbians does not guarantee that it fosters everyone's positive sense of self-identity. There are lesbian bars in which I feel neither safe nor comfortable, because the lesbians in them have customs, beliefs, and values that are different and perhaps even antithetical to mine. The fact is that more often than not, lesbians have very little in common. We may eat and drink different things, dance differently, listen to different music, make love differently from one another. We certainly do not all have the same history. Insofar as we are of different ages, abilities, sizes, classes, and races, our oppression as women, as lesbians, takes very different forms.

The strength of our movement lies in our diversity, and in the fact that we are forced to *recognize* diversity. The power of feminism, its advantage over prior ideologies of liberation, is that it insists on the connections between types of oppression. Particularly as lesbian feminists, we must necessarily recognize the connectedness of our diversity in order to work together at all. We don't have the numbers to act any other way. We have learned that we cannot assert that sexism, or racism, or any single oppression, is always the issue. We increasingly recognize that if we don't work in coalitions across divisions of ethnicity, race, and class, we will not have the power to change society. But this realization has brought us to an impasse. We have become so painfully aware of our diversity that we have fallen back on the bankrupt liberal view that we have to support whatever lesbians do because we're all oppressed together. I never believed that was true for Italians, and I don't believe it's true for lesbians.

Our problem is how to recognize our diversity and still feel enough connected to one another to work together over the long haul. Some have suggested that we don't need to feel connected, that if we recognize that our survival depends on each other we will work in coalitions because we must. But that can't be the whole story. Fear for our survival can motivate us to begin working together, but cannot *sustain* our working together. We cannot be united merely externally, by a common hatred and resistance to those who oppress us. A politics based on common hatred fosters limited and shallow bonds. It creates a commonality that can be co-opted, because it does not create for each of us a felt personal stake in the liberation of the others.

The way out of this impasse is not to build communities, but to develop the ability to create and re-create a communal sense, a connectedness among us, that allows for diversity and inspires us to continue to work together. To sustain our work in coalitions, to transform that work from divisive distrust and mutual recrimination to cooperation and mutual respect, we need skills that enable us to make personal connections with other lesbians and allies who are radically different from us. I suggest that the best methods for creating connections with each other come from feminist spirituality.

Even today spiritual lesbian feminists are caricatured as reactionaries who smile a lot, sing a lot, seek only long-term monogamous relationships, and never lust. That hasn't been my experience. Like everything else lesbian and feminist, spiritual lesbian feminists are marked by diversity and by disagreements. Rather than emphasize these, I want to discuss in a general way the effects on political struggle that result from following almost any spiritual practice. Specifically, I am convinced that most spiritual disciplines make lesbians more capable of and more likely to continue in political struggle throughout our whole lives.

The two main barriers to long-term political engagement seem to be burnout and the development of a divisive anger aimed as much at each other as at our oppressors. Spiritual practice helps prevent burnout in several ways. Many techniques are inner-directed, and as such they provide a needed balance to a life of out-directed activities. And many techniques provide us access to the strength and support of others, so that we do not feel as alone or as overwhelmed by the forces against us. Almost all are forms of self-renewal. Although the mechanism differs with the practice, they have the effect of affirming and strengthening self-identity. Anger is born of pain—the pain of sadness, or of fear, or both. Our experiences of both pain and anger are transformed by spiritual practice. Like psychotherapy at its best, a spiritual practice at its best makes us more consciously aware of our feelings, moods, and emotions, and gives us the perspective that allows us to make choices about whether and how to express them.

One of the major aims of most spiritual practice is the development of a sense of compassion for oneself as well as for others. In this context, both personal and others' pain is seen as a motivation to work rather than an incapacitating fact of existence. In many forms of meditation one has the experience of being in pain and simultaneously being relaxed, centered, and clear. The same thing happens with feelings of fear, terror, and despair. After repeated experiences of this kind, meditators often feel a deeper sense of personal power and courage. By confronting the things that debilitate them, they are able to begin to overcome them. Serious practice of certain forms of meditation enables people to work through unconscious material and make greater peace with themselves and others. Given that many lesbian feminist political groups are torn apart by conflicts that often originate as much from unconscious patterns of family disharmony as from genuine political disagreement, any technique that renders these patterns visible is politically important. When such techniques are free or inexpensively acquired and can be practiced anywhere, their appeal is even greater.

Another politically valuable aspect of much (but not all) lesbian spiritual practice is an insistence on coming to terms with our own bodies. We are creatures of flesh. Our bodies can be the source of tremendous creativity and power. But they also bear the literal and symbolic scars of patriarchy, and we cannot feel connected to one another before we feel connected to ourselves. Each of us mirrors the alienated hierarchy of patriarchy when we try to dominate our bodies. We devalue them. As women, as lesbians, we have good reasons to distrust our misused bodies and the signals they give us. But we will not know how to trust each other until we reclaim trust in our selves. Our attitudes toward and treatment of our bodies often reproduce the dynamics of patriarchal oppression and exploitation. Making these dynamics conscious can be a healing, politically liberating process. Reclaiming our physical selves requires that we learn how to de-objectify our bodies, how to *live* them in an integrated way. I am not referring to getting in shape or learning self-defense or exploring sexuality; these can be important activities and may be part of the process I'm talking about, but they need not be. Regardless of size, shape, physical condition, or abilities, it is important for us to accept our existence as female animals, and even to delight in it. When we value ourselves at such a primary level, our commitment to change the world deepens.

Lesbian feminist politics asserts that we can control the conditions of our lives in nonoppressive ways that do not require domination. But most political lesbians collapse the notions of domination and power. This confusion is pervasive, but most clearly evident in the discussion of lesbian sexuality. Feminist spirituality distinguishes between power over, or domination, and power from within. Without power from within, without the power that comes from an integrated self, we will not have the skills to control the conditions of our lives in nonoppressive ways. Therefore, without this power our political goals are unattainable. Overcoming bodily alienation is one aspect of developing this kind of power. As Starhawk says, power from within "is not something that we *have*, but something we can do."[2] We begin to heal ourselves and each other. We can recognize our connections and build a world that expresses them.

The two primary practices by which spiritual feminists renew their power and their connections with each other are meditation and ritual. Far from being esoteric, most of us engage in these practices in some form. Meditation includes any centering technique. Some people meditate or center themselves by gardening, others by doing the dishes or housework, others by chanting, others by feeling the inhalation and exhalation of their breath. To be centered is to feel a calmness and clarity at the core of your being. It is to feel that actions can come from this core, and when they do they come from a place of power. It is to feel connected to your own power as a fact of life as much as and no more than the existence of the objects around you.

When people meditate together, magic can happen. Whether or not there is magic, there are two immediate benefits. Meditation quiets and settles each person's mind, and it creates connections among them. The "place" of calm and power we each go to when we meditate is the same place. When we meditate together, we draw on and increase each other's power, creating a shared sense of integrity. In one sense, the boundaries between us dissolve. In another sense, knowing that it is only by our own personal actions and dedication that we go to this place of togetherness, our individuality is affirmed. Each person feels centered and knows and feels that all the others in the group are centered. Thus we meet as equals. For twenty-five hundred years Buddhists have used one particular form of meditation to heal anger and negativity in their relations with others. Practiced in a group, meditation is the most powerful tool I know of to enable people to disagree and still feel supportive of and connected to one another. The possibilities for its use in political groups are exciting and comforting.

Ritual, as I am using the term here, is any patterned sequence of actions carried out in order to accomplish a purpose.[3] Ritual calls forth power from within. It is a familiar and integral part of every culture. Most people have rituals for everything from getting up in the morning (lie still for five minutes after the alarm, drink coffee, then shower) to burying the dead. The political importance of ritual lies in its ability to connect people. Rituals affirm the importance and value of the activities engaged in, as well as of the participants. Their usefulness is enhanced by their versatility; they can be tailored to specific situations.

Engaging in meditation and ritual does not require subscribing to any particular belief or set of beliefs. These practices renew and deepen our individual powers and create bonds among us. Their use in the U.S. antinuclear movement, among others, suggests that they are important to the political health of both individuals and groups. My personal belief is that rituals are politically most important for large group actions, while meditation is politically important for individuals and small groups. If every mass action included ritual, and every political meeting and planning session included a time for meditation, our effectiveness would increase dramatically.

Meditation and engaging in rituals together creates a communal sense, even among people who do not know one another. Through these techniques we learn about, define, and redefine our limits. The more skillful we become at these practices, the more they will help us to know when we can and cannot work together. Talking to one another, even when we listen, is not enough to connect us. It leaves out too many aspects of the self. We lesbians are too diverse to work together always. Too much divides us. We have hard questions to ask each other about our differences. When we ask them out of fear, defensiveness, or vulnerability, when we do not ask questions but hurl charges of political incorrectness at each other, we help no one. We could use meditation and ritual to create environments in which it is safe to have dialogues about what divides us. Then even when we disagree irreconcilably, we might prevent the enervating bitterness of our political feuds. For we have only this life, this world, and one another. And not much time.

## NOTES

Many thanks to my heart-sister Iris Young for her criticisms of an earlier draft of this paper.

1. A similar definition is used by Judith E. Smith in "Our Own Kind," *A Heritage of Her Own*, ed. Nancy F. Cott and Elizabeth H. Pleck (New York: Touchstone, 1979), 393–411.

2. Starhawk, *Dreaming the Dark: Magic, Sex and Politics* (Boston: Beacon Press, 1982), 12.

3. Ibid., 155.

# Contributors and Editors

MARTHA BECKER, C.S.W., is a psychotherapist practicing independently in Brooklyn, New York, and in a clinic setting in Nassau County. Her special areas of expertise include substance abuse, chronic illness, and sexual assault traumas.

MARY BRAGG is a professor and practitioner of counseling psychology. She divides her professional time among teaching, training, therapy, and scholarship. One of her major areas of interest is the effect on psychology of feminist theories. She is acutely aware of the repercussions of homophobia.

LAURA S. BROWN, Ph.D., is a clinical psychologist in the private practice of feminist therapy in Seattle and clinical assistant professor of psychology at the University of Washington. She has taught and published widely in the area of feminist therapy and therapy issues with lesbian clients, with recent articles in *Women and Therapy* on women and weight, nomenclature in the development of feminist therapy theory, and feminist therapy in the treatment of survivors of traumas, and in *Psychotherapy: Theory, Research, Practice, Training* on gender-role analysis in psychological assessment. She is active in Division 35 (Psychology of Women) of the American Psychological Association, the Association for Women in Psychology, and the Feminist Therapy Institute, and serves as a reviewer for *Psychology of Women Quarterly, Counseling and Values*, and *Women and Therapy*. She is a diplomate in clinical psychology of the American Board of Professional Psychology, and a Fellow of the Division of Psychology of Women of the American Psychological Association.

BEVERLY BURCH, M.S.W., is in private practice in Oakland and is affiliated with the Women's Therapy Center in El Cerrito, California. She has published articles on lesbian relationships in *Family Therapy, Handbook of Feminist Therapy: Women's Issues in Psychotherapy*, and *Contemporary Perspectives on Psychotherapy with Lesbians and Gay Men*.

SAHLI A. CAVALLARO, Ph.D., earned her bachelor's degree in psychology at Hunter College and her doctorate in developmental psychology at Peabody

College of Vanderbilt University. She studied under a postdoctoral fellowship in developmental psychology at City College of New York. She has published articles on animal behavior, human ethology, the development of language, and communication and social behavior.

SALLY CRAWFORD, M.A., is an outpatient therapist at the Franklin County Mental Health Center in Greenfield, Massachusetts, where she sees individuals, couples, and families. She also has a small private practice. She is a mother and co-parent.

BUFFY DUNKER, B.A., taught at the Woodstock Country School for twenty-three years and trained at the Greenhouse Therapy Collective as a feminist therapist. She currently has a private therapy practice and has been the subject of numerous television shows and a film for her espousal of a lesbian identity at the age of seventy-two, and has published book reviews in *Sojourner* and *Gay Community News*.

ROSEMARY DUNN DALTON, M.S., is a feminist counselor at Pequod Counseling Center in Cambridge, Massachusetts. She is often a consultant for women's programs and founded five feminist projects in her former place of residence, Ashland, Oregon. Her paper, "Understanding the Message of the Father in the Context of our Lives," published in 1984 by the American Women in Psychology conference, reflects some of her work in the study of fathers and daughters.

BONNIE J. ENGELHARDT is a licensed independent clinical social worker and has had twenty years of experience as a social worker/therapist specializing in couple counseling and sex therapy in the lesbian and gay community in the Boston area.

OLIVA M. ESPÍN is a professor of counseling psychology in the Boston area. She has written and consulted widely on the subject of Latina women. During 1981–83 she held a fellowship from the National Institute of Mental Health to study Hispanic women healers. She also works in private practice, primarily with Latina women.

PHYLLIS FISHER is an editor who lives in Cambridge, Massachusetts. A latecomer to feminism, lesbianism, and the book collective, she greatly admires the talents, persistence, and courage of her sisters in the collective.

NORMA E. GARCIA is a Latina woman, Puerto Rican, born in the United States to poor working-class parents. She is a child and family therapist whose major interest lies in the impact of culture in the assessment of disturbance or family disorganization. She has been a therapist for ten years and is presently the associate director of an outreach family program in Greater Boston. She has done workshops on single working mothers, cultural variables in the treatment of sexual abuse in Hispanic families, and on issues in the formation of a lesbian identity by Latina women.

CARLA GOLDEN, Ph.D., has taught the psychology of women for nine years, and during that period has lectured extensively on topics related to the development of gender and sexuality, and psychoanalytic object relations theory. She taught at Smith College for six years and is currently an associate professor of psychology at Ithaca College. Between these two land-based teaching experiences, she traveled around the world on a ship, teaching the psychology of women as part of the University of Pittsburgh's Semester at Sea Program. A Danforth Associate who is committed to excellence in teaching, she has published articles in *Feminist Teacher* and *Women's Studies Quarterly.*

MARJORIE J. HILL, Ph.D., is a licensed clinical psychologist who is currently on the staff at Kings County Hospital and is assistant clinical instructor at Downstate Medical Center in New York. She is in private practice in New York City.

KARLA JACKSON-BREWER, M.S., is the rape education consultant for Soundview–Throgs Neck Community Mental Health Center, New York. She is the chair of the Board of Directors of New York Women Against Rape and a member of SOURCE, a black women's therapist collective. She is an adjunct professor of women's studies at Rutgers University and a therapist in private practice. She lives in New York City with her husband Garry, and her son and daughter, Jamal and Sidira.

CHERYL KENNEDY lives in Cambridge, Massachusetts, with Julia Perez and their three daughters. She works as a business manager in an alcoholism program for women.

LIZ MARGOLIES, C.S.W., is a psychotherapist in private practice in New York City and the clinical supervisor for New York Women Against Rape. She specializes in treating sexual assault survivors.

MARGARET NICHOLS, Ph.D., clinical psychologist and sex therapist, is the executive director of the Institute for Personal Growth, a private feminist psychotherapy center, and of Hyacinth Foundation, a nonprofit center for counseling, research, and education. She considers herself a "bisexual with a gay consciousness" and has a son.

LEE F. NICOLOFF received her Ph.D. in counseling psychology from the University of Texas at Austin in 1983. She is a staff psychologist with the Counseling Center at the University of Maine at Orono, where she is cooperating assistant professor of education. She has made presentations on the treatment of student substance abuse problems and on campus environmental concerns for lesbian and gay students, staff, and faculty. She is also involved in community organizing for lesbian and gay rights.

LORAINE OBLER, Ph.D., is an associate professor at the CUNY Graduate School, where she is a neuropsychologist/neurolinguist among whose other interests are the putative brain-based gender differences in cognitive abilities and the way women relate to language. She has served as spokesperson for the Association for Women in Psychology (1981–84) and worked to set up an alternative insemination program at a lesbian and gay health care center.

LUCINDA ORWOLL, M.A., is a doctoral student in psychology and is active in the Boston Bisexual Movement. She has spent many years studying gender roles and the psychology of women. Currently a doctoral candidate in personality psychology, she is interested in the development of wisdom in later adulthood.

PATRICIA J. PAISER, Ed.M., received her degree from Boston University in 1984. She is currently the clinical director of a substance abuse program and is now pursuing her doctorate in clinical psychology.

SARAH F. PEARLMAN, M.A. (Clinical Psychology) is a psychotherapist who practices in Boston and on the North Shore of Massachusetts. She is also a senior associate faculty member at Antioch–New England Graduate School in Keene, New Hampshire, where she teaches courses on individual psychotherapy. She specializes in female psychological development and feminist theory and is a frequent lecturer on lesbian issues, including relationships and sexuality. She has published book reviews in *Sojourner* and *The Women's Review of Books*, and her article on "A Psychotherapist's View of Rape" has appeared in the *New Hampshire Bar Journal*. Her ambition is to write a lesbian version of *The Clan of the Cave Bear*.

JULIA PEREZ was born in Humacao, Puerto Rico. She counsels veterans and writes in her spare time, and is presently working on an anthology on women veterans. She lives in Cambridge, Massachusetts with Cheryl Kennedy and their three daughters.

FRANCINE LEA RAINONE is a former professor of philosophy and women's studies. She left academia to study Oriental Medicine and has trained in Boston and Nanjing, People's Republic of China. She currently practices acupuncture and craniosacral therapy in the Boston area. She has written articles about sex roles and the role of the body in sexual power.

REBECCA SHUSTER, B.A., is assistant director of Building Bridges, an organizaton that offers workshops and concerts on relations between women and men and race relations. She is a counselor and writer and travels nationally, speaking and leading workshops focused on issues of intimacy and sexuality.

She is past director of Wesleyan University's Sexual Health Information Service, and was a 1982–83 Watson Fellow.

EILEEN STARZECPYZEL, M.A., is a psychotherapist in private practice in Manchester, Connecticut. She received her master's degree in counseling psychology from Antioch University and has taught a course on psychology of the incest victim in the Antioch graduate program. She has lectured on incest psychology at the Wheeler Clinic and at New Britain General Hospital in Connecticut, and has provided workshops for the New England Women's Studies Conference at Keene State College, for the Gay and Lesbian Counseling Service in Boston, and other organizations in New England. Her articles have been published in *Dialogue*, the professional journal of the *Connecticut Association of Counseling and Development*, in *Valley Women's Voice* (Amherst, Massachusetts), and in *Women in Hartford*. She has a monthly column in a Hartford-based journal for the gay community and is working on a book on lesbian families and feminist parenting.

ELOISE STIGLITZ received her Ph.D. in clinical psychology from Purdue University in 1976. She has worked at the counseling centers of the University of Toledo, California State University at Fresno, and the University of Texas at Austin. She is behavioral sciences coordinator in the Family Practice Residency Program at the Eastern Maine Medical Center in Bangor; and clinical consultant at Community Alcohol Services in Rockland, Maine, and the substance abuse treatment programs at the Maine State Prison and the Penobscot Indian Nation. She is also in private practice in Bangor.

KATHERINE TRIANTAFILLOU is a family law practitioner and civil rights attorney, who since 1975 has represented many lesbians facing a myriad of legal issues including divorce, custody, buying and selling houses, starting businesses, and making wills and contracts.

SUE VARGO holds a master's degree in education from Boston University and has trained at the Family Institute of Cambridge. She has a private psychotherapy practice in Brookline, Massachusetts, and consults to human service programs around clinical and organizational issues.

LEE ZEVY, M.S.W., C.S.W., A.C.S.W., received her training from the New York Institute for Gestalt Therapy. Formerly clinical director for Identity House and co-director of the Committee to Aid Women in Crisis, she is currently in private practice.

SHERRY ZITTER, M.S.W., L.I.C.S.W., is a social worker from Massachusetts who works primarily with Deaf and other differently-abled populations. She herself is hearing and a lesbian. She received her master's degree from Smith

College School for Social Work in Northampton, Massachusetts in 1983. She is active in Social Workers for Peace and Nuclear Disarmament, as well as Deaf rights organizations, and is currently setting up an inpatient program for Deaf psychiatric patients in Massachusetts.

# Acknowledgments

The majority of the chapters in this book originated from a three-day conference called "Lesbian Psychologies" that was held in Boston during March 1984. This conference was attended by more than five hundred women and included forty-three workshops as well as paper presentations and training sessions. It was the first conference of this scope to focus exclusively on lesbian psychological concerns.

Both the conference and this book call for acknowledgments and words of appreciation. We would particularly like to thank the Boston Chapter of the Association for Women in Psychology for sponsoring and supporting the conference. In particular, we wish to thank and recognize Sarah Pearlman, who first had the idea of such a conference, proposed it to AWP, and later coordinated the event and put it on with the help of the many women who organized, worked on, and participated in the conference. We would also like to thank all of the women who submitted chapters for this book as well as the authors of the chapters selected, who wrote, rewrote, and revised their original essays. The nine women of our collective read, wrote, revised, edited, Xeroxed, stood in post office lines, and struggled through the numerous meetings and tasks involved in the publishing of this anthology. Special thanks to Buffy Dunker, who held it all together. Finally, we would like to thank our editor, Carole Appel, for challenging traditional forms and working with us.

# Index

meditation, 350, 352, 353
mediator (for lesbians), characteristics of, 327-28, 329-32
medical establishment, and aging lesbians, 80
Meiselman, Karen, 263, 278
men, gay, 32-33, 102-3, 244
Mendola, Mary, 169
menopause, sex after, 78
mental health, gender-biased standards of, 161-62
merging, in lesbian relationships, 107-8. *See also* fusion, in lesbian relationships
minority groups: alcoholism in, 285-86, 289; characteristics of, 230; in coalitions with feminists, 349; communities of, 345; identity development of, 35-48; perceptions of sexuality of, 234; self-definition of, 22; socialization networks of, 185
minority women. *See* women of color
Minuchin, Salvador, 183
"mirroring," 315
money: aging lesbians and, 80-81; lesbian families and, 199, 206
monogamy: of bisexual women, 60-61, 65-66; debate about, in lesbian community, 319; in lesbian relationships, 117-19, 169-70. *See also* nonmonogamy
Moraga, Cherrie, 39, 40
Morin, Stephen F., 237
Morten, George, 36, 42, 46
Moses, Alice, 231
mother: identification of, with children, 134; loss of, in father-daughter incest, 256, 265, 272; power of, 320-21; protection of, by lesbian incest survivor, 274; reaction of, to daughter's coming out, 177, 178-81; in social role theory, 185
mother-daughter bond: damage to, by father-daughter incest, 263, 272, 267-68, 275-76, 280; primary, recreation of by sexual intimacy, 126, 133-34, 140, 264
mother-daughter relationship: betrayal in, 322-23; damage to, under patriarchy, 133, 322; dyadic socialization in, 323; effect of coming-out process on,

177, 192; effect of, on adult female relationships, 320-24; effect of, on lesbian relationships, 127, 138-39
mothering, 196, 321-22. *See also* parenting, lesbian; families, lesbian
mothers: bisexual, 224; lesbian: child-rearing attitudes of, 215-25; invisibility of, 195; isolation of, 199-201; role models for, 215
Mothers & Co., 218, 223
mother-son relationship, 264
Moulton, Ruth, 321
mourning: in coming-out process, 184, 191; in healing of incest survivor, 275; in therapeutic process, 233

Nemeyer, Laura, 164
New Deal, experience of lesbians in, 75
"new psychology of women," 161
nonmonogamy: of bisexual women, 60-61; controversy surrounding, 250, 319; effect of, on primary relationships, 117-18, 250; in gay male couples, 118; and relationship satisfaction, 99-100; and sexual script problems, 249. *See also* monogamy
normal autism, 263
norms, cultural: violation of by Latina lesbians, 49-50
nurturance: of girls, 136; inadequate, 138, 322; in lesbian relationships, 131-32, 138-39; loss of, 180; of mothers by daughters, 179; as source of self-esteem, 131

obesity, 295, 305
object constancy, 263
objective anxiety, 235, 236
object relations: defined, 263; developmental stages of, 263; effect of father-daughter incest on, 262, 270-71; theory of, 132; theory of sexual identity formation, 33; theory of, treatment of incest survivors in, 261-81
Oedipal conflict, 132, 270
Oedipal relationship, mother-son, 264-65
Oedipal triangle, in father-daughter incest, 271
old age, planning for, 80-81